Contents

T0274779

List of Illustrations

List of Illustrations

List of Illustrations

Foreword
by DJ Paulette

My timeline as a resident DJ at the legendary Haçienda starts after the Second Summer of Love. I worked there between 1992 and 1996, happily sandwiched in the halcyon years between the hopeful reopening in 1991 and before Gunchester, bankruptcy and acrimony closed its doors for good in 1997. I held court in the Pussy Parlour (the renamed Gay Traitor bar in the basement) every month at the LGBT extravaganza Flesh, where, besides breaking some taboos, uniting the tribes and changing the licensing laws in Manchester, the Flesh night made money and put 'It's Queer Up North' and 'Gaychester' on the media map. With The Haçienda (FAC 51) being such an integral part of Factory Records, plus this indisputable kudos, one would think that I would have scored a mention in some of the books, documentaries or films dedicated to archiving its colourful history. You would think wrongly. As comprehensive as the coverage is, the Factory Records puzzle has some significant pieces missing.

Now there have always been rumblings; I am not the only one missing from the footnotes and credits. Yet it took me until 2016 to bravely go where no woman had gone before: to wave my red flag at the gatekeepers, find supporters and start talking to the press. At first, the take-up was slow, but the centenary of the suffragette movement in 2018 added some welcomed topspin to my efforts.

It is impossible to have a fair analysis of any situation without taking the full picture into account. In recent years, much has been made of unearthing, acknowledging and crediting women's contribution to world history. In the real world it matters who gets the credit; yet from academia to art, astronomy to science, politics to fashion, religion to radio and from music to management, it is a disheartening statistical fact that women's input in our professions or organisations has been consistently unreported or our credits have been misdirected. How has this happened? Type 'has women's contribution to history been overlooked' into your browser to find Google's enlightening top answer.

> 'The statistics for the lack of women's history being taught can be attributed to the documentation of events throughout history. Not only is the white male narrative still prevalent in modern history classes, but sources being provided to schools are typically the work of white men as well.'[1]

Silence is our confinement, and the gatekeepers hold the key. Since popular authors are overwhelmingly male, it is no surprise that women are overshadowed in history. When a man is commissioned to write a book about what he knows best, we can only expect him to write about the loud, active parts of the machinery he immediately sees — not the smoothly oiled cogs purring away in the background. Never mind that with our direction and with our intelligence and ingenuity, women have regularly saved the day and made others shine. While we have been content to busy our-selves in their shadow or shy away from the spotlight, our humility and lack of ego has made us disappear. Our silent acceptance of the lack of private or public recognition of our achievements simply perpetuates this cycle. Our assumption that people will naturally notice and give us the credit for the time and effort we put in is naïve. The systemic repression and social conditioning of women in the workplace is a tale as old as time. The suppression of our stories is thus a wrong in need of righting and a book in need of writing.

When documenting history, stacking the evidence is essential in its authentication. In basic statistical terms, every employee experience and each piece of data — small or large — is relevant to proving diversity, inclusion and equality. In analysing data, we must temper it with the question 'who says?'. Who and how have they decided what's relevant and what isn't, or who is relevant and who isn't? We must reserve the right to question and to step up with other views and other voices that can equally corroborate and expand on the story. We have the right to show and tell it as it happened for us. We too have the right to be proud of what we represent, of what we have contributed and achieved. As composer, scholar and social activist Bernice Reagon states, 'each one of us is here because somebody before us did something to make it possible.'[2]

Commissioning books written by female historians remains a radical and disruptive act, tasked with addressing and redressing the imbalance and restoring the legacy. Producing and presenting these books is a remedy that counteracts the misrepresentation, as does such speaking out against the mansplaining of history. Writing is a gesture of peaceful, direct action that forces us to confront the issues and dramatises that which can no longer be ignored. It resurrects what is a very significant 'other' from the 'never heard of them' dead zone. It proves our value and worth.

How did Factory and The Haçienda become the '24-hour party people'? In the last twenty years, more than a dozen books have been published on the Factory Records story yet none among them has ever given the women their flowers. These women have been passed over without due attention and disregarded through haste and lack of care. They continue to live boldly and inspire despite imposter syndrome and the invisibility of having been there but not being seen to be there. Tuning these women's stories out, while never intentionally malicious, has done history a disservice and the history makers themselves some damage. And, to those gatekeepers who continue to present an exclusive account rather than offer inclusive revisions, walking the hidden out into the open where they can be seen, acknowledged, accepted and assimilated is a liberating act that seals the holes in the myth.

In a world where misogyny and gender bias continue to subdue women's roles and rights, *I Thought I Heard You Speak* is relevant and timely. This collection of inspiring accounts tells the secrets we need to hear through the voices we've never heard before and probably never knew existed. From this refreshing perspective *I Thought I Heard You Speak* tweaks and reshapes the Factory myth, giving a clearer insight into the experience of working at and for Factory. Through the eighties and nineties, the women of Factory were every bit part of the process and not just a part of the furniture, and it shows just how much women were 'integral to its ethos, its creativity and its massive success'.

How can anything exist before it's created? The Haçienda had to be built. If you can't see it, you can't be it — but when that real-life presence is not acknowledged in print, what then? This book had to be written. Taking in everything from art, design and 'Unknown Pleasures' to live gigs and the Happy Mondays; from Factory Records accounting to The Haçienda management and the DJs, this truth bomb enhances the myth and makes it bloom. Women were normal, not a novelty, at Factory; the world can see and appreciate their achievements, and the women responsible can get their long overdue recognition.

I Thought I Heard You Speak is not simply an essential addition to Factory Records' archive of books, films and exhibitions, it is recommended reading. Period.

DJ PAULETTE
MANCHESTER
DECEMBER 2022

Author's Note

The book is missing some important voices, as is true of any oral history project. I made every effort to locate contact information for: Judy Vermorel, Martha Tilson, Marion Freeman, Serena Lovelace, Su Barnes, Louise Craven, Karen Mason, Barbara Farmer, Alison Lamb, Jane Stanton, Madonna, Raquel Williams, Bridget Turgoose, Penny Cook, Julie and Janet who worked at The Haçienda, Janie who originally ran The Haçienda canteen, Zoe Thompson, and Catrina Cameron. I emailed or called or DMed a number of women whose contact information I obtained and who never responded to invitations to participate, including Jane Lemon, Tina Weymouth, Miranda Sawyer, Ginny Clee, Louise Rhodes, Caroline Lavelle, Kathryn Bigelow, Princess Julia, Lisa Rinzler, Jane Nisselson, and Alison Gilks.

If any of you are reading this and are interested in speaking, I'd still love to talk with you! Perhaps the book will have a second, updated edition down the road. While I did my best to contact every woman who worked for, or did work with, Factory Records and its affiliates, it is certainly possible I missed some names. If I failed to reach out to you and have unintentionally omitted your name here, please get in touch! I was unable to interview Urszula Sabina, Rebecca Knowles, Beth B, Jayne Casey, and Karen Jackson prior to the deadline for the book, and I hope they'll be involved in the mythical second edition.

Several women declined invitations to participate: Rowetta, Pennie Smith, Barbara Kruger, Sue Churchill, Ellie Gray, Elena Massucco, Miranda Stanton, and Susanne O'Hara.

The vast majority of the material in *I Thought I Heard You Speak* is derived from nearly one hundred interviews conducted and transcribed by the author (including multiple and follow-up interviews). In a handful of cases, interview material and text was excerpted from other sources. Karen Jackson of Central Station Design couldn't speak for the interview before the deadline, so I've excerpted material from an interview with her conducted by Lola Landekic for *Art of the Title*. Fiona Allen and Linder Sterling couldn't speak during the timetable for the book, so the text contains material excerpted from a 2006 interview John Robb conducted with Linder, and previous interviews with Fiona conducted by John Cooper and Iain Key. A number of important women passed away before I began writing the book, or in the early stages of its creation. Short excerpted materials have allowed me to include the voices of Ruth Polsky, Lucy Scher, Denise Johnson, Rachel Morris, Annik Honoré, and Gretchen Bender. Beth Cassidy provided permission to use the incredible notes of her mum, Jenny Ross of Section 25. Ben Kelly graciously supplied one of Sandra Douglas's architectural sketches for The Haçienda, allowing me to include her artistic and design 'voice' in this unique way. A full list of sources and credits appears on pages 483 – 485. I want to acknowledge and thank the authors of these texts, which have strengthened and amplified this book immensely.

Interview material contained within the book has been edited and condensed for clarity.

Cast of Characters

Surnames appear as they did then on Factory recordings, correspondence, labels, and liner notes, and in the women's recollections of one another. They are listed here in alphabetical order:

JULIA ADAMSON: Studio sound engineer; former member of What?Noise and The Fall

ALISON AGBOOLA: Haçienda employee

CAROLYN ALLEN: Musician in The Wake

FIONA ALLEN: Haçienda employee; Factory merchandising; actress and comedian

TERESA ALLEN: Haçienda employee

LINDSAY ANDERSON: Musician in Stockholm Monsters

ELIZABETH BAILEY: Film-maker

DIAN BARTON: Live sound engineer

GRETCHEN BENDER: Artist and film-maker

BINDI BINNING: Factory Too A&R

GINA BIRCH: Film-maker; musician and co-founder of The Raincoats

KAREN BOARDMAN: Haçienda employee

REBECCA BOULTON: New Order manager; Haçienda employee and assistant to Rob Gretton

BEV BYTHEWAY: Curator at Cornerhouse; Haçienda programming

CATH CARROLL: Musician in Miaow and solo musician; *City Fun* and *NME* writer

ANGIE CASSIDY: Musician in Section 25

BETH CASSIDY: Musician in Section 25

BRIDGET CHAPMAN: Factory Too employee

HANNAH COLLINS: Artist; artwork commission for The Haçienda

ANNE-MARIE COPELAND: Haçienda employee

NICKY CREWE: Haçienda employee

Cast of Characters

CLARE CUMBERLIDGE: Curator; painted the Gay Traitor cocktail bar at The Haçienda

AMBER DENKER: Multimedia artist; computer graphics for New Order's 'Bizarre Love Triangle' video

DJ PAULETTE: Resident Flesh DJ at The Haçienda

ANNA DOMINO: Musician

TRACEY DONNELLY: Receptionist at Swing in The Haçienda; Factory Communications Limited employee

SANDRA DOUGLAS: Co-designer of The Haçienda and other Factory projects with Ben Kelly Design

CORINNE DREWERY: Musician in Swing Out Sister

LINDA DUTTON: Factory IKON film-maker

RACHEL FELDER: Journalist

SUSAN FERGUSON: Haçienda employee

JUDITH FOSTER: Haçienda employee

GILLIAN GILBERT: Musician in New Order; co-owner of The Haçienda; producer

LESLEY GILBERT: Factory Communications Limited employee; partner of Rob Gretton

REBECCA GOODWIN: Haçienda employee; FAC 51 Productions; promotions

PAULA GREIF: Film-maker; art director

STELLA HALL: Co-founder of the Green Room; Haçienda programming; Festival of the Tenth Summer programming

PAULINE HARRISON: Dry 201 employee; occasional vocals for The Durutti Column and one-time partner of Vini Reilly

PENNY HENRY: Haçienda employee and superwoman

LITA HIRA: Musician in Stockholm Monsters

ANNIK HONORÉ: Co-founder of Factory Benelux; founder of Les Disques du Crépuscule

JAYNE HOUGHTON: Factory PR; founder of Excess Press; *NME* photographer

LAURA ISRAEL: Film-maker

KAREN JACKSON: Central Station Design co-founder and designer

MARGARET JAILLER: Film-maker

ANGEL JOHNSON: Haçienda DJ

Cast of Characters

DENISE JOHNSON: Musician
NICKI KEFALAS: Factory radio and TV PR, Out Promotion (FAC 161)
CARRIE KIRKPATRICK: Film-maker
ALISON KNIGHT: Fashion designer; co-founder of Baylis & Knight
SORAYA LAKHANEY: Sister of Haçienda 'doorman' Yasmine Lakhaney
CAROLE LAMOND: Film-maker
ANNE LEHMAN: Factory US and Of New York employee
MICHELLE MANGAN: Haçienda DJ
CHRIS MATHAN: Peter Saville Associates (PSA) partner and designer
ANG MATTHEWS: Haçienda manager and licensee; Haçienda employee and assistant manager
KATH MCDERMOTT: Haçienda DJ
MARTINE MCDONAGH: James manager; PR
SANDY MCLEOD: Film-maker
LIEVE MONNENS: Factory Benelux employee; Factory Communications Limited employee
CAROL MORLEY: Film-maker; musician; director of *The Alcohol Years*
RACHEL MORRIS: Musician in Hopper
LIZ NAYLOR: Writer of *City Fun* and nonexistent Factory screenplay (FAC 20); Factory PR
MARCIA PANTRY: Haçienda employee
SIDNIE PANTRY: Haçienda employee; fashion designer
ALYSON PATCHETT: Factory Communications Limited employee
RUTH POLSKY: Promoter in New York City
ANN QUIGLEY: Musician in Swamp Children and Kalima; artist and designer
LINDSAY READE: Factory Communications Limited employee; manager of 52nd Street; ex-wife of Tony Wilson; author of *Torn Apart* (co-written with Mick Middles), *Mr Manchester and the Factory Girl* and forthcoming *Nice Boys Were Never Your Cup of Poison*
GONNIE RIETVELD: Musician in Quando Quango; Haçienda employee; *The Haçienda Must Be Built!* (FAC 351) collaborator; professor of sonic culture
JANE ROBERTS: Backline technician
SUZANNE ROBINSON: Haçienda DJ; Haçienda canteen chef

JENNY ROSS: Musician in Section 25

SEEMA SAINI: Factory Communications Limited employee

JANE SAVIDGE: Co-founder Savidge and Best PR; music writer

LUCY SCHER: Summer of Lesbian Love at The Haçienda; co-founder of Haçienda Flesh nights

RENEE SCROGGINS: Musician in ESG

YVONNE SHELTON: Musician in Haçienda Classical

TINA SIMMONS: Director of Factory Communications Limited; employee of Factory Communications Limited

BRIX SMITH: Musician in The Fall

LINDER STERLING: Musician in Ludus; artist and designer

ALISON SURTEES: Co-founder of Manchester Digital Music Archive (MDMArchive)

RUTH TAYLOR: Haçienda employee

GEORGINA TRULIO: Factory Communications Limited employee

CLAIRE DE VERTEUIL: Dry 201 assistant manager; Haçienda employee

MELANIE WILKINSON: Dry 201 chef

JACKIE WILLIAMS: Artist; one-time bass for The Durutti Column and wife of Bruce Mitchell

Introduction

This is a new history of Factory Records told by the women who lived it – of a happening that became a label that became an (inclusive) cultural phenomenon in spite of itself.

LIZ NAYLOR: The idea of a women in Factory Records book piques my interest because otherwise Factory's been a bugbear of mine, and I'm a bit like, *I'm so bored of this shit*, the kind of orthodoxy of the history that's written around Manchester. It depresses and bores me, so I'm excited that something fresh is going to be written to cast a bit of a different perspective on it.

LESLEY GILBERT: I always knew the women in Factory were important — that was obvious. We've been brushed out of history a little bit, but that's coming right.

TINA SIMMONS: There were a lot of women involved in Factory at the time. New Order's got Gillian Gilbert, Section 25's got Angie Cassidy and Jenny. Nicki Kefalas was at Out Promotion in London, there was Liz Naylor doing work at Rough Trade with Factory connections, and Cath Carroll, who had been with Liz and wrote for *NME*, Martine McDonagh had worked for Rough Trade and came up to manage James, and Peter Saville had a Canadian girl working for him, Chris Mathan. At The Haçienda, there was a girl called Tracey Donnelly who worked as the receptionist at the hairdresser's Swing, and of course Tracey ended up working at Palatine Road.

TRACEY DONNELLY: Women have been the backbone of everything in that company, in Factory. There were so many women around the Factory scene. I never felt like there was any sexism, though, but maybe that's because it was the eighties and that was as good as you were going to get ... So I never felt it was a sexist place, but it's other people, isn't it? The writers, the music journalists, the ones shaping the history who just are not interested in women's stories.

GILLIAN GILBERT: I think some of the women at Factory might say they weren't important, but they were. A lot of women in the past, there was the idea that we weren't supposed to have an opinion about anything. There's this idea that you're not supposed to speak up for yourself especially, and so some of us have been conditioned to not speak up ... But if it was a bloke, it would be like, 'Oh, he knows what he wants.' I think with women, you learn you don't blow your own trumpet. And I think because you had men who were big personalities, I think it's only now that people have realised what women have *really* done.

DJ PAULETTE: For me, the hidden histories, the untold histories, are my biggest issue ... these stories just get sidelined and not told, or people put their name on somebody else's work. So it is my biggest mission in life to make sure that the people who actually did the shit get the credit. You've got to be able to use your voice. You've got to use that voice whenever the opportunity arises — use your voice because if you don't, it's use it or lose it.

• • •

Factory Records has become the stuff of legend as far as post-punk, new wave, and acid house music goes. The histories of the label have been told from many perspectives and in wide-ranging formats, from visual catalogues and memoirs written by those who experienced Factory in its heyday to music exhibitions dedicated to the early years of the label, the design work of Peter Saville, and The Haçienda. Yet no in-depth history has ever been told from the perspectives of the women who were integral to Factory's cultural significance and, ultimately, to its success. This lacuna is all the more notable given that Factory Records is truly distinctive because women played key roles in nearly every aspect of the label and its surrounding ethos. So rarely do we hear the women speak.

In the last twenty years, more than a dozen books have been published that circle around Factory Records. Some of those books reference women who recorded for the label or were linked to its founders as wives or girlfriends. Yet even when they're mentioned, women's stories are buried, and their names are sometimes misspelt. Every Factory Records history to date is missing something critical: the authoritative, affiliated voices of the women who ran the label behind the scenes, performed in and managed the bands, worked as onstage technicians, played key roles in the creative design and promotion work for which Factory became known, and became integral to The Haçienda as DJs and in management. How does the history of the label change when those perspectives are placed at the centre of the story? *I Thought I Heard You Speak* is a new history of Factory Records that does just that.

New Order's 'Blue Monday', the bestselling 12-inch of all time, reached the global audiences it did thanks to the women who handled the chaos behind the scenes, ensuring that enough vinyl was pressed while liaising with distributors and negotiating sales and licensing in the UK and abroad. Women designers crafted dazzling images and iconography for record sleeves, posters, and other merchandising materials, while women managers and promoters made the bands famous. Women engineered live and studio sound for New Order, Happy Mondays, and other Factory musicians. Running The Haçienda? Establishing a queer space through Haçienda DJing? Getting Factory songs played on the radio? Making video recordings of Haçienda gigs when male videographers deemed them unnecessary? Developing a viable financial model for the label? *Nearly all women.*

Women didn't just occasionally occupy central roles at Factory Records — they were consistently integral to its ethos, its creativity, and its success. Behind the scenes at the Palatine Road and Charles Street offices in Manchester, as well as at Factory Benelux and Of Factory New York, women kept the label running. The Haçienda (FAC 51) relied on the work of women from its start, and the world-famous club was managed by women from the acid house and Madchester period until its closure.* It also employed the first woman 'doorman' in England. Women directed, produced, and edited Factory music videos that shook the MTV airwaves, embracing new technologies along the way. And, of course, women fronted bands and became electronic music pioneers. Although the trappings of misogynist culture seeped in, women were invited into the central work of Factory Records and were recognised largely as equals at the time of their immense contributions. Indeed, however much Factory grew in popularity, 'it was always like a little family', Tracey Donnelly recalled of her career at the label. At the same time, no history of the label has yet given the women involved their due. *I Thought I Heard You Speak* is an oral history of Factory Records told entirely from the voices of the women involved.

A Note on Narrative Oral History

The genre of narrative oral history is a peculiar thing (and ultimately, never *just one thing*). Few people agree on the proper way to conduct oral history research. Some methodologies derive from academic practices, some from journalistic conventions, and others from literary and editorial customs. The form a narrative oral history book ultimately takes will depend upon the author's own background and experiences, and the methods they've both learnt and chosen to apply.

Narrative oral histories are necessarily subjective. First, you've got the subjectivities of the interviewees — all storytellers — throughout

---

* Factory Records had an extensive cataloguing system that was at once careful and complex, but also playful. For example, every music release from the label received a FAC number, but 'The Haçienda Cat' (FAC 191) also received a catalogue number, as did various Factory events such as the 'Disorder' party (FAC 208) that featured New Order. While most catalogue numbers are designated with 'FAC', albums often had a 'FACT' designation, and CDs a 'FACD' designation. International offshoots of Factory also used their own distinct designations, such as 'FACUS' for Factory US and 'FBN' for Factory Benelux.

the text. Indeed, their accounts can often contradict one another and still be valid. In recounting her experiences in the band Section 25, Angie Cassidy told me, 'I totally understand that each person's Factory memories are sort of special to themselves, so another person might remember the same thing totally differently, but that doesn't mean it didn't happen. It's just that their experience was different from mine, and that's the way it is.' As oral historian Alessandro Portelli explains, 'oral sources are credible but with a *different* credibility'.[1] The truths that arise from oral history work are based on individual experience and memory. They might run counter to details contained in other accounts, but that doesn't mean they're false. Narrative oral histories show us how personal experiences can be authentic, instructive, and meaningful.

Then you've got to contend with the author's subjectivity. I'm with punk authors Legs McNeil and Gillian McCain here. I don't think of myself as a *writer* of this book, but rather as an editor, a sculptor, a collagist, a crafter of the picaresque. In putting together *I Thought I Heard You Speak*, one of my aims was to emphasise how history is never one-dimensional, and no single history can be 'definitive'. There are multitudes of histories that overlap, creating bumps in familiar timelines. Every historical record that exists — including every narrative oral history — is merely one account from many possibilities (depending on who was asked to contribute, who was available, and who declined). The theorist Reinhart Koselleck talks about this idea in terms of 'plural histories', suggesting that each written record always reflects the subjectivities of both the author and the interviewees. Koselleck intimates there are ever-changeable 'inventories' of voices and perspectives that produce plural histories.[2] *I Thought I Heard You Speak* is one such inventory.

The chapters are organised thematically, as opposed to chronologically, with occasional 'mini' chapters that flicker in to highlight a particular moment or idea that shone out across the interviews. By structuring the book this way, I wanted to move away from the idea that there's such a thing as an 'accurate chronology' or a 'complete history', as so many books propose to offer. *I Thought I Heard You Speak* does highlight familiar points on existing Factory timelines, yet in resisting a chronological framework, the book recognises the frequent marginalisation of women's stories from 'official' records that have been organised along a timeline.

So, in the end, I set out to do two things: to create an innovative historical record of Factory and its cultural influences, and to collate an archive of women's experiential knowledge in all its vast, varied, and anecdotal complexity.

• • •

I Thought I Heard You Speak is a new telling of the story of Factory Records that's a corrective and a re-centring. While texts and exhibition materials to date have contributed to the mythologising impulses of the label, this book pierces the lore to reveal an untold but no less enduring legacy: one of extremely hard work and women's labour behind the scenes, and eagle-eyed attention to practical matters that keep a record label and its many-genred arms running. Tony Wilson is often said to have said, misquoting a John Ford film, 'When forced to pick between the truth and legend, print the legend.' With the women at Factory Records, the truth *is* the legend.

CHAPTER 1
FACTORY
ORIGINS

Staff in the Factory office on Palatine Road

Most Factory Records stories to date begin with the vision of Tony Wilson (aka Anthony H. Wilson, AHW), whose work for Granada TV made him a local Manchester celebrity. In May 1978, Wilson and Alan Erasmus put on 'The Factory' nights at the Russell Club on Royce Road, Hulme, featuring local bands that would later be signed to Factory Records – most notably, perhaps, Joy Division. Other early Factory nights happened at the New Osborne Club and the Beach Club in Manchester. Those nights at the Russell Club brought together the soon-to-be directors of Factory Records: Alan Erasmus, Rob Gretton, Martin Hannett, Peter Saville, and Tony Wilson. But that's a story of Factory Records that's already been told. When you dig a little bit deeper, you'll see that many of the women who recorded, designed, promoted, and otherwise worked for Factory Records were present at the birth of the label. Not unlike the canonical Factory men, these women were pulled into lives of music through the explosion of creativity that accompanied the arrival of punk, while drawing their own visionary inspiration from the city.

TRACEY DONNELLY: I grew up seeing Tony Wilson on the TV, and I went to see Slaughter and the Dogs. I was blown away that this man from the telly was there introducing it. He looked unlike everybody else with his long hair, introducing all these punks. Vini Reilly played that night, too, with Ed Banger and The Nosebleeds.

GILLIAN GILBERT: Before New Order, we used to go see a lot of Factory groups at The Factory, of course — me, my sister and her friend, it was like a little gang. Because we lived in Macclesfield, Manchester was the place to go ... We also used to watch Tony Wilson's programme that had a lot of local bands on, *So It Goes*. It was on at teatime. I remember we really liked this group called V2, which weren't on Factory but we'd seen them a lot, and then we'd seen Tony Wilson in the audience, and I said to him, 'Why don't you have Joy Division on?' We'd just started getting into Joy Division, and he said, 'Well, I don't know anybody from Joy Division', so I told him, 'I sit next to Steve's sister in geography at high school.' I passed on the message, and that's how they got onto television. I'm sure somebody else has got a different story, but that's how I remember it.

CATH CARROLL: I used to watch Tony on *Granada Reports* and *So It Goes* before I ever met him, and Liz [Naylor] and I were quite obsessed with getting his attention while pretending to ignore him. Liz knew him a little from the Joy Division film she scripted with Charlie Salem. Tony supported a fanzine of ours that we did before we took over *City Fun*. It went to one issue, and it was massively self-indulgent. Lots of white space. Liz is very gifted at graphic design, so she kind of just put this thing out, and ever since then, Tony was like, 'You kids you owe me £50!' It wasn't a gift, it was a loan, he made sure we remembered. We thought it was a gift 'cause who on earth was going to buy it? We'd put a ridiculously high price on it for the time. £1, I think. Until the very end it was a running joke for Tony, and he persisted with it so much that I kind of realised much too late that he wanted his £50 back regardless of what we thought the terms were. But he never got it back while he was living, so that's that. I've made some contributions since. Making amends.

ANG MATTHEWS: Obviously Factory Records started way before The Haçienda started. I was living in Wales in this small nothing-happening town, and there was a group of us that were into punk. Factory Records had started and there was news they'd got a club in Manchester, so there was talk of Factory Records and it being cool. Tony Wilson was, at that time, on television, and Joy Division then appeared on his show. There was talk about a real new thing that was going on in Manchester. When I was doing A levels, about to start my degree, I chose to do my degree in Manchester in part because Factory Records were here.

LESLEY GILBERT: I suppose my Factory Records story began because Rob and I already lived together from when we were about twenty-one or twenty-two, something like that, and when we saw Joy Division at Rafters. I'm hopeless with years, but it's so well documented — whatever year that Joy Division gig was [31 May 1977]. We both thought they were amazing. So Rob became Joy Division's manager. I still had a job in an office at this point, so it was more of a Joy Division involvement than a Factory involvement at that point.

TERESA ALLEN: When I was sixteen, my eldest sister moved, she went to university. She only went to Salford, so it's not that far away, but it was a great opportunity for me to escape from home. I used to go and stay with her on a street called Great Cheetham Street West. Coincidentally, Joy Division used to rehearse in a building just up the road, and I didn't know who it was, I could just hear music, so when I got to my sister's I said, 'Let's go and find out who it is.' It turned out to be Joy Division. So whenever I was there, if we heard music, I used to go and sit on the stairs in the rehearsal rooms, and listen to them through the door. That's the first part of the start of my own Factory story.

ANN QUIGLEY: At Liverpool art school I wanted to be an artist. In a perfect world that was my biggest dream, besides being with a band, always has been since I was small. So I spent the year at Liverpool art school, and the second week that I was at the art school, this boy called Jon Tuite asked me if I knew any guitarists because he was putting a band together and they needed a guitarist. The following weekend, I began dating a boy in Manchester called John, who played guitar (and he was the only person that I knew that played guitar). So I said to him, 'Oh, this band in Liverpool are looking for a guitarist', and gave him the phone number, and John rung him up and it was Pink Military with Jayne Casey. Jayne was the first female musician that led the way ...

CHRIS MATHAN: I applied to the Nova Scotia College of Art and Design in Halifax, Nova Scotia, was accepted and chose graphic design and photography as my fields of study. NSCAD was a great choice in the mid-seventies: it had a terrific faculty of artists and designers not only from Canada but the US, England, Germany, etc., and a press that published artist books and a great visiting artist programme. Joseph Beuys, for example, did a conceptual art piece while I was there. I also managed a band called the Null Set and a few of us visited London one summer and fell in love with the whole punk/ska music scene, spent nights at Scala Cinema, etc. When I moved to New York in 1981, I spent much of my Saturday afternoons at 99 Records where Ed Bahlman turned me on to lots of indie music, including Factory bands. I walked out of there with armfuls of records! . . .

ANN QUIGLEY: I ended up at Stockport College where I was doing a combined art and business studies course. We all sat around in a circle on the first day we were there. The band had just started, and I stood up and said, 'I'm Ann Quigley and I sing in a band called the Swamp Children.' And this girl on the opposite side just smiled at me, so when it got to her turn, she stood up and she said, 'My name's Gillian Gilbert and I go out with the drummer in Joy Division and they're on Factory.' So we became friends, because it wasn't like an art course, it was more of a business course. And it was awful, and everyone else on it did really well with the business stuff and weren't that great on the art side, and all me and Gillian wanted to do was the art side of it. So for that year, me and Gillian were friends. I knew that she played guitar in a band, and I didn't know too much more than that really.

GILLIAN GILBERT: We got to know Stephen and Ian because they lived in Macclesfield, so me and my sister and her friend started rehearsing with this band who'd phoned us up and said, 'Do you want to be in our band?' They were three blokes from Macclesfield who were a bit older than us. We were only like sixteen, so of course we said, 'Yeah', because we'd been in the local paper saying that we wanted to be in a punk rock band. The *Macc Express* got onto it and put us on the front cover. At the time, I was going to this really posh high school, which is where Stephen's sister was, and we were on the front page! We had to look miserable because there was this idea that punks were miserable. We weren't like that at all, but that's what the paper wanted. So, we got all these phone calls from different people. Even the local record shop wanted to get involved, and we'd not even written anything. My other sister's girlfriend had just bought a bass, I bought a guitar, and my sister and her friend were supposed to be the singers. We ended up doing a few rehearsals with Joy Division. They'd stop in and say, 'Do you want to see our band play, Joy Division?' So that's when I first heard Joy Division, and then because Stephen and Ian were from Macc, so they'd ask if we wanted a lift. We all used to pile into Stephen's car.

JAYNE HOUGHTON: I was an art student in Leeds, and I went to Futurama Festival, which was at the Queen's Hall. One of the bands on the bill were Joy Division, and I photographed them. I was fifteen. I wasn't a photographer at that point. I probably shouldn't have even been allowed to be there! But me and my mate Jill went, and I still have those photographs. I've always photographed New Order when we've been on the road. I've always documented bits and bobs as we've been on our travels.

BRIX SMITH: Way before The Fall, when I was in Bennington, possibly even a little bit before the end of high school, I was obsessed with Joy Division. My absolutely favourite band. I got turned on to all the British music then: Siouxsie and the Banshees, The Cure, Pretenders. I started to play in bands, and some of the people I was playing with knew all about Factory Records and The Haçienda, and spoke of it as if it was Mecca. Like it was literally the epicentre — the coolest label that had ever existed up to that point. It was almost mythical . . . the pinnacle of everything cool. So Joy Division was a life-changer.

ANNA DOMINO: I became aware of Factory Records as the label for Joy Division, who were coming to play in New York City. We were all agog with anticipation to hear them live but then suddenly heart-stricken when Ian Curtis took himself out of the picture. I had great respect for Factory and their bands before I did any commercial recording of my own.

GILLIAN GILBERT: When I started going out with Stephen, I went to Liverpool for the Eric's gig. Ian wasn't too keen on playing guitar, but he was made to play this guitar while Bernard did the keyboards. Towards the end, they were going to come on for the encore, but something happened in the dressing room. I think Ian cut his hand. They all said, 'Oh, Gillian can play guitar'; so they said to me, 'Just come out and play these three chords, just go up for the last number.' And that's how I got to play with Joy Division for one night. Years later, my dad found the coat I'd been wearing that night. We used to wear donkey jackets — what coal men used to wear. They were these big, navy-blue coats with leather patches where they'd put the coal. Anyway, he found my donkey jacket with the set list and the notes from that night in the pocket.

ANGIE CASSIDY: My first exposure to Factory Records was at the house where my brother Larry was living. Rob Gretton and Ian Curtis came round to the house to talk about the early Section 25 'Girls Don't Count' track that they wanted to put out on Factory. I was eighteen or nineteen at the time. They came in the house and went upstairs. I made cups of tea and brought them up so that I could have a nosey at what was going on. They were friendly and cool. Soon after, I went to many gigs where Section 25 were supporting Joy Division and would go backstage. I'd be given a big lump of dope and I rolled joints for everyone. Obviously, this was an important role. [laughs]

LITA HIRA: I was in a band before Stockholm Monsters when I was maybe fourteen, when Tony Wilson was doing the Russell Club, and we played a night there. He came up and said he was starting this new label and would we be interested? Then he found out that we're like fourteen, so we didn't hear from him again. Next thing I knew, Factory's starting.

ANN QUIGLEY: We just started going to The Factory nightclub, me and my friend Cheryl, and it was the most amazing club ever. It really, *really* was. I mean, people can tell you that about all sorts of clubs from Studio 54 to Heaven, but The Factory at the

Russell Club was definitely a breeding ground for what Factory became, both bands and the people that made the record label. That's where everyone started because everyone was recognising people from other things they'd been at that they thought were cool and making associations between different people. What I'd do is I'd spend the week in Liverpool, and then at the weekend, I'd come back to Manchester just for The Factory on a Friday night. It was *that good*.

ANG MATTHEWS: While I was in England, I had been to see Joy Division in Liverpool. I was just a fan then, but that was the start of it, really — of Factory actually being in my life.

LINDSAY READE: I was much more into the music and the songs and didn't much care for the culture of punk that Tony adored. The band that we both agreed on, Tony and me, was Joy Division, and the Factory sample sold well, in my view, because of them. I thought they were great, but particularly after hearing what Martin Hannett did with them in the studio. I didn't really get the whole thing that much immediately, but when I heard their recordings, I thought, *this is fantastic*. And the second album . . . whoa! You just knew this was amazing. But with the terrible tragedy of Ian's death, I couldn't listen to it again. I can't bear to hear it, even after all this time. It's too . . . painful still.

KAREN BOARDMAN: One of my best mates was dating Peter Hook, so in the early days, we were around that scene a lot. They weren't even called Joy Division at that point, they were Stiff Kittens. I knew them as this really cool band we hung out with, and we went to some early shows that are now legendary. If you were a bit of an outsider, which we all were, you suddenly found your tribe, against a backdrop of this post-industrial city that was a bit grim. Going to these clubs was similar to going to a CBGB [famous New York City music venue] in Manchester. It was life-changing for me . . . you suddenly felt you belonged. And then, Joy Division became successful.

LITA HIRA: I mainly remember seeing Joy Division because of Ian Curtis. I used to go to the Russell Club, The Factory, every week, so I saw Joy Division a few times there and other places as well. It mesmerised me, the way Ian Curtis danced.

JULIA ADAMSON: When punk happened in about 1976, 1977, I was sixteen or seventeen, and I started going to see bands. I was also starting art college at the same time, started playing guitar and joined a band, and went to the Factory nights at the Russell Club, where they were putting on some impressive bands. I see punk music and the birth of independent record labels as an arts movement more than anything.

MARCIA PANTRY: I used to go to the Russell Club, and that was in the day when I was young and dressing so outrageous ... you could pick me out in a crowd. You'd see me in a Japanese hat like workers would wear in the fields. I'd dress up and have one of those on. As a Black girl, I'd dress ways that other Black girls weren't. When punk came, I'd dress up with plastic bags and safety pins. You didn't see other Black girls doing that! People thought I was weird, but I was interested in fashion, full stop. Anything. I used to wear a green vinyl like a hat, a halo type, because Grace Jones had something like that. But Black girls then in Manchester didn't dress like that, with that edge.

NICKY CREWE: I had a dilemma of universities to go to. I'd got two offers and didn't know which one to go to. Tony was at Cambridge by then, reading English, and I wanted to do English, and he was one of those people who I'd ask advice, and that's how we became friends. He said, 'Follow the path with a heart', quoting Carlos Castaneda. I followed the path with a heart and lasted a term, [laughs] came back up to Manchester, then went to a different university and enjoyed it.

Tony eventually came back from Cambridge and started working for Granada TV, and again our paths used to cross. I had a boyfriend who was involved as a roadie for some bands in Manchester, and he started doing work for Factory when they were having live bands on and events, and I used to do the door tickets, box office and the guest list. So I was doing the door for Factory at the Russell Club. Alongside that, when I left university the first time — this disastrous term — I moved to live in a big shared house in Manchester, and Martin Hannett was one of my housemates.

MARCIA PANTRY: I worked at the Russell Club before it became anything with Factory, just as Tony Wilson took it over. When I went to work at The Haçienda, one of the guys said, 'This is an original Factory work' — [meaning] me — because I used to work at the Russell Club. [laughs]

SIDNIE PANTRY: I used to go to those Factory nights because my mum knew the owner of the Russell Club, so I could get in for free.

MARCIA PANTRY: I just asked them for a job there, at the Russell Club. I was already going, and my sister was working there, so I got the job. I was at college then, so it just worked. I worked at the bar there.

NICKY CREWE: One night at the Russell Club, Mark E. Smith came in with Brix and said, 'We're on the guest list.' Now, I was very strict, and I think that's why I was popular to be on the door. I never let friends in, and I never pocketed money. So when Mark said, 'We're on the guest list', I just said, 'No, you're not.' He wasn't! [voice impression of Mark E. Smith:] 'Oh, don't you know who I am?' 'Yes, of course I know who you are, but you're not on the list, so you can't come in.' [laughs]

PENNY HENRY: I used to work in a cooperative in Manchester well before The Haçienda opened, and Mark E. Smith once pinched a pair of dungarees. I chased him out of the shop and took them back off him. I think he was going to hit me . . . I didn't know it was him — he was thirteen at the time. When he came into the club, he talked to the hairdresser, Andrew Berry, and said, 'I don't like her (me), she wouldn't let me steal dungarees!' I didn't know it was him until then, but I remembered it. [laughs]

LIZ NAYLOR: My first ever punk gig was The Fall in 1978, and The Distractions were supporting them. I kind of got friendly with The Distractions, and *City Fun* at that point was a collective mainly led by a guy called Andy Zero, a Distractions fan who was at all of the gigs. It was a really small scene, and I kept bumping into this guy. I was sixteen, and I wrote something that was printed in this local fanzine, so I became part of the collective. I met Cath around the same time. It's a long backstory, but in the early days when I first met Andy and Martin X from *City Fun*, I was theoretically still at school — I'd just turned sixteen — but I got expelled. I was a sixteen-year-old kind of truant, running away and going to The Factory. I'd get in at soundcheck and see Joy Division. I would sleep in a flat over the road from The Factory that was owned by another guy involved with *City Fun*, so I was just hanging around. We all started working on *City Fun* kind of seriously in early '79. Me and Cath just hijacked the magazine one day, took it to a different printer, and then just stole it. It wasn't very glorious. *City Fun* was started in '78, and from '81 onwards it's just me and Cath. Manchester felt extremely small, like the whole scene was generated by twenty people, and it felt really competitive, life-and-death. It was like, 'If we don't wrestle this fanzine away from you, Andy Zero, the whole world will fall apart.' Everything felt incredibly serious, and nobody was being terribly ironic about anything because it hadn't been invented yet. Tony was ironic, of course, which nobody understood, but the rest of us were just peasants fighting amongst ourselves on the dark streets of Manchester. [laughs]

CATH CARROLL: Liz and I would go to Factory gigs when we were doing *City Fun* — they would advertise with us, and we would interact with them. Well, actually, I say interact, but Liz and I were just really rude and obnoxious because I think that's how we thought we had to behave. I'm honestly quite surprised that Factory took it for that long. New Order too have always been massively gracious, considering how snotty we were. Factory always seemed like a bit of a refuge because of the support that they offered.

LIZ NAYLOR: We always had a really fractious relationship with Tony and Factory. In its earlier days and later on, it was just Cath and I that were the few dissenting voices concerning Factory ... well, that's maybe not fair because there was lots of grumbling. But we were the people out there taking the piss out of Factory because we thought they needed pulling down a peg. We always existed in this sort of codependent relationship with each other.

NICKY CREWE: One thing I had forgotten until now was the night the feminists attacked Tony. It was at a club somewhere, upstairs, and I think it was a Factory night. It definitely wasn't the Russell Club, though ... might have been the Beach Club. I can't remember who was on the bill, but I have a feeling that it was John Cooper Clarke. I mean, they really attacked him — verbally rather than physically — and it was a very aggressive sort of a thing. People did react to him very strongly, you know? Tony wasn't an aggressive man, and I think he'd sort of step back at something like that. It would be really interesting to know why women took against him that way, and I wouldn't say it was because of his behaviour. I mean, there are people who are creepy, but nothing like that with Tony. He was quite unthreatening, even camp, really.

CATH CARROLL: A lot of the really meaningful interactions with Factory were not actually in reviewing or witnessing performances or hearing records. Although of course having said that, in July 1979, *City Fun* did a fundraiser for a now defunct club called The Mayflower, and I think it was called 'Stuff of Superstars'. Joy Division were the headliner, and we were on the record counter near the stage. I remember Rob Gretton coming backstage and plunking down this big box of albums. We didn't know what it was, and he was like, 'You'll sell them and I don't want the money.' He was being funny, or at least funny for Rob Gretton, because his sense of humour was the driest ever. And that box was full of *Unknown Pleasures*. I remember Liz and I, and I think Pip from The Distractions was there too, just opening up this box and seeing this incredible design — the paper and the card it was printed on, and taking it out and holding it. I love Joy Division and I saw them a lot, but we were just hangers-on.

KAREN BOARDMAN: That was a seminal moment for me, Joy Division becoming successful; indie record stores and clubs were crucial to the 'lightbulb moment'. Suddenly there's a lot of records in the stores of bands that you knew, and suddenly you were around people who were so creative . . . in bands, running venues or doing press for the bands, for example. I started writing for a fanzine called *City Fun*. The bands were here in Manchester, and Factory, the record company, facilitated their journey. When success came, they stayed in Manchester and they reinvested in Manchester with clubs like The Haçienda and bars like Dry. That became an important moment for me: you didn't have to go to London. We created this in Manchester, and London was coming to us.

CAROL MORLEY: Just after Ian Curtis died and Joy Division didn't have a new name yet — so pre-New Order, when I must have been fourteen — I went to see them. They were playing a gig at Rochdale College of Art, and there were hardly any people there. Tony Wilson was there, though, and I went up to him and said, 'When I grow up I'm going to be on Factory Records.' I've never forgotten that because it was something to aspire to. Factory was the heartbeat of Manchester.

LINDSAY READE: Joy Division, to me, was something very different, but a lot of the rest was more fun and games. Almost from the start, Tony and I started to bicker about his managing of ACR, and he and them dressing in battle gear like they did. Then, I loved Magazine, and . . . well you probably know what happened there. [laughs] But I can say that it didn't happen the way it did in the film. [laughs]

LIZ NAYLOR: I remember going to pick up a first pressing of *Unknown Pleasures*. I didn't have a stereo, and we were putting on gigs at The Mayflower, like the Funhouse [a gig featuring Joy Division, Ludus, The Fall and others]. I remember going to Palatine Road, picking up one of these copies of *Unknown Pleasures*, bringing it back, and playing it over the PA system — a very crude system with a couple of basic turntables. It felt amazing to listen to in that perfect setting, a decaying hall. Brilliant.

ANN QUIGLEY: Me and John moved to Hulme, where most of A Certain Ratio lived. What had happened is that the council decided that the flats that were built were totally unsuitable for the families that they'd got in there, and they were moving everyone out and just putting students and musicians and anyone who wanted a freer lifestyle in these flats. So it turned out ultimately the whole block of flats was full of musicians and artists, and it was quite an amazing place, even though it was a really deprived area. You could still see poverty every time you walked downstairs, but a little circle of friendship formed between John, me, A Certain Ratio, an artist called Cliff, and a guy called Eric Random who was in a band with Francis and Pete Shelley, called the Tiller Boys, of the Buzzcocks, of course. That was our friendship group and it was like that for a few years — we were like a little family.

ANGIE CASSIDY: I got on with ACR, with Jez and Simon Topping . . . They used to come up and stay with us sometimes for weekends and stuff because we lived in the country, compared to the flats where they were living in Manchester.

ANN QUIGLEY: A funny thing is that all of this was somehow fated. The area in Manchester called Wythenshawe, which is a massive council estate, was an early home for so many of us at Factory. People like Donald Johnson, the drummer from ACR, Leroy Richardson, who was a manager of The Haçienda, Rob Gretton, myself and Tony, that's where we lived. There was also another band living in Wythenshawe called Slaughter and the Dogs, and they were a punk band that played with the Sex Pistols in Manchester — everyone said they were at that gig, but they weren't. The next one at the Lesser Free Trade Hall, with the Buzzcocks and Slaughter and the Dogs and Sex Pistols, that got Factory started. Anyway, I'd known Mick Rossi of Slaughter and the Dogs since I was about twelve because he liked David Bowie, and I used to do paintings of David Bowie for him. He paid me either with fish and chips or 50p, and then he formed Slaughter and the Dogs. I was on the school bus going home one day, and Wayne Barrett of Slaughter and the Dogs got on the same bus and said, 'Will you come and see our band play in town?' I'd never seen a band before so I said yeah, and he told me that they were going on with a band called the Sex Pistols.

So that was the first punk gig I ever went to, and even though a lot of the boys at that gig said being a fan of the Sex Pistols meant you went out and bought a guitar or a bass and started a band, it had the same effect on me as a girl. My dream had been the same as the boys', so anytime I come across girls in my stories, I'll mention that the girls were important because we were few and far between.

86 Palatine Road

86 Palatine Road

The first Factory Records office was located in co-founder Alan Erasmus's flat at 86 Palatine Road. In 2017, 86 Palatine Road was memorialised with a British Plaque Trust blue circle, marking the site for its significance to cultural history: 'FACTORY RECORDS was founded here in 1978', it reads. Less celebrated has been the role in that founding played by people such as Penny Henry, a woman who was integral to 86 Palatine Road becoming the home of Factory Records and who later played a key operational role at The Haçienda. With several Factory women living in other flats at the address, including people such as Martine McDonagh who worked tirelessly in management and promotion, 86 Palatine Road became the beating heart of Factory's rise.

PENNY HENRY: I moved to Palatine Road in 1972 and was there for forty-six years. I got a flat with my partner then, CP Lee. We also got somebody a flat across the hall, and that's how Alan Erasmus moved in a couple of years after we moved in. He got a flat through the people we'd got a flat for across the hall. He was an actor at the time and was living with a man called Charles Sturridge, who produced a series of *Brideshead Revisited*. Alan was also in a play about a rugby club. That was Alan *then*, and when Factory wanted to start, he said, 'Oh, do it in my flat!' It was just a rented place, for all of us, but that's how he got into the house — indirectly through me and my partner.

LESLEY GILBERT: The Palatine Road flat was in a beautiful old house, and the whole office was a big living room. And do you know what? It worked really well because Alan was very rarely there. There was loads of space, and it didn't feel crammed. Alan never ever got pissed off that it was his living accommodation, never. I mean, he lived quite a bit of the time with his girlfriend at this time, but it never felt like you were impinging on Alan's living space, not ever. It was just a really big room, a couple of settees, a desk, a kitchen, a bathroom. Just a standard flat in many ways. Except Factory Records was being run out of it!

PENNY HENRY: I was just thinking about Martin Hannett, when I first met him. I met him in 1972. He did all the mixing for Joy Division ... He came and lived in my flat in Didsbury, downstairs from where Factory was on Palatine Road.

TRACEY DONNELLY: For a while, I'd see Martin Hannett walking down Palatine Road, and I knew it was Martin. He didn't live far from the office. I remember going to a club that used to put on bands and I saw him there, and I thought, I'm going to go and speak to him. I went over and said, 'Hi, I'm Tracey, I work at Factory', so straight away he looks totally unimpressed. All he said to me was, 'You got any cigs?'

PENNY HENRY: Vini from The Durutti Column lived above me for a bit, and I used to love listening to his guitar playing, which was gorgeous. It would just filter down. Tim Booth from James and Martine McDonagh lived above me as well. Every time Tim and I met we'd argue. One day he came down and I said, 'How's my sparring partner?' He said, 'Oh, that's good' [laughs] and after that we got on really well.

MARTINE MCDONAGH: When I first moved to Manchester, I stayed with Jimmy [bass player for James] and Jenny [Jimmy's wife] for a while, then later Alan Erasmus offered me a flat at 86 Palatine Road that had come up for rent. It was on the same floor as the Factory offices, so even after James left Factory for Sire, I was very much in and out across the hallway.

My only gripe about Palatine Road was that, not long after I moved there, I had this bike I loved that I used to ride absolutely everywhere, and it got stolen from the hallway. I think I'd been there for about two weeks, and the front door was always open. We also had a stalker problem at one point, too. Eventually the front door had to be kept locked.

TRACEY DONNELLY: I actually had a stalker at Palatine Road. I think his nickname was Jinx. He'd be coming in the office quite a lot there, and one day he said he was going to India. You know how some people say they're going to India to find themselves and come back completely lost? When he came back, he was completely derailed. I think he'd really lost his way probably before he ever left. But he tried to attack me in the office. Alan happened to be there and he threw me in a room and locked me in — to stop that guy from attacking me. I don't know what Alan did to get rid of him, but he launched him out somehow, and he never came back. He just had this fixation with me, and he was aggressive. I was just doing my job! If it had been just me there — which it often was — I don't know what would have happened. We always had the door open, so anybody could just come in.

MARTINE MCDONAGH: [There] was someone stalking Tim [at Palatine Road]. Tim and I had become a couple, and Tim moved in with me. There was this guy who kept hanging around in the car park in front of the house. He'd stand by the hedge, just looking up at the windows. At first we thought, 'Oh, he's a Factory fan and he's looking at the wrong window.' But he kept coming back, and late one night he knocked at our flat door and asked to come in. Tim had the presence of mind to come out with a camera. He took his picture and said we'd send it to the police if he came by again. We didn't see him again after that.

PENNY HENRY: IKON also used to be there at Palatine Road, and I got really close with the IKON guys. I've still got a video called 'Bessy's Halloween Special'. He used to get in trouble all the time with the women because they'd say he was sexist, and that was when feminism really started taking hold.

TRACEY DONNELLY: Alan, Tony and Rob, none of them had an office in the flat at Palatine Road. IKON, who were the film production, had the back bedroom (because it was a flat, so the offices were bedrooms). I was in the middle, and then Tina was in the front office. But Alan, Tony and Rob never had an office

— they'd only call in or sit at Tina's desk when they were in, which is quite funny.

LESLEY GILBERT: I think Alan's neighbours found it quite strange to have an office being run from there, because, obviously, people would call in and, you know, musicians would call in. By a certain point, the neighbours knew who those musicians were. Although it was in Alan's living space, it really did just feel like the office until 'Blue Monday'.

CHAPTER 2

RUNNING THE LABEL AT PALATINE ROAD

Alyson Patchett in the Factory office at 86 Palatine Road

Women ran the Factory Records office at 86 Palatine Road. While their roles were behind the scenes and have rarely been recorded in great detail within existing histories of the label, the administrative skills and keen business minds of women such as Lesley Gilbert and Lindsay Reade were critical to the label's cultural ascendancy during its early years. Tracey Donnelly, Tina Simmons, Tracy Farmer, Alyson Patchett, Lieve Monnens, Jane Lemon, and Seema Saini continued that often unglamorous yet critical labour of keeping an ideas-driven label functional until the offices moved to a new location in September 1990.

MARTINE MCDONAGH: Certainly, the Factory women — everyone should know who they are! For all the noise that's out there about Factory — that's *still* out there about Factory — why does nobody know who Lesley is? Why does nobody know who Tina is? Why does nobody know who Tracey is and Tracy was? It's rubbish.

The women running Factory didn't get the credit they deserved. They didn't get any credit for anything they did ... Lesley did *everything*. You know, she ran that label and it's still only the men who get the credit. I've never heard any of the women mentioned, or heard it said that they were doing anything of importance. That's par for the course. As someone who worked in the music business for thirty years, I can say that being a woman, you don't get the credit for the things that you do. I think it's much easier for men to deny women credit than it is for them to deny another man credit. As a manager, you shouldn't expect credit necessarily, but creative input should always be credited and really it's just plain weird — and abusive — to not acknowledge work done by a woman that a man would routinely be acknowledged for.

PENNY HENRY: Lesley was very much a solid person in the whole development of Factory, especially in the early days.

LESLEY GILBERT: We were all by this point very good friends, and Rob was a director of Factory Records. And then Ian died in May 1980. I started work in the office on Palatine Road, Alan's flat, probably in June or July 1980. Susanne O'Hara, Martin Hannett's girlfriend, ran the office for a very short time before me, and I don't think that worked out very well. So they were without anybody to run the office in Alan's living room. After Ian died, I think they really were getting a bit big and there was too much to do. Obviously Tony was working at Granada, Rob was managing Joy Division and then New Order, and I think they needed somebody to just take over the office on a day-to-day basis. I was pretty fed up with my job at that point and looking for a new one anyway, so it just sort of fell into place. Tony just suggested one day that I might fancy running the office. I think I said, 'Yes, as long as you pay me the same as I'm getting now.'

I was there from 1980 to 1985. And in that time, it definitely got busier. Towards the end of my time there, I think possibly in '84, Lindsay came to do all the foreign licensing work and to make sure it was all running smoothly. That completely changed the whole office again because I think Lindsay and Tony's relationship, full stop, at this point wasn't great, so some days were just horrible. I suppose I'm just describing working conditions and people you work with. It's the same in whatever office you work in. The dynamics and the politics.

LINDSAY READE: Lesley sat in what was the living room, and Alan's bedroom was for IKON. I was in the small bedroom, and that was where my deals were done. Musicians often used to wander in and out . . . I had a list of all the licensees, and I've still got the paperwork. It includes lists of the licensees, the FAC numbers and sums of money that were taken. Then there was packaging, sending out the parts to them, after talking to them on the phone and making the deals. I got a taste for doing deals then.

Everyone in my current office says I'm good at doing deals. And I *am* good at doing deals. When somebody wants to buy something, somebody wants to sell it. You've got to do the negotiation, and that can be tricky, but I enjoy it and think I've got a skill for it. It all began with doing overseas licensing deals.

LESLEY GILBERT: This is what I always say to people: it wasn't as exciting as people think because it was my job, and it was basically an office job. For example, just tracking releases coming up. Were the labels ready? Were the sleeves ready? Did we have the test pressings back? Just general stuff like that, and of course phone calls. And we used to get quite a lot of fan mail, so every now and again, I would sit down and reply to the fans. And, you know, don't forget this was before the internet, so a lot of it was done by letter. There were obviously days that were just great because we went through a phase of having film crews in and TV programmes and stuff like that. So that's great and really interesting. And getting involved with the bands when they were touring abroad and having to sort their equipment, making sure they could get it through customs . . . and it was fun when bands would drop in and chill or help out or whatever.

I was aware of the importance of my job because the work needed to be done, but it didn't feel like I was living through history or that history was being created. I was very, very aware of how fabulous and different we were, but at the same time, I had to just do the job.

LINDSAY READE: Within six months of my taking on the job the overseas licensing income had trebled. Yet, even at that time (1984), the Factory bank account was not healthy. People look back and think Factory really did well in the earlier years, but there was never that much money in the bank.

JULIA ADAMSON: I understand Lindsay Wilson was more involved than I initially thought, and behind signing OMD, who were a favourite band at the time for me.

LINDSAY READE: I realised though that I had a gift for the work. It was my persuasion that brought about the OMD record on Factory because Tony wasn't into it at all. I heard a demo tape and I just felt sure they were going places. I got pretty annoyed when Tony got rid of them, actually, without discussing it with me. They were my band, and they did really well, and I really like them to this day. At that point, I thought, I have got a gift for spotting talent. And that carried on because, after I left Factory, I took 52nd Street (the Factory band I started managing while I was there) with me.

ANN QUIGLEY: It was Lindsay Wilson who was our lovely Lindsay, now Lindsay Reade. I thought she was absolutely brilliant, and in the early days, I think a lot was coming from her as to who was recording and what to do. I know that she was so capable, and I think she liked the work. I imagine it came about with Lindsay and Alan wanting our music, but I'll never know.

LINDSAY READE: I also had a bit of a talent for managing, just basic day-to-day affairs. When I ran the overseas licensing at Factory, I had some great product to work with and sell abroad. I was still working at Factory up to FAC 100 and on. I was amazed at all the overseas money coming in as a result of me sitting in that chair running it! I'd never previously thought it my role in life to make money. I'd always thought that was what men were supposed to do. The things I saw my mother doing — that was the role model for women that I took then. Housework and child-rearing, mainly. You didn't think you were supposed to go out into the world and make money.

ANGIE CASSIDY: I'll tell you who was great in the Factory office. Tina, Tina, Tina. She was in command, and I loved her. She always let me take the new albums! [laughs]

ANN QUIGLEY: Tina Simmons was at Factory, Tina and Tracey Donnelly, and they were so important. They also totally loved the music. What Tina and Tracey did was that they worked harder than anyone else in my eyes, it was *them* at the label. When Tina arrived at Factory, it was great because she was someone I could go and sit with and talk to — totally different to talking to Tony Wilson or Rob Gretton — and she really supported the girls.

REBECCA BOULTON: A really important person in the Factory story is Tina Simmons, and she doesn't get the credit she deserves. When

I started working, she had just been taken on, and she *really* knew what she was doing, she knew the industry. Not everybody loved her, but some of the bands really liked her, and other people did too, because she organised things and made things better for them, better for Factory. She instigated proper accounting and made it into a proper business, and she was quite vocal in her criticism of some things that were going to detract from focusing on making the music. She made predictions that ultimately came to be true. She knew, and she said, this is what's going to happen if you do this — meaning it would all go bankrupt, would all end — and actually, it did.

TINA SIMMONS: I was actually an art director, production manager and label manager for Pinnacle Records in Orpington in the early eighties before I came to Factory. They distributed records for independent labels, including Factory. I co-ordinated things in London with regard to Manchester. I left Pinnacle in '83 or '84, but I kept in touch with people, including Alan Erasmus, one of the Factory directors, who'd pop by when he was in London. At that point I worked for another record company, and we operated out of Mayfair to start with, and later Regent Street.

By end of '84, beginning of '85, I got a call from Alan telling me that Factory were looking for an international licensing manager, and was I interested? I said, yeah, I'd be interested. I knew a bit about international licensing because I set up an export arm for the record company where I was, for the records to be exported from the UK around the world. I also knew a bit about the legal side of things because I used to do contract work as well. So it all crossed over.

Long story short, I went to Manchester for an interview with Tony Wilson, Alan Erasmus and Rob Gretton. It was the most bizarre interview I've ever had. [laughs] They wound up arguing with each other during the interview! Tony Wilson had actually offered this job to a mate's wife without telling the other shareholders, so part of my interview was to explain why he should offer the job to someone who didn't live in Manchester. I said, 'I'll move up to Manchester.' He said, 'You don't know anyone in Manchester' and I replied, 'But I know you, and I get on with people. I've got no problem moving to Manchester.'

Then they had this big row — with me in the interview — that started with Tony accusing Alan, 'You've invited her up here because you want to fuck her!' [laughs] I'm just there . . . gobsmacked. [laughs] It transpired because Alan's then-girlfriend looked a lot like me. It was the most bizarre thing I've ever encountered. So I had to say again, 'Yes, I will move to Manchester, I have no problem doing the job, and *no, I will not be having an affair with Alan Erasmus!*' [laughs] Rob's having a go at Tony for having a go at Alan, so I got in the car and just shook my head and thought, I've always known Factory was strange, but that's the strangest interview experience I've ever had. I got back to London and thought, I'm going to immigrate to Australia. I wanted to leave London. Two days before I hand the keys over to leave for Australia — because I'd sold everything by this point — I get a call from Alan, 'You've got the job.' So this is how bizarre things are: I tell him, 'I've sold my flat, I've handed in my notice, I'll see you Wednesday afternoon, but I've got nowhere to stay, so can you find me a bed and breakfast or somewhere to stay?' I packed my car up, put the rest of my stuff in a friend's place in London and drove up to Manchester and started working as an international licensing manager at Factory.

MARTINE MCDONAGH: As manager of James, my communications with Factory were very friendly, especially with the women who ran the office. Most of my conversations would have been with Lesley and Tina, the women in the office who, let's be honest, did all the work. Because I lived there, I'd pop in for quick chats about licensing, sales, etc. They were so busy all the time. So we'd have to make time to just sit and have a cup of tea, talk about this and that.

TINA SIMMONS: It was once I got up there that I learnt I was the replacement for Tony Wilson's first wife, Lindsay Reade, who'd been the international licensing manager but they'd had a big falling-out. So I took over from her. Lesley Gilbert was running the whole office. At the time, Lesley and I worked together in the office, and Alan was there as well.

LINDSAY READE: It was pretty interesting at Palatine Road the day Tony sacked me. That's definitely the standout memory. [laughs] There's a whole background to why he sacked me. Right up until his death, he never agreed with me that it was a total stitch-up and that basically I had become inconvenient to his life. At that point, his first child had just been born. He had been trying to get me back up until the year before his child was born. Afterwards, that was when I was elbowed out. This is how I see it, but he never saw it like that. If he was talking to you he'd say, 'Oh no, no, no, no, it was perfectly fine. She did the wrong thing, she stepped on the toes of Michael Shamberg, who was running Factory in New York' . . . I did kick off in the office the day he sacked me, and I was swearing and saying terrible things . . . but what do you expect? I'd lost my marriage, my home and now I'd lost my job. Anyway, that's my side of the story but Tony would say, 'Oh no, no, no, no. You stepped on the toes of Michael Shamberg, that's what you did wrong.'

TRACEY DONNELLY: I took over Lesley Gilbert's job because she left to have her first child. For the first two or three years, it was just Tina and me. She was made a director in the end, so I was the only office worker, technically. Five directors, and then me — the only employee!

TINA SIMMONS: Lesley became pregnant with Benedict, so she was going to leave, and they said to me, 'You know how to run the record side', so why not have another hat? [laughs]

TRACEY DONNELLY: Andrew [Berry] was looking to go start something else when the job came up at Factory. I applied, thinking I wouldn't get it. I was called for an interview, and I got to The Haçienda, and I was put in a room with everyone else — all the other people who had applied for the job, ten people. Then Tony came in, stood around for a moment and said, 'OK, Tracey's got the job.' A lot of the people who'd applied already worked at The Haçienda. He spent the rest of the time telling them how they could improve their jobs. Then he turned around and said to me, 'I'll see you in the office at ten', and that was it! I was in The Haçienda for two years, and then I worked for Factory from 1985 to 1990.

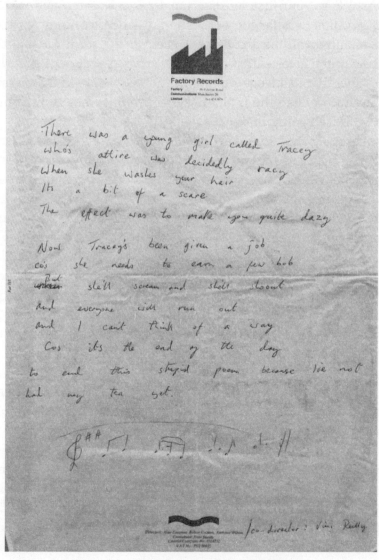

Poem for Tracey Donnelly by Vini Reilly

TINA SIMMONS: A typical day at Factory ... [laughs] I'd never start till ten o'clock, but sometimes not be home till two in the morning. I'd check invoices for production, then check them again. I'd go through everything that had arrived and would pass everything onto accounts. In the earlier days, it was Alison Lamb, and later Chris. Alison was employed by Tony Wilson's personal accountant, Keith Taylor, who also happened to be Factory Records' accountant. [laughs] We got our first computer in 1985, a Ferranti, and it was MS-DOS. Apple was far too expensive at that point. Alison would come in and do all the accountancy book work, which was still by hand. From the invoices that came in, before they went to Alison, I'd make notes. We had ledgers of all the different bands and different records, and we had the fifty-fifty agreement, so I had to note the costs — what's going in, what's going out — with regard to each of those artists and albums. That had to be done on a daily basis, otherwise you'd lose track of it. Then I had to liaise with distribution at Pinnacle, at Rough Trade, to find out what was happening — what had been sold — and this was before there were any computer readouts. The distributors could see those daily readouts — reams of paper! [laughs] They would also phone us quickly if there was a big rush on something. Then I'd have to liaise with the printers and all the pressing companies. That was the start of a day.

I'd also liaise with the studios if we had anyone recording. When we had albums scheduled for release, I had to talk with our licensees, and then I'd have to organise getting all the reels to actually manage sales in other territories. All the packaging and all the export stuff. We made it that the releases would be simultaneous releases, so if we were releasing on one day, all the licensees were releasing the same day. Obviously, I'd liaise with the various bands. Many would drop in — it was an open house, really. [laughs]

TRACEY DONNELLY: One of my jobs was to post records to all kinds of people. I had all the vinyl in my room — my office — because I started off there doing the record production, Lesley's job. Later, I got into dealing with Nicki and being the Factory person who dealt with all the PR. Even while I was doing that, I still did mail-outs, so I regularly sent Morrissey and other people records.

ALYSON PATCHETT: I was in the bigger room where all the records were stored, so there was a big bank of records in some sort of storage system on the wall, the whole catalogue. It was also the room everyone came to, to get free records.

TRACEY DONNELLY: The Factory numbering system had a very practical function — it helped with the chequebook. It was quite literally a cataloguing system. So when you'd make out cheques, you'd use the numbers.

TINA SIMMONS: Turning back the clock, to July 1986, we were putting together Festival of the Tenth Summer. Tony was so involved, and it coincided with the New Music Seminar in New York. He was supposed to be speaking on one of the panels in New York. He came into the office one day and said to me, 'I told the New Music Seminar guy I can't do this, so you're going to have to go and sit in my place on this panel. It's all about independent records.' I said all right, and then he said, 'Oh, and by the way, we're making you a director.' [laughs] He said, 'Rob's standing down, and you're going to replace him.' What I didn't know at the time, and Alan told me this later, 'Tony had no choice because Rob said, "I'm going to step down and you've got to make Tina director in my place."' Rob knew I was the only one who would actually stand up to Tony if he left. Rob was a bit ill at the time, and he wanted to concentrate on New Order. A bit like my interview for the Factory job, it was the most bizarre experience. Not, 'Do you want to be a director?' but instead, 'We're making you a director.' [laughs]

ALYSON PATCHETT: When I started working there, it was '89. I was a fan of Factory but not obsessive. I'd been in London for about three years prior to working for them, and I'd worked in a record shop when *Substance* came out, the New Order compilation. I wrote to Factory to ask if they've got any jobs going up towards the end of '88 and didn't give up for a couple of months. Then I literally had to call them while working at the local hospital, doing admin stuff, and they said, 'We've got a vacancy . . . do you want to come over for an interview?'

A girl called Tracy was working there that was going on maternity leave — not Tracey Donnelly, but the other Tracy — so there was a vacancy coming up. I don't know that they ever interviewed another person for that job. I think they just picked my letter and it was pure luck, coincidence.

TRACEY DONNELLY: Tracy Farmer answered an advert for a cleaner for the office. She was such a lovely person that she fitted right in. That was when it was me, Tina, Tony and Alan there — before we discovered Tracy could type! This is before computers, when typing was a thing not everyone could do. Tracy ended up doing general admin on top of everything else. She did eventually leave to have a baby girl, Cassie, but would call in with the baby to see us. We were all heartbroken when she passed away.

ALYSON PATCHETT: The salary wasn't great. [laughs] I think it was about £7,000 a year which, you know, I had to live on, because I was going to move to Manchester. It paid less than my last job, but I thought, well, you've just got to take a chance. I started working there around Easter '89. I worked there for two and a half years, and it was literally just as the whole thing was exploding in Manchester. Happy Mondays had just got *Bummed* out, had another release planned, breaking them through.

LIEVE MONNENS: I started at Factory in Manchester in 1990, only two years before they went down in their beautiful, sad, tragic bankruptcy. But really, my history with Factory begins with Factory Benelux in Brussels. That's how I ultimately got the job in Manchester. They needed someone in Manchester, and they already knew about me because of my work at Benelux. I was ready to move countries, so when the position came up, it was easy to do it since I already knew all about Factory Records.

ALYSON PATCHETT: When Tracey Donnelly went on maternity leave, I took over what was called the promotions co-ordinating roles, which involved communicating between the press office and promotions people in London. Right around then, we had more people coming on board before the office move. Jane Lemon became Tony's sort of PA. Lieve came in to do the overseas, so she took that over, but on a bigger scale because I think they were wanting to expand the overseas markets.

CORINNE DREWERY: Jane Lemon was important — she was Tony Wilson's right-hand person for quite a few years.

LIEVE MONNENS: There's a picture of me, Seema, Jane Lemon and Simon, who did production, at the Palatine Road office. The photo says 1989, but it couldn't have been since I started there in 1990. It must have been 1990, just before the move.

SEEMA SAINI: New Order absolutely made me want to work for Factory. I'm East Indian, and back then it was very hard for an East Indian person, coming from that type of culture and every-thing, to cross over to work in the entertainment Industry. Back in the eighties, there weren't very many Indians who went in that direction because we were encouraged to be doctors, lawyers, and my family was no different. So I just thought, I'll hopefully be able to utilise my education as a means of going to Manchester and getting involved in the music, kind of like a stepping stone to get into something that was more meaningful and creative to me.

I'm from Wolverhampton, far away from Manchester, so it was like, how do I even navigate to get to Manchester? I went to Salford College and started my Higher National Diploma in business and finance. In one of my business studies classes, the professor said, 'OK, we're gonna do a dissertation on a company, so pick one.' 'FACTORY RECORDS!' I said. I went into the Factory offices and they said, 'Yeah, sure, come in', and that's how I met Tina Simmons. I was so different back then. Tracey said something to me like, 'What were you doing, you showed up in a pair of ankle socks and a skirt?' [laughs] You know, it was the eighties and that was a look. [laughs] Anyway, I remember sitting with Tina, and I interviewed her for this class project. My teacher actually helped me with the questions to ask. I remember afterwards Tina goes, 'Oh, thank God you were asking interesting questions, and not like, "What colour underwear do New Order wear?"' [laughs] I thought, this is good, I've made a good impression! I didn't know what I was doing in the interview, but I knew I was led by my desire, my interest and my love for the music. For the dissertation, we had to volunteer for a couple of weeks at the place we picked, and I remember that I was told no, you can't volunteer at Factory Records, by someone at the company. My teacher called Tina up, and she goes, 'Sure, yeah, she can come for a couple weeks, absolutely.' So I was there for a couple of weeks, just started showing up, and then I got a job there eventually.

TINA SIMMONS: I was once asked to talk about Factory Records at Stockport College, and they were interested in the artwork and the records, and I likened the three directors — three shareholders, I should say, Tony, Alan and Rob — to the three monkeys: hear no evil, see no evil, speak no evil. Hear no evil, that was Rob. He heard everything, and he was the A&R man, really. He was the ears of Factory. See no evil, this was Alan. Alan would always look for new things, for different ideas. He was the first to come up with the idea of using different audio types before anyone else, like CDs and Digital Audio Tapes (DATs) replacing cassettes. He also opened up Russia for us, and Factory Classical, which was a complete off-the-wall thing to do. He always kept his eyes open for new things. And Tony, speak no evil; he was the biggest egotist going, but we had to have a mouthpiece, and he loved being the voice of Factory because he was already on TV and he could be in front of the cameras and *talk and talk*. It suited him, even though his ego got in the way on more than one occasion. [laughs]

Tony once described me as a 'lieutenant'. Not a chief, but a lieutenant. A lot of it is to do with egos, but I think women were always kept apart. At Christmas, for example, we worked together to get all the Christmas promotions out, like the cards which were quirky (and weren't always cards), but when it came to the Christmas do, I'd take the girls out, and Tony and Alan and Rob would go out together on their own. We never sat round collectively. The women went out one night, and the men went out another night. It didn't matter if we all met up later at The Haçienda, we always went out separately, and I always found that a bit weird. It didn't bother me much then because we did our own thing and it was fun. Rob and Alan were the ones who saw women like myself, like Nicki [Kefalas], like Chris [Mathan], as women who were very good at their jobs and didn't see us as 'women' per se.

TRACEY DONNELLY: So much care went into those Christmas cards. But that was true of everything. Even new stationery — so much thought and planning went into *everything*. Tony and Alan were behind all of that.

The Christmas cards were amazing, and they were such a big deal. Tony would usually come up with the initial concept, and then we'd get an idea from Peter, or whoever was designing it, about how it was going to look. Xmas card time was amazing because we'd literally sit for a week and sign Xmas cards, like a conveyor belt where we'd all sit and do them. I loved the New Order book we sent out as a Christmas card. It was so exciting every year to see what the card would be, and when they'd arrive then we'd run out to get silver and gold pens and just spend the week signing the cards. The CD was my favourite one [FAC 145], and CDs were becoming all the rage. I remember Tony saying, 'Eventually everything will be on CD, not vinyl — CDs are the future!' And I thought, *whaaaat?!* [laughs]

TINA SIMMONS: Technology was advancing rapidly at that time, and we were one of the few record companies to issue Digital Audio Tapes. I remember going down to the *Music Week* offices in London to have a look at this machine, which turned out to be a CD player. The idea that you could drop these and they wouldn't break. CDs were coming around that time to replace audio cassette tapes, and DVDs to replace videotapes, Betamax. Since I was in the production side of things, there was work trying to find people who had capacity to produce CDs. Steve Mason, the owner of Pinnacle Records, very astute guy, he bought up masses of capacity, huge amounts of CD capacity. Of course, he had all these independent records he was distributing and could say, 'Oh, I've got the capacity for CDs', making more money. So I did wind up getting CDs done

Factory Christmas card 1985 (FAC 145)

through him for Factory. CDs cost a lot of money at that time to produce, but they were worth it because of the change in quality. As everything progressed, the World Wide Web was also coming in. New Order had an Apple Mac, which was a *big deal*. Just the program — the software — was £10,000! I remember thinking, wow, this would be good for Factory, but it's definitely too much money for the office!

LESLEY GILBERT: Everything while I was there was vinyl, all vinyl. I think the overall feeling from all those people involved in the production and manufacture was basically thank God I was there to speak to them! Trying to speak to Tony or Rob or Alan — to pin them down to have a reasonable conversation — was nearly impossible. I think when things went slightly awry, I really do feel that those people were glad I was there because I wasn't a big personality like Rob and Tony were. I suppose I was just very sensible, that's the way to describe it. But that's why the office ran so well at that point.

TRACEY DONNELLY: The basement at the Palatine Road office, that was where everything was kept. Everything was in that cellar — all the albums, just loads of them and other things — for years. You'd be working, and someone would say, 'So-and-so wants a copy of *Still*.' You could go down to the basement and find — which we knew were rare at that point — loads of the hessian-bound Joy Division *Still* albums. I don't think they realised the true value at that point, not until later on.

LIEVE MONNENS: I was in the stockroom at Palatine, and a guy came in and wanted a couple of records. I thought, well, if someone let him in he must know people. So I gave him a couple of records, and I got told off for doing it. 'He always comes in and wants records! He gets royalties, he gets paid for stuff!' That guy who wanted a couple of records was Martin Hannett. [laughs] I'm glad I gave him those records. For me, he was a hero.

TRACEY DONNELLY: Towards the end of the Palatine Road days, it just seemed like there was masses of accountants ... it seemed like everybody was an accountant! It was crazy days. I felt like I was getting out of my depth to go to Charles Street. It was getting more corporate, and they were employing lots of people, so deep down I always knew I wouldn't go back. So I did the Palatine Road years, and the day they moved to Charles Street, that was the day I left. My brothers had just started a clothing label, so I left to work for them.

I read stories about the Palatine Road office that make it sound like nobody was doing anything! But we took it *seriously*.

LIEVE MONNENS: Factory really was women running a lot of things. It was women finding bands, making connections behind the scenes, and at The Haçienda. Tina Simmons had an important role, and I don't actually know why she left Factory, if she was pushed out, but I always knew there was something not right there. I never met her.

TINA SIMMONS: All in all, I was with Factory for five years and resigned on April 1, 1990 — April Fool's Day [laughs] — but not my choice. I handed in my notice and said, 'I don't want to be here when you destroy this company.' Tony was terribly upset with me at the time because I'd said it was a problem that the early bands, Joy Division and New Order especially, didn't have contracts. What they had were agreements on the back of a napkin, which basically said that the bands owned their own copyright as long as they paid back the money out of 50 per cent of their earnings to pay for the recordings. So how did this work and what was wrong with it?

For argument's sake, let's say it cost £10,000 for a particular album. As soon as it actually earned £20,000 worth, the fifty-fifty split between the band and Factory, let's say Joy Division or New Order, anything after that they start earning money. That's great if you keep getting bigger and bigger like New Order. But then you wind up doing a publishing deal with WB or Warner Music, and from the sale of record one, you are paying royalties – not on the actual record sales but on the publishing rights. When we were in the studio with New Order doing *Technique*, it was overrunning our budget. At the same time, the Happy Mondays were in Barbados with Tina Weymouth and Chris Frantz. Alan had bought a building on Canal Street that was going to be the new Factory Records offices. Fair enough. The costings came in at a ridiculously high level, like £400,000. It only had a commercial office value of £150,000 to £200,000, so we were going to over-spend by at least £200,000. My point to the financial director at Factory, Chris Smith, was 'Chris, do you not understand we can't do this? New Order is costing us £200,000 or £300,000 to pay for *Technique*', which was being done at Peter Gabriel's studio down in the southwest of England. Happy Mondays in the meantime were close on £200,000. So I said, 'OK, from the sale of record one, let me remind you that New Order still recoups at fifty-fifty on the recording.' To recoup that £300,000 it was costing us to produce the album, just for argument's sake, let's say it's £1 for every record sold. If we sell 300,000, they've broken even, but we'll still have to pay an additional 'x' amount on publishing rights with the record sales. Happy Mondays had also done a publishing deal with London Records. I said, 'We haven't got the money. This is going to cripple us. We cannot foreclose or not pay the publishing on those two records.'

That was my major row with Tony. He wouldn't listen and said everything was fine. Alan listened a bit and spoke to the architect, Ben Kelly, on the new Factory office and said, 'You've got to bring down cost, the most we can afford is a quarter million', (which is what the finance guy said) and I told him, 'That's still high!' Ben Kelly is an old mate of Tony Wilson's, so he phoned him in Australia — Tony was in Australia at the time — and says, 'I've been told to change it.' Tony flew home and had a go at Alan, saying he had no right telling Ben to change the costs, and saying that I was to blame. I was extremely upset, and I knew it was only a matter of time before Factory was going to go down.

When New Order did the compilation album *Substance*, we'd sold in excess of a million copies worldwide, and we had a cheque from our distributors for just one month in December for over a million pounds. So, it was a lot of money that was being generated, but you still have to budget for things! I went to Tony's house, and he said, 'You're rocking the boat, and I don't want you to tell anyone anything about costs.' At the time we were also paying over the odds for our distribution contracts with Pinnacle Records. I'd already spoken to our lawyer, and even she said we were paying way too much, more than we had, and I said, 'I know, but nobody seems to be doing anything or listening to me.' Eventually they listened to me about the distribution costs since we were paying for everything. Pinnacle were just a warehouse holding our goods and then selling them out. We were the ones forking the money out. Steve Mason, the new owner of Pinnacle, set up a meeting with Tony, Alan, Chris and I at the Orpington offices, and Tony said to me, 'Do not talk to him about costs. Chris will talk to him about costings. Chris is the finance guy, so Chris makes these decisions. You're only at this meeting because you're a director.'

At the meeting, Steve Mason said we could get distribution costs down to 'x' amount, but I knew it was still too high. Tony looked at Chris and said, 'What do you think, Chris?' Chris shuffled some papers around and said, 'Yeah, we can do that.' I thought, the man's an idiot! He didn't understand the publishing and royalties, and certainly didn't understand distribution. All I could think was: I'm here watching the fall of this wonderful label.

SEEMA SAINI: I was so young at the time, but I knew that Tina was extraordinary. I mean, she obviously knew what she was doing, and she explained everything to me really well for my dissertation, the whole breakdown of Factory — royalties, merchandise, paying for The Haçienda. Tina knew exactly what she wanted. She knew how to get merchandise there and how to make everything work. I remember admiring her confidence and knowledge of the business.

• • •

LINDSAY READE: I think a lot of industries are gendered, and the music industry definitely was. For sure, women have been marginalised in the music business, and probably still are for all I know. I can honestly say I don't remember speaking to a single woman while doing deals for Factory overseas. It was men, men, men. That went right across the world. There were only men . . .

LESLEY GILBERT: The one thing I would say about Tony and Rob, and Rob in particular, actually, was that they just thought women were great and much better than they were. That was the general consensus: 'let's just leave it to women'. Prior to working for Factory, I worked in various offices, corporate offices and . . . it could be horrible. The men would treat you badly. I remember once, in particular, this guy in the office — and I had very long curly hair at that point — got hold of a bit of my hair and said something horrible. That would never, never, *ever* have happened at Factory, ever. There was never anything sexist or inappropriate because I think most of the men involved really admired women.

ALYSON PATCHETT: It felt like a real family atmosphere, and it wasn't like any other job.

TRACEY DONNELLY: It was a very special time, and I think we even knew it then. But I don't think we ever dreamt that all these years on people would still be talking about it.

If you had passion for the music, they'd give you an opportunity. I had no experience, but they saw I had a passion for the music, and they gave me the chance to work for Factory. They were *always* backing and promoting other people. Teaching other people ... If they thought you had the passion for the music, the design, you were in. It didn't matter if you had no experience. Tony would back anything. They were all about helping other musicians, designers, and they really got inspired themselves by anything new. And financed everything. It was like being in a family.

LESLEY GILBERT: The first thing about Factory being different is that Joy Division and New Order didn't go to a major and stayed in Manchester. The fact that the label was in Manchester, that we were all from Manchester and loved our city — we were really proud Mancunians — I think that made a big difference. And the ethos of 'why the fuck would we want to go to London to do any of this' had a massive bearing on it all. It was a chance to try to create and achieve something on your own terms without being tied to anybody pulling your strings. It was very punk, but not in a contrived way. We just thought, why would you do it any different when you can do it like this?

TINA SIMMONS: It was part of the excitement of being with Factory that you could always come up with ideas. Sometimes they worked, and sometimes they'd throw them out, like 'no we're not doing that', and then months later Tony would come up with the same idea that had been your idea six months ago. It didn't matter, really, because it was a fun time to be there. There were no inhibitions about coming up with ideas ... Factory gave a kind of freedom that you didn't get other places, and I've worked with other record companies. There was a freedom about it that I almost can't describe.

LESLEY GILBERT: I look back on it now because this interest in the women of Factory has been building quite slowly for the last few years. I've been thinking about it a lot. And actually, yeah, I think my job was really important. Without me keeping everything running along smoothly, quite a lot of stuff wouldn't have happened. So from that point of view, I'm only just starting to look back on it and to think about it that way after all these years. It's like, wow, actually, you know . . . I was important.

Blue Monday

Lesley Gilbert's 'Blue Monday' anvil

And I thought I was mistaken
And I thought I heard you speak
Tell me how do I feel?
Tell me now, how should I feel?
New Order, 'Blue Monday'

On 7 March 1983, 'Blue Monday' was released as a 12-inch single. It didn't actually cost more to print than it earned in sales.

LESLEY GILBERT: Oh without a doubt, everything changed with 'Blue Monday'. I mean, it just went *bonkers*. First of all, the sheer volume of pressings, and the whole hoo-ha around the sleeve, obviously. Just the interest in it and the way it took off was *instant*. I remember the very first time I heard it was in The Haçienda, and the whole place just went off . . . everybody was dancing. *Everybody*. And most people didn't know what it was, and it just instantly caught on. *Instantly*. And then everybody knew New Order. And of course, because Rob was my partner, work was revolving around New Order at this point and home life was revolving around New Order. So 'Blue Monday' started taking over our lives in a way. [laughs]

MICHELLE MANGAN: I grabbed the 'Blue Monday' 12-inch right away in 1983. I was at school, and 'Blue Monday' was like a benchmark for everything . . . I remember when I first heard it on the radio, 'Blue Monday', and it just went *boom*.

TRACEY DONNELLY: There were a lot of original 'Blue Monday' release vinyl stored at a warehouse in Stockport with other surplus pressings.

GILLIAN GILBERT: 'Blue Monday' was like a big experiment because we got an Emulator, and Martin wanted to get a Fairlight synthesiser

... This story has been told a number of times, so you probably know that they didn't get a Fairlight but got a nightclub instead. I think that upset Martin Hannett greatly. So, 'Blue Monday' was just a complete experiment to see if we could do a song and then just walk offstage and leave it to all the robots. It was quite long, and we never thought it'd get anywhere. It was only our manager, Rob Gretton, who said, 'That sounds like a hit to me.' We all thought, 'What? You can't even dance to it. It'll never make it.' But he insisted, 'No, no, that should be the single.' We had to edit all the tape and then reprogram all the sequencers and the drum machine, which was mine and Stephen's job. We Sellotaped A4 pages together and spread them on the floor so we could count every bar. You had to click every button with a note and put spaces in, so it took a tremendous amount of time. It was a bit like a knitting pattern, if you've ever knitted [laughs] ... *thousands* of rows. We did different sequences in different coloured pens, and then, famously, I left one out and that ended up on the track. It's slightly out of time, but it worked because it was an accident. Because you were actually programming the thing, it's not like on the laptop where it does it all for you. You tell it what to do and it'll do it perfectly, but only if you tell it perfectly!

MICHELLE MANGAN: 'Blue Monday' is definitely in the top club records ever because it laid the groundwork for every track that came after.

LINDSAY READE: With the Factory licensing there was good product, New Order's 'Blue Monday' and *Power, Corruption & Lies* for instance, so I didn't have to work that hard to sell stuff because the licensees wanted it. But it was the amount of money they paid — that's where the negotiation came in and the organisation of it was important.

GILLIAN GILBERT: We went to Australia the first time we played 'Blue Monday' and Bernard was like, 'How can we remember all this, coming in and out?' Because it was all very regimented. On the old acoustic material, we used to say, 'Oh, just play that bit for sixteen bars', or 'Play that bit for eight bars', and you'd remember that. With 'Blue Monday' it was like, 'When do we come in?' At our production rehearsal in Australia, Barney said we'd never be able to do the song live, and me and Stephen knew we could do it because we knew *every minute detail* of that track. Gradually, we all learnt to come in when we should, but of course we couldn't actually walk offstage and leave it to the robots. [laughs]

LAURA ISRAEL: [As a film editor] I always worked with Alex Bingham, who's now my art director, and as soon as she heard I was going to edit the New Order video for 'Blue Monday' '88, we were like, 'Whaaat?!' [laughs]

TRACEY DONNELLY: When the 1988 remix was released, I was in charge of the record production. The track was famously a big success, and I was managing everything so carefully: the sleeves, the labels, the pressings, and trying to avoid overstocking it. We used to get vinyl pressed at a few places, and one of them was in France. Everything was going so well, and I'd got enough vinyl ready to be shipped from France to make the chart position, when I got news that there was a strike. It was a catastrophe. Now there I am, I've got thousands of 'Blue Monday' records stuck at the docks in France, and without these pressings we're not going to make the midweek predicted chart positions. Do I order more pressings and waste money, or go for the charts? I can remember having to make the decision with images in my head of 'Blue Monday' '88 in the warehouse with the original 'Blue Monday' pressings. I decided to go for the charts.

LAURA ISRAEL: I got a studio [in New York] at Broadway and Bleecker Street in this building that was so cool and weird, and the first job I did in my studio was to edit the New Order video for 'Blue Monday'. I was so excited because New Order was my favourite, so when Michael [Shamberg] said, 'I want you to edit this', I was like, 'Oh my God, yes.' I had no furniture in that studio, and I remember I had to run out and buy shades because it was so bright in the room and I couldn't see anything. [laughs] Michael introduced me to Robert Breer and William Wegman [who directed the video], and they'd come in separately to look at the edit, and then they'd comment on their sections. They were both very giving to each other, though, because it was hard for me to mix the two in the video, and it was a real challenge to make their work make sense together. What I was known for in those days was making something that was impressionistic, so that ultimately made sense for 'Blue Monday' and the two of them. They were wonderful to work with.

TRACEY DONNELLY: I got into work one morning, and Tina and Tony greeted me with, 'There's a flight booked for you in a couple of hours to London.' I had to go to an editing suite and choose the stills from the video for press and the *Top of the Pops* chart rundown. Hours spent watching that dog and the ball bouncing around. I'd never done anything like that before and was so unsure if everyone would be happy with what I'd done. I absolutely loved it, and when I see the video now, it brings back some great memories.

LESLEY GILBERT: I was just trying to keep up with the demand for the record — trying to get enough labels, trying to get enough records shipped into the shops. I mean, the more records Factory released, the more stacked with boxes — with vinyl — the office got, until we actually took over one of Alan's bedrooms just to keep all the vinyl. The vinyl was taking over Alan's flat ... Oh God, 'Blue Monday' was intense business, and there was a lot of pressure to get the records out. Rob and Tony seemed quite tense about the whole thing. It was like a rocket taking off, and it took a while to adjust to that for everybody. So, the label printers, the sleeve printers, for everybody. There were lots of really horrible conversations going on between people. That's the first time it felt ... like a proper business.

GILLIAN GILBERT: Lesley worked in the Factory office so she realised how many records she was selling. With 'Blue Monday' we became a proper record label.

CHAPTER 3

THE MUSICIANS

Carolyn Allen of The Wake

Spend five minutes with Factory Records figures, and you're bound to hear that it was always 'about the music'. This was true not just of the men, but of the women who formed, played in, recorded for, and fronted Factory bands, or performed as solo artists. In some cases, they provided vocals on only a song or two, or added notes on keys or strings. Songwriters, singers, guitarists, bassists, pianists, keyboardists, trumpeters, drummers, synth programmers, and all-around multi-instrumentalists, their musical range is vast and varied, and, until now, discussed largely as adjuncts to the male artists whose Factory disc-ographies loom so large. These are resounding stories of women becoming musicians, taking the stage, and recording albums. Their names include Julia Adamson, Carolyn Allen of The Wake, Lindsay Anderson of Stockholm Monsters, Cath Carroll of Miaow, Angie Cassidy of Section 25, Beth Cassidy of Section 25, Diane Charlemagne of 52nd Street, Anna Domino, Corinne Drewery, Gillian Gilbert of New Order, Lita Hira of Stockholm Monsters, Denise Johnson, Beverley McDonald of 52nd Street, Ann Quigley of Swamp Children and Kalima, Lindsay Reade, Gonnie Rietveld of Quando Quango, Jenny Ross of Section 25, Rowetta of Happy Mondays, Renee Scroggins of ESG, Yvonne Shelton, Miranda Stanton, Martha Tilson of ACR, and Jackie Williams. Many of these voices ring out in the pages that follow.

ANGIE CASSIDY: We — Section 25 — went to see New Order play in Reading years ago and stayed in the same hotel as they were in afterwards. Gillian, myself and Jenny were all sat having a drink and decided we were going to set up a girl band — an all-girl band! It never actually happened, but the thought that we would do it was very exciting at the time. We were very made up about it and thought it would be the best thing on Factory since ... well, since anything!

GILLIAN GILBERT: I got to know everybody [in New Order] and the manager, Rob. It was the manager who suggested, when Ian died, to bring another singer in, which they didn't want to do. Eventually he suggested, 'Why don't you just bring somebody in that nobody thought would be brought in?' Especially being a woman, I think it was an appealing idea. I didn't really know much about songwriting, so it was a bit daunting, and they were calling me 'the apprentice'. I thought they'd teach me to write songs, but the more I got to know about songwriting, the more I could do it myself.

When I got asked to join New Order, I was at Stockport College doing graphic design at the time. I did one year there, and I thought, 'I can't ask my mum and dad if I can go off with this band.' I thought they'd never let me go, but they surprised me. My mum, and my dad especially, were like, 'Yeah, go for it.' But recently, my Auntie Linda asked me, 'So, what did your mum and dad think of it when you wanted to join the group?' I said, 'They were really up for it', and she replied, 'That's not what I heard!' [laughs] So I've unlocked a terrible secret now, that all along I thought they were up for it but they weren't at all! So that's funny to me now, looking back.

ANN QUIGLEY: The first gig we did as Swamp Children was at the Beach Club, a small pub in town. Simon and ACR were such a laugh, and we began to follow and support ACR around the country. It was great for my band to get that experience. The reason it happened was Martin from ACR became our drummer. And all that was organic as well. It all came about just from my jamming down there with the whole of ACR, and the Swamp Children fanzine that I did before the band. Jez and Pete and Gillian had all contributed to this one-off fanzine that I did. So they set me on my dream course.

We started doing gigs with ACR around the country, and me and Gillian had a law exam on Monday. We were studying, and she looked really depressed. I said 'Are you OK?' and she just started crying and told me on Sunday, Ian had passed. We both left the course and then, all of a sudden, she was in New Order. They moved out of our rehearsal room into their own space, and I knew at some point they'd be auditioning for new singers. I thought it was absolutely a brilliant idea to get Gillian in New Order because rather than having a singer to compete with Ian and that legacy, a girl added a nice and different edge to the band. My first thought was that Bernard was absolutely brilliant as the frontman, and I think a lot of people knew it. The way that he sings, it's totally different. But I totally appreciate the style, the minimalist style that he developed. I mean it as a compliment: it's like Billie Holiday at times.

GILLIAN GILBERT: After Rob talked to them about me joining the band, Stephen came to me and said, 'You'll never guess what ... Rob asked me if you'd want to play guitar in New Order tonight.' So, it was a surprise, and it's funny because I think it was all channelled through Stephen to ask me what I thought. It seemed like a dream, really. A dream come true. I was a bit daunted because they were obviously songwriting, and I couldn't play keyboards at all, and I thought I'd just play guitar. But they said, 'Well, we've got some keyboard parts.' So, I got my sister's Bontempi organ out. She's very good at music, was in a brass band, and played clarinet. She could do everything. She's so jammy. And she's really good at school as well. [laughs] So yeah, she played all the instruments, and I just played guitar. I started playing guitar with my uncle, actually, who taught me, and we used to do that on weekends when I stayed with them in Manchester. But I got that Bontempi organ and learnt all the songs that they'd already written before I joined. So I learnt all those songs on an organ. [laughs]

CAROL MORLEY: Gillian is really brilliant and made a major contribution to New Order, but at the time, the way it was said around town was, 'They've got Stephen's girlfriend, and she's had to put stickers on her keyboard because she doesn't know how to play.' Certainly from my perception, her introduction to the band never felt like this incredible thing that it was. She obviously proved them otherwise!

CAROLYN ALLEN: Caesar, my brother Steven, Joe Donnelly and Bobby Gillespie recorded a single in 1982 in Edinburgh on their own Scan 45 label, but I wasn't really involved with the recording. I wasn't yet in the band then — just a fan and Steven's sister. They decided to go down to Manchester, take a few copies of the single there to see if anyone was interested in it. Basically all of them, including myself, were really big fans of a lot of Manchester bands like Buzzcocks, The Fall and Joy Division. So when they told me they were going down, I went with them. We got down to Manchester, where they'd decided to go to Richard Boon's office. He was the manager of the Buzzcocks and had a label called New Hormones, so we headed to his office and gave him a copy of 'On Our Honeymoon'.

Richard wasn't really signing new bands at that time because the Buzzcocks were doing really well in the charts, so he was spending his time managing them. But he said, 'Factory may be interested.' So he gave us Factory's office address in Manchester, and he also gave us Rob Gretton's home address. I think we decided to go to Rob's house first because we weren't sure how to get to the Factory office, and he talked to us for a long time about our band. After a while he thanked us for bringing the single and said it was a long way to come to do that. He told us Crispy Ambulance were playing that night, so if we wanted to come we should. We went to see Crispy Ambulance at a community centre in Manchester, and there were a lot of people from Factory there.

Afterwards, we went home to Glasgow the next day by coach, and my brother and Caesar made a lot of phone calls to Rob, to follow up the Manchester visit. I think eventually Rob said, 'Well, if you really want to do this, would you like to support New Order?' Steven said like, 'Yeah, of course.' They wanted to make the sound bigger, maybe have another musician. I think they asked Bobby's friend Jim if he wanted to play bass, and then Bobby would play keys and guitar, but Jim couldn't do it for some reason. They couldn't get anyone else to do it, so they came up with the idea of asking me. That's how I joined the band. They taught me some of the keys. I had no musical ability at all, and I hadn't performed onstage or anything, but that was my first experience performing, and it was in Bristol supporting New Order.

ANN QUIGLEY: Back when I was still in art school, I was going to show my portfolio to a girl called Linder Sterling to ask what she thought of it. I'd heard she was dead nice. She was also forming a band called Ludus and they needed a guitarist, so I went down with John, and John auditioned for Ludus. The following day, I got a phone call that John wasn't in Ludus, but if it wasn't for Linder, I never would have started singing, and my brother Tony would never have started playing bass. So with Ludus falling through for him — and I could see how disheartening it was to him — I said, 'Why don't you try to put on your own band, then? That's what you should do.' This is well before Factory.

John's friend, Dave, an artist, had a studio in Cheetham Hill. We went down there, and a new friend from London who was an art student in Manchester, Cliff, was going to be the singer. They start this rehearsal, and me and Cliff's girlfriend were sat on the sofa. Cliff starts singing, and she starts laughing. I had an idea for Cliff, but I didn't yet sing in front of people. I was really shy about it. So I said, 'Will you come outside, Cliff? I'll tell you an idea that I think might work.' We went outside and I sang him this idea, and he said, 'Why don't you be the singer?' 'I can't sing in front of anyone,' I told him, 'I get really embarrassed.' He asked, 'If I send them all out one by one, will you sing it to each of them?' Which, if you think about it, is harder than singing in front of a group of four people. One by one, the band came out, and they told me I was going to be the singer. So that's how it all started, because John hadn't got in Ludus, all thanks to Linder.

DENISE JOHNSON: I've sung with quite a few Manchester bands . . . The Joy, who remixed my first single. I then ended up singing with people like Electronic — Johnny Marr and Bernard Sumner — and they were friends with A Certain Ratio, who I was also singing with at the time. It's really weird, everything seems to read like a book whereby someone's heard me singing on one thing, and it's led to the next. I've been very lucky like that. [Directed and shot by Alison Surtees for Manchester Digital Music Archive, 2018[1]]

YVONNE SHELTON: I started singing in a gospel choir at church and youth groups. There was a choir at school that was OK, but it was nothing compared to the choir that I was in called the Merrybells, and the group called The Challengers. We toured the whole of England and Europe, went to America, and were on various TV shows. We rehearsed *a lot*. We'd become professional and started getting picked out by producers after certain concepts, and producers would ask me to go to the studio as a young schoolgirl, so then I started to do sessions in the studio with secular artists. We got drawn in by the studio atmosphere, the live gigs. Whenever they asked for gospel singing, I always went back to people I knew who had a gospel background. Even if you don't read the music but have a gospel background, harmonically, you knew. I've always tried to put a piece of gospel alongside my work with artists in the secular field.

ANN QUIGLEY: When Swamp Children became a Factory band, it was organic, and I don't even remember having a discussion with anyone at Factory!

LITA HIRA: I was in a band when I was fourteen — not yet the Stockholm Monsters. Then Shan and the others set up the Stockholm Monsters. I think they may have played a couple of gigs without me at first, but then they asked me to join when I was about sixteen, and that would have been 1980. We played a few small gigs, and it was just something to do, really. It'd just be like, 'oh, we've got a gig tonight', nothing special. It's just what we did. I don't even know how we ended up on Factory Records.

We were one of the first bands to join Factory, and I think we must have got a manager and had to play more gigs. We had a trumpet player join the band, Lindsay. We played a few with New Order and other Factory bands, and it just went from there. With Factory, you could just choose what you wanted to do — you didn't have to stick to things. But I didn't know any different. If you've not done anything like that before, you don't realise how different it is. I was the only girl in Stockholm Monsters until Lindsay joined, but I was never treated any differently.

Lindsay Anderson on trumpet with Stockholm Monsters

LINDSAY ANDERSON: My journey began at the start of 1982, when I was seventeen and joined Stockholm Monsters. Although historically that journey starts much earlier because the high school I went to was actually round the corner from Rabid Records where I'd always pick up badges, and there's obviously a link from Rabid Records to Factory. So I loved music and Rabid Records, but I wasn't going out. I was very much for music education and was busy playing music every night whilst Lita and co were at the Russell Club. I bumped into Shan when I was in college and studying for

A levels, and he said, 'You play the trumpet, so do you want to play with us?' I told him, 'All right, why not?'

ANGIE CASSIDY: I was due to go to study psychology at Manchester University. I got a place and then Larry said, 'Do you fancy joining the band, we're doing this tour of the States?' It was like 'wow, yeah' ... I joined the band, and we did the *From the Hip* album. Touring the States was amazing. I really felt part of the Factory family, being in the band.

ANN QUIGLEY: As far as the Swamp Children were going, we sort of decided that we needed to cut the apron strings from A Certain Ratio and start doing gigs on our own, but at the same time, we still had ACR behind us. It was like a family. With the first record we did, 'Little Voices', friends of Eric Random and Cabaret Voltaire in Sheffield were really supportive. We were invited over to their studio to meet them. Simon produced it, and a tune called 'Little Voices' was born. That particular song is like a magical number — God knows where it came from! Because in terms of experiences, playing our instruments and everything else, we were way off what we were aiming for. With the other side of that 12-inch we recorded in Manchester, you can hear how basic our post-punk style was, whereas that tune had a different element to it, a sort of eerie thing that is something I liked later in Kalima. So that was great, and then Factory said they'd bring it out, which was brilliant and I did the sleeve for the first Swamp Children single.

LITA HIRA: I was a classically trained pianist, so what I was playing in Stockholm Monsters was simple compared to what I was playing otherwise. I can play some other instruments as well. When we started to play, none of them knew how, so they taught themselves. Since I could already play it was easier for me to come up with stuff, like 'let's play it in this key, or that key' ...

I was the only classically trained musician in the band, but we wrote all the songs together. Well, we didn't actually sit down and write songs, but we came up with them when we were together.

It could be me, it could be one of the others; one of us would just come up with some riffs and we'd go from there.

LINDSAY ANDERSON: I'm an obsessive collector, so I've got loads of set lists and things like that from when we played and supported New Order. It was really weird joining the band because I had a formal music education, so going to sit in a room full of people making up songs was really alien to me.

GONNIE RIETVELD: Eventually Quando Quango came about because I was in a relationship with Mike Pickering, who became the creative director for The Haçienda. But when I met him, he was nothing of the kind. I met him on holiday in the Netherlands, on a very wet and windy little island in the north. He was on holiday there as one of the very few English people, and he was funny and knew lots about music, which was really exciting. So we formed a musical partnership, and then my brother Reinier Rietveld became the third member as drummer.

Part of the band's inspiration came from Mike's teenage friend Martin Fry (eventually lead singer of ABC), who had interviewed an electronic music band in Sheffield called Vice Versa for *Modern Drugs*, a fanzine he published with Mike Pickering. They were both friends and music fans. In 1980, Vice Versa came over to Rotterdam to record a couple of tracks for the singles 'Stilyagi' and 'Eyes of Christ', for Backstreet Backlash Records. Backstreet Records was an exciting record shop that sold a lot of no wave, New York imports that no one had ever heard of in Rotterdam. At the time, that kind of music didn't really exist from New York, so to actually have that supply was very inspiring.

Anyway, when I saw and heard Vice Versa play, it made me think, wow, I could actually do that. As Vice Versa were in the studio with their synthesisers, we got interested in the synthesisers. But at the same time, Mark, the singer of Vice Versa, picked up a guitar in the studio and went like, 'Wow, I've not been playing guitar for a while', and hey, Martin actually has a voice! That was the moment they more or less became a pop band after that recording, while we decided to go electronic and bought our first synthesisers. So the start of Quando Quango was really the result of that combination of Vice Versa and no wave, and Mike Pickering being there.

LITA HIRA: Vini Reilly asked me to join Durutti Column once and I said no . . . I don't even remember why!

JACKIE WILLIAMS: I actually played bass on [Durutti Column's] *Deux Triangles*. I'm not a bass player. [laughs] Vini said, 'Can you do this?' and showed me a little bit on the bass, and I did it, but I didn't like it. I went with them to Holland and played one gig. I was supposed to play more than one gig, but I hated it so much onstage, to be in the limelight.

LINDSAY READE: I made this demo with Vini Reilly called 'I Get Along Without You Very Well' by Hoagy Carmichael. Vini played the demo for Tony, but at that point we were separated. Tony was dancing around me then, trying to get me back. Having told me to go away, he was now, very strongly, telling me he wanted to have a family and do this and do that. I think maybe he thought there was a message to him in the song. Actually, subconsciously, there probably was, because I don't think I'd realised myself how attached to him I still was. I was in denial about it because we used to have such terrible fights. But anyway, he encouraged me to actually make the record, but I told him I didn't think it was very good. He was like, 'Well, you just need singing lessons.' I don't think singing lessons work for someone who can't sing! [laughs] I mean, I lived in hope, but it didn't work. [laughs]

GILLIAN GILBERT: One of our New Order producers, Stephen Hague, who produced *Republic* and the Pet Shop Boys, told me to 'have a few singing lessons because it'll give you certain tricks that you can do for your voice'. He said something like, 'Your voice is OK, but you just need a bit of, you know . . . something.' As far as New Order, only Stephen knew about music because he did drum lessons, but Bernard and Hooky were self-taught, so they had their own style. I thought if I did lessons, it might ruin things, but I ended up doing piano lessons first, and I did that with my mum, and she loved it. I got to learn about reading music and doing the keys. So then, when I came back to New Order, Barney was like, 'I can't get my voice to go high enough . . . can you change the key?' I knew what to do. Stephen Hague was very into doing the keys, so that in turn helped New Order as well. So singing lessons made sense, and we experimented with different oral parts of the tracks, instrumentals.

ANN QUIGLEY: Diane Charlemagne was in 52nd Street, and we started taking singing lessons together at this adult education centre with a roomful of people who were just doing it for a hobby. We got the Jazz Defektors to start singing with us, but they were used to dancing — not singing. This was long before they recorded their record. I got them on backing vocals for Kalima for a single, 'The Smiling Hour'. That's how they got their band going!

LINDSAY READE: I did make another record on Factory after that [with] Ad Infinitum, with different musicians, some of ACR actually! I wrote great lyrics to 'Telstar' [the song released by the band] and decided to get a choir boy to sing them this time.

GONNIE RIETVELD: We made a demo, and Rob Gretton genuinely liked it. He always liked dancy stuff. There were just certain bands that Tony Wilson wouldn't have liked, but Rob would push for.

Tony called our music 'Eurodisco' or something, which was supposed to mean something really bad somehow. But we always were slightly danceable, and I think that had partly to do with Mike Pickering's northern soul background. He has quite a collection, and that has been influential. You can hear it in the sound of Quando Quango, but you can also hear the friction because during the early days I was an art college student, and I liked that avant-garde no-wave sound. So it was a bit of a collision between poptastic elements and the experimental sounds, but an interesting one.

Most importantly, Rob really liked it, and he said, 'Well, if you're coming over, then you might as well record, right?' You know, in Stockport, at Strawberry Studios, which was a great recording studio. The very fact that we were present in Manchester made it possible to record there.

ANN QUIGLEY: The editor of *New Musical Express*, Dele Fedele, described us as something like, 'awkward music for difficult people'. That was us! No matter what was thrown at us, we'd just run in there, arms open, and embrace everything that could happen. No matter what people said about us, we'd just carry on doing our thing, and I think Factory liked that — it was a very Factory thing to do.

CATH CARROLL: Our Factory band Miaow began as Glass Animals and we changed it to Gay Animals soon after we first formed. It was mostly me and Liz Naylor and Lynn Howe — Lynn was the singer from the band Property Of ... which was the very first band I joined — and it evolved from there. At that time, Liz and I didn't really present as women. We were really about questioning 'heteronormative reality' and we were not really into performing rock music. There were times we played behind a sheet onstage. We ultimately changed our name after we moved to London, and

Ann Quigley with Kalima

Liz left because when we were asked for our name and I said, 'It's Gay Animals', people kind of went, 'What?' I think they thought that we were mocking, but we weren't. Since we really were now more of a pop band, we became Miaow. I came up with the name ... I think I wanted it to sound sort of camp.

LIZ NAYLOR: Cath and I moved down to London together and had some spectacular falling-out, and then she went off to do Miaow.

CATH CARROLL: We moved to London with our band, the Gay Animals, before it became Miaow. From then, there were a few years of not really having much Factory contact, except I would sometimes interview Factory bands when I was working for the *NME* as a writer. As Miaow, we had recorded a track and for a little bit I was going out with someone who shared a flat with Dave Harper, the Factory promo person at that time. He took it to Tony and Tony called me. It was one of those classic phone calls: 'Kids, we love it!' He'd be on his car phone, and not many people had phones in their cars in those days, but Tony did. So he was on his car phone extremely enthusiastic about the record, and I was just thrilled to bits then ...

Honestly, there was really very little change for Miaow once we got on Factory officially. Our record got officially promoted, and we had a manager called Brian O'Neill (a manager who worked at Rough Trade) who was really helpful in getting us gigs. Factory had a hands-off approach because they weren't the typical record company. Tony believed in giving people artistic freedom.

● ● ●

JULIA ADAMSON: I wanted to become a sound technician from quite an early age. When I met Martin Hannett, I thought he was a beyond top-level record producer. I learnt a lot from him about music, recording and production.

As a sound technician, the Factory people came in the studio, and there were quite a few recordings that I was involved with. I remember Quando Quango, and I remember working with Kalima.

I also worked with New Order. That was an interesting session with John Robie, and musically, that was probably my favourite because there's a lot of interesting stuff going on. I remember John Robie, who's supposed to be the record producer, strapping on a guitar and doing overdubs.

LITA HIRA: The first thing we recorded as Stockholm Monsters was 'Fairy Tales', and we did it at Cargo Studios. We did some demo tapes before that at somebody's house, but then we went to Cargo for a proper recording — a proper studio and a proper producer, Martin Hannett.

GILLIAN GILBERT: I'd been in Strawberry Studios with Martin before, but I hadn't recorded anything. The idea was to get me on to play 'Ceremony' because that was the end of the Joy Division songs. So I went in with Martin, and I couldn't believe how he made you play the same thing *over and over again*. If you asked him, he'd say something like, 'Oh, this is how you record.' Just again and again, and that was how it worked. But then, when we went to London to do *Movement*, I think he wasn't really into producing New Order. I think he sort of got round to thinking, 'Well, it is their first record and with Ian dying ...' I think it was hard for him to work with us, but I thought everything he did was wonderful.

GONNIE RIETVELD: My brother Reinier had his own band, Spasmodique, and they became quite popular in the Netherlands. But he came over to Manchester and recorded that first single with us. Donald Johnson was our producer and, strange thing, Donald is a drummer ... but he wanted every drum to be recorded separately, isolated, as though the drummer was a drum machine. And that's really hard for a drummer because it's the fluidity of the whole ensemble that makes it, you know, *a drum set*. My poor brother. I thought, I hope he forgives me, because he just spent hours going *bang, bang, bang, chug, chug, chug*, with headphones on. It must have been really boring.

It was a good recording, but at the same time, I think because of the way it was recorded there's a certain stiltedness to it, as well.

Maybe it is strange to hear from an academic, but such obsession with detail can make the process of making music too self-conscious, I suppose. It was our first experience of the recording studio, apart from having sat in on Vice Versa. We just thought, you don't argue with your producer, right? Donald also played additional bass, and he was really into funk bass, so there was a bit of slap bass in there. Strangely enough, I don't really remember anything about the singing. I've done 'Go Exciting' twice. I've done it again for our album several years later, and I remember that better than the first recording.

RENEE SCROGGINS: From the moment I met Tony Wilson and then the producer Martin Hannett, it was a wonderful and life-changing experience for me. My sense reflecting back on it was that they made my first time ever in a recording studio a learning tool that I use up to this very day. I think women played a great part in Factory Records, but Factory Records also played a *great* part in this woman's life, and I can never thank them enough for giving ESG a chance to be heard by the world.

LITA HIRA: Martin Hannett was quite strict in terms of doing what he wanted to do. We were just given to him to do the 'Fairy Tales' single, but we didn't really have much say . . . well, none at all, really. It was much different when Hooky was producing on the next single because we could basically tell him what we wanted. But Martin Hannett, he produced things differently. Since it was our first record, we didn't know anything different and just thought that's how it had to be, and that's just how it would always be with a producer. In the end, the work he did grew on me, and it's actually not that bad. [laughs] We only had Martin Hannett that once, and I definitely like 'Fairy Tales' now. You know, I played the piano, the keyboards, the recorder and the handclaps all the way through — I did quite a bit on that single, so I look back with fond memories. It was happy times. I was with the band for 'Fairy Tales', 'Happy Ever After', 'Miss Moonlight' on Factory Benelux, and the video for 'The Longing', a B-side to 'Miss Moonlight.' Then I left the band in 1983, I think it was.

ANGIE CASSIDY: With Section 25, we were at Revolution Recording Studios, Pluto Recording Studios on Granby Row, Yellow 2 and Strawberry Studios in Stockport, Rockfield Studios in Wales . . . Bernard came to quite a few for mixing and was always absolutely amazing. I think Donald also came to get in on the act. I'm honoured to have been exposed to that experience and lucky to have worked with them. It's sad that a lot of people aren't with us any more.

LINDSAY READE: Vini and me, we did that first record ['I Get Along Without You Very Well'] in Cheadle Hulme at Revolution Studios. The poor engineer, who I know to this day, Stewart Pickering, was so patient. Vini wasn't there that day I was doing the vocals, which actually was the day The Haçienda opened.

ANN QUIGLEY: I do remember the first Swamp Children recording session that ultimately came out on Factory. I don't know how it came about — if Factory were paying for us to go to Sheffield — but we were going to the Western Works studio there. I don't even know if they talked to Factory. It was a strange studio, Western Works. It was winter and it was really cold. When I was singing, there was fog coming out of my mouth because of the freezing cold. And everyone asked, 'Do you want your coats on?'

CAROLYN ALLEN: We almost always recorded in Manchester. We stayed a lot at Rob and Lesley's house at first, so we did get to know Rob and Lesley quite well, and they were really supportive of us. We never met Tony on an official basis, like 'by the way, you're now on Factory Records', nothing like that. [laughs] Tony would come along to a recording whenever we were down in Manchester because he knew we were from Glasgow. Tony brought Vini Reilly one time when we were doing 'Talk About the Past'. Vini just spontaneously added some great piano. It was quite good to know people from Manchester, people from the Factory scene, because they'd come into a recording and add something spontaneously like that.

Because we were from Glasgow, and Glasgow had a thriving music scene at that point, we understood that although we were from different cities in the UK, different countries, we had a real connection musically — that we were connected to the Manchester musicians in some way. There was a common language really, and when you have that common language of music, that makes for a really meaningful experience.

ANN QUIGLEY: After our second single, I was constantly ringing Tony Wilson, saying, 'We want to go into the studio again! We've got the songs!' And him delaying it, of course, saying just go and practise a bit more, get a bit more experience. But we were young and impatient, and all we wanted to do was be in the studio. It was the best place on earth.

GILLIAN GILBERT: The Brixton riots were going on outside the studio when we were recording *Movement*, and that was pretty frightening. You could hear all the noise. We were on the second floor. You looked through the windows and you could see and hear all this rioting. That was the backdrop of *Movement*, of going to London to record after we'd done a bit in Manchester.

CORINNE DREWERY: I thought my voice sounded very English compared to what everybody sounded like, singing in an American accent, and I remember thinking they wouldn't use my vocals because I didn't sound very cool. But I thought when you're creating something of your own, you should sound how you speak. I felt very flattered that A Certain Ratio wanted me to sing on one of their records ['Bootsy' on *Force*]. I remember being in Yellow 2 with them and loving hanging out in the studio.

ANGIE CASSIDY: I can remember Strawberry Studios and Yellow 2 in Stockport when we were mixing 'Looking from a Hilltop' and Bernard wanted me to do some lyrics. I was a bit nervous because I hadn't written anything down and wasn't sure what to do. We got to the studio and worked through the night. We'd get there at about eight o'clock, and work into the morning. It was cheaper to have it at night time. Bernard gave me a vocoder, which hadn't been used much at that time. He helped me get over the nerves, and the best part was sitting next to him while he was doing his magic at the controls. He'd say to me, 'What do you think of that?' and I'd say, 'I like that, but I think we should have more of *that*', and he'd go, 'Right, OK, do you mean like this?' and I'd say, 'Yeah, yeah, yeah. Love that.' Being there was important because you could have that kind of input.

GONNIE RIETVELD: For the second [Quando Quango] recording I think Bernard became more of an influence really, and then even more so for the third. We did that one with Donald Johnson, but the nice thing was that Bernard seemed much more into improvisation and encouraged making mistakes and keeping them. I found that really inspiring. But this is where the gender thing comes in because I think if I had been a bloke, I probably could have done more work with Bernard. I think because we couldn't do the 'bloke bonding', that didn't quite happen. But I did feel there was a synergy there, working with him. I learnt a lot from him; he gave me advice about equipment and things like that. So, I think our sound, in that sense, was not that far from New Order, but structured in a very different way. I guess that's true of Section 25 for the same reason, because they also worked with Bernard as producer. In that sense, I think there was a certain synergy there with the music of Section 25, too, but I never met them at the time. So, it was only later on I thought, damn, Section 25, they're awesome!

GILLIAN GILBERT: 'Love Vigilantes' was a little bit about the war in the Falklands, our sort of country & western song, and another one where I did the bass line of the track. One of my first real songwriting things. 'The Perfect Kiss' was a bit like 'Blue Monday', where we just stuck all the bits that we liked together. We bought an Emulator, and we put frogs on that one. Stephen did the frogs. We put sheep on 'Fine Time', which was on another album [Technique]. We liked playing around with that.

GONNIE RIETVELD: I think Gillian really brought a harmonic sound to New Order. She has written entire songs that have never been given proper recognition because New Order always share all of the copyright together, including Rob Gretton being the fifth member of the band. She mostly seemed to create in the shadow of Bernard, who was clearly a creative powerhouse and who at times felt that he should get a little bit more of a share of things.

GILLIAN GILBERT: 'Subculture' was one of those night-time Skin Two songs, coming about because we were staying so late jamming and day would turn into night. These fetish clubs that had started, like Skin Two, opened at 4 a.m., so they were the only places to go at that time if you'd just finished in the studio. I wasn't into that scene, or I don't think so, anyway. [laughs] Barney and Hooky might have been! [laughs] Hooky was wearing his boots back then, and a ponytail and leather jeans, and bondage T-shirts. We used to know a journalist who'd take us out to all these clubs. I remember her coming in with a whip into the studio, because she was taking us all out, and she had a flesh-coloured corset jacket, and was chasing Barney around with the whip. It was so funny because you'd obviously think Hooky and her would get on, but I think she got on more with Barney who wasn't into that and still wore his little white shorts. [laughs] But this was the album where we were working a lot at night, it was dark and sometimes creepy, and I think that reflected in the songs. And it was winter. It was always winter and dark and cold. So when we went to Ibiza, the change in the weather really shows up on *Technique*.

CAROLYN ALLEN: *Harmony* is vibrant for me still because it was the first thing that I ever did, and it was the first time I was ever in a studio. It was like going into unknown territory, an unknown place. It seemed alien in a way at first, but there was something in it that was also quite electrifying at the same time. Although it's basically all machinery, you realise it's all quite human. I remember the smell of being in the studio in Stockport, in Strawberry Studios. We were mixing all the way through the night for *Harmony*, and I remember being really tired. By the time we got to 'Here Comes Everybody', especially, being really, *really* tired and actually having to lie down and sleep on the sofa for a while. I slept in the studio, and while I dreamt I could hear the music echoing all over the place really ... a dreamlike kind of experience.

Those first times being in the studio, I remember I kept thinking, 'I hope I get this right', and putting the headphones on and thinking again, 'I hope I get this right, I hope I don't make too many mistakes.' I did obviously make a lot of mistakes [laughs], because a few of our songs I hadn't actually written the keyboard parts for, and some of the parts weren't how I'd have written it, so I had to just learn in the studio by rote. The ones I'd written myself, I had no problems with those, no mistakes! [laughs] It all felt meant to be.

LITA HIRA: After 'Fairy Tales', we went to Strawberry Studios to do 'Happy Ever After', which was quite a famous studio used by 10cc. I remember playing the Steinway grand piano on that, and it was just *amazing* to play that Steinway. Going back forty years, that piano was something like £25,000, so I just wouldn't have had the chance to play on one otherwise. Hooky produced that, and he also produced *Alma Mater* but I'd left the band by then. But they used all my keyboard lines for *Alma Mater*! We'd had a falling-out, so they carried on and did it without me.

LINDSAY ANDERSON: I remember being at Strawberry Studios, which was very early on, for 'Happy Ever After'. It was like, *What's this world? Why am I staying up all night in a room with a pool table?* [laughs] It was very intense, but it was great. When we were at Strawberry, somebody said, 'Oh, we need some female backing vocals.' I remember Lita and I just looking at each other and laughing because there was nothing we would rather *not* do than backing vocals. So I'm happy someone said for me to play the trumpet.

I became obsessed with music tech once we got in the studio. I was fascinated by things like the Emulator. It was all new to me then, so just watching Hooky when he was mixing stuff, listening to what you could do with tech, that fascinated me. We got to know Hooky really well from gigs and from being in the studio, with him as producer. It was just such a good time.

GONNIE RIETVELD: I can think of a few women working with electronics, like Miranda of Thick Pigeon (also on Factory Records), but not so many women who were experimenting with electronica in the early 1980s. Of course, there was Gillian Gilbert, but her role was more that of a traditional musician, playing guitar and keyboards, rather than experimenting with electronic sound. There were not that many electronic ladies on Factory.

GILLIAN GILBERT: Since doing our solo stuff, Stephen and me — because we've done two solo records and a lot of music for television — realised it's easier to put everything on laptops instead of using tape machines — we can cut it up and move it around. With a computer, you can get loads of synth sounds, but I still like to say I'm a bit multi-instrumentalist. I like trying to do a bit of everything. I've even tried singing, which I found enormously embarrassing. I don't think we had a chance at being on *Top of the Pops* when we did The Other Two with me and Stephen. It was called 'Tasty Fish' and it was frightening because Stephen said, 'Oh, we might enter the Top 40!' If that happens, you have to go to *Top of the Pops*, and I thought, 'Oh no, I don't mind singing in the studio, but I'm *certainly* not going to sing in front of people!' Luckily we didn't make it into the Top 40, so I was saved. [laughs]

CAROLYN ALLEN: On 'Here Comes Everybody', I did some singing, and I'm not confident about singing so I was really nervous. [laughs] I think that the worst thing about recording is going into a booth to sing because you feel so exposed.

LINDSAY ANDERSON: Stockholm Monsters was just a million miles away from what I'd done previously. When I was growing up, I could hear the music and I could sight-read, but I couldn't improvise. So a lot of times in Stockholm Monsters, they used to ignore me and say, 'Just sit there and play.' [laughs] Fine with me, I'll be a session player. I did play the keyboard and the bass on one album, and I played keyboard quite a lot when Lita was not around, on *Alma Mater*. I played some keyboard too, I think, on 'Miss Moonlight' on Factory Benelux.

LITA HIRA: I played piano with The Royal Family and the Poor when they were recording at Strawberry, and Hooky produced that.

GILLIAN GILBERT: I remember I did two notes on that bass line on 'Age of Consent' and I was pretty pleased because we used to record everything on a four-track. We used to record our jams, which is how we worked. Those jams meant everybody playing at once in our rehearsal studio, which Hooky liked doing. So, I think that was one of my first moments of 'Oh, I've done two notes!' It was like, 'Oh, what did you play there, Gillian?' I said a C and an F, and he was like, 'Ooh.' And then it all took off from there . . . But the best one, I've said this before, is 'Leave Me Alone'. Bernard didn't like doing vocals in the rehearsal rooms, so a lot of the time he used to jam the words at a concert and just come up with a bridge, and then we'd listen back to the gig and pick which words we wanted to take to the studio — we'd pick bits of all the lyrics and then write the missing gaps.

GONNIE RIETVELD: I guess when people think about Factory Records, they still lump the bands together with other indie guitar bands. New Order still had guitars, and Section 25 had guitars. And although we had various people recording on rhythm guitar we were not really a guitar band, so that made us different.

CATH CARROLL: When I think of Factory at the beginning, I still think of arty boys and gloomy baritones, but I don't think it's a fair representation because the tone quickly shifted for the label. There was a lot of jazz and dance coming out, amplified when The Haçienda opened, and artists like Ann Quigley of Kalima and Gonnie Rietveld of Quando Quango really typify, I think, this cultural shift in Manchester, going from the deathbed of the industrial revolution with the Madchester bit clearing out the last of the old ghosts, allowing for this cultural turnaround.

ANN QUIGLEY: The story of *So Hot* is this: I was walking across Piccadilly at about ten o'clock in the morning, and I heard someone shouting my name, and I couldn't see where it was from. I looked around and it was Rob Gretton and Lesley. As he got closer, we said hello, and Rob asked why we were bringing the record out with Crépuscule and Factory Benelux and Michel

Duval — and *why would you do that?* 'Why not Factory?' Rob said. So it ended up being a joint record between Benelux and Factory in Manchester.

ANNA DOMINO: I started recording my first LP (*Anna Domino*) at a studio owned by Marc Aryan in the countryside outside Brussels. Marc had been a huge popstar in the 1960s who sort of modelled his look on Roy Orbison. He had that shoe-polish black hair and heavy black-framed spectacles. He'd built Studio Katy right next to his house and Marvin Gaye had recorded the *Midnight Love* LP there. This impressed the heck out of me. I said, 'Yes, yes please, let's go to Katy!' No one had recorded there since Marvin Gaye so I wandered around inhaling the stuffy air, admiring the gold record and hoping to sense Mr Gaye's presence. It was a simple studio with a basic tape recorder, an older synth, some guitars and a vast collection of sound samples on vinyl. Traffic sounds, alarms, running water and ocean waves, crowds of people, automobile accidents . . . they each had their own LP! I used some of these sounds on the 'Take That II, Sing It Yourself' mix we did at the end of a long night.

Marc Aryan came in one day — he always called from his house first — to say he wanted to talk with us about the equipment in the studio because we might have ideas about what it needed. We asked for a Fairlight synth and a twenty-four-track tape recorder — expensive stuff, but he brought them in immediately. And one memorable afternoon Monsieur Aryan dropped by with the Belgian fixer Freddy Cozarts. It was Freddy who'd brought Marvin Gaye into Studio Katy and this time he had Anna Karina on his arm. It seemed Freddy wanted Anna K to record some songs for a new LP . . . She was older and paler than in the films I'd seen, but as striking as ever. She didn't say a word. I was speechless too.

When I could escape from the studio I'd wander around the spooky, neglected gardens and the swimming pool, which had become a sort of primordial pond brimming with new life forms. At night, I could see into his house through the plate glass windows. The whole place was lined with shag carpeting in bright 1960s colours. Everything was shag — floors, walls, doors! Everything except the places with mirrored panels. One room off the kitchen had a row of glass-fronted, ceiling-high freezers full of food, against the day. Parked in the driveway was an enormous sky-blue Cadillac with fins and chrome fittings that looked like rocket launchers. He would get in it once a week, start it up and sit there for an hour or so while it ran. The entire place, the whole situation, could not have been more dreamlike or surreal. I loved working there and came back every time I could.

ANN QUIGLEY: We were in the studio for two and a half weeks, and it was one of the best times of my whole life. I could have lived in that studio. It was the place to be, and we'd recently been joined by a boy from London called Ceri Evans who was fifteen, sixteen, but he was like Stevie Wonder — he could play everything. And played really, *really* well, so Ceri's input on *So Hot* was so important to how it sounded in the end. And the flute player, Elvio Ghigliordini, just popped in on his way to play with the German philharmonic or something. So this German philharmonic guy put some flute down on some of our tracks. This is a band that had only just learnt how to end a song. We were all right playing it, but we didn't know how to get to the end. That's how basic we were. But we chose a genre of music which wasn't just post-punk, it had jazzy elements. And though we wouldn't call ourselves a jazz band by any stretch of the imagination, we were still attempting to do what was probably the most complicated form of these kinds of expressions as opposed to punk, which would have probably been the easiest. So we took the harder way but then with our record, it's like *What are you doing playing jazz?* Jazz doesn't sell records!

ANNA DOMINO: The original recording of 'Summer' was produced by Alan Rankine. Then Michel Duval gave it to Arthur Baker to remix. We were on tour when the remix was finished and hadn't heard it. Duval caught up with us in Liechtenstein and played Arthur Baker's version for me. I wasn't really sure what to make of it as it was so removed from my original demo, which had been more of a dirge. Further inscrutability! We did a video for the song, directed by my brother (Alan Taylor), which was truly a wonderful thing. Then Benoît Hennebert designed a cover for the 12-inch release which was stunning. That was my first official Factory Records release.

The studio, called Daylight, was still under construction, meaning I could only work at night once the builders left. Daylight had some interesting grounding problems, so plugging in my cheap Hagstrom guitar caused a lot of noisy interference, picking up taxi and police frequencies. This was solved by running copper wire from one of my legs to a water pipe across the studio. Then the engineer quit as he was flummoxed by my music, which was fair enough, and Giles Martin stepped in to save the day. Blaine Reininger, of Tuxedomoon, came in to produce, bringing along a small keyboard that wrote out scores on cashiers' tape. Mostly I overrode him on these melodies but his violin playing was terrific! One of the saving graces of this studio, to me anyhow, was a room with open boxes full of great shards of glass which produced phenomenal reverb. We'd put a speaker and mic in there, and the effect was huge. I loved the sound but it was too much and we let it go. Musicians came and went and helped a great deal: Jan Parmentier, Luc Van Acker, Virginia Astley, Erik Michiels and Jan Weuts . . . But I digress, again.

After about ten frantic nights, Michel Duval called it quits and that was that, as far as I knew. My dreams of a glorious career dashed! I wept in Duval's office, begging to be allowed to come back, promising I'd make a dance record next time . . .

• • •

ANN QUIGLEY: Ceri went back to London, and we decided to change our name because we thought Swamp Children sounded too babyish for us in our new sophisticated world of cocktail jazz and little black dresses. We were going into a bossa nova Latin groove and away from the post-punk. So we came back to Manchester and decided to call ourselves Kalima, which was actually after a track on an album by Elvin Jones who was John Coltrane's drummer. It's just a magical word because it means lots and lots of different things to so many different people. It's a word shapeshifter, if you know what I mean.

I don't know if the people at Factory were too happy with the name change because we'd had relative success as Swamp Children, and we were gaining a good reputation as Swamp Children. Then we just changed our name and went back to square one in terms of being recognised and everything. But it's what we did and at the time, it seemed right for us. Outside London, we were one of the only bands in the country doing that style of music. We were from Factory, and there was this odd disjointedness in terms of crossing over into Black music clubs since other Factory bands weren't really playing in those clubs. We were written about in *Blues & Soul*, while Factory was generally written about in *NME* and *Melody Maker* because they didn't know about the blues and soul and all the rest of it. But there was a DJ at the Wag Club called Paul Murphy who was regarded as the one with his finger on the pulse at that time. He was setting up a new label, Paladin, through Virgin, and he asked us if we wanted to sign, and Nina Simone was going to sign with him. I think her song 'My Baby Just Cares for Me' had just come out, and there was a real revival of lounge music. Maybe she didn't have a label at the time or wasn't being treated well by the one she was on, and she was up for it! And we were up for it! But we really loved being on Factory, so we really didn't know what to do.

GONNIE RIETVELD: Beverley is the female vocalist on 'This Feeling' [and] our album, and her vocals were also sampled for 'Genius'. The female voice that says 'quando, quando, quando', that's her. She always had a sort of vulnerability about her, which makes her voice so special. It wasn't a big-belly diva voice, and that made it really lovely. I think she had quite a bad time with men in her life. I can only tell you about hearsay, so I have no evidence of this, but I heard that the guitarist of 52nd Street used to nudge her in her back with the guitar to say, 'It's your turn to sing now' — really rude and really horrible.

One day she woke up, and I think she'd just had enough of everything and flipped. Apparently, she shouted at every man she came across that morning and when she finally showed up at The Haçienda she was still shouting. Staff called an ambulance, and as far as I can gather, Beverley got carted away to a psychiatric institute. I believe she received electro-shock treatments. It was absolutely tragic! I think that's how she kind of evaporated, disappeared from the music world. I wish I would have seen her when she was angry that morning. It's OK for people to flip — and then channel it, put it back into your music!

LINDSAY ANDERSON: I was good friends with Bev who used to be in 52nd Street, and we were at college together. I used to meet up with her quite a bit before she passed away. I remember just laughing with Bev: stories about what was going on at The Haç, and for me, working out who everybody was! She was working part-time at The Haç as well. So I'd always see her when I was there, and we'd have a chat and a laugh. I can just see her face, and I can still hear her.

I think music is a really funny world because it's not always about what you can do. It can be a vacuum of who you know, that type of thing. It's a very lucky world for some people and a very cruel world for other people. I was very lucky that I was in a band that had something to do, that we played good gigs, and that life's been good. For some people, it's just not like that.

CAROLYN ALLEN: Working with John Leckie was a really strange experience, coming from Factory, because when we worked with Factory there was no audition process. [laughs] Factory just took you as you were. With John Leckie, when we contacted him to produce *Something That No One Else Could Bring*, he came up to Glasgow and he basically wanted to audition us in the rehearsal studio. [laughs] He came to our rehearsal studio the next morning, and it was an unusual experience for us because it was a bit like doing a gig, in a way — we were being judged quite directly. Afterwards, he said that there were things he wasn't sure about and there were things he liked, so he agreed to do it. We went to a recording studio in Glasgow but Leckie wasn't happy with the studio at all and he wanted to go down to Manchester. So we had to do a lot more work on it in Manchester, and it became a Manchester record after all.

ANN QUIGLEY: Things were moving fast for Kalima, and around that time Sade had a new single. Apparently they played a demo of ours at a party, and their producer, Robin Millar, was at that party. At the time, everyone wanted to work with Robin Millar because Sade just had *Diamond Life* come out, and it had done *amazing*. So imagine when Robin Millar was willing to close his studio for two weeks and record an album with us! It was probably ten grand to keep the studio up and all that sort of thing, but he wouldn't charge for his services, which was incredible, and we wanted to do it. So this was pitched to Factory. Robin Millar had everyone interested — everyone, meaning people who were at number one that week ringing him up while we were there and saying 'we'll pay you whatever you want if you'll work with us, Robin', but Robin wanted to work with Kalima! And he was doing it seriously on the cheap. So we put it to Factory that we wanted to do this album with Robin Millar. Well, it didn't happen. We found out at a later date that Robin Millar went to university with Tony Wilson — they both went to Cambridge — and I don't know the half of it, but all of a sudden it was 'No, no, you can't do the album in London, it'll cost too much; no, you can't work with Robin Millar, you'll have to do it in Manchester.' So it didn't happen with Robin Millar, which really was like Factory shooting itself in the foot *and* in the other foot, which was a common thing for Factory.

CATH CARROLL: It was quite difficult to move into a solo career. I was in a difficult position where, if I wanted to sound like what I wanted to sound like, I had to change the band. And I really was not in a position to take full responsibility for a solo career. I very much leaned on people, and I made a lot of errors in not taking responsibility for my own life, so it did not always go in the way that I'd hoped it would. But I got to work with Sim Lister and Mark Brydon in Sheffield, and that was such a great experience to work with those two. So there were some good parts, but honestly I was such an intense introvert with zero social skills and a really bad alcohol problem, so it was just a bit of a car crash. I look back at it and I think the songs are something that I wrote and I'm very happy

Ann Quigley and Tony Wilson in Brighton at an indie record conference

with them. But if I'd had my way I'd just keep editing stuff . . . I was not in a position to really fully appreciate what was going on.

Then, of course, I moved to America when it was time to promote it. So, it's not like I made it easy for everyone. [laughs] People were actually pretty annoyed about that.

LIZ NAYLOR: Cath was in Islington around the time of *England Made Me*, which is a fantastic record. To me, it's like the lost fucking great Factory record, it is. She's a really interesting lyricist. Something Wilson had been going on about for the last few years of his life was about how much that record cost him, which is just bullshit compared to a horrible Happy Mondays album.

CATH CARROLL: And actually there's something I'd like to address. There was a book about Factory written some time ago, and for some reason, the author didn't ask me about what he put in there about my album. He'd interviewed Tony for the book, and Tony said that I ran off to America with all the money for the album, like thousands and thousands of dollars, and completely screwed him. I didn't see this until later, when it was published, because I was never asked to interview for the book. Let me say now that that's just completely not true. Tony would tell these stories because I think he liked building up a myth, and I don't actually think it was meant maliciously. He had this way of mythologising people, and he'd do it about Happy Mondays. I think he had a lot more to work with when it came to the Mondays. [laughs] But with me, again, I was at that point where I don't think there was much about me that was interesting. I started to present in a more female way, so there was nothing particularly edgy, and I think he just wanted to do this kind of Sex Pistols mythology to make me sound a bit more interesting. But when I saw that, I was like, hey, you could have asked me about that, because I think people who read it might have been going around thinking I liked to go around nicking stuff, and that's simply not true. I think it was Tony's idea of a joke, but in reality Factory used to pay studios directly. There were some shenanigans with a studio called FON in Sheffield, and I think a few people, including the people I was working with there, got burned. Again, I could have been paying more attention to avoid a really bad conflict of interest, but it also wasn't a completely straightforward process. But I *certainly* did not run off with all the money. I really, *really* didn't. I got some money paid in small increments, but hey, I think again that's a thank you to New Order.

TINA SIMMONS: One of the directors' meetings that comes to mind is about Cath Carroll. We were meeting to discuss Cath Carroll, and Tony had invited her two managers to be at the meeting. We arrived at 86 Palatine Road, two guys turn up, and the first thing they say is, 'This £10,000 advance is not good enough.' Alan and I looked at each other, then looked at these guys, and said, 'What £10,000 advance?!' At Glastonbury the previous summer, Tony had made an executive decision to offer Cath Carroll a £10,000 advance. So it wasn't the directors making that decision, but Tony had made an executive decision because, 'Oh, you weren't there.' Of *course* we weren't in the car park at Glastonbury! So it got a bit heated that night, and her managers weren't sure what was going on because a row broke out between Alan and Tony.

CATH CARROLL: Factory was just running out of money towards the end. I felt slightly aggrieved that much more money was spent on other things, and not just on my project, but people on the outside would say, 'Oh, that Cath Carroll record ruined everything — not Tony, not New Order.' Well, not to my face. But I knew the end was coming. Tony had the grace to call me and say, 'Hey darling' — and he was calling from his car, of course [laughs] — 'it's over, we're shutting it down, and we can't do it anymore. Thanks for the good times.' So I really appreciated that he made that call personally. I wasn't shocked but I was quite upset. It wasn't just my recording association with them ending, Factory had been my first love. Well, after Buzzcocks. So much money went out the door.

CAROLYN ALLEN: We reached a point where we realised we weren't going to be working with Factory anymore. They were moving more into dance music. It was really emotional for us, especially because we wanted to keep going as a group. We knew a band in Glasgow called The Orchids who were with the record label Sarah. They were fans of our band, and through them we got to know about Sarah. They were interested in doing something with us, so that became a new direction for our band. We stayed in Glasgow and we recorded there, working with Sarah. It was funny because we'd made the Factory records mostly in a studio in Cheadle Hulme called Revolution, and when we recorded in Glasgow at Riverside Studios, the owners actually bought the desk from Revolution. So, it was a weird connection that we were still using the same desk. [laughs]

GILLIAN GILBERT: To be quite blunt, our manager said, 'Well, Bernard's doing a solo record with Johnny Marr, and Hooky's gone to work with Revenge', which was also on Factory. So, he said, 'Well, you'll have to get another job because New Order's not going to be happening.' So it was just desperation really, since music was all we'd known. We'd been working on soundtracks, and we said, 'Let's put a soundtrack album out', but nobody was really interested in that, so Rob said we should try to make songs with vocals. 'I think that'll be more accessible to people,' he told us, and Factory would be more interested in that (and so were our American managers). I told Rebecca recently that I remembered Rob saying, 'I'm going to manage Johnny Marr and Barney, and you can manage The Other Two and New Order', and she didn't know what was going on. We'd done quite a lot of music for television, so we had different kinds of moods, genres we could do for soundtracks. Do you want a fast dance song? Do you want a song like 'Elegia'? Or a full-on rock song like 'Thieves Like Us'? That's how we deal with soundtrack stuff. So, if somebody says, 'Can you do Pet Shop Boys?' we'll sort of have a laugh and do the Pet Shop Boys (or a spin on Pet Shop Boys).

'Tasty Fish' was our actual 'let's do a Pet Shop Boys song', but we never played live as The Other Two, and I didn't want to do it! I like being on the keyboards because I don't want to be the centre of attention.

* * *

ANN QUIGLEY: At the very start of Factory it was a little like they were all boy bands, weren't they? And then Tilly joined ACR, so that was my girl. I found that because me and Tilly had the identity we'd adopted — which was sort of asexual — we felt more like it wasn't just boys and girls, it was like *freedom*. Apart from the fact that sometimes, you would just catch something that one boy might say and you'd think, hang on a minute. I remember on one occasion doing a gig, and we were in the van travelling down somewhere. I won't say who it was, but it was someone in the band, and they were talking about a girl's body in a way that I didn't like at all. I didn't want to give them the satisfaction of me responding to it, so I just sat there and listened, didn't say a word. And that was enough.

GONNIE RIETVELD: I felt some sense of kinship with women in
the other Factory bands, but I felt we needed to make more effort
to forge a connection. Everyone seemed to be in their own little
world. Maybe I was too. I've been on tour with New Order, and so
you'd think Gillian and I would be going out on the town, right?
But she was always with Steve, and they'd always go back to their
hotel room and they were incredibly private, on their own little
island, if you like. Then Bernard and Hooky would go out on the
town but they were, like, boys. And then there was Dian, the sound
engineer, who, for a long time — maybe still! — was doing the
sound for New Order. She was also with the PA company that did
a lot (if not all) of the sound for bands in The Haçienda. But again,
she was in her own sort of world with the sound system. With
Kalima, the singer there, she was very girly, and she was younger
than me as well. The thing is, I didn't meet any of the feminist
people associated with that scene. I think that partly had to do
with the fact that I was married to Mike Pickering, so even I was
in my own little world, with Mike, whether that was right or not.

JULIA ADAMSON: When we formed a girl group, I asked Tony
Wilson if he'd be interested in signing us. He baulked at the fact
when I said we admired Courtney Love's band Hole and downright
refused, galvanising my opinion of the sexism in Factory. It was an
all-girl band, the Thrush Puppies. At that point, I'd been in a few
bands. I thought maybe working with female artists would throw
a different light, a different writing style. I think women have a
different perspective, which I have always wanted to explore more.
With the record label now (Invisiblegirl Records), I have a policy
that at least 50 per cent of the artists on the label are female.
There are so many really good female artists out there. With the
Thrush Puppies, we were putting tunes together, and we knew
what we wanted to do. Grunge was just happening, so we were
into our guitars.

I was down at a gig when I saw Tony Wilson. I don't think the
girls were with me that night. I approached Tony and said I'm
in a girl band and we're doing a single — would Factory put it
out? We'd love to be on Factory. It's guitary stuff, we quite like

Courtney Love (she'd just done *Pretty on the Inside*). He just baulked completely, like, 'Oh no, not that, absolutely not.' I thought, you know, at least you could give it a listen. But it was like you had to meet some kind of magical criteria with Tony Wilson. If you weren't a man in a grey coat, and if you weren't mimicking a sound that was similar to Martin's on the Factory releases already, you know . . .

ANN QUIGLEY: I've tried to introduce the girls that I meet along the way in the music industry because we are few and far between, and we've all sort of been told to bow down a bit in one way or another.

That's the thing. It's almost always the boys' story. With Tony Wilson, if you were flavour of the month, he'd do anything for you, but if you weren't flavour of the month, it wasn't very nice. That's why I think people like Tina and Tracey, and also Rob and Alan, were so important, too. When the Factory compilation album *Palatine* came out, Tony put one comment about us at the bottom of the thing, and what did it say? 'Never got the credit, blame the company.' That was true because of the success of Joy Division and New Order, which meant all the smaller bands found it harder to get any attention. You have to work harder to be noticed and stand your ground. We lasted ten years and we didn't compromise for anyone. And you know, we did five albums, which is great. If we would've signed to a major, if our first album hadn't gone top ten or something, we'd have been dropped. But if Tony Wilson would have let us go in the studio with Robin Millar, we might have made a much bigger contribution.

CAROL MORLEY: When I interviewed Tony Wilson, Anthony H. Wilson, I've never forgotten asking him, 'Is Manchester a white working-class boys' town?' He got furious with me even asking that question. He didn't want to answer it, and he actually got very angry that I was even questioning him about the role of women within that time. I was surprised he was unwilling to talk about it — how I mean, it's pretty basic knowledge that within the patriarchal world, women are marginalised and excluded from those histories, the histories he was so much a part of.

JULIA ADAMSON: Factory also became a label of white boys, as well. When you look at the catalogue, there are a couple of Black artists there, and there are some women, but that wasn't what was 'iconic' about Factory. Factory could have had stronger female representation, in my opinion. It was labels like 4AD and One Little Indian [now One Little Independent] who took up the baton for that. The Thrush Puppies ended up releasing material with 4AD.

CLARE CUMBERLIDGE: There was amazing Black music happening in Manchester at that time, but they weren't getting signed by Factory, and I think that made me more frustrated. Politically, that's problematic to me. Most of the women I knew that were involved in music at that time were in the performance and visual arts area, so omissions weren't as apparent. Whereas I knew a lot of Black musicians who were in the music sector (or should have been), so that lack was more apparent.

GILLIAN GILBERT: The first thing that comes to mind about being a woman is when we worked in Cheetham Hill, this bloke came up who was fixing the boiler and said, 'Oh, do you know where the boss is, love?' I was like, 'I *am* the boss.' There was always a lot of the typical 'Oh, are you the singer?' No, I'm not the singer, I play instruments, you know, *he's* the singer . . . that kind of usual stuff, of course.

ANN QUIGLEY: Over the years, you did come across sexism from male musicians, and a lot of the time, it would come in the form that you were 'just a singer'. I remember I once asked a sound guy for more reverb, and he said, 'If you have any more reverb on your voice, you'll look even more stupid when you're on stage.' This is my very first soundcheck outside Manchester, and Alan Erasmus was with us, so I went crazy and he said, 'Go tell that PA guy that he can't speak to someone like that because he'd never speak to a boy like that.' It would have been so easy to get swallowed up in the onstage play at being 'the girl singer', with ideas of the low-cut top and 'this is what girls do'.

GILLIAN GILBERT: But I never got that at Factory, and I think it was a lot to do with Rob. Rob had vision, and he had a big vision for New Order. He really believed in us, and he was very clever, and I never felt like an outsider. There was never anything about macho blokes. We were all one, and I wasn't any different to anybody else, and the whole Factory thing was like that. Tony was very clever, but there were a lot of women in Factory that gave as good as they got. His 'oh darling' wasn't like *that*. It was never us and them — it was all just one big family. There were a lot of girls at The Haçienda who were running the door, girls doing loads of big jobs like Rebecca, Tina, so many others. Maybe not getting the name recognition, but doing really big jobs.

ANGIE CASSIDY: I was never made to feel unwelcome or not part of what was happening. It was very inclusive, and my personal experience was very inclusive.

GILLIAN GILBERT: It was so good how so many women worked for Factory because in those days, in most other industries, it was still 'Benny Hill country' with mother-in-law jokes and men running around making fun of women. But it was *never* like that in 'the bubble' I'd say, the Factory bubble. Other record companies were like that, but not Factory. I remember when Factory collapsed, we went around record companies in London, basically being interviewed by their boards. At one of them, I felt really small because someone said to me, 'What are your ambitions? What do you see yourself doing?' And I said, 'Writing for New Order', and the whole room burst out laughing. It was like, 'You? Writing for New Order?' as though it was a big joke. At that point, I felt like I'd come a long way and I was not someone to be laughed off.

Section 25: A Factory Family Affair

Section 25 when Jenny Ross and Angie Cassidy were in the band

Section 25 was a family affair from the start, started by brothers Larry and Vin Cassidy. With the addition of their sister Angie Cassidy (aka Angela Flowers) and Larry's wife, Jenny Ross, the band became a Factory sensation. As other band members departed, Jenny and Larry continued to record as Section 25 in the mid-1980s, including while Jenny was pregnant with their children. After Jenny tragically passed away in 2004, their daughter Beth Cassidy stood in her mum's stead when the band reformed in 2010. Shortly thereafter, Larry Cassidy passed away, while Beth continued singing with the band. At a Factory fortieth-anniversary gig, twenty-first-century New Order additions Phil Cunningham and Tom Chapman saw Beth sing, and together they formed a new kind of Factory family band, Sea Fever.

ANGIE CASSIDY: If you listen to the *Always Now* album, if you listen to some of the tracks, it was so ahead of its time. It sends shivers down your back, and I'm glad I was involved on later albums. I feel blessed and honoured to have been part of something so cool. Thank you, Larry, for asking me.

BETH CASSIDY: Before my mum joined [Section 25], the *NME* hated them. They were more like noise. Then my mum joined, and she was really musical. She's from a musical family, so she actually brought the talent. She could play multiple instruments, and she used to have to tune my dad's bass. So when they moved into electronic music and melody, my mum was a real pivotal character.

ANGIE CASSIDY: Section 25 at that time was made up of my brothers Larry and Vin Cassidy, Jenny Ross, Lee Shallcross and myself. Jenny obviously brought a female beauty to the music, a majestic intelligence that only women can portray. Her contribution is even more visible now because the music has got that longevity to it.

BETH CASSIDY: She played mainly piano, which also means keyboards and synthesisers, and she could play guitar as well. Years later, she started making her own music when the band disbanded. She was doing it all, a one-woman band, through this Yamaha M80. She created patches and drum sounds, doing the work of a whole band herself. She had this innate ability to do that, and I think that's what made her very pivotal in terms of Section 25's direction. I don't know if that's properly recognised. Maybe in some ways it is, but when my mum joined, they became really big. They went to America for the first time and they did really well. She gave them that electronic edge and she created that route.

Jenny Ross in Portmeirion, Wales c.1984–85

ANGIE CASSIDY: Larry gets lots of recognition, and I think it would be so lovely for Jenny to get recognition because she was such an important character in the band — so influential, writing the music. She carried so much on her shoulders, and she did it so easily, even with having the kids. It was probably quite difficult to do that, and she made it look really easy. Love to Jenny and thank you!

BETH CASSIDY: The band eventually decided to part ways, so it was just my mum and dad. They had a load of material for *Love & Hate*, and this was in '86. I remember her telling me this later on because I remember thinking, 'Wow, you did this all when you were really heavily pregnant.' She was in the studio, recording the album with my dad, just the two of them, when she was seven or eight months pregnant with me. She was pretty hard core.

JENNY ROSS: These are a mixture of tracks [on *Love & Hate*]; some developed from riffs which would inevitably crop up while we were jamming, as far back as the three of us, Larry, myself and Vin in Larry's attic bedroom, with views far out into the countryside through one window and way over to a busy — hippish at the time — pub through the other.

I always thought, depending on the collective mood of the group at any given time, our music either meandered melodically or attacked frenziedly, the more ferocious of the two being demonstrated in the main at gigs or taped band rehearsals and which I never felt quite came out in recording sessions at a studio. It was an altogether different flavour once on vinyl. This bothered me and I was never heard to be completely satisfied with the result.

However, more than ten years on, I wonder whether we tapped into something specifically because the germ of our music could not be pinpointed. The lyrics sought out an understanding and left a struggle. Can one be confused and enlightened? Now I hear a million voices (I'm rather hopeful there with the number) hum in unison.

BETH CASSIDY: That's my brother and me, with my parents, on the [*Love & Hate*] album cover. They never said anything at the time, so

I didn't know anything about it. When I found the record, it was like, *I'm on a record!* A defining moment. [laughs] I remember going into primary school, saying to all my mates, 'I'm on a record!'

It was Ian Tilton who was doing the photography for *Love & Hate*. He was coming down to the house to meet my parents, to bounce ideas around. Me and my brother were mooning about on that settee in the hallway by the door, and I believe Ian came in and was just like, *that's the shot.* So he just started snapping away, and he did a whole shoot at the house that day. I found all the negatives in the attic, and even my granny's on them — my mum's mum — because she was asked to come around and mind us, so there's even a photo of her holding my brother. My brother's wearing that tracksuit because he wouldn't change into his outfit. He was supposed to wear a shirt, bow tie . . . my mum used to love dressing him up. But he just wouldn't wear it. He was insistent, so they had to let him wear the tracksuit. So from what I can gather, it was a very natural process to get the shot that's on the cover. I found out years later from Ian that it's one of his favourite shots ever, and he shot everyone.

JENNY ROSS: In the beginning it ['Bad News Week'] was 'Boogie Beat'. It must have been 1983, around the time when we practised at Singleton Street, a huge — what seemed to me — part-derelict building, but what in actual fact was just and still is an old ware-house with crumbly paintwork. That is not to lessen the creepy fascination this building held for me.

The room we rehearsed in was big with an open fire and stone floors. We had old rugs hanging on the walls to try to help deaden the sound. We were surrounded by guest-house landlady neighbours from hell. This is why we eventually gave up hiring it out as a rehearsal room. Petty, picky people posing problems. A pretty puzzle!

Then we recorded it as a single at Yellow with Bernard from New Order. I was still breastfeeding and 'Boogie Beat' became 'Bad News Week' with an altogether different drum beat and rhythm.

We kept coughs and sniffs [in the song] as I remember simply to save time, but the effect was comical as well.

BETH CASSIDY: It's a bit of a double story, Section 25 reforming and me ultimately joining the band. When I was fifteen or sixteen, the band started having rehearsals — well, jamming sessions, I would call them, or a lot of noise in our downstairs lounge area [laughs] — and these went quite late into the night. This first resurgence of the band was when my mum was still around, and it was mostly the line-up from the eighties.

Factory is so worldwide, and because it's so known, so many people have so many things to say about it. So there were always talks about reforming again, anniversaries. Over the years, interest in Factory, and in Section 25, sparked something with my parents where they thought, 'Right, we can do this again.'

They were always very humble about the whole thing and never really discussed it, so interestingly, as a teenager, I didn't know anything about the ins and outs of the band or what my parents had done. I started to pry and I would ask questions, but they were so private about it. Once they reformed, my mum became ill, so the whole project stopped again.

JENNY ROSS: This one ['Crazy Wisdom'] is complicated for me. It was about two things which coincided. One of them was the wars going on in the name of God [e.g., the Iran—Iraq War from 1980 to '88]. The ridiculous paradoxical notion of holy wars! It made me angry.

And the second — all around me friends were trying to free up their minds with Buddhism. This on the one hand and Catholicism, from whence they came and which was reluctant to let them go, on the other.

Larry and I have never seen eye to eye when it comes to God. When I met Larry my view of religion as an irrational, irrelevant irritation supported itself, I thought. (I am no longer so dismissively arrogant.) We had endless discussions about the existence of God and Larry's line that you have to believe something exists before you can argue its nonexistence would drive me nuts.

I was brought up not believing in God and when I discovered at the age of about nine that there was a title for me — atheist — I was adequately satisfied. I would feel strongly and state proudly that I did not believe in God and secretly enjoyed the unusual status this brought to me; I remember being taunted by my best friend telling me that if I hadn't been christened then I didn't really have a name and me saying well actually I must have been christened as I had a birth certificate, but that I had just not been baptised. The derivation of 'christened' was lost on me.

And then I had this other friend who tinkered with people's heads. (He was older and wore the mantle of a wise man.) He became the guru in our area and was disingenuous but he was controlling in such a way that it could never be pinpointed. They all became so wrapped up in themselves they could not see further than the ends of their noses. They could not see the pud for the peas!

Everyone's kneeling if they could see themselves afraid to stand up.

Dabbling piously, dipping a mere toe into dark water. It made me angry. My father had died New Year's Day 1979 and I had seen this body being carried away on a stretcher in deep, crisp white snow through glorious, dazzling sunshine and realised I had to pack all my realisations into that moment — then panicked because the moment was too big and I knew I would never see him again. That was frightening. This was crazy wisdom.

● ● ●

BETH CASSIDY: My family were overcome with my mum's long illness. After she passed — I was just so young and had lost my mum, and we were so close — I basically ran away to London as an art student and did the art thing, and then I went to Berlin and didn't want to go home. While I was in Berlin, I got a call from the label that the band were on at that point to say they wanted a female vocalist. They'd started recording again and realised, 'oh, shit' — because my mum wasn't around, there was only so far to go with what they had without a female vocalist. When I got that call initially, I was terrified at the thought of doing it. It was so far removed from where I was at the time, doing performance art and certainly not making music. But they wore me down and I agreed to go and sing on the album they were making at the time. I remember it was one of the most terrifying experiences of my life. It was really intense. I felt like, I don't know what the fuck I'm doing, so just fake it till you make it. That was 2007, and that's how I joined Section 25.

When I recorded the vocals, everyone was almost in a trance because I do sound a lot like my mum, so I think they really thought, 'Oh my God, is this ...?' It was a very intense experience for everybody. I didn't quite realise it at the time, but when I look back, it's still quite visceral memories and I know now that it brought up a lot for everybody.

ANGIE CASSIDY: Bethany is playing now with Tom and Phil from New Order in Sea Fever. After she played a Section 25 gig, Phil and Tom were like ringing her up — or most likely Rebecca, actually! — asking if she'd want to come in.

BETH CASSIDY: We were recording an album that was called *Retrofit*, which, as the name suggests, was like retrofitting the old classics: *From the Hip*, *Always Now* ... we were kind of reimagining them as a band and how they would sound in that time. I was on the edges, really, since this was music they'd already recorded at one time, but I went into the studio, and I did some vocals with my dad, as well. We played a couple of gigs together as Section 25, and then he passed away suddenly. We were in the middle of recording. When he passed, my uncle came to speak to me and basically said, 'The ball's in your court, Beth ... do you want to carry on?' I needed to think about it and eventually thought, why not? Let's see what happens. We did a few shows, and I found my feet in terms of live business, and then we went back to the studio and started recording *Dark Light*. That was when I started to write my own melodies, lay down my own lyrics, and figure out how to do this.

I always feel frustrated as a woman, because I do wonder whether that self-doubt would have crept in for me otherwise. I think about my dad and how much ego and bravado he had, and how he came from a similar place to where I came from, in terms of having no musical experience. He just had something he wanted to say, and he thought, 'Well, everybody wants to hear what I've got to say.' There was never a point where he doubted himself. Whereas certainly with me, there was a long time where I was wondering if what I was doing was any good. I don't know if it's a female thing, but I think it must be. So that kind of self-doubt made for a difficult introduction to the band, but I think that was also tinged with the fact that I was having to stand in my dad's shoes in a way, while also standing in my mum's. There was a lot of self-doubting, worry and nerves, and a lot of trauma.

From certain fans' points of view, I was taking over my dad's role because my mum never got the chance to perform live in the reformed band, and there were loads of fans who had seen my dad in the reformed Section 25. So I had to deal with the fact that he's gone now, and they're there for him. Then there was also this likening of me, obviously, to my mum and my mum's voice. I found it easier to sing the songs that she sang because we have the same vocal range. I was dealing with my own grief while I was stepping into both their roles for fans of the band.

ANGIE CASSIDY: I think they [Tom and Phil] feel safe with her because she's organic grown-from-Factory. She was born into it and has grown up through it. It couldn't be more perfect. Larry and Jenny would be so proud. And Bernard — they call him Uncle Bernard [laughs] — I don't know if they floated the idea by him, but I know he would have gone thumbs up because he'd know she'd be right.

BETH CASSIDY: I think everything with Sea Fever, it's been written in the Factory stars. Section 25 were slowly going our separate ways. But we played one last-hurrah gig. Martin Moscrop of ACR called and said, 'We're doing a fortieth-anniversary show in Manchester, and we'd love you to play. Are you up for it?' Obviously I thought, brilliant, let me ask everybody. It took a bit of persuading because we hadn't played for a while together, but everyone eventually agreed. We had a few rehearsals and got back up to speed. At the same gig, Shadow Party were playing, which is Tom and Phil from New Order. They were in the audience while we were playing, and I got an email a few weeks later from their management asking if

I would like to collaborate. I was like, 'I'll just have to check my diary' — you know, really nonchalantly. [laughs] I was actually catching my breath! But I realised then, everything is absolutely connected. So Sea Fever has become the next chapter.

CHAPTER 4

OPENING THE HAÇIENDA

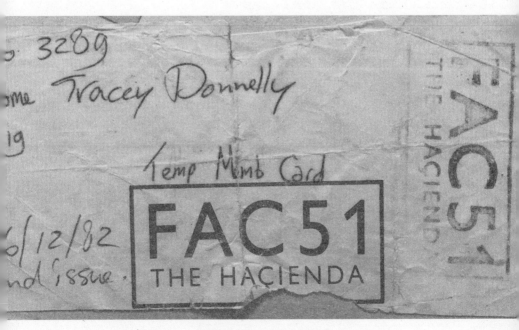

Tracey Donnelly's original Haçienda membership card

Factory opened The Haçienda in May 1982 with Howard 'Ginger' Jones as the first manager and licensee. But women played vital roles even before its official opening, as Penny Henry oversaw the practicalities of running a club. Through the early opening years, women laboured behind the scenes in myriad ways: at reception, on the door, in the coatroom, behind the bars, and, in Penny Henry's case, even on the roof! Many of the women who made the club viable before the Madchester days have not been fully recognised in the histories of The Haçienda to date: Teresa Allen, Karen Boardman, Rebecca Boulton, Nicky Crewe, Tracey Donnelly, Susan Ferguson, Ellie Gray, Penny Henry, Rebecca Knowles, Ang Matthews, Marcia Pantry, Sidnie Pantry, and Gonnie Rietveld, to name a few. Centring them here reveals a social world that existed among the women who shared the night-in, night-out experience of making The Haçienda hum.

ANN QUIGLEY: Factory knew we needed a club that was for our people. There wasn't a single club in Manchester that catered to young people like us, and there were all these really horrible discotheques with horrible carpet. They were like bingo halls or arcades, penny arcades, and that's why The Haçienda *had to be built*.

ANG MATTHEWS: We started hearing about this new club that was going to open. Until then, people like us had nowhere to go. There'd be odd dates in venues, but people like us didn't go to pubs, and we didn't go to discos. We just weren't into that, and we just liked live music, so that's what we presumed The Haçienda was going to be. We'd heard about it and knew that Tony Wilson was going to be involved, so it was quite exciting because it was going to be somewhere for us to go — a whole revolution.

PENNY HENRY: I got into The Haçienda because I'd worked at Rafters, for a man called Roger Eagle, who used to bring all of the R&B bands over, and he'd put them on in Manchester. He was around in the early days — he used to be a DJ at a club called the Twisted Wheel. He was then responsible for all these reggae artists coming over, which I think really enriched the music business in Manchester more than he was given credit for. I was working for him when he was doing an R&B night, where I met Alan Wise who was connected to Factory. Since Alan Wise was so bad at running Rafters — he used to just let everybody in and leave me there at the end of the night with all these irate people who didn't get paid [laughs] — I started going round the club at the beginning of the evening, asking everybody how much they were supposed to get paid. I'd also read books before the club opened, and I'd hit Alan with my book and say, 'Stop letting people in the club!' [laughs] He did it because he was very kind: if someone said they couldn't afford to get in, he'd let them in. But as a result, all these people never got paid, so that's how I got started.

When I started working at Rafters, my boyfriend was in Simply Red. I thought he was having a glamorous life and decided I wanted a glamorous life in music, too. Then you realise, of course, that it's not really so glamorous at all because it's a lot of just hanging around. [laughs]

In the days when it opened, there wasn't enough money to cover the expenses, and it was quite dire at the beginning. When Peter Hook wrote his book, he said they only employed friends. I was really upset about that because I had a lot of experience working on doors before that. It wasn't as if I was new to it. I had experience.

GONNIE RIETVELD: Mike was offered a position to give creative leadership to a new club in Manchester, The Haçienda. This was because he'd organised a set of nights in a venue called Hal 4, within a complex called Utopia, which was an old water treatment facility in Rotterdam. The abandoned industrial buildings and water tower had been squatted and had a huge hall where you could put the stage, and you could put on a party. Mike Pickering basically became a creative director there, if you like, and invited

New Order over. It was one of their first gigs — definitely their first gig in Europe — so that was quite something. Due to shared football and music interests, Mike was friends with Rob Gretton, the manager of New Order, and before that of Joy Division. Rob decided, with Mike being a good mate of his and having gained experience in Rotterdam, that he'd bring him over as creative director for The Haçienda. So, we both went over to Manchester, which was totally new for me, and totally alien to me as well.

GILLIAN GILBERT: Since Rob, our manager, was very much involved in Factory as was one of the partners, we got pitched the idea that this was 'not a club'. I think because we'd been to so many clubs in New York, it was like, 'let's have somewhere that we can go as well, that doesn't have dress codes, that's not like the clubs in England'. I'd been to some of the clubs, like Pips in Manchester, and it was just girls dancing and blokes looking at them, like an awful cattle market. It wasn't fun, to me. I'd rather go see a band live. So I think when Rob said, 'Why don't we get a club we can all go to?' we'd imagined a small club like the Peppermint Lounge or somewhere else like in New York that was small and dark. When they came up with the idea of buying a marina, it was like: *What? How? Why?* It's so massive, why would you do that? I think we were all in shock, really, when we went to see it. We were so busy with New Order, and I think we just thought, well, that's what your managers are for, it'll work out. I think it was too late to say anything by the point they'd found the marina. We were all taken in and shown around, and it was just such a . . . big place for a boat. Does anyone really have a yacht in Manchester? You can't fit them on the canals! [laughs] It was just ridiculous.

PENNY HENRY: I started three weeks before The Haçienda actually opened, and I walked in and said, 'Where's the cloakroom?' They said, 'What do you mean?' I said, 'Where are people going to put their coats? You can't not have a cloakroom!' There was also a set of very steep stairs, and I said, 'You *have* to have a railing, you can't have people running up and down those stairs without a railing.' It was all these practical things, and I noticed there were five doors all around the building. I told them people were going to just let their friends in, so they put a board by reception with lights on it that would show which doors were being opened. Obviously, otherwise anyone in the club could just open those doors and let people in. A very beautiful club, but a complete shambles. It was all the men designing it who hadn't thought of anything practical at all, really. That was the beginning.

LIZ NAYLOR: I love the way with The Haçienda you've got really important people like Penny Henry, Gonnie Rietveld and Suzanne Robinson in the kitchen — these amazing powerhouse women. You've got Wilson patting around like, 'This is an homage to Constant', and the women kind of go, 'Well, right then, so who's going to be doing the door? And who's been going to be providing the food? How are we going to get the shit on the road?' These great women making shit happen. It feels like it's like an age-old history, doesn't it? Women are there making sure stuff happens and being quite protective of the people in that community.

CATH CARROLL: At the start of The Haçienda, Liz and I were invited over to do a piece on the club just before it opened, and the manager, Howard Jones, took us in and showed us around. They gave us the first public membership cards.

SIDNIE PANTRY: I remember getting my membership card when it opened in '82. The intention was for it to be free to get in at the very beginning if you were a member. My boyfriend at the time and I were some of the first people to join.

PENNY HENRY: When the club opened, cult magazines like *Face* used to put articles about it in, and what a wonderful club it was because of its unusual design. It was my son's age group who were really keen on going to the club. My son used to come to all the soundchecks and bring his friends when he was around fifteen, and he had signed copies of all the posters of the bands, and he managed to lose them all somewhere. Would have been worth a fortune now. [laughs] It was his age group that really started going to the club in the later Madchester years. Before then, the club was often empty.

LINDSAY READE: Tony took me to see the building when it was a boat room. I wasn't especially for or against it, really, probably a bit for it. I actually really enjoyed going to The Haçienda when it was empty. When it was busy, I didn't so much like it.

PENNY HENRY: Howard 'Ginger' Jones started after Rob Gretton and Tony asked him if he'd want to run a club, so he was in at the beginning of The Haçienda. He'd been putting on gigs to make money for Scope, a disability charity. He'd seen what I did at Rafters and asked me if I'd go and set up the door. If you use your intelligence, you can see what needs to be done, and Ginger knew I could do that. He took me along to start at The Haçienda, and he and I recruited quite a lot of people to come work in the club — on the bar, everywhere else. I'd been working in lots of public places anyway and knew lots of people.

NICKY CREWE: I was involved in a very alternative shop called On the Eighth Day, both before and after I left for university. I went off to Morocco for a year to teach English, and when I came back, The Haçienda was planned, so I sort of slotted back into doing the door for a couple of promoters alongside a day job. I ended up working at The Haçienda when it very first opened for the first seven or eight months, and then I kind of lost touch a little bit because I went off and had babies.

LINDA DUTTON: In 1982, The Haçienda opened. By this time all the IKON film equipment had been moved to Tony Wilson's cellar. Unfortunately, or fortunately as it turned out, the cellar flooded and the camera and portable recorder were quite badly damaged. The insurance paid for replacements and the damaged ones were repaired, giving us two useable cameras — ideal for The Haçienda when it opened. At that point, Malc said to me, 'Do you want to do the second camera?' I had done the camera before a couple of times at The Ritz, so when he asked me if I'd want to do the second camera, I said yeah, and it went from there.

TERESA ALLEN: I'd been a hair model for a while for a Manchester hairdresser called Ray Wilson and he took us to his hair shows in a little minibus with a local band called The Thunder Boys. Their manager was Ginger, Howard Jones, first Haçienda manager. This would have been a couple of years before The Haçienda opened. He used to talk about how he was going to be managing a new club, and that's where I first heard of it.

Fast forward to May 21, 1982, and I was at college and I went along with a friend of mine to join a new club she'd heard about — and, lo and behold, it turned out to be The Haçienda. It was the opening day and the big loading bay doors were open and I could see The Thunder Boys all in there painting — the painting was still happening on the opening night. [laughs]

GONNIE RIETVELD: There are a lot of memories because I was working at The Haçienda six, seven nights a week, basically. I helped out with setting up the membership system, together with my colleague Penny Henry, and we both then ran the reception as well, in the early days. We got some extra people, like Teresa Allen. And there was the cloakroom. I started to work a little bit in the cloakroom, and that's very much frontline work. Some people are slightly crazy, to be honest with you, like people who didn't want to pay the extra pound because they forgot their membership card. There was one guy who actually managed to headbutt the glass through the ticket office! I still remember it. When adrenaline shoots up, everything goes in slow motion. That's definitely a very clear memory still: the slow motion movement of broken glass, this strange rain of breaking glass, coming in. Then everything speeds up again and there is still a queue with a guy at the front just wanting to get in, like: *What are we waiting for?* There were very strange moments like that.

CORINNE DREWERY: Gonnie Rietveld let me sleep on her floor when I was coming up to Manchester to do demos. I didn't really know anyone and needed somewhere to stay. She had a flat and she had a pet mouse. She said, 'If you'll feed my mouse while I'm away, you can stay at my flat for as long as you like.' So that's how I got to know her.

PENNY HENRY: I admire Gonnie enormously because she's absolutely remarkable. She's a one-off, Gonnie.

TERESA ALLEN: I asked Ginger for a job a few visits in, and he took me to Penny Henry, who put me on the cloakroom. That started my Haçienda journey. Penny was a very good friend for many years. She's very much a nurturing person, and she looked after everybody. She was great to work with.

PENNY HENRY: Teresa was so young when she worked in the club. One Halloween, she decorated the cocktail bar and it was absolutely stunning. She is so creative. She's quite shy in some ways, but she did so much for The Haçienda — more than a lot of people. She was beautiful in every way, a really special person. But she's never been one to blow her own trumpet, not ever, but she did so much and doesn't get the proper credit.

TERESA ALLEN: It was like a family, really, and working at The Haçienda was the first time that I ever felt fairly normal and not on the fringe because I'd always stuck out like a sore thumb. It was the first time I was with people that didn't treat me as if I was weird, so I loved it from the first.

REBECCA BOULTON: I think my Factory Records story began when I came to Manchester in 1981, and I wanted a part-time job. So when The Haçienda opened, I just got a job behind the bar. That's where it all started, really. I worked behind the bar, and I met loads of people doing that. I also worked on reception at The Haçienda, and then I worked for a brief time helping out Kevin Cummins [photographer known for his work with Joy Division, New Order and many other bands]. He obviously didn't work for Factory, but he had a big association with Factory, of course. It's funny, isn't it — I've still got friends I met when I was at university, but some of the most significant people I've met in my life have been through Factory.

ANG MATTHEWS: Strangely enough, as they say, there's always coincidences: the day I came to Manchester to register as a student, stood behind me was Rebecca Boulton registering to be a student. All those years ago, and she also had got over to Liverpool for a few months, so had actually lived in my house for about four months when we were students, as well. That was a strange connection before we became so close because of Factory and The Haçienda.

KAREN BOARDMAN: I was going into The Haçienda most nights as soon as it opened with my mates, and finally I said to Ginger, the manager, 'Look, I come in here every night anyway, you might as well give me a job so I'll get paid', and he said OK. That's how most of the people who worked there got jobs in the early days. That job gave me the key to the door even though I was technically just working behind the bar. I was working in this seminal club, and that job gave me permission to go there early. Even though I probably didn't start till nine, I was there to help bands load in and load out, and I gave myself this artist-liaison job that didn't technically exist. It was then that I realised these bands have got people around them who are all carving a career in the music industry: a manager, a tour manager, a lighting person, a sound person, even the person who drives the van. That was the next lightbulb moment for me. I realised you could have a job in the music industry despite not having any talent in terms of playing or singing or writing, building the foundations for my future career.

NICKY CREWE: On the first night The Haçienda opened, Penny, myself and a woman called Ellie Gray were in the box office. I honestly don't think anybody would remember that we were there because . . . Peter Saville and Ben Kelly-like people were there for the opening, along with all the other people you see mentioned. The box office was in the foyer, so we didn't get to see any of the acts, but it was so busy and so abuzz. Then you see it mythologised, and I *was there*, but in the written history, the mythologised history, I'm *not there*.

STELLA HALL: Ellie Gray was really instrumental in the early days of The Haçienda because PR was a huge part of what got the place attention. She didn't just do the PR — she had a managerial role as well. She was an astonishing presence.

BEV BYTHEWAY: Ellie was so significant in the early formations of The Haçienda.

CAROL MORLEY: Ellie Gray was on the door at the start, and she was fantastic and ran a strict door policy. It was rumoured that there was a Fun Boy Three song, 'Too Much Too Young', that was written about her allegedly. She already had the status of a myth!

STELLA HALL: I found her to be a deeply impressive woman who really shone out in a very male environment. She was very confident, very skilled and very sure of her own talent. You saw a woman like her as a role model. And she was a fierce negotiator. My God, it was scary trying to do a deal with Ellie. [laughs] Blimey, she really knew her stuff. That's what she was there to do, and she did it.

SUZANNE ROBINSON: Ellie was the biggest bitch in the world, but I had so much admiration for her. She was very stylish and very strict, and she absolutely got the job done. I just admired her so much.

PENNY HENRY: I did have a nemesis at The Haçienda called Ellie Gray, and she tried to undermine me quite a lot, which I found very difficult, but there's always somebody somewhere. [laughs]

CAROL MORLEY: [Then] there was Susan Ferguson who was at the cocktail bar and there was also Suzanne in the kitchen. These were quite significant people because, literally, if you got to know them, which I did, you might get a free plate of chips or free drinks! And great conversations about so much!

SUSAN FERGUSON: I was living around the corner in Robert Adam Crescent in Hulme and I heard that Factory Records were opening a new venue (they had been using the PSV Club in Hulme and Rafters on the Oxford Road but this was going to be their own place). I went down with a friend a week or so before the opening and joined. I always say the joining fee was £5.51 but I think that is one of those false memories. Anyway, we paid our money, got our membership cards and then were invited to the opening night. Which I am pretty sure was on a Thursday — the day before it opened. We turned up and it was just amazing. Massive. And full. Full of people from the indie music scene. Not just locals. Packed. I loved it ... At the end of the night I went up to the bar and asked if there were any jobs going. They didn't think so, but they pointed me towards Chris — a huge guy who was the bar manager. I went and spoke to him. I was still beaming. I asked if he had any jobs. 'Sorry, no. We've already got everyone we need.' Me, still beaming: 'Oh, never mind. I just really love it here.' 'Sorry,' he repeated. Me, still beaming: 'It's OK. I just think it's such a great space.' 'Oh, OK then. Go on. You can start on Saturday.' So I did. That was when Cabaret Voltaire played. I worked behind the bar from the night of Cabaret Voltaire until about 1987.

LITA HIRA: I was at The Haçienda on its opening night. We had honorary membership, being on Factory Records, so we used to go at least two, three times a week. In the beginning it was like going to somebody's house because you knew everybody, so it became a second home in a way.

LINDSAY READE: Although Tony was trying to get me back, he was dating a woman called Roz. He took her to the opening night, but invited me to the second night, the night after, which didn't have such a big attendance. They played 'Me and Mrs. Jones', that old track. You wouldn't think of that song at The Haçienda, but Tony asked me to dance with him to it. So we slow-danced on The Haçienda dance floor to it. As we were doing that, I thought, 'This is really symbolic.'

TRACEY DONNELLY: December 1982 was my first time at The Haçienda. Me and my friend Cath knew Thomas Dolby was playing. We didn't have enough money to go to the gig, but we sat on the step hoping to get in somehow. Eventually this man came out and said we could go in for free. Once I started work at The Haçienda, I realised that it was Mike Pickering that had let us in. It was mind-blowing going into the club; it was like nothing we'd seen before.

• • •

ANN QUIGLEY: In the first two years of The Haçienda, it was a really odd place because it was too big for the nightclub it intended to be.

ANGIE CASSIDY: The Haçienda was something else. We used to go quite regularly, and it'd be this huge, empty, almost echoey space.

JANE ROBERTS: If you went to The Haçienda, you got to know everybody. I worked as a backline technician for New Order, but I got to know them before I started working for them, mainly in The Haçienda. For a big city, it's quite a small sort of family in a way.

LIEVE MONNENS: I actually started going to The Haçienda when it opened in the early 1980s because I had a good friend in Manchester. It wasn't trendy at all then, and it was actually quite empty, full of students. It was a completely different atmosphere from what it became. I still have some posters on my wall from The Haçienda at that time. The space was so different from all the clubs I'd gone to in Europe. There was electricity in the air.

LINDSAY READE: I thought the space was stunning. I thought the idea for The Haçienda was a bit ambitious, and it was. I mean, it was part of the downfall of Factory perhaps. Like the decision to move to the big building in Manchester as well. But everybody goes on about The Haçienda, even now.

It was like a youth club in the beginning, you know. We were older, but you'd see all your friends there, and then you'd go and sit in the Gay Traitor bar, which was cosy. You wouldn't sit in that cavernous space, it was just empty. It was an empty cavern. There were gigs, but the sound was terrible. It never worked as a live venue.

NICKY CREWE: I'm sure people have said this, but it was not a club that suited live performances. The sound was awful. [laughs]

REBECCA BOULTON: Everyone thinks about it as Madchester, and it being really crowded, but there were really busy nights before that, too. Certain gigs were obviously packed out.

BRIX SMITH: When I came to Manchester for the first time, Mark took me to The Haçienda, *obviously*. That was before I ever played there, and before I was actually in The Fall (at that point, Mark wanted to produce my solo stuff). Immediately, I was taken to the hot seat for a night out. Mark was definitely a VIP there, one of the kings of the Manchester scene. I remember going to The Haçienda and feeling breathless upon entering, as if you were going to the Taj Mahal. Within the walls, there was so much massive creativity — everybody that was walking in, working there, playing there and involved in it. It was the collective consciousness of a real happening. And you could feel it every time you went there in the early days.

ANG MATTHEWS: My first experience of being at The Haçienda at night time wasn't as exciting as I was expecting it to be. I went on a Saturday night, and it was still quite dressy and disco-dancing music. It was John Tracy who was the DJ. Although it was OK, I didn't find it as exciting as I expected, and it was dark, so I couldn't see what was actually going on. But I was getting involved. I wanted to work in the music business, so I was on the guest list then everywhere in town. I was also starting to book gigs at our student union building. Around then, I started going to The Haçienda in the daytime and I was getting to know people like Tony Wilson and Tim, who used to book gigs there. So, the first time I went in the daylight, it was ... life-changing, really. I had never seen a venue like it. It had a glass roof, so if you experienced it in the day, you saw everything that Ben Kelly had done, and it was just astounding, really. From then on, I'd say that nearly every day, I had some reason to just pop in there even though I was also working there.

GONNIE RIETVELD: There is a canal behind The Haçienda, so if you would be behind the venue, you could see Manchester's old industrial past. When we first moved in, there were still a lot of empty warehouses with broken windows at the back of the building. We had some goth, post-industrial, black-and-white, huge backcombed hair, early-eighties pictures made of us back there for Quando Quango's publicity purposes. [laughs]

BRIX SMITH: I felt that we were a house band at The Haçienda then and now. It was Factory's club, New Order's club, but it was also our club. We were such a major part of the scene, and of course The Fall and Joy Division went way back. Tony Wilson was so supportive of us, too, so we really felt that this was our clubhouse too. It's even where we went on days that we didn't play, when we would go to the Gay Traitor to hang out. And since we were working with IKON, on Factory's video arm, we really did feel like we were part of Factory and the scene in that way. So ultimately, we were one of The Haçienda's house bands.

TINA SIMMONS: The Haçienda was absolutely number one, *the* place to go. It was always something bizarre in there, fairgrounds inside The Haçienda, swimming pools ... brilliant. [laughs]

* * *

PENNY HENRY: I tried my hardest at The Haçienda. I was the building manager, and I'd be doing five things at once at any given time. From the start, lots of money was being wasted on things like tablecloths. I tried to make it work better because it was losing so much money.

GONNIE RIETVELD: The cloakroom for me was torture because the acoustics in The Haçienda were terrible. It's got a factory-style roof with glass, and all the walls were just bare brick with a lick of paint. So the sound just bounced. Glass is the worst for reflecting sound, but so are bricks and concrete. Then, with all these different directions and angles, sound waves would all arrive at the

I THOUGHT I HEARD YOU SPEAK

cloakroom at slightly different time intervals, and so the music starts to sound like a white noise. Everything comes with a slight delay, and then you have to shout over that from the cloakroom. That wasn't for me. After a few months of that, I switched to looking after the bands backstage, and that was quite rewarding in a way. It was a good learning curve, and I did that for several years. I met a lot of bands. And I made a lot of sandwiches. I personally made the sandwiches for a lot of bands, got them their headache pills, and made sure that they had the drinks that they wanted and that they had flowers in the dressing room. I never had graffiti in my dressing room. It was polished, it smelled nice and it had flowers, which is something I learnt from Paradise Garage in New York, which really had a lovely feel as well, and that's what I wanted to reproduce in the dressing room.

NICKY CREWE: The other thing I sometimes did was the cloakroom, and that had you more within the body of the club than working in the box office because you could see what was going on, and it was more sociable, really. You could certainly hear the music.

TERESA ALLEN: The cloakroom was a really weirdly configured thing. There was a little cloakroom desk, and then there was a few steps up to a room that had scaffolding poles configured to hang coats on. I'd take someone's coat and money, give them a ticket, go and hang it up. Quite often, it was really quiet, so there wasn't a lot to do. We used to do stuff like hanging upside down on the poles in the back, and I remember doing that with Mike Joyce from The Smiths. Hanging upside down sends blood to your brain and makes your brain activity better. [laughs]

NICKY CREWE: I have a friend in Sheffield who recently showed me a photo on her phone of herself and Johnny Marr from a record-store event. Nobody else among her friends knew who it was, and she showed it to me and I said, 'That's Johnny Marr. I did the cloakroom with him at The Haçienda.' So I definitely did the cloakroom with Johnny Marr! I remember that I thought his name was a stage name because I'd come back from working in

Morocco, and obviously French is spoken there. It's spelt different, but in French, the sound of his name means 'I'm bored'. So when he said he was called Johnny Marr, I just thought, 'You've got a stage name — "I'm bored".' [laughs]

SUSAN FERGUSON: [I remember] The Smiths doing what I thought was their first gig — where, as usual, there weren't many people there — as their first single had just come out and he had boxes of gladioli to throw out to the 'crowd'.

ANG MATTHEWS: I started working behind the bar in 1983 when I was a student. I immediately asked for a job because the first time I walked into The Haçienda (in the daylight, as I said). I thought, this is life-changing, this is amazing. The next day, I phoned up and said, 'Do you have any work? I'm a student so I can work nights.' The first gig I worked on was The Smiths, their first Manchester show. That was manic. It was my first night working behind the bar, and I couldn't believe how busy it was (and couldn't believe that we were allowed to smoke cigarettes behind the bar while serving people). The stage got bombarded, and it was just packed and so hot. Although it was a night's work, it was still really exciting. I worked about four nights a week there from 1983 for about two and a half years.

PENNY HENRY: I'd be putting the slats back, climbing onto the roof to stop the rain from coming in. I was under the stage doing repairs, I was in the toilets in the cocktail bar. They built the toilets below the level of the canal, and it'd be six o'clock at night and the canal would be regurgitating out of the toilets if there'd been a heavy rainfall. I had to sweep it all down a manhole and disinfect the whole place. That shouldn't even have been allowed! And these are things that *nobody saw*. After I was done working there, I knew the canal had come in because I could smell it. It was really badly built! [laughs] It was beautiful, but it was *really* badly built in other ways.

KAREN BOARDMAN: I was working the night Madonna was there recording for *The Tube*, and she came over and asked me where the bathroom was and because the toilets were flooding (again), I had to take her upstairs to a different set of loos. [laughs]

TERESA ALLEN: We all worked really hard. Every time it rained, the roof would leak, and we'd have to sweep all of the water out of the back doors, dodging customers. The cocktail bar toilets used to overflow and we used to have to sweep that out, and that was Penny and me in the main. We ruined lots of pairs of shoes!

PENNY HENRY: Me and Gonnie, if we worked during the day, we never wore makeup. Then we'd go to the women's toilets and put our makeup on for the evening. I remember listening to Alison Moyet, who I really loved, warming up during the soundcheck, and I preferred her soundcheck more than the set later, while we were putting on makeup. There are some very little moments like that which are still so special to me.

GONNIE RIETVELD: There's one black-and-white photo where you see these two blokes sitting there, really depressed, putting their coats on. It was really cold in The Haçienda most of the time, except during the summer, so people used to keep their coats on, and besides, they didn't want to pay for the cloakroom. So they'd just sit there in this cold space, being all droopy.

SUSAN FERGUSON: I was a student and I did about two or three nights a week. It was open seven days a week. Unless New Order were playing, you'd be lucky if there were a hundred punters in there. And it was cold. Not helped by the fact that it was empty. People sat in their overcoats and brought board games to play. It had the feel of a (rather cool) youth club. The bar was busy enough (like any pub), with plenty of time to talk to punters.

CORINNE DREWERY: When The Haçienda first opened, I made a pilgrimage to Manchester with a friend. It took us great trouble, and it was snowing. When we arrived, it was like this huge, empty box. It was really cold and a lot of people had their coats on, but that seemed to be part of the Manchester look. [laughs]

It was freezing until it was filled with sweaty bodies, but that came later.

PENNY HENRY: I kept trying to do all this housekeeping: to cut down on the costs to keep it running. It was a boat showroom before, so when it poured with rain, the water would come pouring in, down through the light fittings. That was why I had to go on the roof to try to shove the slats back in, to fix it. You can't have water with electricity! I learnt a lot about buildings by looking after the basic building issues, the roof, the emergency lights. We all put our heart and soul into that place. I worked seventy-hour weeks, and all my relationships broke up over it. I was putting so much time into it. I paid a lot for working there, and I don't think it was particularly appreciated by the people who owned it. I'm sure it must have been a terrible headache for New Order, having to play gigs because we were always running out of money. In the winter, it was a *huge* place to heat. Most clubs aren't as big as that, and the sound wasn't particularly good, either . . . the sound was dreadful, actually. [laughs]

TERESA ALLEN: I was moved on to the reception desk after working in the cloakroom for a while. I used to work with mostly Julie, and it seemed everyone who worked there were family members. Her eldest sister was Janet. She did all of the accounts in the office. Ellie Gray managed the door staff. Reception was just taking people's money, letting them in and looking after the guest list. I was really strict. If you weren't on the guest list, I didn't care who you were, whether you were famous or not. If you weren't on the guest list, you paid.

I think the only times I ever came out of the cocoon of the reception area was when, in the early days, there was someone playing that I particularly wanted to have a look at. William Burroughs came and did his readings, and they had Throbbing Gristle on. Amazing to see, and a standout event for me throughout the years.

KAREN BOARDMAN: I was often in the Gay Traitor bar downstairs, making myself busy thinking of new wacky cocktails to invent. There were a few regulars like Pete Shelley around that time.

SUSAN FERGUSON: Initially, there was just the Kim Philby bar at the end of the main space and the Gay Traitor bar downstairs, which was mainly cocktails. I usually worked on the main bar. It was great. If we got a five-minute break we'd go out the back to the canal for a cigarette. A longer break and we'd go either to the Briton's Protection or the City Road Inn. Then they opened Hicks bar, selling just cans. It was on the mezzanine level where the DJ box/VJ box/lighting box were. I worked there for a bit. The Gay Traitor was named after Anthony Blunt and run by Glenn and Gerry, two older gay guys, probably actually only in their later twenties or early thirties. I would sometimes work with them if it was very busy . . . Barney and Hooky from New Order drank tequila sunrises. (I *know* — but it was the 1980s!)

MARCIA PANTRY: The truth of the matter was, I was never hired at The Haçienda. I had two friends called Brendan and Glenn, who were a couple, and I'd known for quite some time. They worked at The Haçienda, so I used to always be on the guest list when I was going to see them there. One night, Brendan was working on the Hicks bar, and he said, 'Jump round', because I'd worked at bars before. So I jumped round, and the following weekend did that again, and the following week again . . . He shared his tips with me, and then eventually they started paying me — someone who was never actually employed. [laughs] Eventually I was on the payroll officially.

TRACEY DONNELLY: I ran Hicks for a while in the early eighties and Rob had the idea for me to do Haçienda merchandise. I sold it from Hicks bar. I used to have all the T-shirts set out and hung around the bar! [laughs] It was quite cool for back then. Mainly polo-type shirts with a small logo. Wish I had kept some.

MARCIA PANTRY: I think I was there at Hicks from '83 to '88. First it was hippie-like, young people, and then it started to get to be a trendy thing. The thing about The Haçienda was that you could wear your ripped jeans or you could wear your ball frock — that was The Haçienda. It was anything you were into, and it made no difference. It was just a vibe rather than a club. All genre of people were there. I even took my mother there a couple of times!

TERESA ALLEN: After a certain amount of time, they moved me to the office. Janet, the woman who did the accounts, left and they brought me down there and taught me how to do double-entry bookkeeping, and I started doing that work.

My role morphed and expanded over time, and I did lots of other things like getting the merchandising started in the early days before other people came on to do it. Everybody just did everything. I'd work in the office in the daytime, go home and have a bath, get changed, come back, and then I'd be the go-to person at night. If anybody needed anything, if there was any trouble, I'd sort it out. If there were bands on, I'd be liaising with them and sorting out the dressing room, getting them onstage, and all that stuff.

KAREN BOARDMAN: I worked at The Haçienda for three or four years before I decided, that's it, I'm moving to London to go to drama school, but that didn't last very long. I decided I was on the wrong track — I didn't want to be an actor — music is where I needed to be. I taught myself to type, and I got a job at London Records, and that was the official start of my career, but it really started in Manchester because I was swept along in this wave of excitement ... There was always the air of possibility. It changed my life, the whole Factory scene.

TERESA ALLEN: In the early days, it was fun. People used to come and escape from the crowds in the cloakroom. Morrissey used to come and hide. [laughs] Because it wasn't so busy, I used to write poetry and we'd stick it up on the notice board, and people used to steal it. Somebody somewhere has got some of my terrible poetry. [laughs]

NICKY CREWE: I had a day job simultaneous to working at The Haçienda, which was in the history department within Manchester Polytechnic, which is now Manchester Met, so I'd get off work there and go to The Haçienda pretty early, about six o'clock, and get ready for the evening. I'd be there till quite late, which was one of the reasons I stopped working there. I didn't drive. My boyfriend at the time used to come down and meet me after work, so it could be two o'clock by the time I got home, and obviously I'd got a day job. One night, he dropped me off at work and went to watch *Raiders of the Lost Ark*, and his lung collapsed. He came to pick me up at two o'clock and was in a lot of pain, and it was an emergency. They kept him in hospital, and he was there for about a week. At that point, I thought, 'I can't expect him to come and pick me up from work. I can't do this anymore.' And that's why I left.

PENNY HENRY: All the people who knew people from Factory were very irate that it was a 'members only' club because they couldn't get in, and that was a nightmare. Somebody did headbutt the reception window over me once for not letting them in. There were some terrible things that happened at The Haçienda as well as the good things.

GONNIE RIETVELD: Penny was a very supportive person, so I want to thank Penny for supporting me in finding my own path and completing my studies. She has been a great friend, and someone I could always talk with at any point of crisis. I owe a lot to Penny's support.

NICKY CREWE: Penny and I were and are friends . . . Female friendships have always been really important to me. I'm one of three girls, my mother's one of seven girls, and I went to all-girls schools. So female friendship has always been really important and supportive, and working somewhere like The Haçienda — I'm more aware of how men work where I work at the moment — there it felt very equal. I'd also been involved in On the Eighth Day, so I was used to a work environment that was like a worker cooperative where, as men and women, we were absolutely equal. I've had a bit of a charmed life in that respect.

REBECCA BOULTON: I spent half my life at The Haçienda. If I wasn't working, I'd go see a gig. I can remember going there and sitting and being freezing cold in a big and empty cavernous space. And

I can remember going and being jostled around, pouring in sweat because there were so many people in there. I remember seeing New Order . . . that was really special.

SUSAN FERGUSON: I think like in every walk of life, the women did a lot of the lifting and carrying and took little of the glory. I think the Madchester thing was very laddish, but I don't think the indie scene that preceded that was. There were always women at gigs. Women in bands. Maybe they didn't hit the big time in the same way. In a society and a world that was very male, The Haçienda felt very different.

SUZANNE ROBINSON: Women were the force behind a lot of what went on, they were the powerhouse. They kept it all going, kept it all together.

CAROL MORLEY: I felt all the women at The Haçienda were pretty feisty and up to something really, really interesting: in a band, writing, inspiring you to think and to have ideas.

PENNY HENRY: We were all very passionate about making sure the club worked, and to do that, we worked our socks off. Very often, during the day, we'd sleep underneath the mezzanine. People didn't go home — they worked all day and then worked all night.

TERESA ALLEN: We were paid a pittance, but I think the people who worked there loved working there, and we did it because we loved to be in there. It was the only place to go in Manchester of any note, so I was there twenty-four hours a day. [laughs]

PENNY HENRY: Peter Hook never bothered to speak to me for his book [about The Haçienda]. You can do the research properly. If people are there and are willing to talk — it's not like I wasn't there and wasn't willing to talk. In 24 Hour Party People, they suggested if the facts aren't that interesting, just make it up. I guess everybody could have the same experience but have a different view. You could all be at the same place, and you could each have a different view of an experience we all went through because you see it from your own perspective.

GONNIE RIETVELD: Penny Henry is older than I am and at the start of the club we worked together, and stayed in touch with each other. When I hear her life story, her experience has been pretty harsh on her. She's one of the forgotten women of Factory even though she has lived in the very same house on the ground floor of where the Factory office was on Palatine Road. In many ways she's been embedded in the whole thing, but she's another one of the forgotten women of Factory.

This Is a Stick-Up!

Among the highs at The Haçienda, there were lows, as well. A horrific armed robbery occurred in 1984, which revealed the dangers of running a club and ultimately resulted in Penny Henry's unjust dismissal. The Haçienda carried on.

PENNY HENRY: There was a terrible robbery that cleaners set up. They'd set it up for these people to come in, and they thought Ellie was going to be doing the money, but of course that particular day she didn't come in, so I was doing the banking on a Monday morning after the weekend. I was too busy talking to the other cleaners about the jobs that needed doing after the weekend. The other cleaners from Salford let these three guys into the club, and I thought the robbery was a joke. They came in and said, 'We're going to rob the club.' I banged one on the chest and said, 'OK, you've had your fun, now take your mask off', and he said, 'We're serious.' They had guns, which they then put at my head. We were on the floor and I pretended I didn't know how to get in the safe. The woman who usually did the banking had all the money out on the table every Monday, but with money, it's best to not have a routine. It's easier for people to rob you if you have a routine. I was a bit unorthodox, so thankfully I didn't have the money out. The club's weekend takings didn't get taken. They got the float, and that's it. I got blamed for it and Rob Gretton sacked me, which was pretty awful. After the robbery, since I lived on Palatine Road, the directors would walk past my door every day, and not one of them came by to see if I was OK, which I think is pretty dreadful. They thought you should be loyal to them at Factory, but you have to earn loyalty, don't you? You can't just assume you'll have loyalty.

TRACEY DONNELLY: When I worked at Swing hair salon in the basement of The Haçienda, it also doubled up as the dressing room in the evenings. The main office where Penny, Ellie, Louise and Teresa worked was next door to us.

I can't remember what day it was but I know someone must have been in the dressing room the night before, as I was using the vacuum. The next thing, someone came running in to tell us that they had found Penny tied up and the office had been robbed. She had been restrained and threatened while they robbed the safe. It must have been horrendous for her. They had a gun. I felt terrible. I'd been playing music, cleaning around while Penny was being held up. There was an armed robbery in the office next door and I was in the next room and never heard anything.

LINDA DUTTON: In the video booth at The Haçienda, we had expensive equipment. We turned up one day and it was all gone. That was the start of the gangsterism because cleaners had stolen it. I remember Penny being held at gunpoint around that time for the money. Everything was changing. The Haçienda was a happy family, really, and then it all changed. It started to get darker.

GONNIE RIETVELD: I wasn't there when the robbery happened, so all I know is what Penny told me. Apparently the people who did it were the partners of some cleaning ladies, so some cleaning ladies were considered part of it, as well. They were people who were trusted, but they let people in to do the robbery.

TRACEY DONNELLY: Go back a couple of weeks prior to this. A cleaner called in Swing (I know it was a Saturday) with a man. She introduced him as her husband and said could he have a look around as she had told him all about the place. I mentioned this to Ellie, saying I'm sure it wasn't her husband as she had shown me some holiday pics of her holiday, and her husband in the pics wasn't the same man. I suppose I told Ellie in a gossipy way, as I thought she was having an affair.

Back to the robbery. Ellie remembered what I had told her and told the police. I then found myself at Bootle Street police station being questioned for hours. It turned out that cleaners had set the whole thing up and I'd busted them with this flippant bit of gossip. I did have to go to court with Penny as a prosecution witness. I was never called to give evidence but spent the whole time in a corridor outside the court while two detectives bullied me. I come from a notorious-type family, and they had it worked out that I was related. I wasn't very assertive at that age, and I was so upset and confused. This ends on a positive, though. I was working a night in the club and Rob gave me a cash reward.

PENNY HENRY: When I got held up, they presented Tracey with some money to say who had robbed the club, and even when she told them what happened, I still got sacked. I was told I'd have to change my personality if I wanted to keep working there, so I said forget it! We're paid less than £1 an hour, and we were all paid equally. There was a point where there was a management committee, five or six of us, and we all got paid the same — that part was good. I'm still friends with Ginger, and we still talk nearly every day. We both value each other very highly.

GONNIE RIETVELD: Penny is a really generous and nice person, so she probably felt very concerned for the cleaning ladies and didn't know how the situation had developed. I can imagine that the owners were perturbed with Penny for being nice to these people who had done this horrible thing, but for Penny, she sees the human being before she sees their role. That's the way she's wired — she wants to look at people for their humanness.

CHAPTER 5

LIVE GIGS

Gillian Gilbert, New Order, Manhattan Club,
Leuven, Belgium, 17 December 1985

Playing live gigs as a woman is difficult work. You've gotta know your stuff sonically while contending with the realities of gender-based discrimination and violence. Accordingly, women in Factory bands remember a range of experiences performing throughout the UK and abroad while honing their craft. Once The Haçienda opened in 1982, Factory bands played regularly (The Fall essentially became a house band), and women onstage left their mark on what was quickly becoming Manchester's legendary live venue.

ANN QUIGLEY: Sometimes our fashion onstage had to be practical. We did an early gig in Leeds ... Have you ever heard of the Yorkshire Ripper? At that particular moment, he was killing women around the country. He'd sent a tape to the police saying his next attack would be in Leeds on a street called Chapel Street on a particular night. So, on this particular night, all the girls in Leeds were told to stay indoors and no one was to go out. But Swamp Children had one of our first gigs and it was on Chapel Street in Leeds! So Eric Random was in a band called Jell at the time that had two girls, a girl called Lisa, and Lynn, who I think was Eric's girlfriend at the time. The three of us were the only girls out in Leeds that night and that's because we had to do this gig. One of them looked really dodgy and I didn't like it at all, but I wore army clothes too big to avoid getting noticed, adopting a sort of asexual identity. I felt weird being a girl that night. We were really lucky, but we shouldn't have had to be lucky. We wanted to play our gigs.

CATH CARROLL: I think I had this internal sense of myself as not being female, of this intense discomfort with being female and being in a female body. I was also with Liz, who was out, who is a lesbian. We were living in a flat with a trans man, creating our own reality, and we presented as kind of androgynous. It was a bit of a nightmare in northern England in the late seventies. You'd step out of the door and you'd get followed, and sometimes you'd get stoned, pushed, shoved, beaten up. That happened all of the time. We were constantly running. We didn't just walk to the bus, we'd run. We'd watch for the bus from our flat until we saw the bus was already coming and then we'd just run, run to the bus stop to avoid getting hurt physically.

I had discovered that in cutting off my hair and putting on men's clothes and wearing everything on the outside — being masculine by looking it — helped something. I didn't particularly want to be a man because I think I looked at the person that we were with, who was a trans man, and I sort of instinctively understood that we had differences. They wanted to transition, and I did not. But I found it intensely freeing. It was a relief to not feel like a woman because, you know, every time you'd walk out the door in the seventies as a woman, it was just . . . a nightmare. You didn't get beaten up by the pack quite so often, but it was a different kind of fear. Because as a woman going onstage, I just cannot imagine how vulnerable that feeling must have been at the time, and wearing female clothes. But each of us was in a very different situation. Liz is a lesbian, the other person is a trans man, and me, I was ultimately just a heterosexual cross-dresser I think, but it did take a long time to come to terms with being female — being in a female body and understanding I had [gender] dysphoria, but I didn't think it made me trans.

LIZ NAYLOR: It was tough. I'm a butch lesbian, and in a way that helped, but it was also very, very hostile. I spent most of my late teens and early twenties trying not to get beaten up and occasionally getting beaten up, and gigs weren't particularly safe places. It wasn't like, 'here we are — an alternative indie gig'. Fast forward years later, I organised the first Bikini Kill tour of England, and it was fine in London because it was all a bit like 'Oh, Riot grrrl!' But as soon as we hit the Midlands and Sheffield, it was fucking horrible. Blokes would turn up looking for a fight, and it was frightening and quite violent. A lot of those early punk gigs in Manchester were like that.

I coped with that by being quite aggressive. I was a traumatised young woman, but how I managed that was by being aggressive and 'fuck you'. I think Cath and me, we dealt with it differently, but it was there for both of us. We used to walk around together as a little unit of protection.

CATH CARROLL: We considered ourselves feminists, but others who considered themselves hard-line feminists didn't think we were. In fact, they would routinely scold us when we took *City Fun* into a store called Grassroots (a great bookstore). It was really progressive, but the women there were like, 'you two, you're just male identified, and you're a disgrace to the cause'. And we'd just go, *oh fuck off*. I think I understand now where they were coming from, but when you tell someone who is not comfortable in their own body that they're just a stooge of the patriarchy, all it does is make you double down. We were quite immature about it. And it's actually been quite helpful in finding out what I am and what I am not. We definitely considered ourselves feminists because we were and I am. But I suppose it depends who is defining the word. The people who beat us up were men. There were no lesbians or feminists chasing us down the street; the feminists just had words with us and left us alone. But we also met so many good men who helped us without looking for anything in return.

ANN QUIGLEY: Since Tilly was there [after joining ACR] with both of us, it strengthened our resolve to break down that idea of 'sexy girls onstage'. We wanted a harmony with the idea that if the boys can have it, the girls can have it. We can wear army clothes ten sizes too big for us, and if the boys do it, we can do it as well.

● ● ●

DENISE JOHNSON: It's actually good being a singer in a band because you've got the least equipment to carry. In fact, you don't even have to carry anything because there's always a mic there ready for you at the gig. I remember doing an interview when I was with Fifth of Heaven, and the interviewer asked me,

'So what kind of microphone do you use?' And I can't believe I actually sat there and said this, but I said, 'It's black on one side and silver on the other, and it looks like an ice cream cone.' And as I'm saying it I just thought, 'You sound like an idiot — why do you not know what mic you're using, you know? What, you just turn it up, and just singing and then going home? Know what you're doing!' So I now know that [microphone] was an AKG-C414. And so since then, I've always been interested in microphones and how they work. I always vowed that if I could get one, my ultimate microphone would be a Neumann D47, so I got one. [smiles] This is my favourite all-time microphone. The U87 is great as well, but this microphone makes my voice sound really good. [Directed and shot by Alison Surtees for Manchester Digital Music Archive, 2018[1]]

GONNIE RIETVELD: I was doing schematics for each song, and then I'd make a drawing with different settings for the instrument I was using at the time, along with rhythm patterns. I made structures as well, in terms of numbers of bars, which functions as the electronic grammar of the song. Mike always wanted to be spontaneous, but this was not possible because these machines need to be programmed. I also had a sequencer (with my Pro One Sequential Circuits monophonic synthesiser keyboard) that could remember just twenty 'events' — which isn't much. An event is either a note on or a note off. Even the pauses between the notes are events. For this reason, I used a drum box (the Roland TR 808) as a trigger, so I only needed to program the notes as events. That way, the rhythm of these notes — the spaces between — didn't need to be programmed in as events. Since it was only twenty notes, in between songs, I had to program the thing in between each song onstage during a performance! [laughs] Other bands can start their next song straight away, but I had to program it live in front of an audience, and used my notes onstage — some of these are still glued to my keyboard.

CAROLYN ALLEN: At first, I think I was just there temporarily to fill a gap for the New Order support gigs, but I hung around and learnt

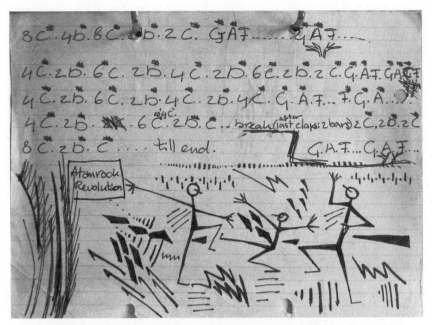

Sketch from around 1984, made by Gonnie Rietveld during
the recording of Quando Quango's track 'Atom Rock'
at Revolution Studios in Cheadle Hulme

more keyboards. I got the hang of it and what it was all about, and I thought, *I can do this*. We played another gig in Newcastle at the Soul Kitchen. New Order were great that night and I thought we sounded quite good too. Afterwards, we were in the dressing room and Rob came over to us and said, 'Would you like to do a recording at Factory? What about a single or an EP?' and Caesar said, 'Actually, could we do a mini album?' He just sort of laughed, 'Yeah, if that's what you want to do.'

LITA HIRA: With Stockholm Monsters, we did play quite a bit with New Order, and we went on a European tour with them. That was the first proper tour we did so it was exciting at the time. But again, Factory weren't like normal record companies, so there was nobody saying 'you have to do this' or 'now do that'. We didn't have a manager at the time, so Rob Gretton, New Order's manager, must have sorted everything for us as well.

Lindsay Anderson's setlist for a Stockholm Monsters gig

LINDSAY ANDERSON: One minute I was sat in a room being asked, 'You want to play on this song?' The next minute we were touring Europe with New Order, seeing Belgium and France, and playing festivals like Futurama — things that I would never have got the opportunity to do. At Futurama, I ended up doing a spotlight on some scaffolding.

ANN QUIGLEY: I think I was a bit scared of New Order even though I'd known Gillian from before because someone told me years ago that they liked to scare the support band! They liked to play tricks on them. At one gig, they told someone to open a flight case or a guitar case, and it was full of maggots — that was the rumour, anyway. So I got it into myself that that's the sort of trick they'd play on us, and as a result I was always really wary of them. When they asked if we wanted to support them, I was the one who said no, and that was the reasoning. I don't think we ever played with them! We must have been the first band to say we didn't want to play with New Order and didn't even give a reason. We were just this little band from Manchester, and they're like the bee's knees. Obviously, we should have played with them!

CAROLYN ALLEN: With 'Here Comes Everybody', I remember New Order's live sound engineer, Oz, really showed us how to do live sound. On the first gig with New Order, there were four of us playing on, like, mega equipment, and he really pushed the sound up and put lots of echo on it. The more we gigged with New Order, the closer I felt we were getting to our own sound. He ended up producing 'Something Outside', 'Talk about the Past', 'Here Comes Everybody' and 'Of the Matter' for us.

GILLIAN GILBERT: 'Sunrise' stands out to me from *Low-Life*. I particularly loved playing that live, and that was my dad's favourite New Order song, he told me once.

SUZANNE ROBINSON: I did go on a big British tour with New Order, and that's when I kind of realised *how good they were*. We'd feed them while they were rehearsing at the Apollo. There was about seventy people to cater for in total on that tour, not small numbers. Because I'd been doing catering for such a long time, I knew what worked and what didn't. I think they did six days of rehearsal at the Apollo, and I was astounded at how good the show was. They had people up in the gantry doing amazing things with the lights. You know, I'd never seen riggers up in the gantry. And the sound was amazing . . . shivers-down-your-spine stuff.

ANN QUIGLEY: We started to tour with ACR, and obviously that's how we got to know different people involved with Factory behind the scenes . . . At that point, Tilly had joined ACR as well, which was great because she was a lovely girl. When we'd go out and do dates together, Swamp Children and ACR, another girl in the back of the van makes a big difference to the enjoyment of being there when you're with so many boys.

JACKIE WILLIAMS: I didn't used to travel with Durutti Column at all. I'd go to local gigs in Manchester and would maybe go down to London when they went there, but I had too much of my own life. I've got my own work at Cosgrove Hall — a full-time job — and I've got children. I was incredibly busy, so I wouldn't have had time to just go off on tours.

LINDSAY READE: I've got a strong memory of the very first gig I went to with 52nd Street in London. I remember getting in the front of the van and Diane was in the front, wrapped up in a black cloak. Diane Charlemagne was kind of like an Aretha in terms of voice, and she's another woman who never got the credit she deserved. She did this amazing song with Moby ('Why Does My Heart Feel So Bad?'), for instance, such a powerful vocal, but she was really only visible as a session singer. Anyway, when I got in the van that day, I couldn't see her face, and she stayed like that the whole journey, didn't say a word. I thought, oh my God, this isn't going to go well, maybe this band isn't happening after all. [laughs] But then at the gig she did great. I thought, she's got a great voice but I'm not sure about her personality. It turned out she'd had a very difficult life. She ended up giving birth herself age thirteen. She went through hell, but we became very close friends, long after I stopped managing her, until her death, aged only fifty-one. She was also wise. On another journey to an early 52nd Street gig, I got in the van, probably wearing something nice, and Diane completely distanced herself from me. I didn't understand why but she later confessed, 'Those guys, they just see you as a piece of meat, can't you see that?' Of course she knew what boys/men were like, and I didn't. I was innocent and naive, unlike her, and thought that men weren't like that. But these men were, and I think a lot of men are. Which is why it's nice to think about a history of women.

BETH CASSIDY: Growing up, I never really knew anything about Factory or what my parents were doing. What's so bittersweet about the whole thing is that by the time I've become interested in it, they're not around to ask, and they're not around to discuss it. When I was recording with the band [Section 25] and doing live gigs, there was that sense of knowing that my parents have been there, doing the same thing I'm doing now.

CATH CARROLL: I went to England to perform [for the release of the *England Made Me* promo box set FAC 315]. Factory hired Ronnie Scott's Jazz Club in London, so I did that in the Factory days when there was still money around, and it was a full house. I was petrified to perform, but the audience were very kind. I didn't drink when I was performing, but I couldn't wait to get offstage and drink. I remember sweating a great deal, and the next day, Tony Wilson's partner Yvette came up to me and gave me some Shiseido mascara and said, 'You should try some *waterproof* mascara.' I thought, oh God, I missed out on that girlie lesson, growing up. I think that was my first time back in England since I'd moved to Chicago.

BETH CASSIDY: When I would sing during the gigs, I would cry sometimes singing 'Looking from a Hilltop', which is my mum's song. That didn't happen initially — that I'd shed a tear — so a shift occurred in me where it became emotional and cathartic to sing that song.

A real defining moment for me was at the Alfresco Festival, where that Benelux album was recorded. Andrew Weatherall was playing, and I'll never forget it: we were on really early, at like two in the afternoon, the graveyard slot. I was thinking we might just be playing to ten or fifteen people, and then my now-husband, who is a big Weatherall fan, nudged me and said, 'That's Andy Weatherall there!' And there he was, at the front of the queue to go into the tent, just to watch us play. He was clapping like a superfan; it was the most amazing moment. It goes to show the reach that Section 25 managed to make and the band's really special legacy.

• • •

DIAN BARTON: The Haçienda was a very difficult space for live sound for various reasons, firstly the stage position which was on the long side of a rectangle rather than the short axis, due to the bar occupying the optimal space. This made it a very wide area to direct the sound into and the back wall being a lot closer producing a slap-back effect. The roof was also a problem because it wasn't flat and would cause strange reflections. Then the walls were painted brick, which the sound bounces off. With all these different responses the room would appear to be very noisy and cavernous unless it was totally full of people who could counteract the effect. To top all that, the stage itself was very small and low, making it hard for the band to hear themselves.

The main difference between a static venue like The Haçienda and touring is obviously the change of space; each band is a specific challenge so the approach is the same really. On tour, because you are working with the same band, it becomes easier in that you begin to know the songs, whereas working in a venue it is an unknown band every time. So there are pros and cons for either situation: you might know the room but not the band or vice versa.

Lita Hira's setlist for a Stockholm Monsters gig

Having said all this, we had some phenomenal gigs in The Haçienda, including New Order (of course), The Smiths, Happy Mondays, and the first British show by Madonna. The Haçienda was a wonderful place in which to learn my craft because it was so difficult to mix in. I also met other engineers mixing whom I could observe and learn from; it was fantastic.

BRIX SMITH: Playing the first gig at The Haçienda, I remember being out of my mind with excitement and feeling like, *I've arrived. This is it*. Only a few months earlier, I was living in Chicago, playing in an abattoir with my band, talking about this mythical place, The Haçienda. And here I was in The Fall, playing guitar onstage at The Haçienda.

LITA HIRA: At the first birthday party at The Haçienda, Tony Wilson asked me if I would play the piano onstage, like on my own up there, playing a piece of classical music — not the kind of thing typical for The Haçienda. I said I'd play because he was acting as though he was under duress and needed someone onstage. [laughs] I asked for the lights not to be on me, but I'm sure they were. They had a few different instruments on the stage, including a piano. I don't think he got that piano for me because he asked me to do this sort of last minute — you know, he asked me on the night! I remember going home to get the piano music. It would have been Mozart or Beethoven or Chopin — one of those. I was only nineteen, so just to be on your own, on The Haçienda stage, playing classical music that you know isn't gonna go down well with that audience . . . It wasn't his best idea. Everyone was booing me off because it was a piece of classical music! So, never again!

CAROLYN ALLEN: The first time we played at The Haçienda was January '83, maybe '84. Tony was there, everyone was there. The Haçienda was such a beautiful club, super stylish, before it became a mega club. At the end of that night, I remember Tony asked me to take part in *The Tube* at The Haçienda, which was a few nights later and was going to be one of those eighties programmes with bands onstage at The Haçienda on TV. I think they wanted New Order to play, to do the whole show, but it ended up [with] Tony picking at least one member from each band, and then we picked some songs to perform as Factory All Stars. I don't know why Tony asked me, but I think it was maybe that he just wanted more women, girls, involved, so I said yeah, of course I want to do it. It was chaotic, really; Bernard was setting everything up, and Rob and Lesley were there. I spent the day working on the keyboards I was meant to play because I thought there's no way I'm going on TV not knowing what I'm doing! [laughs] Bernard showed me the keyboard parts he wanted me to play, and I did a bit of singing too. I think he was really frustrated by the end of the day because he had so much work to do.

LINDSAY ANDERSON: I was involved in the Factory All Stars for *The Tube*, so I've still got the guest pass from that one, and it's so funny because I look back and say, 'I shared a dressing room with Madonna but she didn't speak to us.' [laughs] Actually, I had no idea who Madonna was or how important she was because everybody shared a dressing room at The Haç. We just didn't think anything of it. But that was an interesting night because it was like two worlds meeting: the dancy, funky people were busy dancing away and I was sat there just playing my brass bit.

Ticket for *The Tube* night at The Haçienda with the Factory All Stars

CAROLYN ALLEN: I got my hair cut at the hairdresser's Swing for the gig, and it was good fun. It was great being on TV, and we were all in one big dressing room. It was so noisy, and I think Madonna was there and had to share the dressing room, too . . . I don't think she was happy about it. She was trying to work out her dance routine and everyone was going, 'What's she doing?' No one really knew who she was but Factory were really into it. They thought she was going to become really big.

All the songs were in different keys, but because we were doing it for TV and it was a medley, we had to just unify everything. When it came to 'Love Will Tear Us Apart', I don't think it was in the right key for Bernard to sing, because obviously we were doing a load of other people's songs as well. So then someone just says, 'We'll get Caesar to sing it', and he got dragged up at the last minute and said, 'I don't think I can sing it!' Everyone said, 'Just go for it, you'll do fine.' He did it and he didn't get paid for doing it, of course. [laughs] It was all pure accident because it was just thrown together, but it was also great fun and very memorable.

LINDA DUTTON: I filmed Madonna at The Haçienda, but I don't know what happened to the film. The cost of tapes was so high, yet somehow so much stuff was lost. Anyway, it was for a TV programme called *The Tube*, and the Factory All Stars played. I filmed it for IKON, but the TV company obviously filmed it themselves, too.

CORINNE DREWERY: I was auditioning for a band called Working Week and they said, 'Hey, do you want to come and see us play in Manchester at The Haçienda?' I had a job as a fashion designer at the time, and I had to take a day off work, saying I was sick, and went up to Manchester. On the way up, they said they hadn't got anybody to sing 'Venceremos', which Tracey Thorn from Everything But The Girl had sung when they recorded it — and did I fancy singing it? I thought, 'This is a test', so I said, 'Yeah, sure.' I listened to it on a cassette all the way up to Manchester. At The Haçienda, the band started playing and beckoned me onstage. I thought, I won't know anyone in Manchester at The Haçienda, so it doesn't matter if I mess up. When I looked into the audience, the first face I saw was Andy [Connell]. I'd met Andy before, as he played with A Certain Ratio and I used to go and see them play quite a lot. Then I saw a few more faces, like the Jazz Defektors, and I thought, 'Oh no, there's people who know me here, and I'm singing this song that I don't even know.' So I did a gig at The Haçienda, and by chance, I met Andy, and that's how Swing Out Sister came to be. We wouldn't have existed if it weren't for A Certain Ratio, and if it weren't for The Haçienda.

JANE ROBERTS: I think we played at The Haçienda just once while I was working for New Order. That stage was tiny. By that point, I'd done at least one American tour and a few festivals, so we were used to having this vast space. You'd get on The Haçienda stage and it was teeny-tiny. To get all our equipment on was just ... ugh! Oh my God, I mean you could've filled the whole area with just the keyboard set-up. I think Andy [Robinson] was offstage with some of the racks.

GILLIAN GILBERT: My mum and dad used to come down to The Haçienda after it opened, and they loved it. We had a party in the cellar, which was the underground bar. I've got some early pictures of it, which my sisters took, which are really funny and black and white. Going to the marina to start, the one thing you did notice was that it had big windows and skylights, so there was daylight pouring down. It's like, who has a club with daylight? It was really hot in the summer and really cold in the winter, and the stage had a very funny set-up, a very low ceiling. But there were hundreds of people when we played there — I think we played three times. The Haçienda was one big party.

REBECCA BOULTON: I remember that first New Order gig at The Haçienda was very hot and packed, and I brought my little brother, who had not really been to any gigs. I think he was about fifteen. I loved it, and I thought it was absolutely brilliant!

ANNE LEHMAN: Chris [Mathan] and I went over to England, I think it was for New Year's Eve at The Haçienda, and Angie [Cassidy] was with us. We were ... *insufferable* when we were over there. [laughs] I remember the exact jacket I'm wearing, which is this ridiculous hip-hop jacket. I brought over a bunch of them because someone at Factory wanted them. [laughs]

CHRIS MATHAN: One funny thing that happened, I think the following night after New Year's, was that we went to The Haçienda with New Order. They weren't going to let us in without tickets ... funny since New Order pretty much bankrolled The Haçienda! It got sorted out and in we went.

GONNIE RIETVELD: There was a huge single-floor basement in The Haçienda, and part of that basement was not The Haçienda's. Although the entire floor was once squatted for a weekend for a party called 'Disorder'. This might possibly be where the 'catacombs' or 'secret tunnels' idea comes from? New Order did a gig at the G-MEX, and they had an after-party at The Haçienda. They brought their entire sound system that they always used — Oz PA — down into the cellar, and it was much more powerful than you'd need for that space. So it was a very rich sound that didn't need to be on full volume for it to be effective. A hole was knocked at one side of the cocktail bar so people could get in there. People could also get in from the dressing rooms, and those dressing rooms had big triangular beanbags made for the occasion, with the word 'disorder' spray-painted on each of them using a stencil. That was quite hilarious because the party went on until ten in the morning or something, and by 6 a.m. people started to crash out there, and you'd see legs just sticking out of these huge beanbags.

SEEMA SAINI: Before I officially got the job at Factory, when I was volunteering, New Order were doing the show in the G-MEX centre. I actually bought a ticket. I mean, there I was volunteering for Factory, and I still bought a ticket, and I still bought the album even though there were all those albums right there, and I know they'd have given me one if I had asked. I think that's a thing they liked about me, that I didn't go in there trying to wheel or deal. I was just me.

I went to the concert, and I met up with a friend there who I was studying with. She was friends with Gillian's sister, and she had an extra ticket for the after-show party. I'd seen these after-show tickets because I was mailing them off for Factory Records, but I never asked for one. [laughs] This girl I met up with there said, 'Meet us after and we'll get you in because we have an extra ticket.' I remember getting this ticket, oh my God, and getting to go to this after-show party at The Haçienda, which was in the basement of the club. You know, I remember telling Rob Gretton this story a couple of months later, downstairs, when I started working at Factory. I told him I felt like I was like Charlie in the movie *Charlie and the Chocolate Factory*, but my ticket was silver, it was actually silver, and said 'disorder' on it. The bouncer asked if I was on the guest list, and I just held up this ticket, like Charlie. [laughs] That experience kind of drove something inside of me because when I got downstairs where the party was held, I realised there were other people from Factory and I was part of this now. Sometimes when you put things out into the universe, and if your intention is good, you receive beyond what you imagine. I've often heard that, and I've seen it happen in my life a couple of times now.

BRIX SMITH: I remember Nico opening for us solo at The Haçienda — Nico opening for The Fall. Her manager, Alan Wise, who has since passed away, was very involved and I believe was promoting it and put that together. I remember downstairs at Swing that night, it was just rammed, and I was so nervous that I had an upset stomach, which was not abnormal for me. In my early days in The Fall, I didn't want to be the person that stood in the front and took over . . . I was very much Mr Spock to Mark's Captain Kirk. I stood in the back and let the captain take control, like the first mate, and just worked my way slowly into the band. But on that night, I remember thinking I'd made it. Even if it seemed like it was in a small way for other people, it was in a big way for me.

YVONNE SHELTON: By the time we were doing gigs at The Haçienda, you knew that if you got big there, special things were happening.

Record labels and promoters came to see people there, so getting a gig there ... we knew we were happening at the time.

TRACEY DONNELLY: Me, Jane and Rebecca have all performed on The Haçienda stage — together! We rehearsed a few times at Jane's flat. When karaoke first came over, it was like, if you were no good, you got booed off. I remember Tony introducing us as the Factory All Stars of the Big Stage, and that was the worst thing we could have been introduced as, because straightaway people were like, 'Booo! Booo!' So we never got all the way through a song.

JANE ROBERTS: We did a karaoke thing where we were like a 1960s girl group at The Haçienda. Oh my God, we were so shit! [laughs] None of us knew the words, and there was no screen — it wasn't like proper karaoke. We were supposed to learn the words, but instead we got all dolled up and, you know, sixties beehives and all that crap, pointy-eye makeup and everything. [laughs]

LITA HIRA: Once when we were playing at The Haçienda, there was some guy in the audience waving his hands about, taking the piss out of our singer, Tony. I was annoyed because, in time to one of my solo bits, Tony, who had a bit of a short temper, ran forward and booted this guy in the audience in the face. Tony Wilson wasn't happy with us at all.

DIAN BARTON: The Haçienda brought a very diverse genre of acts, obviously lots of 'normal' bands, but also a lot of acts from different parts of the world like Africa and South America. These acts often brought traditional instruments, which presented their own challenges, not least in how to mic them up. For instance, traditional drums, panpipes and homemade xylophones. The chance of encountering this kind of act is very unlikely anywhere other than The Haçienda.

We did an act from Bolivia, in South America, called Rumillajta who were this type of band. They were tricky being totally acoustic — that is, nothing electric — but I found them very interesting and enjoyed their music enormously.

YVONNE SHELTON: It was all different types of music. It wasn't just dance music in the beginning. It was every kind of music, and it would change throughout the night. We were always like, 'If you dance, I'll dance', then, 'No, I'm not dancing!' We watched it transform into an electronic dance music room because, in the beginning, you'd see the reggae guys and the punk rock guys all in the same venue. The punk rock guys would be dancing to reggae music, the reggae guys dancing to punk rock, and then it became about hard-core dance music in the late eighties and into the nineties. It changed completely.

JULIA ADAMSON: With What?Noise, we played for a TV recording at The Haçienda for a show on Granada hosted by Bob Dickenson. Our album had just come out on One Little Indian. I was absolutely terrified performing live because I wasn't that used to it. I was more of a 'working in the studio' person, so I actually found it quite nerve-wracking doing live performances. But once I joined The Fall, they were all about live performance — much more than working in the studio, and they really excelled at live performance. So I actually played The Haçienda twice, first with What?Noise and then at the very last night with The Fall, before it shut down permanently.

BRIX SMITH: Mark was absolutely falling apart by the last show at The Haçienda [30 May 1996], and the addiction had gotten so out of control. The man was almost impossible to work with . . . violent . . . literally had to pull him through every show, if he even made it onstage for ten minutes. I feared for my own mental health. By the end of it, I couldn't even handle it. In my mind, I remember playing The Haçienda that day and it being one of the last shows, but memory is subjective. I don't remember a lot of it because literally I was just trying to get through everything alive.

Linder's Meat Dress

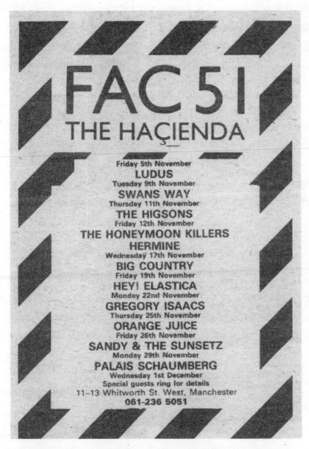

Ad for the Ludus performance at The Haçienda

On 5 November 1982, Linder Sterling's band Ludus played at The Haçienda. That show, often referred to colloquially as 'the meat dress performance', was Linder's response to casual pornography being screened at The Haçienda and the objectification of women performers onstage. The dress made of meat and poultry – complete with the reveal of a 12-inch dildo beneath the skirt at the end of the show – paid homage to women artists such as Lynda Benglis, who in 1974 appeared nude in an Artforum ad holding a cast-latex, double-headed dildo between her legs. The performance has become legendary, giving rise to acts in the present like Lady Gaga's 2010 appearance at the MTV Video Music Awards in a dress made of raw beef. It was an act of resistance, a feat of performance art, and quintessentially Factory.

CATH CARROLL: I remember Linder as the first woman I met that I felt was artistically supported. My memories of her are quite personal, like the memory of the room she rented in Whalley Range, how magical and exotic and glamorous it was. It felt like Linder at the time was not a woman of the 1980s. It was 1982, but felt ... I don't want to call her a woman out of time, but *she's just a woman out of time*.

LINDER STERLING: Cath Carroll and Liz Naylor managed Ludus for a short while. Importantly, they were instrumental at the concert at The Haçienda in November 1982, when I wore a dress decorated with raw meat ... I am a vegetarian, but was prepared to be bloodied for protest; I insisted that all of the meat used had to be that which was normally discarded ... My seamstress and I worked very quickly in the hour before I was due to sing, embellishing my tulle skirt and bodice with the sorry remains of innocent creatures ... Liz and Cath — or the Crones, as they were known then — handed out small packages of leftover raw meat wrapped in pornography to the audience. Then they tied bloodied Tampax to the bannisters of The Haçienda, and at this point the management really panicked . . . We carried on regardless, and for the last song I triumphantly removed my skirt . . . to reveal not myself, but the black dildo which I was wearing beneath it . . . This was my retort to The Haçienda's casual and interminable showing of porn films. [Linder Sterling, *Linder: Works 1976–2006*, ed. Lionel Bovier, 2006[1]]

LIZ NAYLOR: When Linder wanted us to manage her — we had no idea how to manage Ludus — our job was to walk around looking menacing behind Linder. We just walked around together, clinging together in a way, because it felt really tough. Cath and I would dress in men's suits, and Linder would just get thrilled by the idea that she could walk around with these two weird, strange characters.

LINDER STERLING: Ludus ran on pure anxiety and frustration. Various line-ups at various times, always fragmenting, but capable of great beauty as well as the necessary ugliness too. We went running through popular culture at such a speed. [John Robb, personal interview with Linder Sterling, 2006[2]]

CATH CARROLL: I remember The Haçienda gig that Ludus did very well, where Linder wore the meat dress. It actually went off entirely as planned. Actually, as I'm talking right now, I can see a picture that we took that night when we were in Hulme, just outside of where The Haçienda is located. It was a huge event, and somehow it just went entirely as planned. Linder was amazing. When she ripped off the . . . lamb chops, I think it was, that she was wearing, stitched onto a leotard, it was extraordinary. In those days, and even now, it was edgy. I think we were hoping for horror-struck faces in the audience, but people were just like, 'hmm, I don't know what that is'. Some people were really interested, and I think some people were there for the art and for the band. There were a lot of casual members who'd come in, too, and at that point it was not a dance club. It was this weird place that was open all the time. So people were looking, trying to figure out what it was, but they didn't seem shocked, unfortunately. They were faintly baffled and not terribly impressed. But the concept of it had a life way beyond the performance. Typical Linder, I don't think she was in it for the audience reaction. As a female performer, I think she must have been used to seeing people look at her baffled and not getting it.

LINDER STERLING: I was doing a combination of feminist statements and looking at things like pornography, which was very hidden away at the time. Weirdly, a lot of people thought my early work was done by a man. They seemed to think only a man would work with that kind of imagery, and were genuinely shocked to discover it was created by a woman . . . I was trying to decode pornography: pornography as a sexual shorthand and the way it's very formulaic. And I was fascinated by the way pornography was very hidden. Britain was so prudish then. I remember sending off for fetish-wear catalogues and they were not remotely sexual. They had everyday clothes made out of rubber, such as flared trousers. Really vile! Now, sexual imagery is part of everyday life. [John Robb, personal interview with Linder Sterling, 2006[3]]

LIZ NAYLOR: The Linder meat-dress gig was very much a response to how laddie it was . . . I was making the dress, mate! I was adding the meat because at that point we were her managers. The belt was made out of chicken claws, and it was quite horrible to do. I wasn't a vegetarian, but God, it was quite horrible to handle that level of meat.

ALISON KNIGHT: I must have been nineteen at the time when we made Linder's meat dress. It was when Affleck's Palace first opened, and I had a unit in there with Adrian Luck and Carol Lee. I can't quite remember how we were asked to get involved, but we made the skirt and bodice. Carol Lee was one of the people that had a place within Affleck's Palace: her parents ran a Chinese takeaway. So we had bits of offcuts of meat from there, and chickens' feet. We were really mindful of trying to get meat that we didn't have to buy, if that makes sense, but we did have to buy some steaks even though we were hampered by cost . . .

LIZ NAYLOR: I went with Linder to buy the dildo for the gig, too. We got it at the Harmony Centre on Cross Street in Manchester. Dildos weren't that easy to come by. The guy at Harmony Centre obviously thought we were a couple, and I felt deeply embarrassed by the whole thing because he was a bit like, 'Oh, you want the 12-inch one, love?' Then we created the dress from this offal.

ALISON KNIGHT: Adrian Luck, Carol Lee and myself were down in the basement of The Haçienda with weird needles, trying to sew the meat with fisherman's twine onto the bodice. Then we nail-varnished the toes of the chickens' feet and we sewed them around the edge. I think we were tasked with fitting it on Linder there because I can't remember other fittings. We must have had to put Velcro on the skirt so she could rip it open during the performance.

LIZ NAYLOR: The response felt quite angry, and The Haçienda were furious because there were bloody tampons in the men's toilets and offal everywhere. The response was angry beyond reason. It wasn't just like, 'the cleaners are gonna have to clean this up'. It was like, 'you have invaded the men's toilets'. It felt like boundaries had been sort of broken, and the atmosphere was quite antagonistic. It's the same hostility I saw towards Bikini Kill later on. When I saw that happening with Bikini Kill, it really resonated. It was like, 'whoa, I've been here before'. That strength of a female statement elicited exactly the same kind of response both from the audience and from the venue.

GONNIE RIETVELD: I was doing the backstage management for the Linder performance, and I had to deal with her rider. On the rider, they asked for tampons, either liver or other bloody organ meat, and ironically it was me that had to deal with that, so they could make bloody tampons from them. I thought it was hilarious. In some ways I thought they put it on the rider to annoy a whole bunch of Factory boys, but that didn't quite work out since I was the one dealing with their rider. I created small plates with liver and with tampons — and I think they might have hung some of them on their ears? That's the memory that stands out to me for that particular performance

— what they had on their rider . . . Reflecting on this, it's somehow a precursor to Lady Gaga's flesh dress!

TERESA ALLEN: Linder — I remember that night. You couldn't see the stage from the cloakroom, obviously, so we used to nip out if there was something that we wanted to see. I remember going out to see Linder because I'd seen people sewing meat on her clothes that day. I didn't have a clue what was going on, and I was really curious to see. I don't remember what she was like musically at all. I just remember the fact that she was pretty outrageous — even by our standards, and we were all quite outrageous, she was off the scale. She was really outraged, apparently, that they used to play porn on the video screens. I don't remember this at all, and I was walking to and fro in the club a lot. I never remember seeing any porn. I remember weird images that the IKON guys used to put up there, but I don't remember porn. I read later on that's why Linder did it, but I didn't know the reasoning behind it at the time. I thought she was trying to outrage people, which was fine by me.

CHAPTER 6

THE HAÇIENDA:
MORE THAN MUSIC

Suzanne Robinson's Fifth Birthday cake for The Haçienda

The Haçienda is most often remembered as a music venue and dance club, but it was so much more. Its space gave rise to cultural production that helped to put Manchester on the global map, and women across various creative industries were key figures in making it happen. Fashion, merchandising, visual art, theatre, literary drama, performance art, gastronomy, hairstyling, design, experimental sound. This chronicle of The Haçienda is one of the distinctive storylines that emerges from a Factory history told by women.

ANNE-MARIE COPELAND: The Haçienda was a Pandora's box of creativity, waiting to be let out.

SIDNIE PANTRY: With The Haçienda, a lot of people talk about the music, but they don't talk about the art that went on there. I did fashion shows there as well. I didn't just work there. I used to put on these fashion shows that were part of the art happening at The Haç. The art, and the artists! Nobody talks about the art, but there were installations, acts, fashion shows, much more than just music.

BEV BYTHEWAY: The Haçienda's design was so radical as an interior event space: it wasn't meeting any kind of tradition of what a nightclub was supposed to look like, or what a club was supposed to look like. Because of that, it actually created a space which became a new free space. It wasn't already defined. People could use it and interpret it in the way that they wanted.

REBECCA BOULTON: I've never been anywhere like The Haçienda ... but I don't think anybody had. I'd never been in a nightclub like that before, and I've never been since . . . As soon as it opened, I knew I would probably not really go anywhere else except The Haçienda, and that was kind of it, really. It was fantastic.

The design made it different. The design was unbelievable. It was completely unique, new. It was completely different to anywhere else that I'd ever been and, actually, completely different to most places now.

ANNE-MARIE COPELAND: The Haçienda had an aesthetic to it that I just couldn't describe at the time. It was like walking into a piece of artwork.

HANNAH COLLINS: The Haçienda had such an agenda — a social agenda, political agenda, musical agenda. All of those things combined to make it, and people were really loyal to The Haçienda. I thought I was privileged to have something to do with it, at the time.

LINDA DUTTON: The Haçienda wasn't just bands and music, so we'd film everything. There was a drama put on by CP Lee, who did *Tales from the Newgate Calendar*. It had to go ahead after a deluge of Manchester rain leaked in through the roof of the club and blew the electrics — the play went ahead using only emergency lighting. I think that was the night that I filmed the whole thing on my VHS camera and recorder. The lighting gave the play a particular atmosphere.

CORINNE DREWERY: Tony Wilson made The Haçienda an educational space, a place for a meeting of minds, and it wasn't just highbrow. It was about introducing people to all sorts of spontaneous stuff. There were fashion shows and great film projections onto the big, empty walls.

CAROL MORLEY: I never went to university, but The Haçienda became a kind of complete education in so many ways. I mean, I saw William Burroughs! The acts they put on were not just bands — it was so much more. It totally opened my eyes to ideas beyond Manchester.

DIAN BARTON: We also did spoken word at The Haçienda with people like William Burroughs. He was very difficult as he spoke very quietly. This was all a learning sensation, being exposed to such diverse experiences.

SUSAN FERGUSON: William Burroughs and Psychic TV. Everyone sat on the floor. You could hear a pin drop. You could also hear the tills 'ping', so we stopped serving while he read.

PENNY HENRY: I didn't get to see William Burroughs when he came, but I took a picture of him when he left. I have a picture of him leaving. [laughs] On the door, you're so removed from all the action because you're trying to deal with the people coming in.

GONNIE RIETVELD: There were lots of experiments at The Haçienda regarding what you could do in a club space, and that made it a really interesting venue. It wasn't just a music venue. They even got William Burroughs to read from his work. They just tried out different things really, and because it was set up by musicians for people who love music, and who just loved being able to bring back something to Manchester that they encountered in the world at large. So for Mancunians at first, it was very much like a spaceship that landed ... it was so alien to them, the design, the programming. It really was not Manchester at all. It was very much about bringing the culture from outside *into Manchester*.

SIDNIE PANTRY: Nowadays people talk about experiential events that are kind of like experiments, and The Haçienda used to do those. I can remember one event, upstairs near the Hicks bar where my sister Marcia worked, they had a tattoo artist inking tattoos. Back then, that was experimental.

MARCIA PANTRY: I was still into fashion at Hicks! I had hair like a pineapple at one time, with random and lovely ends, and different colours. Grace Jones, David Bowie, they were my fashion icons.

BEV BYTHEWAY: When I first arrived in the northwest, I worked at Rochdale Art Gallery, which was this extraordinarily radical experimental space in the eighties. We did live performance and set up the Rochdale Performance Collective. One of its first events was Whirled Music at The Haçienda (Richard Wilson, Paul Burwell), and that was at a time when The Haçienda was absolutely desperate, it was empty. It was the most beautiful interior, and we made use of that creative space before it became this hugely successful nightclub. I think we were given a bleak Monday night and the place was empty − maybe twenty people at the most. But the Whirled Music performance so suited the space, it was fantastic.

CLARE CUMBERLIDGE: I lived in Manchester for five years, and I was the founder and writer of a women's feminist performance group called Spinsters. There were nine of us, and we all had different disciplines. I used to go to The Haçienda, and for me what was always really important − and perhaps is not talked about because it's a different narrative than how The Haçienda is usually talked about − is that at that time in Manchester, there was a really fertile, rich and diverse culture of young practitioners, and The Haçienda was part of that. I was living in Hulme in a squat with a friend from the performance group, a way of living where you didn't need a lot of money and nobody had a lot of money. There were three key places − the Whitworth Street 'triangle' − where everybody went: Cornerhouse, the Green Room and The Haçienda. The Cornerhouse was visual arts and film, the Green Room was the widest definition of performance and live arts, and . . . you know The Haçienda! It was a really exciting time to be in Manchester and to occupy those cultural spaces.

STELLA HALL: In 1982, I was independently producing and presenting − I ran something called 'Women Live' in Manchester (there were Women Live programmes all over the country). I was introduced to somebody who started presenting work in various venues in the city, Jeremy Shine, and together we established an organisation that was supposed to move into a venue called the Green Room, which had been a theatre somewhere in the back end of the Castlefield area of Manchester, but they lost the title deed. So we started casting around. We wanted to be part of the art centre that was Cornerhouse, but the then-chair didn't want performance in there. So we thought Whitworth Street West with

Cornerhouse at one end, Haçienda at the other end, and a whole load of derelict railway arches — what a great place for us to put ourselves! We negotiated with British Rail to take over two railway arches, one of which became our office and one of which became our bar and performing arts space. We had three members of staff and a volunteer board, one of whom was Tony Wilson. In the years between '83 when we were established and '87 when we opened the venue, we presented performances all over the city in other people's theatres, in found spaces, including bringing the ICA's *Performing Clothes* [a fashion collection and exhibition] with Leigh Bowery to The Haçienda. We continued that relationship informally because we were quite a small tight-knit community of people working in the cultural sector at that time.

BEV BYTHEWAY: Cornerhouse was an independent film and exhibitions centre. It had three floors of galleries and three cinemas. It opened October 1985, and I worked there as one of the exhibition organisers, one of the gallery programmers, from '84 to '94. I was there for its opening decade, which obviously was when The Haçienda was also part of the cultural landscape of Manchester.

CLARE CUMBERLIDGE: The Haçienda was part of the cultural infrastructure. It had a role for after-hours in the same way that the Cornerhouse played that role earlier in the evening and during the day. The Green Room had a really inspirational programmer called Stella Hall, who had this fantastic international perspective on performance and live art, so the Green Room was bringing in an international network. Beverly Bytheway, who clearly has the best name in the world, was the curator at Cornerhouse and was there for the whole of The Haçienda. So you'd go to Green Room for a refreshed and outsider type of encounter, or to the Cornerhouse for political and international art. Then you'd be at The Haçienda later on. Those were the places that were really producing exciting new art and culture, and yet Beverly's and Stella's names aren't known and recorded, and their work at Cornerhouse and the Green Room isn't celebrated in the history of Manchester the way The Haçienda has been. It was really a creative triangle.

STELLA HALL: If you'd been in that street, Whitworth Street, back in the early eighties, you'd have seen a row of derelict and empty railway arches, but not a great deal else. Once the three of us were established — Green Room, Cornerhouse, The Haçienda — it spawned a whole range of other small venues and artists' spaces popping up all the way along the street.

GONNIE RIETVELD: I think the other interesting thing is that there were already plans for Manchester, urban planning for gentrification. For example, there was the big central station around the corner, which became the G-MEX Centre with exhibitions and big performances and things like that. And The Haçienda was meant to slot into that kind of urban redevelopment. Rob Gretton really had that vision of wanting to be a part of that renewal of Manchester. It was really dilapidated, and in 1982 parts of the city centre were just *empty*. Yes, there were shops, but much of the central part of Manchester had many empty buildings with bushes just growing out of their walls. It was very much a deserted city, without urban dwellers, so the city planning was about needing to bring people back in, and asking, 'How do we do that?' The Haçienda was almost too early but very much part of that process.

BEV BYTHEWAY: It was a very industrial northern street with an overground railway line, so all the railway arches ran the length of Whitworth Street. Cornerhouse was an old furniture store which had been empty for years.

You've got Haçienda at one end of the street, Cornerhouse at the other, and Green Room in the middle. But it was also really close to the university, which is important because Manchester is a young person's city, with three or four major universities right in the city centre. Most of those students came to Manchester because of its reputation: there was a very important fine art department at the poly (now MMU — Manchester Metropolitan University), and an alternative independent music scene. Most students were attracted to Manchester because of Joy Division and the pull of Factory Records.

GONNIE RIETVELD: Later on, when I was a research assistant for the Institute for the Study of Popular Culture, some of my colleagues were involved in advising the Manchester Council about how to repopulate the city. They used Zukin's *Loft Living* as an example, about the repopulation of downtown Manhattan . . . that book was a big influence on getting Manchester back on track. I don't think Rob Gretton actually read Zukin, but he did have a sense of vision. What he did read, which was interesting, was *The Third Wave* by Alvin Toffler, about the information society. That actually made him feel that with New Order, they needed to go in a different direction than with Joy Division, and continue using new music technologies. Joy Division had already experimented with a drum machine, a little primitive one. They started buying synthesisers and also started coding their music on a Macintosh computer, which was really hard; it's probably the wrong thing for it, but anyway, that's what they did. It was all about looking forward, being part of the re-urbanisation, the repopulation of Manchester, wanting to be part of that process. You see that with The Haçienda, but you also see it in the way New Order were using equipment and technology. People had been using electronica in music in the sixties and seventies, but such instruments became more accessible during the eighties, which enabled the whole electropop thing. So I think that goes hand in hand really, the electronic sound and the urban planning ideas for The Haçienda — both features of a post-industrial age.

BEV BYTHEWAY: It's an ongoing legacy about collaboration between creatives, producers and makers — look at the Manchester International Festival now and maybe that wouldn't have taken place without The Haçienda, Green Room, Cornerhouse. And the pioneering appointment of a Creative Director for the city — Peter Saville.

STELLA HALL: What Bev and I are keen to do is a repositioning: it's not just a music story. The Haçienda wasn't just a music venue. It wasn't just about the bands. We presented performance, dance, theatre, music, visual art.

•   •   •

TERESA ALLEN: We did fashion shows at the club, and we used to work with the hairdressers and Vidal Sassoon. Nick Arrojo was a stylist there, and I taught him how to properly backcomb hair, to make big hair. [laughs] The women designers were great, and I was in awe of them. Su Barnes was one, and she made the most amazing fitted stuff. It was very eighties, high-waisted panelled fitted skirts. I've still got one of them but can't get it past my knees, sadly. [laughs] I can't get rid of it because I just loved it so much.

LINDA DUTTON: One of the most fun nights was a fashion show organised by the club and the hairdressers from Vidal Sassoon's. That was pure fun, and I got my hair done for free!

ANNE-MARIE COPELAND: The fashion shows got me because it was Mancunian talent on stage.

ALISON KNIGHT: I was already doing fashion design at that point. I can't remember whether we were selling clothes in Affleck's Palace or the Royal Exchange then (I don't know whether the Royal Exchange would have been open then), but definitely selling clothes that people wore at The Haçienda at that point!

TERESA ALLEN: Then there was Baylis & Knight, with Alison Knight doing the fashion shows, and she's still a designer.

ALISON KNIGHT: I remember getting ready for the Style in Our Time night, with Frankie's Angels, making the clothes and being in The Haçienda basement with the other people in the show, and the hairdressers doing our hair. It was all quite ad hoc, and the basement was massive. I remember curling my hair on these really old curling irons. My hair was really super curly, and the hairdressers were really jealous of the fact that I had such curly hair. [laughs] We were wearing the clothes we made, and Frank and I, and a few others, did a walk to Marc Bolan's '20th Century Boy'. That was what we danced to.

We would have made the clothes in our flats in Hulme, with Frank. He looked a little bit like Boy George and was quite a big character, and he used to work on the cloakroom at The Haçienda, so he knew a lot of people there. So when he would have been asked to do the fashion show, I helped him out with it.

CLARE CUMBERLIDGE: My very good friend Edward Gibbon, who I met when we both worked at the Green Room bar, used to work at The Haçienda where he was staff representative. He's now a very successful costume designer for film, but he used to make me rather outrageous outfits, and we'd go and parade at The Haçienda after we'd spent a night working in the Green Room bar. What I'm describing, in a way, is the completely joyful playground that Manchester seemed to be at that time.

SIDNIE PANTRY: I'd finished college and knew a few girls that were potential models. Since I had my designs, my friends said, 'Let's put a fashion show on.' The first one we did was in London, and then we did one in Manchester in The Haçienda. Since art events were happening there, it was easy to have people gather around. Mike Pickering DJed it.

It was on the dance floor — we put a catwalk on the dance floor. People sat around for a while, then the fashion show happened, and then everything was taken away and it became a dance event. There were daytime events in The Haçienda as well, but this was evening. It would have started at maybe six o'clock, and would go till twelve. It was all advertised by word of mouth. Because it was a Haçienda night anyway, it just opened earlier for the fashion show. The way we did it was a two-part show. In the first part, it was daywear. We had the Jazz Defektors during the break, and then the second part of the show, which was evening wear.

ALISON KNIGHT: Baylis & Knight started maybe one or two years after the fashion night at The Haçienda. Everything was so boring . . . the clothes that you could buy were just so dull. We either wore second-hand clothes, or if you wanted anything interesting whatsoever, you had to make it yourself. That's why we all started making clothes. We were making a lot of 1940s-looking pieces

I THOUGHT I HEARD YOU SPEAK

and then everything went a bit more modern. Not really Vivienne Westwood, but things that weren't made before.

I was mostly self-taught just from making clothes myself. I'm five foot eleven, so it was always very difficult for me to actually buy clothes. I did do a year-and-a-half clothing technology course at Hollings College, where I learnt a bit about pattern design. Then Affleck's Palace opened, and it seemed like a good idea to just make my own clothes. I'd had a baby in 1984 in January, so I stopped for a little while, but soon just started up again, making and selling clothes.

SIDNIE PANTRY: Because it was the eighties, my designs involved a little bit of power dressing. I was influenced by African prints, so imagine merging that sort of eighties power dressing with African prints. That was the influence. A bit forward for the time, and it was received quite well.

ALISON KNIGHT: We always tried to make things that were wearable and interesting, and were well made that would last. At that time, you could walk out in Manchester and you could buy everything interesting — fabrics, trimmings, it was all at your fingertips. Really old fabric or really new fabric. You'd go round all the old warehouses, and it was exciting to pick out things to buy for making clothes. So there was some clothing being made in Manchester, but there were a lot of things like dish cloths and massive mills that made belts and covered buttons — you could have a lot of materials done very locally then. We'd go to those places to buy fabrics, buttons, and we'd make things out of tablecloths. There was one place that used to sell loads of crochet tablecloths, so we made a lot of stuff out of that, which was really popular.

SIDNIE PANTRY: Manchester back then had a lot of independent designers. Some were in the Royal Exchange, where I had my shop, and some were in Affleck's. I was part of that, of the independent designers. I was making stuff at home and putting it in the shop, and then working on the hatcheck at The Haçienda at night. I thought, it can't be that hard to open a factory myself, so I opened it with two machines, then it went to four, and then I switched from doing fashion shows to running this factory and selling commissioned designs.

I left the job at The Haçienda because I developed the factory and started doing work for other fashion companies. We did stuff for Bench when it was owned by James Holder, like their first T-shirts. So I was doing stuff for other people while I was also trying to do my own design stuff. Then the bomb came [the IRA detonated a bomb in Manchester in 1996] and I closed down the retail part of it and only kept the manufacturing part of it.

Fashion by Sidnie Pantry of Sidnie Co Couture

ALISON KNIGHT: I made the New Order 'World in Motion' clothes. We did some shorts that were all printed, and hooded T-shirts. I've still got loads of Factory clothing labels that I was given to put in them. That was a bit of a mission, those 'World in Motion' clothes, because we had to make quite a lot. I was doing Baylis & Knight at that time, and it was hard work trying to get it all done. I must have made probably 200 of the 'World in Motion' pieces.

FIONA ALLEN: I was a United fan, and a Bolton Wanderers fan (sorry!). Tony Wilson was obviously a massive Man United fan, and we'd often get a load of tickets to all the games — generally in the stands but sometimes we'd get a box. I used to look at their merchandise, but it wasn't really to our taste, it wasn't very Factory, so we came up with the idea to make something of our own. Merchandise even then was tied up in knots, but I managed, with some perseverance, by talking and pushing the people at United, explaining that it was going to be ubercool; it wasn't going to cross markets or probably even make any money, it was just a creative thing using the emblem and a statement. No one was going to 'get it' unless they were a music fan and a United fan, so people buying the other merchandise wouldn't want to touch it anyway. They were brilliant T-shirts. Three in the end. There was one with the United emblem and Factory logo, another which had 'Are You Man U' plastered on the front and another with 'the Saint' which was a stick man one. [Iain Key, personal interview, 2020[1]]

SUZANNE ROBINSON: Every year, they used to pay for The Haçienda blokes to go and see the cricket, and every year I'd have to do hampers for them. So this one year — and I really like cricket — I said, 'Is there any chance I can come? Instead of just doing the hampers? Can I come as well?' 'We didn't even know you like cricket,' they said. So I went out with all the lads, and it was a day of excess, shall we say? Starting at the White Lion, in a pub around the corner, at nine o'clock for beer, and then on to the cricket. So yeah, it was a good day, but a very boozy day. [laughs] I just don't think it had crossed their minds that women would want to come.

TERESA ALLEN: When merchandising was just kicking off at the club, Manchester was buzzing with all of this creativity. We used to work with a lot of local fashion designers, and a lot of them were women.

We got to choose our favourite designs for the T-shirts. So the first Haçienda T-shirts, I started all of that working with Glenn, and I think Trevor did some as well. We did loads of them, and we did them for all of the different nights we had. We used to take our nights around, and we did T-shirts for those as well. We went to a club in Blackburn, and we had T-shirts made up for that, and we used to go to the Moulin Rouge and do nights in Paris with Laurent Garnier [music producer and DJ], and we made T-shirts for that. I loved the pollen T-shirts [an abstract pollen spore graphic], and I loved being able to play with the printing: getting things printed in different ways, using foils and printing down sleeves.

JUDITH FOSTER: I was asked if I'd be interested in selling T-shirts in the nightclub. I used to bag the T-shirts up and bring them down, where I had a table inside the club. I'd sit there and sell T-shirts. After I sold T-shirts for a while, I was asked, would I be interested in taking the money on reception? Somebody else took over the T-shirts for me.

Between the dance floor on the left-hand side and the door entrance to reception, there were one, two, three stairs up, and then you were at the front doors; so I was in the middle of the club selling the T-shirts. I'd be there all night because people would come to look at the T-shirt, probably be thinking about it after they'd had a look, then come back later to buy one.

ALISON AGBOOLA: I started doing some of the merchandise because I was at college in those days and had that flexibility of being able to come in Monday to Friday in the daytime, go upstairs into the offices, and wrap up stuff like the T-shirts or sweatshirts and hoodies. We used to have all these badges and memorabilia that people were requesting and we'd send out.

FIONA ALLEN: My sister was working at The Haçienda, so then I did. Obviously, like everyone else who worked there, it was a really good time. Then, when it closed, I said, 'Well, I've got an idea, let's open a shop.' 'Cause I actually came up with an idea for a Factory label, which Wilson thought was a really good idea, for clothing. But they didn't do it in the end because it was gonna be really expensive. But you should've seen some of the draft stuff that they designed; it was really good. I can't remember the team there but it was lovely. [John Cooper, *Scream City*, 2010[2]]

ANG MATTHEWS: Fiona Allen, who's since become a comedian, had opened a shop in town. It had its own Factory number actually, 'The Area' [FAC 281]. She was selling merchandise there.

GILLIAN GILBERT: There were lots of women working at The Haçienda, like Fiona. I remember her working on designs. She designed some T-shirts for us. I remember her saying, 'You haven't got a T-shirt, so I designed one for you!'

JUDITH FOSTER: My sons keep trying to get my Haçienda T-shirts off me because I've still got them. I'm like, 'No, you can't have that!' [laughs]

ANNE-MARIE COPELAND: The most memorable nights for me were the Zumbar nights [a mix of fashion, arts and live music] on Wednesday. You'd have a fashion show, and then you'd have a performing artist.

BRIX SMITH: There has never been a moment where I haven't thought in huge depth about fashion and planned what I was going to wear — ever. And that's true to this day. Everything was really thought out. At that point in time, I didn't have a lot of money, but there were a few pieces that allowed me to create a juxtaposition between what The Fall wore. Think about the background of the rest of the guys in the band: they were just blokes wearing normal, off-the-street clothes. It was almost *non-fashion*.

In the early days, I had a job in Chicago at Marshall Field & Company, which was a big department store. I worked as the lowest person on the totem pole in the window display team,

but I was influenced by edgy fashion designers, avant-garde artists and photographers like Helmut Newton. Basically, I wanted
to shake up the window displays at Marshall Field's and shake
up the tired windows, which were multiple and prominent,
into the artistic zeitgeist moment, countering the beige, bland,
Midwestern conformity that was the old-school handwriting of
the store. I wanted to disrupt and shock. I wanted the windows
to be eye-catching works of art, to make people stop and look and
think about fashion in a modern way. I came up with all these
wild designs for the window, like creating a motorbike crash with
the mannequins on the floor in pieces. But obviously they never
let me do it. My every concept was shot down and overruled.

Anyway, the one perk of this job was that we got a massive
discount at the employees' shop, where the 'faulty' clothing was
sold. One day at lunch, I went up to that shop where there was a
blue sequin top. It was a little bit more than I could afford, but I
thought, one day I'm going to wear this fucker. So I bought the
top. I wore it a lot in The Fall, including in the video for 'L.A.',
and I wore it at The Haçienda.

JULIA ADAMSON: The official last night of The Haçienda, Brix had
re-joined the group [The Fall] too — she is really into fashion and
design — and I remember she had her clothes co-ordinated, wearing the colours of The Haçienda, black and yellow, with platform
shoes, dressing to celebrate the venue for our concert.

BRIX SMITH: I believe that we are non-physical energy in a physical
body, and when we die, our physical body dies, and our non-
physical energy goes up and out. But people that are extremely
intuitive — probably everybody, if they're open enough — can
connect with that non-physical energy, and at points can learn
to channel it through to get ideas, stimulation and all that
creativity. This is what I firmly believe in and how I work. I
am a receiver and a filter. So when I go on stage, I do that, too:
I bring it down, and I inhabit more than who I am. With the
music of The Fall, I've often described it as a musical Rorschach
test. What happens is that everybody who listens to it hears

something else that relates to their own psyche, to what they're going through as a human being. Quite often, each time they listen to a song, they will hear *different* things that relate to them along their journey of life that they'll pull out of the music. So The Fall is working on multilevels, and I think that's exactly what's happening when different people have different memories of the same thing, whether it's the fashion I wore onstage, whatever it is.

STELLA HALL: I've noticed that some of those stories get reimagined. I was looking online earlier today, and somebody was saying, 'When I saw Leigh Bowery at Flesh, one of the queer nights . . .' No, you didn't! You saw Leigh Bowery at an event that the Green Room co-presented at The Haçienda with the ICA. Things get shifted into one another, histories morphed.

CORINNE DREWERY: Brix Smith used to have a shop around the corner from our studio in London called Start, full of amazing designer clothes. When we were rehearsing I'd go in and say, 'We're going on tour in a week and I haven't got any clothes!' When I realised it was Brix who owned the boutique, we had all these conversations about Manchester. Then it'd be, 'Have you got anything in the sale? I don't want to spend too much because it'll get sweaty and ripped up, or I'll leave it on a tour bus.' She knew exactly what would work and along with Lizzie, who worked there (and was the partner of Andrew Weatherall), they would sort out my tour wardrobe. It's great to have a rock 'n' roll contact for someone who runs a shop like that. They were designer clothes, but they'd always find something I could shove in a bag and put on in the tour bus. There is definitely still a Manchester camaraderie, cemented by Factory and The Haçienda, no matter where you are.

JANE ROBERTS: Speaking of fashion, for the New Order American tour we had a programme — you know, a typical New Order programme with Peter Saville's designs. It was very cool, amazing; no content to it at all, just odd little sayings. I was the centrefold in that. I've got my face in quite a lot of things because the press sort of picked up on my job, 'Yeah, not many women doing what she does.'

TRACEY DONNELLY: Vini Reilly took photographs of me while I was working at Swing. He came into Swing and needed to get his hair cut. I thought he was involved with Factory, and I knew he was a musician, but I didn't know who he was. He kept asking me, 'Will you let me take your photo?' In the end I said yes, but I realised I was going to this strange guy's house. I was living at home at the time, so I gave my mum his number, told her to ring me there to check I was OK, and said, 'I'm going to this man's house to have my photo taken.' [laughs] He lived with Bruce Mitchell at the time. When we sat down to take my photos, my mum rang. I was embarrassed because he said, 'You told her to do that, haven't ya?' Yeah, I was having her check that I was alive! [laughs] We're still friends today, and I absolutely love Vini. Those photos were taken in the back garden at Palatine Road.

TERESA ALLEN: I got to know Tracey when they opened up the hairdressing salon, Swing, in the dressing room. It was next to the downstairs office, so we were all underground all the time. We never saw daylight. We were like vampires.

TRACEY DONNELLY: When The Haçienda opened, my best friend Cath, her brother Andrew was the hairdresser, and he approached Tony Wilson about opening a hair salon in the basement of the club. This was in 1982. So, Tony gave the go-ahead, and then Andrew asked me to work there. It was called Swing. So we used the changing rooms during the day, and then the bands would come in at night and use them. But Swing was more than a hair salon. *Everyone* got their hair done, you know. The Fall, New Order, Psychic TV, The Smiths, and it was a place people just hung out — all day — and it was Andrew running it. He was twenty-three at the time, I was nineteen, we were all really young.

Tracey Donnelly photographed by Vini Reilly

NICKY CREWE: There was a hairdresser's downstairs, Swing, and Bruce Mitchell's wife, Jackie, had done the murals for that part of the building.

JACKIE WILLIAMS: I always said that they pinched the idea for The Haçienda colours from my work. [laughs] That black and yellow with those hard sides . . . a lot of that was in my vision. There used to be a painting of mine in the hairdresser's at The Haçienda. They bought one of my paintings, and it hung on the wall there. That had the black and yellow with the chevron shapes, which The Haçienda used, and I'd been doing those from the sixties on, those shapes and colours.

TRACEY DONNELLY: The first moment I remember having an inkling of how special Factory was, was at Swing.

TERESA ALLEN: Swing was great. I got free haircuts, and it made the daytimes more lively, for sure, because I just had my head stuck in books, doing wages and accounts.

TRACEY DONNELLY: Factory did a week at Riverside Studios in Hammersmith and Tony sent the Swing hairdressers there to do everyone's hair. Durutti Column played, a whole week of Factory bands. We brought Factory badges with us and we started selling them, and the stuff was *really selling*. Tony got excited and he'd come back each day with his car restocked, and we'd sell more and more of this Factory stuff. But I never took any of them! Badges, etc. A funny story from that: one night, we finished work doing haircuts and left all the stuff lying around — scissors, towels. The next day we went in and found out that someone from Riverside thought the hairdressing stuff was an art installation, talking about the placement of the scissors and

Tracey Donnelly at Swing in The Haçienda

I THOUGHT I HEARD YOU SPEAK

towels! [laughs] But no, *we just didn't clean up!* The pretentiousness of some people! [laughs]

JANE ROBERTS: We had our own little group, a group of Factory girlfriends. We used to get our hair cut at Swing in The Haçienda. Neil used to cut my hair and he'd take great pleasure in making me look like Johnny Marr. [laughs]

BRIX SMITH: Downstairs in The Haçienda in the dressing room, there was a hairdresser called Swing. Andy Berry cut all our hair, and I remember having my hair cut there into what we would now call a mullet. *A severe mullet.* But it was super cool ... it was more like a loose Mohican. [laughs] Everyone got their hair cut there, which meant there was so much creative energy swirling ... vortexes everywhere. Johnny Marr, the rest of The Smiths, New Order and Nico, too!

GONNIE RIETVELD: Around '86, '87, there was a shift in the management. Paul Cons arrived with a socialist, queer activist background. He introduced set design and special lighting for themed weeknights. This approach was quite successful. He always wanted to have a queer night at the club. One of those iterations actually became 'Hot' in 1988, which was very much influenced by the big warehouse-styled party scene that he witnessed happening in London at the time. He used to go to parties in London, and he'd come back with ideas, and the Donnelly family had been on holiday in Ibiza. Almost overnight, in 1988, The Haçienda turned from this kind of ... avant-garde cult space to this sort of bizarre 'holiday on a Wednesday', with a little swimming pool and beach balls — and people were in their swimming gear.

TERESA ALLEN: For the club night Hot, when we had the swimming pool up in the club, we came in one day and there was a fish in it. We had to go out and buy a fish tank for it, and we had it in the office for years. We bought another fish to go with it. He was called Herbert. [laughs] I mean, who puts a swimming pool up in

– 182 –

a club? It's ridiculous. [laughs] You wouldn't be able to do it now, for health and safety. There's no way that you'd be able to have a great body of water in there under lights.

SUZANNE ROBINSON: One summer, we did ice cream. I bought an ice cream maker. It was not boring ice cream. You know, we tried to do something outrageous. Then Paul Cons came along. He'd have wild ideas about what we could do and how we could do it, and he organised a barge trip because obviously The Haçienda backed onto a canal. He wanted me to take all this food onto the barge, and I just said, it might be better if we all eat in The Haçienda before we go on the barge. [laughs]

BEV BYTHEWAY: We did a number of collaborations with The Haçienda, presenting art installations as part of the club. I mainly worked with a guy called Paul Cons, who was the programmer of Flesh and various other nights. There were three big art installations that happened at The Haçienda. The first one was David Mach, where they used a column of Factory Records vinyls [4 December 1986 to 11 January 1987].

TERESA ALLEN: I remember once getting sequin appliqués and making a curtain that went the whole way across the bottom of the mezzanine for an 'under the sea' theme. I realise now they were like art installations, using your creative abilities. It didn't occur to me at the time that we were actually creating art pieces, these temporary installations, and I wish that we'd recorded it.

CLAIRE DE VERTEUIL: I wanted to go and flex my creative muscle creative muscle ... I had a boyfriend. I had a boyfriend at the time who loved to make films, so we decided to do something which was quite new at the time. The Haçienda was having problems and promoters like Ross McKenzie from Most Excellent started doing nights in smaller clubs around Manchester and the north. We started doing projections in all the little clubs, and then we got into lighting, and then we developed into dressing, and production. People were going less and less to The Haçienda because of all the trouble there, so small clubs and promoters really took off. We became in demand, so we started doing it full-time and started to work for a couple of different promoters. I was approached one day by Paul Cons about his nights at The Haçienda. They had a lighting guy, Jonathan, but when Paul Cons and Lucy Scher had Flesh nights, they wanted to dress up the club. For Flesh nights, we made these giant rainbow flags and dressed it up. Once we turned Gay Traitor into the 'Garden of Lust' with fake plants and a swing. Each month was usually a different theme, which all added to the amazing vibe. From a Miss Flesh beauty contest with lots of glitz and a special throne, to a Halloween night when I commissioned a local artist to make a massive flying bat with lit eyes, to the *Flesh* record launch — it was all potty, camp, and great fun.

BEV BYTHEWAY: The one that I liked the most was Hannah Collins, who is a photographer. Tony Wilson, and I think Paul Cons and myself, went to Hannah Collins's studio together in London and met Hannah.

HANNAH COLLINS: I never pitched anything to Factory or The Haçienda. At the time, I was making quite a lot of work about music, so there was a relationship to that. I don't know where they would have seen it. I had a gallery called Maureen Paley, then called Interim Art, in London, so maybe she [the gallerist] said something, but I had a visit from the boss, Tony Wilson, to my studio late one night. I was developing a print at that time, which I used to do myself by hand. I had a flood because I was talking to him for so long that I left the water running. [laughs]

The fact that the boss was somebody who had a political agenda to some extent, that was opposition to the mainstream, made me interested in doing the piece for them. Although I realised once I was in it that the music industry was then much more structured than art, so that I think Tony was trying to move into art, vaguely, but maybe not that actively ... I also liked what The Haçienda represented because it was about young people. You know, the thing is in England, young people never get much of a say in anything. Not really. They have to be rebellious to get any say, and The Haçienda gave them that. My piece spoke to that in a way: it was jovial, but it was also in your face.

BEV BYTHEWAY: She did this fantastic huge hanging, sort of like a stage curtain, which was a staircase to heaven. It was extraordinary. I often wonder what happened to that. It's interesting because none of those things get documented in the usual stories around The Haçienda.

HANNAH COLLINS: The piece for The Haçienda started as a picture of a Nash terrace building, so it had a big staircase going up — like a staircase to heaven, but in a sort of British establishment sort of way since it was a staircase from the Nash terrace at the back of the ICA in London. There's a group of Nash-designed buildings, and they have these amazing staircases that are very solemn and very establishment. I think I did two five-by-four negatives together, so it was this quite big negative and a great, big staircase. Then I went to Westminster Abbey, and there was a shop there that sold religious stuff. I got this ribbon that they use for religious purposes, a red ribbon. I had these ribbons going all the way down the sides of it. The work I made was very handmade-looking and still is very handmade-looking. Most photography has a very clean-cut, hard aspect to it, but this was mounted on fabrics. It was like a hanging but an original artwork, and it referred to something classical but it wasn't classical. It had a backing on it — a big flat colour — and it was probably twenty feet high by about seven or eight feet wide.

I used to make these huge prints by hand, so they were very much hand-processed, and maybe what Tony liked when he came to my studio was the fact that it was this big handmade object. In that sense, it was more similar to music than the visual work most artists were making.

The Haçienda had an opening, and I went up to Manchester. 'Stairway to Heaven', this piece of mine, was hung so that it went up to the top of the building. When they were hanging it, I remember thinking, this won't last two minutes here in this heavy environment. Then years later, somebody told me they'd been to

The Haçienda — and guess what? There was this piece of mine hanging in the middle of The Haçienda.

BEV BYTHEWAY: I've always felt that it was very difficult to get the visual arts on the agenda because Manchester was defined so much as a music city, and that's to do with the legacy of Factory Records. It always felt like you were the second sister, added to the fact that it was completely dominated by the male voice all the time. I know every city has its own culture that defines it, and it's very much music that defines Manchester, but it was extraordinarily frustrating. Tony Wilson sat on Stella's board and on the board of the ICA in London, but he didn't really engage with Cornerhouse as a cultural venue.

HANNAH COLLINS: I don't think they were prepared for art in general. I think what happened was they established themselves as a music venue, and then really wanted to break into art. But in reality, most art at that time was very contained: it was in little frames, it was small, or it looked nice, whereas my art was explosive and didn't really fit into anything. I think that's what they liked, but I'm not sure then that they knew what to do beyond having this thing there, which was really different to the rest of the club.

GONNIE RIETVELD: Part of the culture shock for me was that Manchester was incredibly traditional about gender roles in a way that in the Netherlands may have been like the 1930s. Even the clothes they were wearing, the wallpaper and the furnishings, to me it was a total shock. You look at the artwork Factory was creating, and that's really modern, but you go to Manchester in the 1980s and you have roses on the wall, porcelain saucers on display and flowery brown carpet, wall to wall. Even in the bathroom it's wall-to-wall carpet. Brown bedding, brown this and brown that. Pastel and brown ... And that was a shock, as well as people wearing what I thought of as quite old-fashioned shoes. A real pride of how you shine your shoes, and I'm like, I'm from a kind of hippie/punk background. So there was a certain old-fashionedness about all of it. And the guys would go out and do gigs that pushed the boundaries of music, but then they'd go home to places like that.

CAROL MORLEY: There were these hangover attitudes that felt very 1950s, I'd say, and so my artistic desires got mixed up in the prevailing views of women at the time but also my own 'am I not good enough?' thoughts. It felt very empowering to make a film and go back to that time — a messy time, a complicated time — in *The Alcohol Years* and to make something of it that ultimately did reveal the attitudes towards young women in a way that we didn't question at the time we lived through it. I remember being very aware of feminism at the time and challenging people — mostly men — but they weren't really interested in what I had to say. Some of those key players thought of me as being literally 'nuts'! Crazy! Or, mostly, too 'mouthy'!

HANNAH COLLINS: I went and had a look at The Haçienda in the daytime, before they hung my work, in its grittiness. I also went to Tony's house, and that was surprising to me because it was very middle class. He'd come to me in my studio in London with this very glamorous girlfriend and he appeared late at night, around eleven, which I think he thought was cool. I was busy working because I used to work all night, and that was when I used to develop photographs (at night). So I had these huge prints, a lot of water and big rolls of paper. I think if you'd walked into my studio at that time, it would have been quite dramatic in a way. Then when I went to his house, it was this very middle-class house on the outskirts of Manchester. So he had several identities, let's put it that way.

BEV BYTHEWAY: We also collaborated with The Haçienda on the installations presented by Marty St James and Anne Wilson, who were a performance artist duo. They did an installation in the Gay Traitor bar and the steps going down to the bar.

CLARE CUMBERLIDGE: I was writing a show for Spinsters. Paul Cons had previously lived in my flat in Hulme, and Dani Jacobs, who was one of the swivel boys who did the videos, had also lived there for a bit. I was very good friends with Dani and friends with Paul, and I believe it was Paul who invited me, Sarah and Belinda to paint the Gay Traitor. Sarah Cameron was the technologist for Spinsters and Belinda Meredith was the visual artist. They invited us to paint out the Marty St James and Anne Wilson installation, which covered the Gay Traitor. I seem to remember fake grass in that installation. Anyhow, it took us two days on a scaffold to paint that installation out, and in return for doing that, we got membership cards to The Haçienda. It was a very good deal because The Haçienda became our after-hours free club forever after.

STELLA HALL: You've got the Gay Traitor, so you could happily sit down there all night, just chatting if you didn't want to be upstairs dancing. Or you could find nooks and crannies all over the place, just to be with two or three people or to throw yourself into the middle. It wasn't always thronged, particularly in those early days. So you got to know everybody. It was very different people — very different from me, I mean — young, working-class people from Hulme, who came to dress up and dance, rubbing up alongside university lecturers who shared their interest and enthusiasm. The mix was really quite extraordinary.

CAROL MORLEY: I have this very vivid memory of Stella Hall. At that time, when I was going to The Haçienda, I was used to going home with men (and I would go home with women as well, sexually), but it was a lot of going back with men and doing whatever would have to happen. Once, Stella said, 'You can stay at my flat tonight' — obviously completely non-sexual. (I think it began with a group of people going back to her place and I snuck along!) I slept in her living room, and she gave me this amazing nightdress to wear from the fifties. I remember this feeling of absolute safety, and getting my first reality check that there was something beyond what I'd got used to in Manchester — some kind of way out. I don't mean a way out of the town, but a way out of where you felt stuck. I went from going, 'OK, the only way I'm going to get ahead in life, whatever that means, is to sleep around', to being given a nice nightdress and treated really well — I realised there could be more than what I'd learnt up to that point. That always stayed with me.

CLARE CUMBERLIDGE: Another aspect of The Haçienda that is not sufficiently spoken about is the way it became an after-hours club for creative production. Sarah, Belinda and I weren't going to The Haçienda only because we wanted to dance. Rather, we used it almost the way that gentlemen's clubs operated, but *not for gentlemen*. And *a lot of people* were using it in that way. It was a place where you met different creative people and had the kinds of conversations that were generative for cultural production, supporting emerging practices.

TERESA ALLEN: There was a series of nights called Shiva. Tony Wilson's best friend Neville did that and I've still got some of the little flyers we made out of printed fabric. Neville used to go round and put the little bindi stickers on everybody, and I had loads of those stickers stuck all over my mirror at home. In the office, we would be commissioning flyers all the time like that, and T-shirts and artwork. We'd be working with people like Glenn Routledge from Anagram, Trevor Johnson, Keith Jobling. We used to do all sorts of commissioning, getting the posters for fly-postering. I even got to design one once, and I've actually got that artwork. It was for a guy called Paul Haig who came to play.

SUZANNE ROBINSON: Tony used to come into the club with food ideas, and he'd just gone over to Japan. In Japan, they have plastic replicas of the food that's to be served on a display, and he wanted to do that at The Haçienda. I was like, 'Come on, Tony', and he just said, 'Darling, it will be fabulous-looking, just fabulous, darling.' I obviously didn't do it. I let him run away with his ideas and then he'd just leave me alone. [laughs]

TERESA ALLEN: Suzanne ran the kitchen. Before her it was a woman called Janie and her partner, Dave. Suzanne was great. I gave her my recipe for parsnip soup. [laughs] She was very good friends with Rebecca Knowles, who is still a very good friend of mine.

SUZANNE ROBINSON: Janie ran the canteen and Dave was the electrician at The Haçienda. They were my neighbours. We would meet up and go in there for a few drinks after we finished work, just to unwind. One night they said they were going to Greece, just upping sticks. They suggested that me and my close friend Liza Ryan Carter and Steph Rollins, who was managing it for them at the time, come together and buy the equipment, which they were selling for £300. That sounds like nothing, but you're talking thirty-five years ago, so it was quite a lot of money for a young person. So we did. I couldn't cook, and then Liza went to Sheffield uni, and Steph just gave up the ghost. So suddenly that autumn I was there, doing it with staff, all the riders for the bands — and obviously they ramped it up in the autumn months.

SUSAN FERGUSON: Suzanne Robinson ran the kitchen. Not from day one but from quite soon into the history of the place.

SUZANNE ROBINSON: I was a little bit of an entity on my own there. I really did have free rein to do whatever I wanted. Back in those days, if you wanted a two o'clock licence, you had to serve food — it couldn't just be chips. So they wanted a late licence but they didn't want the bother of doing the food themselves. In the very early days, a guy called Laurent did it, then Janie took over, and then I took over and served really, really unusual food for a club. We used to do veggie samosas, homemade hummus, vegetarian chilli . . . it was quite an extensive menu.

ANNE-MARIE COPELAND: In the canteen, I used to eat vegetarian food, and I'm not vegetarian! The food was just that good. It was something completely new that I'd never experienced before.

TRACEY DONNELLY: Suzanne's canteen was so good. It was unique at the time, and I can't think of any other venue that had a food place like that: the food she served, the atmosphere and the set-up was all really different and very cool. Served with a smile, too.

SUZANNE ROBINSON: From me being at The Haçienda and doing work for the bands, all their riders, I started doing outside catering. I did catering for Roger Eagle, who was a promoter doing gigs at The Ritz, which is down the road from The Haçienda. At one point, I was catering for The Boardwalk, for The Cellar . . . They were tiny venues and they couldn't afford a full-time person to do it. I did the catering for the Manchester festival when that first started. Bruce Mitchell got me in on that one, another of the cohort from Palatine Road. I also did Jon da Silva's wedding, the DJ at The Haçienda.

TERESA ALLEN: Rebecca and I used to do loads of really arty things together at the club. We used to decorate for big occasions or Christmas and stuff, and we had a couple of weddings in the Gay Traitor. I got bolts of fabric for a wedding and made crazy stuff that was just to last for one night, or not even a whole night because everyone pulled it down. We decorated all the tables in the Gay Traitor. We sprayed everything gold, and we had old-fashioned tele-phones wired up, so that you could pick up and talk to someone at a table across the way. Those were all sprayed gold, too. We'd been out to some suppliers and sourced a load of shells and sand, and we decorated the table tops with those. We poured epoxy resin on there and decorated them. They were absolutely beautiful. We've got no photographic record of this at all. No one had cameras then, but now it would be splashed everywhere with people thinking, 'How great is this?' Sadly, it's all lost now.

MARCIA PANTRY: That last New Year's at The Haçienda, 1988, Christmas swag was still hanging on the walls. I still have two items from the Christmas decorations from The Haçienda: I kept two silver string things and a red string thing. I used to use them a lot, hang them up here.

RUTH TAYLOR: One Boxing Day in the early days there was a huge fight at the club, with people throwing furniture at each other and you had to duck under the counter. They got in the canteen and just started chucking furniture. I think it was Suzanne from the canteen who had to deal with that! I still wouldn't change any of my time working there for the world. Maybe Suzanne would change that day. [laughs]

SUZANNE ROBINSON: I had free rein, but the management would ask me to do special stuff for The Haçienda birthdays. Once, I made a ten foot by six foot cake for the Fifth Birthday. That's *huge*. [laughs] We did it in black and orange because that was the poster. So we had to use black food dye in the icing. Quite a lot of my friends said, 'Uh, I had green poo the next day.' [laughs] I'm like, 'It's the black food colouring!' We got some square 12-inch cake tins, about ten of them, and we made batches of cakes in bricks. I think it took six people to move it into place. Six men, not me. [laughs]

BEV BYTHEWAY: There was a big show about The Haçienda at Urbis and there was none of the story about these events, these collaborations. It's always the main story that's promoted, always the 'main characters' that are promoted, even though there's a lot of other stuff which went on around it. Manchester is very good about mythologising itself and mythologising the male leads.

GONNIE RIETVELD: In 1992, I worked with Jon Savage on editing the collection *The Haçienda Must Be Built!* to commemorate ten years of the club's existence, for which I collected an archive of materials that ultimately led to an exhibition that I curated on the club, also in 1992, at Manchester Met ...

At the time, Jon Savage was a known journalist ... I mean he was an authority, he'd written for established indie music magazines, and was known for his music reviews. He was regarded as a knowledgeable person and was probably a marketable name as well, to be associated with. They didn't consider me to be of that ilk, even though I'd been involved with The Haçienda from the moment they started looking for potential buildings in the early 1980s ... It felt a little bit like being an invisible member of the management, a 'woman in the shadows' kind of thing. Maybe many wives feel that way. [laughs] On an informal level, I was very much part of conversations, so for a few years I'd been part of that. And, of course, I recorded music for Factory as well, during the early to mid-1980s.

In 1992, though, I was just at the start of my academic life, so I was also a research assistant for Steve Redhead's research at the time, but for Factory and The Haçienda, that kind of thing seemed of little value. Reengaging with academic study was like I had *dropped out* as far as they were concerned. It was like, what are you doing, getting a *degree*? In the end I actually collected all the materials for *The Haçienda Must Be Built!*, and Jon Savage did the interviews. Then we spent a day actually editing all of the text, and Jon was more like chief editor in the sense that he'd say, 'I want this picture in there' and 'that's not going in my book', that kind of thing. So I learnt a lot from the process, put in a lot of time, and I had a lot of input. If I collaborated now with people on a similar project, I would give them more credit though.

BEV BYTHEWAY: I think Carol Morley made the best thing to come out of The Haçienda. Her film [*The Alcohol Years*] is so brilliant. It exactly illustrates that absence of women in the story.

CAROL MORLEY: When I finished *The Alcohol Years* and we screened it in Manchester, somebody said to me, 'If I'd known you were going to finish it, I wouldn't have been in it, I wouldn't have been interviewed.' He obviously thought I wouldn't manage to get to the end, to be able to complete it, based on my reputation as a young teenage girl.

In *The Alcohol Years*, Dick Witts says something like, 'We didn't judge you in terms of your artistic aspirations, but purely in the sense of how many things have gone up your vagina.' [laughs, sighs] But he was very honest! It was true . . . Factory created a sense of desire for something — not just the music, but the energy and a way of looking at life. So as a young woman growing up in that context, or with that organisation of Factory Records around you, it was very inspirational, but getting to be truly part of it in one way or another felt almost impossible. As time went on, it felt more and more elusive. So any woman that was a part of Factory is superhuman in my eyes!

STELLA HALL: Her film encapsulates that era and the absence of women in the stories that are told. Carol Morley was an always-there figure, with so much potential and so much talent, but of course, she wasn't viewed in that way. She's a real illustration of how women are . . . in the shadows.

CAROL MORLEY: I felt like I'd got so much from being in Manchester, but I also felt like I'd given so much of myself to that place and that scene, and it all sort of evaporated. I did feel like making *The Alcohol Years* was the beginning of an exploration into being visible again.

BEV BYTHEWAY: Where are the women in the story of The Haçienda and Factory Records? It's always been an issue. It was an issue when I was at Cornerhouse, and it's still an issue now. We all played roles, and I still don't think that's ever been properly looked into. The story never changes. It's the same lead characters every time. It's all the same voices and they just perpetuate each other's myths.

Festival of the Tenth Summer

ALL INQUIRIES REGARDING MERCHANDISING FOR
FESTIVAL OF THE TENTH SUMMER, THE HACIENDA,
AND FACTORY COMMUNICATIONS, SEND SAE TO
TRACEY DONNELLY
FACTORY COMMUNICATIONS LIMITED
86 PALATINE ROAD
MANCHESTER M20 9JW

Tracey Donnelly's Festival of the Tenth Summer business card

Held across the city of Manchester in July 1986, the Festival of the Tenth Summer (FAC 151) celebrated a decade of punk. It foregrounded the way in which Factory, in part through The Haçienda, forged pathways into much more than music. Through the Festival, the label summoned forth nearly every element of contemporary culture, emblazoning the interplay among myriad artistic forms.

TRACEY DONNELLY: Festival of the Tenth Summer got started because there was this idea that every ten years, there was a musical revolution. Tony wanted to celebrate ten years after punk, and I got involved. I used to leave the office to go to these Festival of the Tenth Summer meetings in town. I think I may have been the only woman there, with Tony, Alan, Paul Mason from The Haçienda ... I was given the role of doing the merchandise and getting The Smiths to play.

CHRIS MATHAN: The Festival of the Tenth Summer, conceived of and organised by Factory, took place in July 1986 in Manchester. There were citywide music and art events (numbered one to nine) that culminated in the tenth event on 19 July, held at the Greater Manchester Exhibition Centre (G-MEX). Factory and non-Factory bands played from noon till 11 p.m. New Order were last, ending the festival.

STELLA HALL: I presented an element of the Festival of the Tenth Summer in The Haç. Other events took place all over Manchester — ours was performance and fashion. We focused on bringing young, up-and-coming local fashion designers with models and music into the space with performative elements. We had some solo performers mixed in with the fashion, so it was a reflection back to the *Performing Clothes* show that we brought with Leigh

Bowery to The Haçienda, but it was also a nod to the 'Off the Rails' fashion show we did with Cornerhouse at The Ritz. It was about opening out beyond just the music scene. I'm looking at the names of the designers now: Andrew Obaje aka Jelly Universe, Breed 86, Su Barnes, William Tailoring, Dawn Campbell, Geese, presented by The Haçienda and the Green Room. There was a film programme at Cornerhouse and an exhibition of Kevin Cummins photography.

JANE ROBERTS: For the Festival of the Tenth Summer, New Order played at the event. It was brilliant. We did a fashion parade for that. I dressed like a punk, punk fashion . . . I thought I looked amazing!

SUZANNE ROBINSON: I did the food for Festival of the Tenth Summer at G-MEX. That was 120 plus, and that was over three days.

TRACEY DONNELLY: The Festival of the Tenth Summer meetings were ground floor, Saint James's building, 89 Oxford Street in Manchester. I got a little card with my name and contact just for the Festival of the Tenth Summer. I went to a meeting with Tony and the guy from Acme making the actual merchandise. Those little cards of mine were thrown about, and people got in touch to buy the Festival of the Tenth Summer merchandise.

CHRIS MATHAN: The marketing of the event revolved around the ten numbers. The inspiration for those came from the first computer alphabets and numbers that were created on grids. There was, of course, no post-script yet. So, for example, there was OCR-A and then OCR-B [a monospaced font developed in 1968, designed to be read by electronic devices]. I admit I wasn't all that familiar with computers then. That was more Brett's department. Once we had the ten numbers, I designed a lot of the applications, the logo, the stationery and the number posters, which were teasers — a sort of count-down of what was to come. They were really big, about forty by sixty inches, black and white, just the one giant number on white with the logo underneath, and were sniped all over Manchester, one per week. So these mysterious numbers offering no real explanation appeared all over Manchester. By the last week, posters describing the events went up. The numbers were used for everything — graphics, merchandise and an art installation of giant, fabricated, three-dimensional, plastic resin numbers. We had postcards silkscreened, T-shirts, bags, etc.

TRACEY DONNELLY: Chris Mathan did a bunch of the design work for Festival of the Tenth Summer and did a lot of work on those numbers. I think Chris designed the number posters, and I've got one framed still. The posters were beautiful, silkscreens in beautiful colours. It was like they were taken from the air of Manchester.

CHRIS MATHAN: I don't know what happened to the gallery numbers. I guess Factory sold them. In my collection of Factory memorabilia, I found price lists for various Factory products. One list is entitled: Merchandise —Tenth Summer. The last thing on the list is the price for merchandise item #10: installation. The price was £32,000.

TRACEY DONNELLY: In the notes I've got here, we had plans for all these people ... Jerry Dammers, Steve Diggle, Virgin Prunes, The Smiths, Pete Shelley, Gil Scott-Heron, John Cale ... We also arranged art exhibitions. I remember Jamie Reid did some art, and Malcolm Garrett did some stuff. Then there were ten pieces made of the numbers, big sculptures, and I think Tina's still got #4. I didn't manage to grab one, and I'm still upset about that.

CATH CARROLL: I had forgotten about that Festival of the Tenth Summer booklet [merchandise item #4]. I do actually remember writing that piece on Linder. I think Richard Boon from New Hormones contacted me to write something. Richard had been so very supportive of Liz and I. He would buy us drinks when things were bad and we were broke. Which was all the time.

NICKI KEFALAS: We used to drive up to Manchester all the time. Everybody was working at 200 per cent but inevitably combined with a good time. I'd stay at least once a month in Manchester at Rob's or in a hotel, or at Rebecca's later on when she started working for Rob. We stayed at the Britannia quite often in the early days, which was a terrible hotel in those days, and very rock and roll. [laughs] The Britannia was in a really big and beautiful old building, but was run-down back then. I was always bringing radio and TV people up to Manchester for things and we stayed up for a full week when we covered the Festival of the Tenth Summer. When we arrived for this trip, somebody had shit in the bathtub of one of the rooms we'd been given. That was ... shock. [laughs] There were always parties in the hallways too. One time The Rolling Stones' crew had an all-night party in the hallways there. Eventually I refused to stay there as I increasingly valued my sleep as I got older. [laughs]

BRIX SMITH: My biggest memory of the Festival of the Tenth Summer is being included with all those iconic bands, being part of something that was game-changing in terms of the nucleus of music that was coming out of Manchester, and being a big part of the nucleus. For me, that was huge validation and a 'pinching yourself' moment. In those days, I used to get incredibly nervous before shows and felt a lot of pressure, so I would have been laser-point focused on what I was doing, going through songs, rehearsing, putting my hands on the right strings ... very isolated and in a focused place. But afterwards, after the gig, then all bets are off. [laughs]

Everyone was smoking pot, and we all had to evacuate the Hotel Britannia en masse when the fire alarm went off, which is hilarious. It felt like every rock star in the world was standing out on the fucking street. [laughs]

CAROL MORLEY: TOT was one of the bands I was in, with Debby Turner. We were going to play at the Festival of the Tenth Summer — or we thought we were going to play. Bruce Mitchell from Durutti Column was our manager and he got Tony Wilson to agree that we could play — but Tony changed his mind. So instead of playing at the Tenth Summer, we made badges and T-shirts, and ran around giving these T-shirts to 'influential' people — we were determined to make our mark. But we were not allowed to play, and I don't remember many women on that bill. I internalised that, and even now I would say, 'Well, it was my fault, I wasn't good enough, I didn't have what it took.' But I remember that night at Festival of the Tenth Summer feeling a fury and a frustration.

SUZANNE ROBINSON: For Festival of the Tenth Summer at G-MEX, that was on a different level. I was in hospital because I'd had a miscarriage before my boys were born. I had my favourite cookbooks with me and a clipboard, and that's all I did: planning, planning, planning. The proximity to The Haçienda helped with the G-MEX planning, but I was still back and forth, back and forth, because they were cooking stuff at The Haçienda and bringing that up, as well as what we were prepping at G-MEX.

Then they decided to have an after-show party in the basement of The Haçienda where they wanted all the food. I had never worked as hard in my life.

TINA SIMMONS: At the Festival of the Tenth Summer, Happy Mondays were on the same night as New Order. They were on the stage directly before New Order. Need I say more? [laughs] They wrecked the place and New Order was going *mad*. I remember Rob turned to me and said, 'That's the *last time* the Happy Mondays *EVER* appear onstage with us again!' They used to let all the people come up onstage and dance with them, and New Order would be panicking because all their gear was set up onstage and these people were just rampaging across the stage. *Absolutely wild, absolute mayhem.*

CHAPTER 7

HEY, DJ!

DJ Paulette at The Haçienda

Self-taught sensations, self-starters, scene-makers. Women DJed at The Haçienda from the early days through the Madchester years, but you might not know it: they've been largely written out of the club's histories to date. Through DJ culture and themed nights – Flesh in particular – women firmly established The Haçienda as a queer sanctuary in the heart of Manchester. On its dance floors, the club became a safe space for LGBTQIA+ dancers and music lovers who could thwart the hazards of identity politics outside and create their own narratives on the dance floor to the sounds reverberating from the DJ booth.

ANG MATTHEWS: Earlier in the days, I think Suzanne Robinson was the first woman to ever play a record at The Haçienda. She did indie music and that would've been '82, '83, maybe '84. I had a great working relationship with her. She was crazy, she was brilliant, and during that mad period gave birth to twins! I mean, that is just so unbelievable. She was a single parent with twins. I used to think, how's she even doing this? But she did it! She ran the canteen when I was the manager there, so I didn't have to think about that. She paid her rent, but if you speak to Hooky, she never paid a penny. But she was absolutely paying rent.

SUZANNE ROBINSON: I started DJing on the local radio pirate station, and that got me in contact. Manchester at that time had such a small-village feel to it, so I knew a lot of musicians. My best friend was a sound engineer for Simply Red, and everyone knew each other. So I knew members of ACR and Biting Tongues before Factory, and then when I started DJing, I used to go to Factory because it was around the corner from me on Palatine Road. They would give me records to play, and I'd have a cup of tea with Tina.

I was doing the pirate local radio, and Mike Pickering heard me interviewing ACR. He contacted me and asked if I'd be interested in DJing at Haçienda as they had gigs on. So obviously I went down and saw the place. It was such a beautiful building, and it was so different to anything else, to any other club at the time. After that, I started DJing when they'd have gigs on. I was the first female DJ at The Haçienda. Now this is well before house music. Tony Wilson was very much about promoting local music and bands, and he asked if I would organise a night for local bands, and I said yes. There were four bands on every Tuesday, and I started getting more and more demo tapes. I'd have to listen to the demo tapes of the bands, organise the backline, and DJ. The first week Alan Wise did it, and after that it was down to me. In total, I worked at The Haçienda for over fifteen years, and I was there at the end.

I knew what I was doing when I started DJing and running the local band night. Mike Pickering had showed me around the DJ booth. Next to me was IKON video and next to the video guy was a lighting guy called Tony Martin. I ended up going out with the IKON guy, Tim Chambers, and having children with him.

It was mainly students coming to the Tuesday night, and people that would go and see gigs. So quite a diverse kind of range of people, and they weren't there necessarily for the dancing because they were usually there to see the bands. My DJ sets were maybe thirty minutes, and then the local bands would come on. That night ended because they started bringing in more nights. Friday and Saturday were always classic nights, and then Thursday, my friend Dave Haslam started doing the student night, and they stopped booking as many bands.

KATH MCDERMOTT: There was DJ Michelle [at The Haçienda], and she was really important. She's a lesbian who used to play Tuesday night at the No. 1 Club, a kind of pop music student night, and it was so, so good. All the young gay people would go to that, and I loved it. She had some great records, and she really knew how to rock. People don't give her the credit she deserves and she's not properly recognised like she should be, but she was actually the first woman to DJ at The Haçienda, and she DJed at the Summer of Lesbian Love.

MICHELLE MANGAN: Before I moved to Manchester, I started DJing as a teenager in Liverpool at a time when it was all blokes DJing. I remember I used to go to this club in Liverpool on a Saturday night — they had a lesbian night or a women-only night. I remember going not long after I came out, and started to go to gay clubs. At this club, they had this guy DJing with gaps between the records! I remember going up to the owners and saying, 'Your DJ is awful.' They were like, 'Yeah, we know.' I had so much music and I loved music, so I said to them, 'I'll do it — let me do it.' There were hardly any female DJs at the time. There were people like Janice Long and Annie Nightingale who were radio DJs — I always taped Annie Nightingale after the charts on a Sunday night, and that's where I got a lot of musical influences — but there were just no role models for women who wanted to be club DJs at that time, in that side of the DJ business. There were no female DJs as far as I knew.

So the club in Liverpool said to me, 'We'll give you a ten-minute trial on Saturday night, a ten-minute trial.' I was like, ten minutes?! That could be just one track if you're doing a house set! I think I mixed in about four tracks. I'd never, ever touched a set of decks before, and they weren't even Technics. They were like old-school things. But they gave me my own Friday night, which I did when I was at school, and I handwrote my own flyers. I named the night after a Debbie Harry B-side, a track called 'Feel the Spin'. I drew all these 12-inch records and wrote, 'DJ Michelle, Feel the Spin, Fridays'.

KATH MCDERMOTT: Obviously there's DJ Paulette, a real, proper DJ. Amazing.

DJ PAULETTE: I learnt on the job. I never planned to be a DJ. When I became a DJ I was studying for my degree, and at the same time I was a clubber, so I was known on the scene for dancing. I was dancing on podiums before I was DJing behind the decks. I was also modelling a lot, and people kind of knew my face before I started to DJ. I'd been singing in bands before then as well, so I had a bit of stagecraft, but I didn't have my own decks or anything like that, and I never, ever set out with the idea that I was going to be a DJ.

DJing at The Haçienda was a bit of a no-brainer. It's not so much that I wanted to DJ there as I was just *there all the time*. I knew it like the back of my hand. I went to gigs there, I went to club nights there, I knew the people that worked there; I knew the people behind the bar, on the door, the security. I knew bands, I knew Tony — it was just a very Manchester thing. So as soon as I was offered it, it was like yeah, great, I'll work here because I'm here anyway! [laughs] It was home.

I went to loads of gigs at The Haçienda because I'd been going there since 1987. We always went to the Nude night. I have a memory — a very strong memory — of a moment when Mike Pickering played Wally Badarou's 'Kiss of the Spider Woman'. Me and my twin, it's just one of our favourite records, and we were dancers. We just took over the dance floor to this particular record. We'd just had our hair done and the thing is, when you get Black hair relaxed, really for the first week you can never get it wet. Do not sweat in it! Never get it rained on! We just ruined our hair because we danced so hard to this record. By the time we finished dancing to the record, the relaxer had reverted and our hair had shrunk. We were just like *crying*, 'My hair, my hair!' It's a Black girl thing, and it was just one of those moments. Then there was the Mantronix gig which was off-the-scale energy.

The Haçienda is absolutely where I learnt to DJ. I wasn't a DJ before! I'd never played records before, and I didn't have decks at home until '93 anyways, so I really learnt on the job — how to sequence records, how to keep people on the dance floor, how to entertain people, how to present myself, how to perform. I had to think about what I was going to do when I was behind the decks to perform. I'd been a singer before, and I've always lip-synced to records, always sung along to records since the day when I started DJing. That became an integral part of who I became behind the decks, and I still do that now. So The Haçienda is where I created this person who is DJ Paulette.

KATH MCDERMOTT: My DJ story begins long, long ago. In about 1989, a friend of mine in Liverpool wanted to put on a World AIDS Day benefit, and we couldn't find a DJ that would do it for nothing

— we just wanted all the money to go to charity. My girlfriend at the time said, 'I've got *loads* of records, so why don't we just do it?' So we did it, and everyone loved it, and we really enjoyed it. After that, everyone was like, 'do another one'. So we started doing a monthly night and that got quite successful because it was the only queer night in Liverpool. Every club was very traditional and very separate. There'd be women over here, men over there, with the gay scene totally separate from the straight scene. So we were like, let's just mix it up and play loads of house music. It was all really cool, and when I say it was cool, it was kind of cool because it *wasn't* cool. Do you know what I mean? There were no posers.

ANGEL JOHNSON: Every single moment after I'd drop my son at school, in the few hours before college, I was on those turntables. (I was going to college as well, at the time. I'd decided to enrol myself back into college to try and further my qualifications.) With the turntables, it got to the point where it was such an obsession that I'd be mixing the same records over and over to get it right. It was such a beautiful feeling when they did lock in, like, wow, you're creating something new. Hook, line and sinker, I fell in love with the whole concept of DJing. When I did go out to play, I could mix because I practised so hard. I'm quite a perfectionist, and if I'm gonna do it, you know, I'm gonna do it well.

GONNIE RIETVELD: I DJed at The Haçienda, but not in the main room. DJ Paulette was playing there regularly during the early 1990s. She made a career from DJing. Paulette was one year behind me, studying for the same degree as I was. When she was doing her exams, I did her gigs. Apart from that, I DJed at a place called Strangeways, named after the local prison, which was a queer, gay after-hours club in the gay quarters of Manchester. I would actually start at 3 a.m., and finish at 7 a.m.

TERESA ALLEN: If DJs were late, sometimes I'd have to peg it up to the DJ booth and put a white label of some description on there and get some music going.

ANGEL JOHNSON: I kind of fell into DJing. I was your sort of prover-bial 'club diva', out dancing from a very early age, from about age sixteen. My friends and me, we discovered the nightlife, and that was it — we wanted to go out every week dancing. I was working in a factory at the time. We got our wages on a Friday, and some of it would go towards buying a new outfit, and then we'd go out. I had to take a fake ID, so I used to pester friends' older sisters, 'Please, please, give me your birth certificate so I can get in!' At first it was dance clubs. It was a very Black scene, all the first clubs I went to, with breakdancing and jazz funk competitions on the dance floor. It wasn't really about drinking, but more about the music and the dancing. So, I was introduced to a very soulful kind of sound and became a great lover of divas, vocals and funky instrumentation, all mixed in with electronic music.

Some years later, I fell upon some underground clubs in Not-tingham and was introduced to house music. I became a lover of house music. So I used to frequent the underground clubs in my city of Nottingham, and then I got a job working behind the bar at this club called Venus. They used to bring in the best DJs to play. By this time, I was actually a single parent, and my son went to his father's at the weekend, so I got a bar job. Working in the club gave me a little bit of a social life at the weekends. I was mad on house music, but I wasn't a record collector at that point. Apart from the obvious records I couldn't tell you the artists that I was listening to . . . I just loved the music.

My best friend, who I'd go dancing with, we saw this TV pro-gramme on a Friday evening on Channel 4 called *DEF II*, watching that while getting ready for work. There were these female DJs from Bristol! It dawned on me for the first time ever: oh my God, women can be DJs! It literally was like that.

So then I knew, OK, I want to be a DJ, I want to do this. I started asking, does anybody know anybody who's got any decks? Someone said, 'Oh, I know this guy who's unemployed and he's got some decks.' I said, 'Can you hook me up with him?' We went around to his house, me and my friend Nina — because we were both going to be DJs, the pair of us — and the first week he showed us how to mix. The second week, Nina was on the bed reading the magazines.

And the third week she fell asleep. She got bored really quickly, but I was just absolutely hooked — hooked on the concept of a mix, and how two records could sort of turn into a different record.

I didn't know anything about DJ culture, even though I had learnt to use the decks, so the first thing I did was go out and buy a load of records that I liked, that other DJs had made big. I said to this guy, who'd been teaching us to use his decks, 'Can I hire your decks?' I had them for about three months, I think, and literally every spare moment that I had, I was on those turntables. It was such a frustrating journey because it's such a craft to learn, but I was so determined. After sort of burying myself at home and sweating over these belt-driven turntables that didn't do the job very well, I produced my first mix — a sixty-minute mix.

With another friend of mine, Sam, we'd arranged to go to this underground night. As I sat in his car I said, 'I've done a tape.' We stuck it in the car while we were driving; he didn't say anything. Then we pulled up in the car park at this venue and we were supposed to go inside, and Sam said, 'I want to hear it again. It's so good.' So we played it again and again, just the two of us sat in this car park having our own little rave! Then I presented it to the promoter of the club Venus, James Baillie. This guy had a reputation for being one of the top promoters in the industry, really knew his shit. The best DJs in the world came to play for him. He called me the next day and said, 'You're a DJ, you're a DJ!'

Just before my first gig on New Year's 1991, he said to me — because my name is Angela — 'What's your DJ name?' And I said, 'Angela', and he said, 'You can't be DJ Angela.' So I said, 'Angel — just lop a letter off the end?' 'Yeah, that's better,' he said. So I became DJ Angel. From then on, I developed my craft, if you know what I mean, because I am a true music and house music lover. I thought, I'm gonna do this properly because when I went to play a gig, there was competition with some of the guys, and some of them didn't like it. One thing they were never going to pull me up on was my mixing; one thing I could do was mix.

MICHELLE MANGAN: I moved to Manchester in September '89, I think. It was definitely a boys' thing going into a record shop in

Manchester that sold dance music or club music. It was always blokes behind the counter back then, being intimidating, but if you were passionate about something, you went for it. In Manchester, I started DJing at Archie's Bar underneath Oxford Road station, and then the Tuesday nights at the No. 1 Club, and then Thursday nights at the No. 1 Club. The No. 1 Club had the only queer alternative night outside of London at the time. It was the cool gay club to go to, and there was a DJ there, Tim Lennox, who was amazing. The No. 1 was a real mix of people, as well. It wasn't just gay people — it really was the beginnings of gay clubbing, and the forerunner of Flesh at The Haçienda.

There's a massive progression from what used to be considered a gay club. What I've seen over the years is that back in the day, the gay clubs, especially the ones that were in New York and Chicago and Detroit, were influencing what the music was on the club scene in general, whereas I find these days, a lot of the gay clubs have become really formulaic. At the time of the No. 1 Club, and then of Flesh, there's a feeling that was really, really special, and we felt like we were part of this unique scene. It felt like a family, you know? I'm sure everybody has their own tribe and their own place, but that really did feel like that.

I was kind of known as the queer alternative DJ, I suppose, from DJing at Archie's and the No. 1 Club, and a woman called Lucy Scher approached me and said, 'Look, we're going to do a big women's night, and we can get The Haçienda.' I was like, 'Yeah, let's do it!' So I remember us all having meetings about this night that we're going to do at The Haçienda, and it was called the Summer of Lesbian Love. It was the time of Madchester, so all the media were calling it the New Summer of Love. That was what was great about moving to Manchester at that time, the Happy Mondays/Stone Roses etc., and all of that stuff just exploded alongside a lot of the cool clubs.

KATH MCDERMOTT: I started going to The Haçienda in early '89. I'm from Manchester. I'd moved away, but I moved back to become a student. It was just unbelievable. When you walked in, it felt like, how the hell are they getting away with this? Because you're on a big street in Manchester with lots going on, and everything's totally normal. And then you open a door and it's kind of like when Frodo puts his ring on. [laughs] You're somewhere else. It had the scale of an illegal rave, which would take part in a warehouse or an industrial building, but this was inside a club. That vision — obviously Rob Gretton and Tony and everybody had that New York vision — meant they had years of disaster, really, until its moment came. It was exactly the right shape and size and utility for that job. It was quite an overwhelming experience. I used to go on Fridays, which was Nude night with Graeme Park and Mike Pickering. Then on Saturday, we'd go to the No. 1, which was absolutely phenomenal, very underground, very small, totally queer, completely mixed gay night that was the precursor to Flesh. So when Flesh came, it was both elements coming together, and I was completely in the middle of that Venn diagram at that point.

The first time I DJed at The Haçienda was at the bar downstairs, the Gay Traitor. It's probably 200 capacity, but if you're all wedged in together — which you were [laughs] — a lot more. The main room was maybe 900, 1,000 capacity. The downstairs was an absolute shithole. The toilets always leaked and overflowed, so of course that first night I DJed the toilets were leaking. I was so nervous. It would be like if someone said to you now, in the present, that you're DJing at The Haçienda tonight. It was that big because it had been such a big part of my life as a punter. One of the resident DJs who was really experienced, DJ Tim Lennox, who we all adored and we all owe a lot to, really saved me that night. The decks weren't working, and I was just like, 'Go and get someone! The decks aren't working!' Tim came downstairs — bless him — and just looked at the decks and said, 'Oh, the lever's not there all the way over.' I mean, that is a measure of a) how panicked I was and b) how inexperienced I was.

There was no ventilation in the basement and it had these shelves for you to put your drinks on. I remember everyone and everything, everywhere, was just drenched with condensation. It had mirrors, and all of them were just *drenched* with water rolling down. Everyone was dancing on the drink shelves ... It was like a health and safety risk assessment disaster film! Everyone dancing behind me on the shelf eventually flipped it, and they all fell down, as did all my records. That's a measure of the chaos [laughs]. Normally the Gay Traitor was just a chill-out room, but not when you've got loads of queer people that are high and you're playing disco and soul music!

DJ PAULETTE: I DJed in the Gay Traitor downstairs. Whenever I arrived there, you'd come in the main doors, through the meat-packing fridge sheets, and that was the main floor. But in order to get to the second room, you'd take a left past the cloak-room, go down the first set of stairs, and there was a mezzanine that looked over onto the floor, and the bar downstairs, and then you go down another set of stairs — and I tell you this set of stairs was only safe at the beginning of the night because by the middle of the night there was no air conditioning and there were a lot of people in there. Those stairs were lethal! [laughs] So if you were coming down those stairs, like all the drag queens and everyone dressed . . . well, let's say we saw so many casualties on those stairs, people coming down the entire flight of stairs on their backsides.

Anyway, so you come down this really high, almost vertical set of stairs, down to the Gay Traitor, the toilets were on the left and as you turned in right into the room, in that corner there were corner sofas there where they set up the DJ booth. It was basically two decks and a mixer on a wobbly table — a very, *very* wobbly table, and that was where I DJed for four years. I mean it's mad, just totally guerilla. Because as I was DJing, I'd always have all the dancers, the drag queens and fans in a race to see who would dance behind my decks. They were dancing on the bars and they were dancing on the sofas behind, and they would dance so hard on the sofas behind that my record boxes were always falling on the floor. All the vinyl would go skidding on the floor! But it was part of the fun. It just really was part of the fun, and I'd know I was having a really good set if I was rescuing my records all the time because people were dancing the cushions off the sofas.

ANGEL JOHNSON: I was starting to understand the concept that the DJ is the person who introduces new music to the dance floor, and as the DJ, you create your own sound. I started experimenting with that, and it was so much fun — is so much fun — to see what you can get away with. The crowd, they're in your hands, and you know that, they know that and you can take them on this journey, and they know that they're safe with you — even if you shake things up a bit you're always going to deliver some lovely surprises. The journey has a beginning, middle and end, and it is a great privilege to stand there, to be in a club, and to be able to take these people on this journey and watch them enjoy it . . . it's just beautiful.

DJ PAULETTE: There's a John Tejada record which was out so many years later, but it's called 'Sweat (On The Walls)' and that was just exactly how it was. It always rained inside in The Haçienda. It was wet, it was hot, it was busy and it was *totally decadent*. People were tops off, tits out and just getting wild. And they'd just get wild down there all night. Some people never went upstairs. But then again, some people didn't ever come downstairs. You know, you'd find your level; whichever room you wanted to stay in, you could stay in, or you could pass between the two all night, however you wanted.

KATH MCDERMOTT: The first time that I did the main room, I remember being as scared as I've ever been in my life. I was so petrified being behind a system that big and knowing everyone can hear everything that I'm doing. I never thought I'd wanted to be a DJ, so in that moment, being at the helm of The Haçienda dance floor in the main room, I just thought, 'This is it, I'll just do this one and then I'll die happy.' I didn't think that I would ever do it again and assumed this was my one moment, so I took it. Then, lo and behold, the next month, I was asked if I wanted to play again. I didn't even know if I had it in me to find the nerves of steel to do it again! But it's great now, some thirty-odd years later, that I can still enjoy that connection with brilliant people in great spaces.

LUCY SCHER: The lesbian social scene was dreadful . . . There were a couple of worthy clubs that advertised themselves as 'safe spaces', and a couple more authentic Manchester clubs with bad lighting, bad music, bad booze and sticky carpets. The Summer of Lesbian Love was the opposite: music, dancers, sex, proud, far from safe, and at the fucking Haçienda! I spent a total of £35 on publicity for the night, and it sold 1,000 tickets in advance. [Kamila Rymaldo, interview in *Dazed Digital*, 2018[1]]

KATH MCDERMOTT: The Summer of Lesbian Love was probably more lesbians in one place than I'd ever seen in Manchester. Being in that big space with loads and loads of women — and it was just all women — it just seemed like New York in that space. By that I mean it was kind of like all my dreams coming true because, at that time, New York was just *everything*, and I'd never been. It felt like a door opening.

MICHELLE MANGAN: So it was 1990, and we did the Summer of Lesbian Love. There were about 900 lesbians in The Haçienda. Could you imagine? I've been to some of the Prides over in New York, but back then in Manchester? How the heck did we even find 900 lesbians on the planet, let alone 900 lesbians in Manchester?! People came from *everywhere*. It was just a flyer and word of mouth, and the flyer wasn't even about the graphics. It wasn't a Peter Saville Haçienda design flyer. It was literally a red piece of hard paper — not even card! — with a little illustration and words on it. So to get that response with that flyer ... It was clearly the time to do it. It was the time to come out and celebrate.

With every kind of lesbian night or women-only night, there's a whole cross section of people. You'd have real ultra-feminists, then you'd have the ones that are a little bit cheeky, the rebel dykes, the S&M types ... I remember some of the lesbians getting offended, but it literally just was somewhere that girls could come to dance.

So the Summer of Lesbian Love was so successful, and then after that, there was a night where we did a mixed night as a follow-on called 'Attitude'. That was meant to be at The Haçienda, but something happened, so we did it at The Academy in Manchester. That imagery, that iconography from that night, was amazing. It was political. It was out there. It was provocative. The slogans were things like 'Rough Dyke', 'Psycho Queen'. It was part of the gay political movement, reclaiming the word 'queer', reclaiming the words 'fag' and 'dyke'. It was so important to reclaim those words because they were used to abuse gay people, so we wanted to say, 'Yeah that's what we are, let's celebrate it.'

KATH MCDERMOTT: Lucy and Paul got me my start at The Haçienda. Paul Cons was the in-house promoter at Haçienda, and Lucy Scher, she's a really important character who is sadly often forgotten. Paul was the entertainments manager at The Haçienda, and he was gay. He was good with crazy ideas. Lucy was really practical – a hedonist to a degree, but really practical. At this point, she was bookkeeping for a living, so you can sort of get the measure of what she was about.

MICHELLE MANGAN: Lucy was somebody that was wanting to make a difference, to do something different. She really pulled the lesbian scene up by its coattails to create something new . . . Lucy was brilliant. I remember sitting in her flat in Hulme, having all these conversations. She was a real galvaniser of people, and an ideas person. She made it feel like everyone was coming together, even though everyone was a bit different.

Hats off to Lucy for keeping on and making sure that the girls got a say because I wouldn't have gone to The Haçienda and asked to DJ, to put on a night. I was too shy. I did the music, not the business side. I mean, I did have the balls to say 'your DJ is crap and I can do better' when I was sixteen or whatever it was. And that was when I didn't know if I could do better. I just knew that I knew music, so I did it.

DJ PAULETTE: Had it not been for Lucy Scher – she died in 2018 of cancer, rest her soul – there wouldn't have been any women on the Flesh night because it was Lucy who brought the women and the lesbians in. Without Lucy, I wouldn't have been there and I wouldn't have become DJ Paulette. I'm very grateful that I got the chance to say this to her in person before she died: I am absolutely grateful to her. I owe everything about my career to Lucy Scher because without her, I wouldn't have existed at all — there were no straight nights that were employing female DJs in Manchester. I wouldn't have been a DJ if it hadn't have been for her saying, 'We want women, and we're gonna put women in the second room every month.'

KATH MCDERMOTT: Lucy lived in Hulme, and I lived in Hulme; there was a massive queer community there. It was a riot, amazing. It was young, political, very mixed male and female, which was unusual. We'd all fought against Clause 28, a local government act that basically outlawed council-funded bodies to promote homosexuality. So libraries, schools, anything that was being paid for locally couldn't promote homosexuality, and we'd all campaigned against it. We'd all campaigned against prejudice regarding HIV and AIDS, and we got involved in ACT UP, so we knew each other, we wanted to come together and do something socially: put on a massive event at The Haçienda called the Summer of Lesbian Love, which was a women-only event. It was crazy. Lots of politics around that, lots of ups and downs, but it was like, wow, this is different, especially the scale of it.

Paul and everybody who worked at The Haçienda bar were like, 'Bloody hell, the lesbians are drinking loads of beer!' because no one else was drinking at The Haç. Everyone was getting high, and no one was drinking alcohol. That's where you should make money — on the bar. But they weren't making a penny on the bar! They were just giving away tons of free water, so they were like, 'Get the lesbians back in here — they're the only people that are drinking!' They went to Lucy and said, 'Please come back and do another event.' And Flesh was born.

Then they thought, 'Well, hold on, we still need to get it to 1,200 capacity.' At the time, the Manchester gay scene was small, then your percentage of people in that scene that want to go and listen to house music is smaller. It's not like now, where the gay scene in Manchester is huge, partly because of Flesh, of course. We had to build that — there was no Gaychester then. So what they thought was, 'We'll get buses coming in from Leeds, from Liverpool, from everywhere.' They also thought, 'Let's get a coach

Flesh flyer

from Liverpool to bring everyone from our night called "Loose" to The Haçienda.' Lucy said to me, 'We need you to come and DJ to bring those people in.'

Lucy was hell-bent on having women represented on that bill in a way that nobody was. She was like, 'I want women right at the centre of this. I want them on the door. I want them in the DJ box, performing. I want them to do stuff around the edges, even. I want them representing us.' Paul was a bit like, 'Well . . .' but Lucy stood firm: 'This is what we're doing and this is how it's gonna be.' So she got a lot of women DJs involved and invited me to play the Gay Traitor as part of the Loose DJs — that's what we were called from our club night Loose. After a few months, I played upstairs in the main room and did a mix of both for four or five years. Lucy left after about three years, and that changed the essence of it. No disrespect to Paul, but the vibe became about gay men, so you just lose a bit of something that relates to women, and women being at the forefront of something.

MICHELLE MANGAN: Putting that first record on at the Summer of Lesbian Love and then putting the first record on at Flesh . . . it was an electrifying feeling that you were like part of something special — that you were at this place that had been in your cultural consciousness for so long and there you were playing music in it.

I did play some Factory records there and I obviously would have played 'Blue Monday'.

KATH MCDERMOTT: Flesh nights were quite wild, and people would dress up to go to Flesh. Some people did come in jeans and T-shirts, but loads of people would dress up. People would go to an after (after Flesh) and talk about what they were going to wear to the next Flesh. It was the sort of kingpin of your whole social life, and everything revolved around it. You'd walk in, and it was strikingly different. The energy was different.

MICHELLE MANGAN: Lucy and Paul Cons set up a company called A Bit Ginger, and they were the ones behind the Flesh name and the Flesh nights at The Haçienda. At that first Flesh, there was huge anticipation, you know. The first night it was Tim, me and the Attitude dancers (the people we had dancing at Attitude) alongside those incredible visuals that Homocult put together and projected. The feeling of going in and knowing that it was the first one, and getting into that DJ box at The Haçienda ... It was the biggest DJ box that I'd seen. You were so far away from the dance floor, really high up, and the lighting guy was in the next box. You overlooked that amazing dance floor with the stage, you could see everything and you could feel it, even when you were short like me.

DJ PAULETTE: [Before I started at The Haçienda,] What happened was that a friend of a friend was running a party at the No. 1 Club in Manchester, which was a really cool club, but it doesn't exist any-more. It was an underground club, and she was putting on a night there. Ridiculously, she paid for the hire of the club, the promotion of it, the posters, flyers and everything, and she'd run out of money. So she needed to book a DJ and she didn't have enough money to pay any of the big boys to do it, so my friend suggested to her that I do it because he knew I had lots of records. I'd been buying records since I was seven years old ... So I said yes, I'll do it! I'd never DJed before, but I had lots of records, and I had a vague idea of what to do because I'd been clubbing for years, and understood what DJs did that made me stay on the dance floor. I think that's what I used as a benchmark for how I was going to do whatever it was that I did. So I accepted the deal, and then I went out and spent my entire grant for that term, which was £150, on vinyl.

I did the night and I played it all on my own from nine till two, no breaks. I went from never having DJed before to playing a really long set. A lot of DJs don't even play that long a set *ever* in their lives. So I started off playing long sets, and nobody left — everybody enjoyed it, everybody was on the dance floor!

That was my baptism by fire, really. I went from ten minutes one go, moving the fader from one deck to the other, to DJing at a really cool underground club for five hours, nonstop, no breaks, no toilet. Then people talked about the party because they'd enjoyed it, and news got back to the people who were running Flesh. They were moving Flesh from The Academy to The Haçienda. The girl who'd put on that party — my first DJ experience — said, 'I think we should ask them if we can host their second room.' They liked the idea of having something different downstairs because I was playing a mixture of house, hip-hop, disco, funk, rare groove, so it was really vastly different to what they were offering upstairs. They said yes, and the rest after that is history. Flesh was a monthly party and I hosted the second room. I started off in 1992, and I stayed with them until 1996.

MICHELLE MANGAN: By the end of the night at the first Flesh, everybody knew something really special had happened and word got around. It became an absolute sensation across the country, and Europe as well.

DJ PAULETTE: The crowd? They were wild and cheeky and rude. And I say rude because there was a crew from Sheffield — who are now really good friends of mine — who were always first down in my room because they were really big disco, funk and soul fans. If ever I played a record that was not their vibe, they'd give me the time-out sign on the dance floor. And I'm telling you — it's just the biggest training for any DJ because, if you get that sense that people are not enjoying it, well, it's an immediate barometer that says 'We don't like what you're doing, and if you don't change it, we're gonna go.' So if ever I saw that T-sign, it was like, OK, switch, do something different. Really good training, but rude. If anyone did that to me now, they'd get a punch. [laughs] In their defence, they were there every month, and they danced hard, and they brought their mates, and they kept people down there. They were very much responsible for the vibe — screaming, whooping and loving it, and they dressed up as well. They were always really beautifully turned out, so I thank them very much for helping me create the vibe for that second room. There was always such good energy from people in that room.

RUTH TAYLOR: Flesh nights at The Haçienda were probably the most exciting because everyone was so dressed up, it was so new, and it was a *proper party*. People in full Vivienne Westwood who looked incredible. And it wasn't restricted to a certain clique of people. There were so many different people, and everybody was mingling — nobody stood out. Everybody just got on with it.

SORAYA LAKHANEY: The night Yasmine Lakhaney [Hacienda door-woman] really loved at The Haçienda was Flesh for the LGBTI+ crowd. She said to me, 'You know, Baby, that's just the best night ever. The crowd gets high on life. They didn't need to be high on anything else.' Many people in the faith circles she was part of were horrified at the idea of an LGBTI+ night, and said things like, 'Why on earth are you involved in this kind of thing?' Yasmine said, 'God is loving, and God loves all people. Isn't that the heart of what you believe as love? Regardless of what any writings may say about what people's private interests are, and what they do in their own private lives, isn't that their own personal choice?' My sister challenged people's beliefs and their own prejudices.

MARCIA PANTRY: The guys used to come to the Flesh night in chaps. It started out quiet but then it got weird and ... more naked. [laughs]

KATH MCDERMOTT: The whole experience at Flesh was so completely unique. We kind of took it for granted because it was this crazy kind of beast that you couldn't compare to anything that was happening in Manchester, to anything happening in London. But it wasn't really a thing that people outside it noticed, and it was never commented upon, or spoken about at all. The *right people* noticed it, of course, but Flesh hasn't gotten its due. It's crazy because I was there for a long time, and DJ Paulette was there for a long time, but there were never comments made about women DJs at The Haçienda. Now there's a sense that you need to get women and gay people on your line-ups, so the phone rings thirty years later, but it's like, I'm not really 100 per cent sure I want to get involved in what you're doing. Why didn't you ring me up ten years ago?

I'm definitely not somebody that looks at The Haçienda through rose-tinted glasses and says, 'Oh, it'll never be the same, the glory years.' There should be less of the nostalgia around it and more comments on the stories that haven't been told, like interesting women of the house, women DJs, or somebody like Hewan Clarke, who was the first Haçienda DJ, a Black DJ who played soul music. Why don't we hear much about those stories?

LUCY SCHER: Someone gave me Peter Hook's *How Not to Run a Club* and there is a small section on us . . . I guess Flesh didn't work with the narrative arc, as we ran it brilliantly.

DJ PAULETTE: Peter Hook's Haçienda book — and this is one of my biggest arguments — I have said, relentlessly, that book is factually wrong. Because it doesn't talk enough about the women, and it doesn't talk enough about its Black history. But as you and I both know, when you write a book, you have a word count and a particular agenda. You have a particular or a personal story that you want to tell, and anything outside of that story then gets missed or redacted or 'I don't want to talk about that bit', or 'I'll talk about that person, but not *that* one'. But my issue with Peter Hook's book is that he made a point of listing every party that had run through The Haçienda — in the back of the book he gave those through every night, or the parties that ran over a period of years, and every time he mentions the Flesh party, he never mentions me. He never gives me credit. He gives a DJ from

London, Luke Howard, the credit for playing that second room and he didn't play all of those parties. I think in four years Luke might have played four or five times. I played *every fucking party*. And my name is on *every single flyer*. So, if I'm having my name on every single flyer, to be completely erased from that book . . . it was like, wow, now we know how histories disappear. Because if someone simply doesn't remember, never saw or partied with you, or maybe doesn't feel like mentioning you, then they just don't mention you. If an employee says, 'Oh well, she wasn't that important', that's how the history changes. That's how the story gets mangled and twisted, because it depends on the honesty and the factual correctness of the people that are interviewed.

YVONNE SHELTON: The night that stands out to me was one where I wasn't naked, but a lot of people were in just trainers. Only trainers. [laughs] Eye-popping DJ Paulette doing Flesh night . . . I'd say 'oh my goodness', but it was just so non-threatening. The nakedness wasn't threatening at all. It was just people having fun. It reminded me of the way people talk about the seventies. DJ Paulette and Flesh night should be remembered like that.

• • •

GONNIE RIETVELD: The DJing itself really came about because I was doing a PhD on house music, and I felt that that was the best way to get to know the subject area because you get to buy records, you get to know people. And then, I also started to DJ at a late-night radio station — Funky Female Radio, we were called. Very late-night. That's actually where I learnt my mixing as well. That's another thing, beat mixing. So mixing is, again, one of those kinds of skills that guys teach each other, but as a woman to get into that, you need a bloke to volunteer to teach you. The advantage of radio is that you can listen in to the monitors because, normally, you just can't hear what a DJ hears in their headphones. As an audience member, you just don't know what a DJ is doing. It's all like magic, like 'what on earth', you know? But at the radio I could actually hear what they were doing via the monitor headphones, and how they were queuing as well. So that's what helped me with learning to DJ. Then I just had to make time in the afternoons, going into a (male) friend's house to try it out. That was part of my PhD project, really. With Vince Lawrence, I also made a record in Chicago. That's the last released recording I've made, I think.

ANGEL JOHNSON: I started playing at The Haçienda because a pro-moter from Leeds recommended me to Ang, and she hired me to play there. By '89 The Haçienda was legendary even to go there, so to actually be asked to play there, I'm not from Manchester (I'm from Nottingham), and apart from resident DJs Paulette and Kath McDer-mott, I was one of very few female DJs, I believe, that were invited to play in The Haçienda as a guest. It's a great honour, but really fucking scary. [laughs] But obviously, I was considered worthy of gracing the decks. One very significant time I played was The Haçienda's eleventh birthday party, where they had a line-up of eleven DJs including the likes of Frankie Knuckles, Tony Humphries, David Morales, Mike Pickering, Graeme Park . . . I was the only female on that line-up.

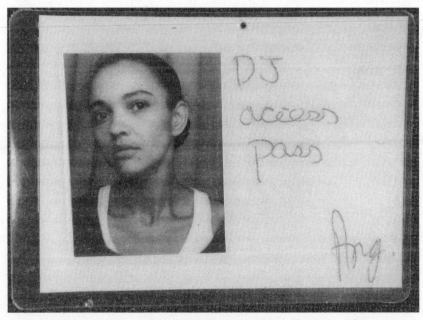

DJ Angel's pass for The Haçienda, signed by Ang Matthews

ANG MATTHEWS: The eleventh birthday party stands out to me because it was my first time to be responsible for the bookings — Paul Cons had started his Flesh nights by then. So, on the eleventh birthday, what we did was not 'A Day in the Life' but 'A Night in the Life Of' and I booked every DJ that I had booked the previous year that had played at The Haçienda. I have a photograph of them all. The only woman in the photograph, unfortunately, because there were no other women I'd booked, was Angel.

ANGEL JOHNSON: I do have sensory memories of being behind The Haçienda decks, actually. When we did the eleventh birthday, all the DJs had to go down in the daytime to have this group photograph taken and get guest passes. I can remember it being quite peaceful, the calm before the storm; a bit surreal without the music pumping out, the club somehow felt less vast. On the eleventh birthday, I had imposter syndrome, and I think it shows in that photo that I mentioned, because I felt out of my depth with these other DJs who are legends.

DJ PAULETTE: I remember the first Flesh birthday I DJed was incredible. There were a lot of pictures taken of that one because we were getting a lot of press attention, and the popularity of the Flesh night was filtering down into London. By 1993, the time of the first birthday party, I had started presenting a TV programme in Manchester, so there was that edge to it as well, where I had a certain level of celebrity. A lot more people knew about me, and a lot more people knew about the night. I can remember the outfit. I still have the knickers on my wall that I made for it. It's a silver-sequin pair of knickers, which have like forty metres of silver sequins, and twenty-five metres of red sequins, and I sewed every single one of them on myself. They took me about two weeks to make. I had to do them twice because the first time I sewed them too tight and couldn't get them over one leg. [laughs] Then I had to unpick it all very carefully because the shop didn't have any more sequins! I had a pair of silver-leather, thigh-high boots, which were incredible, from Carl Twigg in Manchester, and I had a silver waistcoat, which was actually a denim waistcoat I sprayed silver with car spray. [laughs] So creative.

ANGEL JOHNSON: The DJ box in The Haçienda was up in the gods. The first time I played I remember being totally alone in there, feeling like, OK, you've got this, you've got this. Nobody was stressing me; you're above the crowd, not surrounded by them. I felt like I was floating on this cloud. Although I think some people got on the balcony, I was on my own there in the DJ box. It gave me time to get my thoughts together, to give me a chance to sort through my records, get my bearings. I think the build-up to it would have been full of anxiety but the response I got when I played would have cancelled out all of that.

DJ PAULETTE: The Haçienda underpins everything about my career. You have to remember that The Haçienda is legendary. It's like worldwide legendary, so how much has it got to do with who I am and how I DJ? It's got *everything* to do with who I am and how I DJ, because I've had the good fortune and the honour of being able to play at one of the best clubs that ever existed in the world. It was a club that brought in a lot of incredible talent from all over the world, with a reputation such that in 2019 The Haçienda site was made a heritage site. And the club doesn't even exist anymore! So, how much does it have to do with who I am as a DJ? It gives me the kudos, gravitas and profile that you cannot pay for.

Anyone that worked there will tell you that while we were working there — it's like anyone who works at one of the big clubs — when you're working there, you're just working at a club. You don't think, 'Oh, in twenty years this is going to be a legendary club or a legendary club night.' It's a busy night, and it's great, and it's a fantastic party, but you don't get the legend until years later. So at the time, we were all just working at really great club nights and having a great time, just having a ball doing what we love to do — entertaining people and playing music.

• • •

ANGEL JOHNSON: I was ... aware that people would see me as a female DJ, as a novelty. When I started playing at venues, then other promoters started booking me. Sometimes you'd get the feeling they're booking you just because you're female, as a novelty. They weren't actually expecting me to be able to mix. So there was a great deal of satisfaction that I actually got from being able to do that, and that shook up some of the other guys.

DJ PAULETTE: It's that question about 'woman DJs' that keeps rolling back, and I kind of wish it wouldn't. But it's intriguing that it still does because it shows that, no matter how much we think we've moved on, we've not moved on enough.

In 1992, when I started DJing, there weren't *any* Black female DJs that I knew in Manchester, and there were nowhere near as many female DJs as there were men at the time. You could actually probably count, quite easily, the few women who were headlining. And I know I can name the ones who were regularly on the line-ups in England: Lisa Loud, Nancy Noise, Smokin' Jo, Princess Julia, Rachel Auburn, myself, Mrs Wood, Jo Mills, Angel from Nottingham, Girls on Top in Liverpool and then Sarah HB in London ... and then you start to struggle to name any more. We've not even got to twenty yet. And with men, you've got all the names. So, in one way, it was difficult because you're not the immediate choice — you're never going to be the immediate choice — but you are a quick choice because there are so few women around that if you're good at what you do, you get the work. So, in one way, it was difficult because there weren't many women doing it, but I always worked. I could play records, I can mix, I can sequence tunes, I can mix and blend, and I can play anything from disco to funk to house. So I always worked to a degree. But now, even now when there are so many more female DJs, I think it's getting even harder because you will see that there are continually line-ups with no women on them even though there are far more female DJs.

I'd like to think of myself as a DJ, not as a female DJ. But every time that question comes back, the separation is just like — boom! Back in your face — the idea that you're a woman before you're anything in this industry. And you're a woman in a place where there aren't many places, y'know. Any job you care to mention is not really constructed for women, and the spaces for women are few and far between.

KATH MCDERMOTT: I do think Lucy saw her work as political. She was quite a political animal ... It was about creating a space for people to be allowed to be who they wanted to be. We'd have people coming in who might be trans, or cross-dressers, queer, and they could literally be the butterfly for the night before getting the bus back to Rochdale, Oldham or all the places where they couldn't be who they wanted to be (and probably can't even now in some of those places). When people talk about Flesh, they say, 'I had the space to be who I was.' And that is a political act.

MICHELLE MANGAN: I may have even been the first female to put a record on at The Haçienda. Even if there might have been somebody else who'd done it once before me, it felt like I was the first because I'd never seen a woman do it before.

I didn't feel like I was changing the world. I just wanted to play this brilliant music. I always used to say, as a DJ, you're only playing somebody else's records, so don't take yourself too seriously. But at Flesh at The Haçienda, the Factory atmosphere behind it, it was special. It was like the whole world came to Manchester.

DJ PAULETTE: You have to remember that when I started to DJ in '91, '92, it wasn't a popular job. It wasn't a career choice because there weren't superstar DJs. There were DJs for sure, and there were parties that had a certain amount of kudos, but the DJs really weren't anything special.

And certainly, also, there weren't any Black women doing it. So there wasn't any sort of prototype for me to base whatever I was going to do on. So I don't actually know how I made the quantum leap from there not being someone that represented who I wanted to be to actually *being* who I wanted to be and who I am. I don't know how I did that actually, but I did it anyway.

ANGEL JOHNSON: I think I earned my respect as a DJ, and I felt respected as a DJ. Ultimately, that respect doesn't come from the promoters — it comes from the dance floor. People on the dance floor dictate that. And I always had a fantastic relationship with the people on the dance floor. I'm actually quite a shy person, which people might be really surprised to learn. I think that's why DJing has always really suited me — I'm a shy person, but I'm also a performer. When you're behind the decks, you can do that at a distance, you know? I'm very interactive with my crowd, in terms of really acknowledging them and making eye contact. I've been told that I always smile when I'm playing. I think I do, and I think I can see every single person individually — I don't see a crowd. So from the perspective of the dance floor, I don't think I ever experienced any sexism, but definitely from other DJs and definitely from promoters at times. I can remember playing in Ibiza on a couple of occasions, and DJs who I was taking over from messing up the decks so that when I came on, I didn't sound right . . . things like that. Or, for example, when I'd turn around to go change the record, messing with the pitch. So when I'd come back, it's out of time — just to try to sabotage me.

I think that in society, we're still susceptible to the kind of stereotypical role models that males and females have. This goes back to me saying that it took me seeing other female DJs to realise that DJing was a possibility for me — it hadn't entered my head. When I started, there were hardly any female DJs, only a handful of us in the UK, and I just always put it down to the fact that there's a stereotype of the DJ who's male, and it's a case of needing to change that stereotype. Not just young women becoming DJs, but also sound engineers, producers, those roles where the stereotype is male.

DJ PAULETTE: DJing is not gender specific — it's not a gender-specific job. And it's not like heavy lifting or anything like that, so it doesn't require a particular physical strength or force . . . Well, it does when you're playing long sets. But in general, it doesn't require any amount of force to do the job. So male, female, he, she, they . . . there's no limit to who can do the how or the what. The thing that makes a DJ is the selection, the music, the personality, the profile. And that again is not gender specific — it can be male, female, he, she, they; it doesn't matter. But what does change it is the systemic sexism, racism, misogyny — call it what you will. Those things that are there in society also exist in the music industry and the music world. We can't get away from the fact that we live in a patriarchal society. We are ruled by men, the rules are made by men, the conditions are made by men — the way we do things are determined by men. The way things are set up, even in terms of clubs and toilets and DJ booths, and *everything* — the design of it is very much more male-centric than female-centric. So, those are the things that make it a bit more difficult.

ANGEL JOHNSON: It has always been an old-boys' club, and it still is to some degree, but I've pretty much always ignored that and it never fazed me. I used to get an amazing amount of appreciation from the crowd, and all they were concerned about is that you dropped the tune that made their night. The crowd is all that matters. For them, and for me, it's all about the music.

KATH MCDERMOTT: And then, who's running the night? It's Lucy. I suppose The Haçienda was quite a masculine space, normally, but it also really became a space that opened itself to trans people, to cross-dressers, queer people. There was a real openness, and a sense of inclusion, maybe even in spite of itself, thanks to Flesh.

To compare, when The Haçienda closed briefly, a club called Home opened. I worked there and used to warm up every Saturday in the main room. Every single week, someone would come over:
'Where's the DJ?'
'I'm the DJ.'
'Yeah, but where's the DJ?'
'I am the DJ.'
'Where is the DJ?'
'IT IS ME. I AM THE DJ!'
I think they thought I was doing the lights or something. They just didn't understand at all. Home was a club run by men, with men on the door and men on the bar, so that could explain the

difference a bit. But it was quite notable that at that same kind of time, I was having two very separate experiences on the decks: at Home, completely not comprehending that a woman could DJ, whereas at The Haç, it was like, why wouldn't a woman DJ?

Yasmine, the First Woman 'Doorman' in England

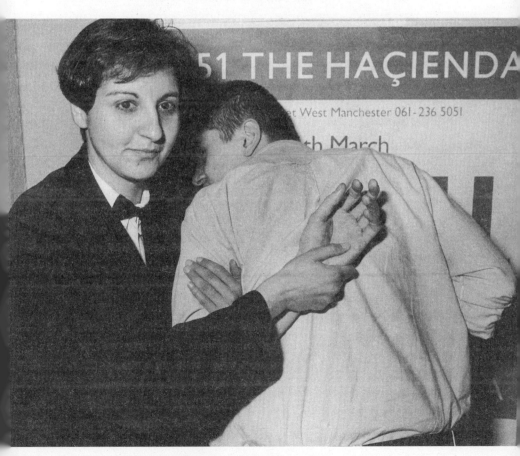

Yasmine Lakhaney at The Haçienda

Yasmine Lakhaney was, by all accounts, the first woman to work as a 'doorman' or bouncer in the UK, and that happened at The Haçienda. She's remembered as a groundbreaking, compassionate, and fierce figure on the scene. Yasmine passed away in 2011, but her memory lives on.

SORAYA LAKHANEY: My sister Yasmine was a very strong, loving and caring person. She had a very resolute and determined streak in her, and she was quite a formidable woman in her own right. But she also had this beautiful, gentle, very compassionate nature.

TERESA ALLEN: Yasmine was really unusual at the time — you never saw a female door person. She must have been one of the first ever.

SORAYA LAKHANEY: It was a very unusual opportunity that presented itself at The Haçienda, to work on the door, because she was the first woman to work on the door in the UK. So it was really groundbreaking ... it was revolutionary. She was very much into empowering women, but she wouldn't have seen it or said it that way. She never saw herself as a role model, a ground-breaker or as any kind of a vanguard, but she was always ahead of her time in her music tastes and in her attitude. Yasmine's approach was very forward-looking, very future-thinking. It was old news and she was moving on to the next thing by the time everybody else in the crowd caught up.

To be able to hold your ground, to be able to work on the door and to receive people, but also to be able to be delicate and diplomatic with people ... divas who weren't allowed in because they weren't on the list, and individuals who were a bit high on life and other things, who weren't in the best kind of state of mind. Yasmine could say to them 'sorry, not tonight' without them losing control. It was a very, very fine line at The Haçienda. It was a volatile time, and you never knew from individual to individual what they might be carrying, what might trigger them ... She could automatically read people just like that, get a sense of how to approach things.

She had a love of people and care for people because she trained as a psychiatric nurse, which gave her that experience of dealing with all the unexpected events that can happen. Always being vigilant, being able to read people carefully, to understand what's going on, being a real person who has a curiosity about human nature. She loved psychology and wanted to understand people and what motivates them. She loved martial arts as well, and she had training in it. When you spoke with her, you thought she's really soft and lovely, but there was this really hard core of steel as well. So, in many respects she was perfectly qualified to work at The Haçienda.

GONNIE RIETVELD: Yasmine the bouncer, the doorwoman! She was a really matter-of-fact woman who had really good people skills. She had a good sense of humour and she was really strong within herself. She could actually deal with difficult people without getting angry or aggravated, and thereby could diffuse any stressful situation. I think her family is from South Asia, so she was a woman of colour on the door. But she was simply one of the gang, really. I won't say 'one of the boys' because why do you need to be a boy to work on the door? But she was definitely part of the door team.

SORAYA LAKHANEY: Yasmine used to get all kinds of artsy publications with advertisements, and she read they wanted somebody in The Haçienda. She had no hesitation whatsoever in applying for it and she went for it. From what she told me, in the interviewing process I think they were looking for people with the right kind of personality and profile, to work as part of a team that was very highly pressured. I think they made a strategic decision to hire a woman because they wanted to present a different face of the club and its scene, about what was possible in Manchester for women.

I think they really wanted a woman who'd be able to stand her own ground, working with men. Not a woman pretending to be a man, but a woman who could be a woman in the company of men: a strong woman, a resourceful woman, an empowered woman without necessarily knowing what that word empowerment meant. They were really ahead of their time, breaking the ground, and my sister was really drawn to that — she saw it as an opportunity. Not just for her, but for other women as well.

ANG MATTHEWS: Yasmine has died, but she was great. Absolutely fantastic. I think she's the first woman in the UK to do that job as a 'doorman'. She dealt with lots and lots of incidents in The Haçienda, and she was a really integral part of everything. After she finished at The Haçienda, it was usual to have three women working on the door, and that became a normal thing, but it was very unusual to have her there at the time as a woman. The women I employed after tended to be into bodybuilding or trained in that sort of thing, and Yasmine wasn't.

ALISON AGBOOLA: Yasmine was lovely and kind, and she also had this core of steel. I've never seen it before.

KATH MCDERMOTT: Yasmine was brilliant, even to stand in that space physically, the eye of the storm, outside the queue that was maybe three hours long. She would be so firm but fair with everyone, so careful and so calm. At that point, it was pretty radical to have a woman bouncer, and not many people could occupy that space with those men, you know? It was a bit of a Wild West and Yasmine was phenomenal.

SORAYA LAKHANEY: Yasmine was in her element at The Haçienda. I used to say to my sister that she used to burn the candle at both ends and in the middle — because it wasn't just enough to burn the candle at both ends! My sister was so extra she had to do the middle as well. She loved life that much. She had such an energy and a passion for life — loving the music and throwing yourself into the scene, but also being very mindful about the policy and safeguarding the door crew and safeguarding individuals. It was all very much on her radar and on the team's radar. She gave so much and she received a lot also.

SUZANNE ROBINSON: Yasmine was the doorman, and I remember one New Year's Eve, she came into the kitchen with a customer and says, 'Suzanne, can you do anything for this girl, she's not prepared to go to hospital.' I said, 'Why?' 'She said she's fallen on the dance floor and she's got a piece of glass in her bum, but she won't go to hospital.' So in the kitchen, there were stairs that went up to Hicks bar; behind the wall, I had a big chest freezer. I remember saying to the girl, 'I've got some tweezers and I've got some antiseptic.' I said, 'You're gonna have to hold still while I take this glass out of your bottom, or you can go to hospital.' 'I'm not going to hospital,' she said, so on New Year's Eve, in the back freezer in the kitchen, I was picking little bits of glass out of this lady's bottom. But Yasmine was such a lovely, lovely entity, you know? She spoke to everybody, and she got support with all those doormen all those years.

SORAYA LAKHANEY: My sister was there when ecstasy was really taking off and acid music was starting — the Madchester days. She was working there when, unfortunately, someone had a very bad time with ecstasy. Yasmine was there tending to them and called the ambulance, and unfortunately it was a fatality. My sister was holding the girl's hand and was with her, trying to keep her centred, being with her in the last moments of her life.

Yasmine used to call me 'Baby' and she'd say, 'You know, Baby, when I say prayers about there being peace in the club, it's a good night, and people have a good time, and when I don't, it's a rough night.' I thought that was really interesting, how her beliefs played into that, were very important to her in keeping her grounded and centred. She felt that kind of hand of protection in a non-physical sense that resourced her to do her work at The Haçienda in a way that was helpful.

ANG MATTHEWS: She was very religious. That was the thing about her when the drugs became more prominent, with ecstasy and that. She didn't want to be involved in that sort of thing. But she was very, very kind and she didn't have a bad word to say about anybody. I don't actually think she had any form of social life at all other than going to The Haçienda. She loved soul music, what we call northern soul music. I kept in touch with her and saw her a couple of times after The Haçienda. The customers loved her — they all knew her name.

REBECCA GOODWIN: In my time working on the door, we had three eras of doormen: the originals with the bow ties, including the lovely Yasmine. Then there were your ordinary Joes in the second set. When money was being made and drugs were being sold, The Haçienda became a centre of territorial battles of power in the city, and that was reflected in who was employed to run the door in the third set of doormen. We had Cheetham Hill gang-type associates who came next, and they wanted us to pay them off by running off extra tickets early to get a bit of extra cash. The police were getting increasingly interested and coming into the club in plain clothes. Then it switched to a Salford group who were nasty pieces of work, really. We had the Noonans, a sort of crime family, on the door. The whole thing got darker and darker, really. With customers, they'd kick people's heads in on the street and there'd be violence.

SORAYA LAKHANEY: Martial arts was something that fascinated her. She loved all kinds of religions, and she loved Eastern philosophy, that sense of peace and self-discipline, and the idea that the martial arts moves had meanings. With the body in a certain position, it showed her power and strength. You could do a lot with very little — she told me that — and she could throw a man who was much, much heavier than her . . .

ANNE-MARIE COPELAND: We'd always wondered, how could she be a bouncer? She was the one who would try and calm down tricky situations, and I asked her once how she could do the job and she said, 'Don't worry, I have a black belt!'

SORAYA LAKHANEY: Sometimes Yasmine would do a door shift at The Haçienda, which would finish at two o'clock in the morning, and then she'd drive to Liverpool for a northern soul gig! Can you imagine how draining that must have been — on your feet dealing with the whole evening's drama, full throttle, then to drive to Liverpool? She'd creep in about seven or eight o'clock in the morning, get a couple of hours' sleep, and then she'd be off again. She loved the music. For my sister, the music was like breathing, like oxygen. The soundtrack of life would have been very silent without it.

RUTH TAYLOR: Women were always there in Factory, weren't they? There were probably more women than men working in The Haçienda: Ang was running the place, Suzanne was running the canteen . . . women were all over the place. Sure there were blokes on the front door, but even Yasmine was on the front door. Because there were women all over the place, it wasn't a patriarchal place — there was no room for patriarchy there. It wasn't a job-for-the-boys kind of place at all.

SORAYA LAKHANEY: I'll pick up the story some years after The Haçienda. Yasmine became unwell. She was living in Manchester with my mum, and I had my own life and career in London. It was too much for my mum, so I left my life and my career in London and moved to Manchester to care for my sister. We'd talk about The Haçienda days and her fond memories of it. She was so proud of the work she did there. You know, it wasn't perfect, and there's nothing perfect in this world. But she was so proud that she was part of that club and was part of such a strong female team.

Yasmine loved being part of The Haçienda, and when she was buried I had her buried in one of her Haçienda T-shirts and her favourite denim jacket she used to like wearing when she'd go to northern soul all-nighters.

CHAPTER 8

FACTORY GOES GLOBAL: NEW YORK AND BENELUX

Anne Lehman and Michael Shamberg at
the Of Factory office in New York

Factory formed relationships outside the UK that led to the creation of various regional arms of the label. In New York, the off-shoot that would eventually become Of Factory New York began in 1981 as Factory America, followed by Factory US, fronted by Michael Shamberg and based at 325 Spring Street in SoHo. While Shamberg largely played the role of Tony Wilson in America, women managed the New York wing of the label. Anne Lehman ran the office through much of its heyday, her name listed among the 'directors' on the Of Factory New York stationery designed by Chris Mathan. Miranda Stanton did behind-the-scenes work in the early days of Factory's New York wing while also writing and recording music as her musical alter ego Stanton Miranda and with her band Thick Pigeon. Over the years, the city of New York itself played a vital role in the development of Factory Records, from Ruth Polsky's zealous promotion of Manchester bands at clubs that inspired The Haçienda, to the annual New Music Seminar (1980–1995), which highlighted the dearth and necessity of women in the music business.

Across the Atlantic in Brussels, Annik Honoré had been promoting Factory bands in mainland Europe with Michel Duval. They went on to form Factory Benelux (**Bel**gium **Ne**therlands **Lux**embourg), along with their own distinct label Les Disques du Crépuscule, which released music by Factory artists like The Durutti Column, Anna Domino, and Thick Pigeon. Outside Europe and North America, references are made occasionally to another Factory arm, Factory Australasia. This Pacific wing largely served as a licensee but was the only Factory company to release the soundtrack to *Salvation!* (catalogue FACT 182), a film by director Beth B.

ANNE LEHMAN: The Factory US office was in the old Port Authority trucking building. It was gorgeous. We were on the south side of the building, and the windows overlooked Spring Street. It was very small inside (the Factory office), there were two or three tables made from doors — you know, doors on sawhorses. I don't even think there were chairs, quite frankly. The hallways were long and dark with those wide staircases. I love that building. The office was room number 233, so we were on the second floor. At the very end of that hall were the offices for White Columns [a contemporary art gallery]. If we needed to make photocopies or send faxes or anything like that, we were able to use their machines. I spent a lot of time just sitting on the floor in the hall outside of the office because Michael was not a very punctual person. I think I learnt to always travel with a book because there's not really a whole lot else to do. I smoked a lot of cigarettes in the hallways waiting for him. [laughs] I think I eventually got a key.

That building on Spring Street is a historic landmark, but you wouldn't know it because the office was *a mess* when I first got there. Michael Shamberg was never punctual, and that office was in ruins. Piles and piles and piles. Piles of paper, piles of ticket stubs, letters from people, piles of . . . I don't even know. [laughs] When I started, I took *all those piles of paper*, and I sorted them into more piles that made sense. And then I created files for all that stuff because Michael could never find anything, but he also never threw anything away. I organised everything — every piece of paper. If it had anything to do with New Order, it was in a pile. If it had anything to do with Quando Quango or anything like that, another pile. At some point in time, I started doing Doublevision and IKON, the video arm, and more piles. I've started piecing everything together in my memory, too, and I realised all of those piles must now be in the New York Public Library in the archives of Michael Shamberg. They still exist because I was there to sort them. I'm just so curious to go to New York and see those files again.

MARGARET JAILLER: I didn't even know there was a US Factory and, if I had, would probably have assumed it was Warhol-inspired. The only interactions I had with Michael Shamberg were in 1988, first as director of photography (DOP) on New Order's 'Fine Time' promo, which Richard Heslop directed and shot, and then on the

Brazil/Argentina tour job. I remember that Shamberg was always calm and polite, very nurturing really and not fazed by surprises (e.g., when we filmed bloodshed on the street of Buenos Aires when the festival for democracy was cancelled).

ANNA DOMINO: I had more direct contact with Factory through my friends Michael Shamberg and Stanton Miranda.

I met Miranda at the Mudd Club, where there were many insanely creative people knocking around. She was one of my first real friends in New York and she then introduced me to her boyfriend Michael. Over the years, while Miranda was writing and recording her own music, we made attempts to start a band together but couldn't quite hit on a winning combination of our distinct talents. I watched Miranda perform several times but didn't yet have the bravery to get up onstage myself. Miranda also contributed to two of my favourite songs from those days: 'Caught' and 'Dreamback'. Michael made a great impression on me, as he was one of the very few people I met in NYC who wasn't consumed with cynicism. He could find the good in anything and everyone. This was completely radical in New York as the downtown scene ran on sarcasm. Michael rarely said an unkind word, even once he fell sick. Extraordinary.

GINA BIRCH: Michael was an incredible communicator. He'd come to town and knew more people in three weeks than you'd know in twenty years. He was always putting people together, and introducing me to all sorts of people.

AMBER DENKER: I think of Michael Shamberg as being very much a feminist, empowering to Gretchen [Bender]. I think she felt he had her back, and there was a lot of trust and support there.

ANNE LEHMAN: I moved to New York in 1984 when I was twenty-four. I was born and raised and had lived in California my whole life until that point. From 1980 to '84, I was working at Rough Trade Records in San Francisco. That's how I first met Tony Wilson, Rob Gretton and New Order. I think 1981 was New Order's first tour of the States, so I met them all at that time. Tony came to visit Rough Trade because they were manufacturing and distributing all of Factory's records in the US. We were Factory US at that point . . .

I have a vivid memory of spending an entire day with Tony Wilson in San Francisco. I just drove him around. He wanted to see the city, so I spent a day in the Rough Trade car taking him wherever he wanted to go. He wanted to see City Lights, so I took him to City Lights. He wanted to see the Cliff House and the beach, so I took him there and across the Golden Gate Bridge, took him across the Bay Bridge. Just drove him around until it was time to go to the airport. I loved spending that time with him. He was so incredibly open, and I thought he was brilliant. You know, I was just a kid, twenty-two or something, but I felt really respected by him because he picked me to drive him around the city.

When New Order were in New York in '83 recording with Arthur Baker, doing 'Confusion', I went to New York with my boyfriend at the time, Steve Montgomery. Steve had opened Rough Trade in the beginning with Geoff Travis in the US and then got . . . estranged or fired or whatever. I don't know why we were there when New Order was recording with Arthur Baker, but we were in the studio the whole time. It was horrible. There was so much tension because Arthur Baker was kind of a fascist in the studio. That's when I first met Michael. Anyway, we moved to New York because Michael Shamberg said, 'You should come to New York and work for me.' I pretty much jumped at that opportunity. I left home, sold everything I had — mostly a record collection — and did one of those drive-away companies where they just have you drive a car from point A to point B and they pay for everything if you just deliver the car. So, we loaded all of our stuff in the car and drove to New York.

We turned up at Michael and Miranda's place on 6th Avenue and he said we could stay with them. He lived in a massive open loft with Miranda and a big dog. We slept on the floor for one night and I said, 'This ain't gonna work!' [laughs] So, we stayed in a really shitty hotel that smelled like roach spray and it turned out there was no job for me. Eventually I did end up working for him, for Factory US, but a little bit later on.

ANGIE CASSIDY: Anne ran that Factory office — she kept Factory afloat in bloody New York. She could do it on her little finger — she was so good at it.

ANNE LEHMAN: I went to visit Michael Shamberg at the office on Spring Street, and it was clear to me that ... organisation was seriously lacking — of money, of accounts, of files and of *every-thing* in that office physically. I didn't have a degree in accounting and was completely self-taught, but I'd been doing it since I was sixteen, and I was really good at doing that kind of work at Rough Trade. It was all pre-computer, of course, so it was general ledger and manual accounting work. So when I went to Michael and said, 'Hey, look, I can get you organised', that was probably very appealing to him. Because the place was, in my recollection, *a mess*.

CHRIS MATHAN: I don't remember when I first met Anne Lehman, probably through Of Factory New York where she worked for some time. Anne was involved with many other indie bands both in the US and England for many years. Same with Angie Cassidy (then Section 25), I don't remember when we first met but she, Anne and I became close friends when I returned from England and continued to work for Of Factory New York. Anne and I shared a loft in Tribeca and Angie lived in NYC too for a while. I did know Angie when I lived in London. She was squatting in a flat in London. I met her there to have her cut my hair ... she had worked as a hairdresser. I had to wear a beret for about a month after that! [laughs]

ANNE LEHMAN: I worked with Chris when we did *Young, Popular and Sexy*. I did whatever she needed done. She did this video cover packaging mock-up, and I loved working with her because she was so crazy about font. So she did this mock-up in Italian, and Michael thought it was really cool that she did it in Italian. But the thing is, it was supposed to just be a mock-up. But because it was Factory, Michael said, 'It has to be like this, it has to be in Italian.'

ANGIE CASSIDY: New York and Chris! Her apartment was an amazing place in downtown New York with one of those lifts where you'd pull and the thing goes up. You'd think you were going up into some sort of crazy warehouse, and then you'd come out into this amazing apartment.

ANNE LEHMAN: For two of those years in New York while I was working for Factory, I didn't have a place to live. I met Chris at the White Columns show, the *COMPACT* exhibit. So, I was living with Chris.

CHRIS MATHAN: The *COMPACT* exhibit was in the same vein as the *Brotherhood* campaign [marketing for New Order album and singles], and the Festival of the Tenth Summer stuff, the numbers and what we termed 'meta language'. Personal computers already existed, the first Mac was launched in 1984, but no software had yet been developed to do graphic design work on computers. But what was to come, digital fonts, etc., was fascinating and opened up a whole new visual language. I don't remember exactly how that fit in with Peter's fascination with, for example, Benson & Hedges cigarette packaging. If you took the Benson & Hedges cigarette pack apart, you'd see the hidden colour bars, registration marks, etc., [that] printers use. Benson & Hedges cardboard cigarette packs were metallic silver or gold, and, if I recall, that led to the use of the *Brotherhood* metals. And it inspired the gold-leaf *COMPACT* art piece manufactured in England, then flown to NYC for the art exhibition at White Columns in Soho, as well as the invitation to that event. *COMPACT* was an enormously enlarged tiny flap of a Benson & Hedges cigarette pack. I still have the unfolded cigarette pack mounted on black board. Who would have kept such a thing?!

ANNE LEHMAN: That *COMPACT* show, I had never seen anything like it. I remember being in the office around the time of *COMPACT*, and I remember Chris was there with Peter Saville. He was talking about where all those ideas for the construction of the 'Blue Monday' sleeve came from, and how if you break apart a cigarette pack, there were all those Pantone colours in there. For *COMPACT*, the idea was similar because the gold for the invitations

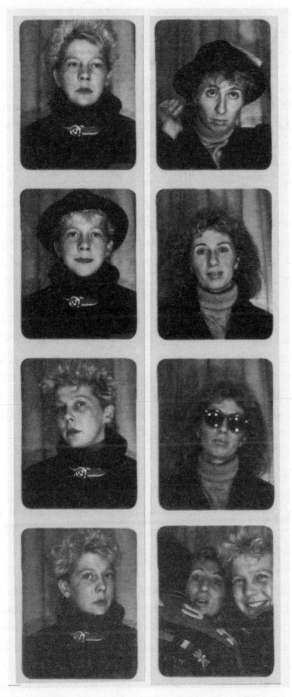

Angie Cassidy, Anne Lehman and Chris Mathan

was all about the packaging of cigarettes. I was thinking, 'You're so far out.' [laughs]

CHRIS MATHAN: I was hired to create the Of Factory New York stationery, so in keeping with other Factory division marks, I designed it to be part of the Factory family. The American flag star and the stripes over the factory building symbol was created for Michael Shamberg. I felt it should closely resemble the Factory logo because they were releasing artists like Miranda. The various Factory Communications logo marks predated my working at PSA. They were already using iconography to represent the different facets of the Factory Communications Ltd brand. The Of Factory NY icon was part of that brand. Later, the stationery for Factory was redesigned based on the Of Factory New York stationery — except the Factory mark was blind embossed.

ANNE LEHMAN: In the beginning, I felt really respected and like I might be contributing to something. I was just looking at the Factory stationery that had my name on it. I remember when that happened I felt like, 'Wow, I'm getting some recognition for being there at that time.'

• • •

GILLIAN GILBERT: I don't think people in England could get their heads round New Order at the time because it was still Joy Division fans going, 'It's not the same.' So we tended to play in America a lot, and then we started getting into club music in America and I thought, 'Why can't we do that over here in England?' I liked playing America because they didn't know who you were and the audience was just there. They were very interested in your music for the music itself. England's a bit more stern, and you could see in their eyes, 'This isn't Joy Division, how dare you?' Every time we went over to America, the audiences got bigger. We started playing little clubs like the Peppermint Lounge in New York City, where everybody was staring at us because they didn't know who we were. We were just some band from England, but there also wasn't the same sense that we *weren't Joy Division*. So people accepted us a bit more in America.

GONNIE RIETVELD: I felt a certain affinity with New York City in the early 1980s, and it was nice in New York: they really liked our music! We did actually end up at Paradise Garage and Danceteria. We visited the Fun House, and we visited The Roxy as well when it was the big sort of electro night, Friday nights, which brought together this Anglophile scene with the hip-hop scene — so, electropop people and the electro people from uptown. That was really cool. I guess there's always been an affinity with New York in one way or another with our music.

Then there are nonsense lyrics in our song 'Go Exciting' that seemed to really go down well with some of the Latino crowd. They were like, *I know what she's saying, but I can't hear it! What is she saying?* It had everything to do with me growing up in the Netherlands and not being able to hear English very well in my first encounter with Latin music, which was through my granddad. It was a very strange reinterpretation of what may possibly sound slightly Latin. But it seemed to work for that crowd, so . . .

RUTH POLSKY: At one time it seemed unlikely that new wave music would find mass acceptance. Besides, the zealously uncompromising bands which began the movement were all too willing to voice their contempt for commercial success; not to do so would've meant a serious loss of credibility.

The popular culture has an insidious way of devouring and assimilating any cult that survives more than a season, and adapting it to suit the needs of the moment. Right now [in 1979], people need to dance — not the well-oiled, machine-like dancing of a bland, conformist half-decade, but the individualistic style of a crazy new era, where we could just as easily blow ourselves up as create the future world . . . It's time to face the modern age. [Ruth Polsky, *The Aquarian*, 1979[1]]

RACHEL FELDER: Ruth Polsky was an integral player in the American success of many bands from England, and particularly bands from

Manchester. The fees she was able to pay at the clubs she booked enabled those bands to tour America. She was their launch pad to American success, and it goes beyond that, because the cachet of American success, even if a band played just one night in a tiny venue in New York City, reverberated in the UK and beyond. It's easy to say 'they played a cool gig at Danceteria', but that's just one part of the importance of what those gates [to success] were.

Her intense love of British music — and Mancunian music in particular — gave a lot of these bands a feeling about America that was so positive. I think Ruth took such a personal interest in making sure that every gig was a success. She really instilled a love of America and acceptance of touring here in a way that otherwise wouldn't have been the case.

CHRIS MATHAN: Ruth did so much to help the UK bands get bookings and promoted in the US. When I still lived in NYC, it was hard to even pass by The Limelight where Ruth was killed by an out-of-control taxi that pinned her against the former Episcopal church in 1986. Her death was so tragic, such a freakish accident. I have the invitation to Ruth's birthday party at The Haçienda from just the year before.

RACHEL FELDER: I think being a female promoter was challenging for Ruth because it wasn't the norm at the time. But with most of those Mancunian bands, when they'd come to New York, their attitude was if someone could do the job, that's all that mattered. So she was able to be treated with great respect and equality by the British people she worked with — not just the bands, but the labels like Factory, too. She was great at her job, and everyone knew she'd get the job done.

I think a lot of the people she worked with in the UK were just so happy to have a kindred spirit over here. She really understood Mancunian humour — surprisingly so for someone who wasn't British. She went out of her way to make sure that when these bands came over, they really were taken care of and felt comfortable.

Ruth Polsky on a train en route to London for a gig with Certain General (who she managed, and who toured with New Order), lecturing the band on the British music press, 1985

GILLIAN GILBERT: In New York City, we used to all go back to Ruth Polsky's flat. Ruth Polsky was great, and she took me to loads of antique dress shops. She bought me my 'Blue Monday' dress!

AMBER DENKER: Oh my God, of course we were New Order fans! The whole downtown New York art scene, I think, was just all about New Order. For me, they epitomise that era.

GILLIAN GILBERT: Going to America was like a dream. We were just dragged out of clubs after the gigs, and it was great because they used to close at like four in the morning, and Michael Shamberg and Miranda, who we've worked with, knew the best places to go. I mean, Danceteria was famous, wasn't it? I remember playing there, but it's weird 'cause everything was so dark inside. [laughs] At Danceteria, I remember we got very hot and the sequencers didn't like hot places ... the New Order sequencers didn't like Danceteria!

RUTH POLSKY: This [Danceteria] is a place where anything goes, from oompah bands to Diamanda Galás to the funkiest thing happening on the street. We try to do as much variety as possible and to present music from all over the world. [Ruth Polsky, *The Tube*, 1983[2]]

ANGIE CASSIDY: I remember being in a nightclub in New York where Mark Kamins [resident DJ at Danceteria] was DJing. We were stood up in the DJ booth, and Section 25 'Looking from a Hilltop' came on. I look over and there's a guy stood next to me. I said, 'Wow, I'm so excited!' He said, 'Oh, do you like this?' I said, 'Oh my God, yes! This is my band, and all these people are dancing to our track!' 'That's cool,' he said, and someone came up and asked if I knew who that was. Just some guy, right? Johnny Marr from The Smiths.

ANNE LEHMAN: I remember Section 25 at Danceteria because I became really, really good friends with Angie. Angie and Lee Shallcross moved to New York and into our place on Sixth Street. I loved that band, and I maintained contact with all of them. Larry and Jenny, and Vinny ... I went and stayed with Angie and her family in Blackpool numerous times.

I also remember contacts with Lawrence Weiner, who did the beautiful Section 25 poster. When the band came over to New York, they were expecting to see the posters all over town. I remember them coming into the office saying like, 'Uh, where are the posters?' 'They're right there in the corner,' I said. There was this huge stack of posters, and this is what Michael did so often: he was a really brilliant facilitator, but there was no follow-through. So yeah, the posters were just sitting in a huge pile in the corner, and I remember thinking, what's the point of this? They were *so* expensive to produce. I mean, they were beautiful, massive posters, and that's how shows were promoted at that time. But they weren't hung, and I don't remember there being that many people at the show.

GONNIE RIETVELD: I don't think we actually played that one at The Ritz with Section 25 [for which Lawrence Weiner designed the poster], and I'll tell you why. We put all our equipment into the

Angie Cassidy in New York

Factory New York office, but Michael Shamberg was locked out of the building when we went to pick up the gear. There was no way to get in! He was phoning and tried what he could, but the caretaker wasn't picking up. What a disaster! So we never played The Ritz! It was really, really strange, and that was very much a lost opportunity because some rather important people turned up for that gig. They never got to hear us or see us.

ANNE LEHMAN: Michael was also working with Crépuscule and Benelux, with Michel Duval and Anna Domino, and I saw Anna Domino play.

ANNA DOMINO: When my test pressing came in the mail [from Crépuscule/Factory Benelux] I took it over to my friend Jean's place (Jean-Michel Basquiat) because I couldn't listen to it alone. The record was unlabelled and came in a corrugated cardboard sleeve with no return address. Over at Jean's, I put it on the turntable and waited. He listened for a while, then turned back to his work. After I'd played both sides and taken it off, he said, 'It sounds English.' At first I thought this was a good thing, despite his tone, which was pretty flat. But what he meant was, 'It's a European sound and not New York. It has no cred. It is puffery.' He was the first person to hear that test pressing and his opinion meant a lot to me. Maybe too much. He was always saying I should just do the thing instead of complaining about being unable to do the thing. And by then he'd already made a record himself ('Beat Bop') so he didn't see a problem. After this pronouncement, though, I wasn't sure I could do anything at all. I was too *English* but I lived in and loved New York. I didn't fit in anywhere.

ANGIE CASSIDY: I moved to New York because the band seemed to just go quiet for a while. I stayed with Anne there and met Michael Shamberg.

• • •

TINA SIMMONS: Before the Festival of the Tenth Summer, I flew to New York and met up with the team there, Anne Lehman and Michael Shamberg of course. I had to sort out the finances for New York because they were getting the royalties from Rough Trade in San Francisco for the album sales in America, but the royalties weren't coming into England. They seemed to have halted at Factory New York. For New Order, and Joy Division, this caused a lot of trouble because the taxman said, 'They've earned these royalties . . . tax them!' Hence Rob being poorly because these tax issues should never have happened. It was all sorted eventually, but that caused a bit of a rift, to say the least. Factory thought, 'We're going to give the people what they want', the roots of the independent record label idea. It's great working with that idea, but you can't let the finances just go.

BINDI BINNING: I remember being at New Music Seminar in New York City. I was working with In the City and Factory Too at the time, so I would have been looking at it from both points of view.

Alyson Patchett and I went to New York with Tony. Originally it was just supposed to be me. Alyson and I just did everything — we really *did* New York, and that trip inspired me so much that it became the model for In the City. I loved the idea of being able to go to all these different places, from one club to the next to hear bands every night. So I told Tony I wanted to recreate a version of that in Manchester, pick multiple venues, with four or five bands in each of those venues every single night. Which, of course, did happen. It made it so buzzy to be able to recreate a little bit of New York but with a Manchester twist.

LIEVE MONNENS: I remember the first time I went to the New Music Seminar in New York. I knew a couple of other girls from Rough Trade, and from Play It Again Sam in Brussels, and it was interesting to see the ways some record companies were more progressive (in dealing with women, I mean here) than Factory. Maybe it was England, because in Belgium I had the feeling I was equal to men. I didn't have that feeling that I was to know my place as a woman, but I felt that much more in England. They could be progressive musically, but I found England to be remarkably

Tina Simmons's New Music Seminar pass

old-fashioned, chauvinist. For example, I would be asked to wear short skirts, and I had to say, 'I never wear short skirts, not ever.' I used to be straight in people's faces, 'Get lost!' — you know? The male chauvinist attitude that came through shocked me, actually. I'd worked with English people before, but the contrast between working in a modern and alternative industry while still coming across those conservative attitudes . . . it was the feeling of shock that I remember. In Belgium, there were some issues, but I felt equal. Or if anything happened, it didn't feel like it happened because I was a woman.

TINA SIMMONS: At the New Music Seminar at the Marriott Marquis, I remember sitting next to the guy who was at an independent record label but he'd done a deal with Polygram, so he wasn't *really* independent, and we had a big discourse about what true independence is versus selling out to the big boys. I stood up for what true independence was, a true independent record label. I was the only woman on that panel, and a lot of people came down from the audience afterward, asking me questions about what it was like being a woman in the music industry. It's probably the same today because it was very much a male-orientated place. It stems back to America, where it started, but even the people running the companies here in the UK, it was all men. There were very few women. The women who came forward wanted to do what I did and asked if they could succeed. I said, 'Well, I've done it and there's no reason that women can't do it.' I think around that time, a lot of independent record labels started appearing around America.

• • •

ANNIK HONORÉ: It all came so naturally. I knew Factory for a long time and got on well with the people, and I liked all their bands. It was the same for Michel. Both of us were promoting concerts at Plan K, and we got in touch with Factory, with A Certain Ratio and everyone. We thought it would be a good idea to put out records ourselves, we could do a single together . . . Instead of just doing a single, we said, 'Well, let's start Factory Benelux.' [Akiko Hada interview, *Rock Magazine*, 1981[3]]

ANNA DOMINO: And then there was Annik Honoré! A founder of both Factory Benelux and Crépuscule. She left shortly after I began working with Crépuscule but she remained a friend and I admired her greatly. After she died I wrote a song about her, in a non-literal, poetic sort of way.

ANNIK HONORÉ: That was one thing, that was Factory Benelux, but obviously we liked other groups and we wanted to start a label of our own, so we started Crépuscule at the same time ... I don't think people know that Factory Benelux and Crépuscule are run by the same people. It doesn't matter that they don't know. They are two separate things — Factory Benelux deal with Factory artists, Crépuscule is something we look for, we have to look for what we want to do.

ANNA DOMINO: There was a connection between Crépuscule and Factory Records as they released each other's material. Crépuscule — as Factory Benelux — also arranged their own releases with Factory artists. I met Factory's top brass once when Michel Duval was going to Manchester to see them and took me along. This promised to be unnerving as Duval was not a great driver at the best of times. Navigating cities from an unfamiliar side of the road proved to be somewhat heart-stopping.

There were a few women working in music publishing in those days — perhaps because it demanded patiently explaining the vagaries of publishing to angry artists. As far as I could tell, heads of labels were all men, though the occasional woman might be procured as adornment. The women I met mostly made coffee, did secretarial work, manned the front desk. Translators always seemed to be women who joined us at dinners to interpret the questions and comments of the men at the next table and to soften their demands and occasional cruelties ... Of course, there were plenty of women actually making music.

LIEVE MONNENS: I got to know the people at Les Disques du Crépuscule and Factory Benelux. While I was still in college, I went to work every free minute for them. When I finished my studies, they had a job waiting for me, so I could start straight away. I was twenty-two. That was my first job, and it was in Brussels. It was great. I was assistant to one of the people who started Crépuscule, Michel Duval. I'd basically do anything: work on a schedule for the recording studio, help with international press coming around, paperwork, royalties, authors' rights, etc. At Crépuscule and Benelux, I worked with Michel, but Annik was there, and there were women handling promotions, etc. Then I worked for different record companies in Brussels. But I could only do that up to a point before I thought, I need to leave, I can't stay in the music industry after six years. I loved Brussels but I wanted a change.

BETH CASSIDY: I had very brief interactions with Annik. I literally played two gigs with my dad — one God-awful gig in Düsseldorf, which I would like to forget, which was my first, and then a second in Brussels, a Plan K gig. It was obviously a Factory night. So everybody who was anybody was there. I was introduced to Annik and noticed she was talking to my dad, but I was young and didn't really understand the situation. When my dad passed away, I received a really lengthy email from Annik out of the blue. She'd obviously worked to track me down, and it was a beautiful and intuitive email, a eulogy of my dad and his relationship with Ian. I respected it so much that she just reached out to me to pay this beautiful tribute and then, not long after, she passed away. I realised she must have been ill when she wrote to me. She had no need to reach out to me, but she did, and it's those little moments that mean the most.

ANNA DOMINO: Miranda [Stanton] was already recording for Crépuscule and introduced me to Michel Duval one night at a show in the East Village. I remember it as Africa Bambaataa and Soulsonic Force playing at the Ukrainian Hall, but it may well have been elsewhere; my memories from that time are a blur. I asked Duval if I could send him some demos made on my four-track cassette recorder — with borrowed instruments, pots and pans, a small synth. He said yes and I mailed him a cassette of eight to ten songs. Several months later he got in touch and proposed that I come to Brussels and spend a week in the studio. I'd never done anything like this, so a week seemed reasonable.

My first studio sessions in this life were for Crépuscule Records in Brussels. Two weeks into recording I was unceremoniously shipped home. Songs were unfinished, nothing was mixed and the label's head, Michel Duval, seemed indifferent. Back in New York, I was talking with a friend on the phone late one night about whether to have an alter ego as a sort of remove, in case my songs ever did come out and nobody noticed. All we could think of were goofy names that fell flat. I was staring absently out the window at the massive sugar refinery across the East River. All you could see at night were the gigantic illuminated letters that read DOMINO. Now there was an idea!

PAULINE HARRISON: I started going out with Vini in 1983, I think, and we went out together for eight and a half years. That record *Short Stories for Pauline* was made around then because I was still at university. It was on Benelux/Crépuscule. I remember Vini decided he was going to make an album for me, and that was it. He just said, 'Do you want to do a few vocals?' I'm not a singer . . . at all. So I did those vocals in the studio. We were in Brussels, in Belgium. On the album cover, there's the drummer they used — normally it's Bruce — because Bruce must have been busy. They used a guy called Alain Lefebvre. He was really lovely. He showed us around Brussels, and it was just a really lovely time.

There's actually two different covers for that album. One of them, it's the three of us: there's Alain, me and Vini, and then there's another cover that's just me and Vini. I recall that the album wasn't released because Tony didn't think it was good enough. I could be wrong, but that's what I remember Vini said: that Tony didn't think it was up to his usual standards, so he wasn't going to put it out. I had a copy of it myself — I had a cassette of it. So I'd heard everything as it was done . . . I liked some of Vini's music, but I was more into Echo and the Bunnymen and bands like that.

[laughs] Of course, I recognised how talented Vini was and still is. He's a very, very talented human being.

LIEVE MONNENS: Someone recommended I stay in the music industry but change environments and move countries. So that's what I did. I saw the job advertisement at Factory in the UK and moved from Brussels with my then-boyfriend, Stefan de Batselier, who has just recently passed away. We had a year of exploring a new world together.

CHAPTER 9

TECHNOLOGY

Gonnie Rietveld's initial drum grid for 'Bad Blood',
for one of Quando Quango's final recordings

In the third decade of the twenty-first century – the future! – fewer than 5 per cent of people working in music tech are women, and women are credited as producers on fewer than 3 percent of all studio records.[1] In the story of Factory, technology – and advances in technology – was a catalyst for women to carve out new niches: from live and backstage sound to operating the controls in the studio to pioneering computer and film technologies in cutting-edge music videos. Di Barton is a live sound authority who honed her craft at The Haçienda and at gigs featuring Factory bands. Jane Roberts was a backline technician who pushed back against assumptions concerning the roles women can play behind the stage. In filming live performances and creating music videos, women such as Linda Dutton, Margaret Jailler, Carole Lamond, Amber Denker, Carrie Kirkpatrick, and Laura Israel mastered new video technologies. Gonnie Rietveld and Gillian Gilbert pioneered electronic sound onstage and in the studios. At the controls, Julia Adamson learnt about music production at Strawberry Studios and produced records at Yellow 2 Studios in Stockport, while Tina Weymouth produced the Happy Mondays in Barbados and Gillian Gilbert produced Miranda Stanton and Thick Pigeon in New York. Most of these women were self-taught, grappling with both implicit and explicit sexism in their respective fields to create lasting works that cement their legacies.

BRIX SMITH: There's a way that women work differently than men in certain aspects of tech, which I find really interesting. There's a kind of a spiritual looseness – a freedom – to the way they work, and they're more open to ideas and possibilities, and you can see the same thing in fashion shows. It might just be that women weren't formally trained in tech because they couldn't be. I believe it's right that gender is fluid and nobody is just one thing or the other, but at the time, it was a different world when women were coming up in tech, in music and theatre, and I think they learnt and responded differently. Women were a *novelty* in so many industries in those days, and it was very, very hard for most women coming into a very male-dominated industry. We were an anomaly, and I think that changed how we learnt to do our jobs. We had to be as good or better in order to play in their sandbox. But there's also the passion for doing something that was considered a non-traditional job for a woman: that meant we did the job in a new way. With that passion comes spectacular results, and that's the fucking bottom line of it in those days.

LINDA DUTTON: We were shooting on U-matic. We had one camera with the sound coming from the mixing desk, and then there was an ambient microphone, which Malc would mix together. But there were always problems one way or another with it; either the video lead didn't work or the sound didn't work. I took it upon myself to try and fix the technical things because nobody else was really interested in doing it. The whole thing of IKON was a very 'do it yourself' attitude. So if you wanted to learn something, then you had to just have a go. Nobody was helping.

MARGARET JAILLER: Regarding the job of cinematography, as many roles on a live film crew require considerable physical strength, particularly in the photography department (the lights were very heavy before LED), these roles were — and may still be — filled by working-class men. Film, like many crafts, operated through an informal apprenticeship arrangement, so someone might start as a spark in the lighting department and then become a gaffer and perhaps eventually a DOP [director of photography], and runners might become clapper loaders, then camera assistants/focus pullers, then camera operators. There was resentment when young film school upstarts entered the industry at the DOP level after only three years (or in my case six years) at art school, walking into roles that men who had served time in the lower ranks might eventually have gone into. So being female *and* film-school trained was an affront. I must acknowledge that the industry-trained gaffers were a wealth of knowledge and experience that I didn't have, so

I had some sympathy for them, but (in my experience) they were also more conservative in their ideas/sensibilities because they had neither the same vast and eclectic range of visual references that art students are exposed to, nor the same experimental instinct that is fostered in them, so there was an element of duress for them in the working relationship which could manifest in blatant disrespect.

BRIX SMITH: Mark was also a big champion of women in the band. In the working process, there was pretty much always a woman in and out of The Fall, and we had a *great* sound engineer called Di Barton who does The Charlatans now, and did New Order and so many other bands. We absolutely had women on our team. It was important to be not only inclusive but very much supportive of women.

GONNIE RIETVELD: Dian Barton, the sound engineer, to be honest with you, she's seen it all, too.

SUZANNE ROBINSON: There was a woman called Di who was the sound engineer for us, Oz PA, who was and is great.

DIAN BARTON: It all started in 1978 when, with two friends, we began providing a small PA to mates doing gigs in pubs around Manchester. The PA, or public address [system], only consisted of one microphone and two speakers, one for each side — i.e. stereo — and was just a hobby to begin with.

As the gigs became more frequent we bought more equipment, learning as we expanded. We all had day jobs at this time but were being asked by bands and venues to travel further afield. This was all through word of mouth and recommendations because we didn't advertise.

We had no formal training but since we started with basic minimal equipment, as we grew bigger we gained an understanding of how to use it in stages. When we bought something new — for example, a crossover or amplifier — we found the best way to use it and its specifications. In this way, we slowly built up our knowledge without the need for formal training. I don't think there were any specific courses at that time anyway. We also met a few other sound engineers, watching them and quizzing them for anything they could teach us.

At first I was just helping set up, driving and doing the accounts, learning all the time; this sparked my interest in wanting to actually mix live sound. I finally got the chance to do this in 1980, in a club in Leeds called The Limelight, for a band I had never even heard before. It was daunting to begin with, but you are so busy once the gig starts you forget the nerves and just get on with it.

By 1980 we left our jobs and were doing the PA full-time; my partners took redundancy, receiving quite a substantial amount of money, which we invested into the business. Our reputation grew, travelling all over the country, working for bands doing tours and with promoters at specific venues. This is how we came to work with Joy Division on a few gigs before Ian Curtis sadly passed away, coming into contact with Rob Gretton who was their manager and co-founder of Factory Records. It was Rob who realised how fastidious we were as a PA company, employing us for all future New Order gigs and ultimately the live sound at The Haçienda.

When The Haçienda opened, the PA that was installed was OK for DJs but not suitable for bands. As a result, our company was employed for all live gigs, where we met even more bands and engineers, so extending our platform to increase our knowledge and experience even more.

JANE ROBERTS: New Order were headlining Glastonbury [1987], and I really wanted to go. I was working at a little place called The Corner-house which was an art house cinema. I saw Andy [Robinson] walking past, and I chased him down the street, 'Andy, Andy!' He stopped [impersonates Andy's voice], 'Hey Jane, whaddaya want?' and I said, 'I really wanna go to Glastonbury and I was wondering if I could come with you lot. Can I just come in the bus, make tea or whatever?' He said, 'Actually we were talking about asking if you wanted to do the backline for us, do Bernard's guitars.' So of course I was like, 'Yeah, course I do! Yeah, I can do that!' They were in Strawberry Studios at the time, and I think they were doing a bit of remixing. Andy said to me, 'We'll go through stuff and see how we get on.' I turned up at Strawberry Studios in Stockport, and I was supposed to be doing Bernard's guitars at first. Andy passed me a guitar and said, 'Do you want to change the strings on this?' Andy had quite a deep posh voice, that's why I keep doing that voice. [laughs] And when he asked me to change the strings I just went, 'Yeah, sure', kind of looked around, and he said, 'You've never done this before, have you?' I had to admit, 'No . . . fuck, no, I haven't.' I had to hold my hands up, so it went from there and it's not rocket science. You know, if you've got a bit of common sense, you can do it.

I was totally unmusical. I learnt *everything* on the job. The thing is, if you meet backline technicians now — roadies, whatever you want to call them — if you meet them now, you say, 'Oh, what did you play before you started?' and they all play *everything* . . . I can sing, and I did a couple of backing tracks on some of Hooky's Revenge work. He had a couple of remixes done by Moby, and they came back and it was all my vocals. He was so fucking annoyed . . . he was really pissed off. So I did that, but I have no talent musically. *I love music*, you know? Just can't play it.

DIAN BARTON: Some of the most challenging gigs are festivals, especially before the introduction of digital desks. After the US tour with New Order most of the gigs for the next ten years (or so it seemed) were festivals with no soundcheck.

My first festival was with A Certain Ratio at Glastonbury in 1983, very early in my career. I was not familiar with any of the equipment at front of house (FOH), it was before the use of two desks (one for the band onstage and one for the band coming on next) — we call this flip-flop. In fact there were three desks, which I found out later were each for a specific use: the first for drums, the second for percussion and brass, the third for guitars, keyboards and vocals. There were a lot of effects (reverb, echo, etc.) and rows and rows of gates and compressors, none of which I had seen before — I didn't know how to use any of it.

I was out of my depth and panicking so I went backstage ready to tell the band I couldn't do it. I walked up to each member of the band but realised they couldn't handle what I was about to say, until I came to Donald Johnson, the drummer. So I took him to one side and whispered to him that I was out of my depth. He put his arm round my shoulder and whispered back, 'It's all right, Dian, we all are.' Luckily, we had arrived early so I kept going back out front, watching, asking a few questions and looking at the equipment. Eventually, I realised you couldn't use everything, just choose what you needed.

I formed a plan, asking the engineers running the system to set up what I required and help me operate them. It was a very windy day so the sound kept blowing away then coming back, but was a pretty successful gig. This taught me how to mix a festival and still to this day I keep going out front, looking, listening and forming my plan. Thank you, Donald!

JANE ROBERTS: Before we went to Glastonbury, my first gig with New Order was on a small tour they did, a tiny little tour in Spain. It was like bullrings and arenas, but there were only about two or three shows, if I can remember right. I definitely remember Valencia, but I don't really remember much else. [laughs] We might have done Barcelona and then Valencia. Playing bullrings is quite common . . . You know how you do arena tours in America? Bullrings were kind of like that in Spain. It's quite horrible to think about now because they still use them as 'bullrings'. Hopefully, that will eventually just fucking stop because it's disgusting . . . just turn them into places for gigs! But at the time, I think bullfighting was seasonal, and we were there when it was summer, so it was hot. I remember being onstage with bright sunlight, feeling like I'm boiling. The back bits were also a bit smelly, where the dressing rooms were. Not that I mind smelly, because I'm a country girl at heart, so I don't mind the smell of shit. [laughs] But when you think about death, that's a smell I mind. At that gig, I was just stood onstage, and Bernard keeps passing me things and throwing melodicas at me, and I'm going, *this is fucking surreal, what am I doing here?* But you sort of get used to it, and it's a job. But it's also good fun.

By that point, I was in the thick of it, and I'd actually started doing Pete's basses. I wasn't doing Barney's guitars because an old crew member came back, Jacko, and he always looked after him. So in the end, he did Barney and I did Pete's basses, which I think was always the intention, because Pete's bass tech at the time, Dave Pills, was just about to leave. So they got me in to train me up to do the bass.

MARGARET JAILLER: The crowds at the Brazil gigs were thrilling — New Order played very big venues and there was so much love for them. I'd be in the wings, capturing that, and in the daytime I'd just be a flâneur, wandering the streets alone, shooting B-roll on my Super 8 camera.

When I got back to the UK I dutifully handed over all the film to the production company to be telecined. I was at the telecine, grading the shots, but I never got the film back because technically it wasn't mine.

JANE ROBERTS: For us backline people, it should be pretty straight-forward because everything's been done by the time you get there. Somebody's built the stage, erected the PA, all that's been done, so our power should be there and taken care of. There will be a stage and power waiting for us.

At that point, and we're talking nearly thirty-odd years ago, you wouldn't find an earth pin anywhere (in Spain, South America). When you'd go to big stage gigs, big arenas or big outdoor gigs, they're supposed to put an earth pin in. You've got all the power, which has to be earthed, so basically people can't die from elec-tric shock. Still happens. But in Spain, you wouldn't find them, and South America was the same. You'd be lucky if you had an earth pin. You'd have to just knock one in and roughly attach the mains power to it. That's the start of my career, almost getting electrocuted. [laughs]

MARGARET JAILLER: The New Order gigs were in big sold-out arenas, and there was a real feeling that the circus was in town. As I recall, the film production was intended as in-house (I have no idea for what purpose), so it was low key. There were just Richard Heslop and myself shooting handheld camera at each gig — I don't even remember the format, probably Hi8 (which was relatively new in the mid-eighties). I can remember shooting from the wings, and I think Richard was front of house somewhere — we may well have filmed soundchecks too (I certainly remember being present when they occurred).

New Order were due to play an outdoor festival celebrating five years of Argentinian democracy: Raúl Alfonsín had been freely elected on 10 December 1983 after years of military junta-appointed presidents, so it was to celebrate the fifth anniversary of that, but it was cancelled at short notice.

DIAN BARTON: The first band I toured with was Cabaret Voltaire from Sheffield. We had done a few gigs with them using our PA and at The Haçienda, when they asked me to do a tour of Europe, then the USA in 1984, I think. It was a new experience, using another PA system, but I tackled it as I would my equipment, following the same procedures, making sure everything is working properly, ultimately trying to imitate the sound of my own system.

Having served my apprenticeship running a PA company from the basics gave me great insight into what makes a gig. I gained so much experience and confidence working at The Haçienda with different bands week in, week out, it allowed me to realise I could go on tour and thrive.

I progressed quickly, being asked to do more and more bands we had worked with at The Haçienda, especially supports such as James and Inspiral Carpets and some main acts like A Certain Ratio, The Fall and Marc Almond.

Eventually in 1993 Rob Gretton asked me to do New Order for a tour of the US.

I was three months pregnant but by the tour I would be six months. I told him this, but he still wanted me to do the tour, flying me to each gig with the band so I wouldn't have to travel on a tour bus. I had a fabulous time. I continued to do their sound for the next twenty-three years, travelling all over the world.

JANE ROBERTS: Andy, who has the posh voice [laughs], was the keyboard technician. Andy had the worst job because, obviously, a lot of their [New Order's] music was electronic. So he had all these amazingly complicated things to deal with. For me, I'd get there and I would have two huge speakers to set up. We'd all have these things called 'rolling risers', which are a sort of mini 'stage onstage'. A rolling riser raises the equipment, and it's easier for the band to see what they're doing. I had two massive speakers and two racks, which were basically two boxes which all the effects units went into. I had those to set up. It was like spaghetti in the back of the racks, and the keyboard set-up was very similar. Andy had about six racks and they were all joined, but it was all neat and tidy. Pete never sorted out the bass set-up, so that's one of the things I did, and that's how I learnt my job. I sorted it all out so that it was easier for both of us to deal with if anything happened onstage (and it always did because his equipment was that old, and some of it was so weird!). But things would go wrong, just cut out, and I'd be in the back, unplugging stuff and trying to patch it back. Eventually I sorted it all out and had very nice patchbays, and it was much easier. First, I'd set that equipment up and then I'd get his guitars out.

I think there were six guitars, and what he had was twins — two of the same sort. He had his favourites, and then the others were backup, basically. I'd tune those, changing strings if I needed to, and make sure everything was working. I'd get it all working and test it. Then they'd turn up, and everything would go wrong. [laughs] I think I weighed about eight stone the whole time — and I'm five foot nine, so I'm quite tall — because I was always fucking scared things were going to go wrong, so I never ate properly. It was stressful, but it was amazing fun, as well. I had (probably) the best time of my life.

DIAN BARTON: One of my most memorable experiences with New Order was at Reading Festival in 1998 when digital desks were in their infancy. The desk I used only had a few elements that could be saved on a floppy disc. We had a rehearsal with it before a few upcoming festivals and so I was taking my hired desk to these. But when I got to the first Reading Festival, the desk provided was a different version, resulting in the floppy disc not working and me having to start from scratch.

We weren't headlining so didn't get a full soundcheck, just a line check, but it was before the festival opened in the morning. I did my usual checks and everything was working as I wanted, but when we came to the actual show my VUs (main output level of the desk) were not. I asked the guy who had provided the desk to find out why, while I worked on other channels. I could see him looking down the section of the desk where it should be, down and down he went. Near the bottom of this bit was a large red button which is large and red for a reason; it means danger, and mutes the whole sound. Guess what he did . . . he pressed the big red button! I knew he was going to and was ready to hit it straight after, which I did, but the sound went off for a split second. The BBC recording engineers asked me about it afterwards but I don't think many of the crowd heard it thankfully. Brilliant gig nonetheless.

JANE ROBERTS: Stuff went wrong a lot. Pete had two racks, so he had two of each effect unit, but one was the ghost of the other. So, it had the same effects in one as in the other, and there were just a couple of things that were different. It's far too complicated to explain fully because, really, it was a pile of shit. [laughs] He had two piles of shit and I had to have it working for somebody who wasn't that technically minded. [laughs] I did really fucking well, actually. I'm quite proud of myself, how I managed to cope with it. What would happen was if one effects rack went down, you should be able to change it and the other one should work instead, the ghost. But of course it never did. *Never* did, so I'd panic, Hooky'd come round the back, and there'd just be leads flying, and then we'd stick 'em all back in, and eventually it would come back to life. We'd usually bypass a lot of stuff and it'd go straight into the amp. But his sound was really specific because of certain equipment, like an amp he liked from the 1950s . . . you couldn't get them anymore then! They were just completely obsolete. But that was his sound, so if you had to bypass all that, his sound would go. He had foot pedals he could still use to do stuff, but it wouldn't be the same.

Before we went to America, Jacko, one of the other crew guys who did a lot of the technical bits and bobs, got me in the rehearsal room and I made these new patchbays. I soldered everything, and I loved it. God, I loved that work. It was really interesting, and there was no stress because it was just me and Jacko, and everything worked. It got a lot easier after that because, instead of going into the back of things, as long as everything was plugged in and you'd checked that everything was plugged, if anything went wrong you'd just re-patch it — so much easier. But of course, if you let shit-for-brains Pete get round there, it'd be like, for fuck's sake, this isn't working again. We didn't get on at the end.

DIAN BARTON: The most exciting aspect of live sound engineering is it's never the same twice, no matter the circumstances. Every day is a new environment, every room is a challenge; even if you do two gigs with the same band in the same venue two nights running, each night has its own vibe. The most challenging times are when you can't get a 'hold' of the sound or things go wrong, making it appear you haven't had a good gig. Live sound is very subjective, you may feel you haven't done a good job but the audience love it — or the opposite may happen. Thankfully those times are few and far between and generally I am happy with the sound I produce.

BRIX SMITH: I loved the fact that Di was a woman doing sound at The Haçienda — we all did. We loved it so much we hired Di and her partner Ed to go on the road with us. So they did many, many tours with The Fall. She was one of our right-hand people. It was too rare to see women doing jobs like that — women in production jobs. I came from a bit of a theatre background, so I was really into doing lights. Before I actually joined The Fall, I used to do their lighting design. I knew how to have the lights amplify the music because when you're working with light and sound at the same time, you can really affect the vibration and the frequency of what is being absorbed by the brains and the bodies in the audience. It was really important to get those lights right, to enhance the show with light frequencies and colour. So I was super into women doing technical work, and Di was an absolute must-have because she was the best, and it made complete sense.

DIAN BARTON: As regards being female in this industry, I do not entertain sexism. I am a person before a woman and have always believed that, acting accordingly. I grew up in a family with four brothers and no sisters, my parents treating us equally, therefore have never felt intimidated by the opposite sex. I think having this attitude along with my experience enables me to compete on a level playing field. The Haçienda was also very open in its treatment of women giving high positions on merit, not gender.

This industry is very male-dominated but different in that it is an unusual and almost new profession with the people in it being more non-discriminatory.

I'm sure I have been treated differently at times, but I feel my knowledge, experience and especially my confidence has carried me through, enabling me to ignore it or show their lack of knowledge. This can be dangerous, as you need them to help, so a bit of psychology is needed to bring them back on your side, eventually making them do what you need. I have had a fantastic life, fortunate to commence my journey as the music scene took off here in Manchester and with Factory Records a springboard to greater heights.

LINDSAY ANDERSON: Di was doing work that I think people thought at the time was work men did. So seeing Di as part of the crew, lifting equipment . . . I didn't see a difference. But now, with the work I do, and looking back, I do see that gender is a factor in the industry.

For me, it's a bit of an obsession that there's not enough women in music technology. I've been involved heavily with a Brighter Sound project called Both Sides Now, talking about women in the industry and looking at why it's different in the north and the south. So back in those days of Stockholm Monsters, I didn't think of it at all, but nowadays I'm very conscious of it. I work really closely with DeliaDerbyshireDay [a Manchester-based organisation named for electronic music pioneer Delia Derbyshire], trying to address the issue in schools of women in music technology. There's still this 'what's a woman doing in music technology' idea, so even nowadays we're still having to fight that barrier.

GONNIE RIETVELD: Linear music composition software and the way the patterns are shaped on the screen look, to me, like knitting patterns — the way that knitting machines run particular patterns. Sometimes I used to joke with the guys by asking, so how's the knitting going? [laughs] If you actually look at how knitting machines operate and how they're programmed, they have a really abstract way of thinking about how patterns are actually put together. Weaving machines do it, too. So there's a certain precursor in pattern computing that's not necessarily exclusive to the female realm, but women in the domestic domain have long been active in the creative practices of knitting and weaving. There are a lot of abstractions in there. Can we call them algorithms? Whichever way, it requires an abstract way of thinking, to imagine a pattern in advance and actually program this in lines.

GILLIAN GILBERT: I think with the help of computers now, you can pretty much simulate a string orchestra, but when I first joined the band, I used to write notes about how synthesisers worked. You know, Bernard used to tell me [what he was doing] and I'd think, 'Why did you do that? You just get on a synth and start twiddling the knobs around.' That's how you basically get going and doing plugs, male and female, in and out. I used to have to wire everything up before we did the soundcheck. Now we use laptops, which is a lot easier for playing live, but in the very early days, there wasn't that technology. Bernard had started getting into technology, and Stephen with drum machines. And Martin Hannett was really into electronics. That sparked an interest, and me, Stephen and Barney used to stay behind after rehearsals and work on electronic stuff . . . that's how we got into it.

GONNIE RIETVELD: The programming of electronic music is not uniquely 'men's work'. When I think about how many men in the early eighties started to engage with that type of work when the digital technology started to become available, affordable and domesticated, the marketing of those devices seemed very much geared toward a male consumer group. If you look at music technology magazines, for example, in terms of their advertising and what they focus on, they definitely have a male user group in mind, and possibly a heterosexual one at that. And if you look at DJ magazines in the early eighties, such as *MixMag*, they used to have a page devoted to a Miss Wet T-shirt, supposedly the girlfriends of the DJs, pictured with their boobs showing through wet T-shirts. In this context, the DJ is presumed to be male and heterosexual. It's a certain pitching of assumed identities around those new music-making roles. To be honest, I would not have known about the Roland 808 drum machine or the Roland 303 bass synthesiser if it wasn't for Bernard Sumner being an avid reader of those music technology magazines and being able to recommend these to me. So, knowing a few men in the music business was quite helpful for me.

JANE ROBERTS: It was really rare for women to be working as backline technicians then, yeah. When I came to an end working in the music business, there were girls starting to work on the local crews, but you didn't always come across them back then, so it was rare.

As backline crew, you'd tend to turn up at these massive venues, and I had ways of doing things because the speakers and racks I had were huge. They weighed a ton, but I could do it, no problem. I might have been eight stone, but it was all muscle. I've always been strong. And I knew what I was doing because it was my rig, my set-up. But on maybe two occasions in America, I had somebody pushing me out of the way as I was doing something — male obviously: 'Oh, here honey. I'll do that for you. Oh, here little lady.' I was like, *fucking hell*, I'm bigger than you, you cheeky git! Eventually, everybody knew me in the industry, so nobody patronised me. If I needed help, I would ask for it. I'm not stupid. But when it's my stuff and I know what I'm doing, it's like, *don't fucking treat me like that*. And in that same venue years later, I'm getting pushed out of the way because apparently I can't do my own work because I'm 'just a woman'. And it's like, *I'll rip your fucking balls off and shove 'em down your throat, love. Would you like me to do that for you? 'Cause I'm really good at that.* It's where I learnt to be a real ballsy gal and it's also where I learnt to have a really foul mouth. I swear a lot and it's great, very empowering!

LINDA DUTTON: It was a very masculine environment. A lot of male egos whizzing around and, at times, it made things a bit uncomfortable, to be honest.

• • •

JULIA ADAMSON: In the recording studios in 1978, women didn't work in control rooms. I was one of the first female engineers employed in a recording studio.

AMBER DENKER: There were not many women doing computer graphics work then. Rebecca Allen, who I also worked with, did pioneering work on Kraftwerk music videos at the [NYIT Computer Graphics] Lab. She and I were the only women doing production at the Lab.

JULIA ADAMSON: Working in a predominantly male environment, I adopted an attitude of pretending I was a bloke. I tried to adopt a male mindset to fit in and work as a good team. Or at least study that and respect that, as working in the recording studios was what

Julia Adamson at the controls

I'd always wanted, so I wanted to do my best. I loved the job. It's still the favourite job I ever had. But you would get the odd ones who would tell some horrid jokes about women, and you'd have to just laugh along, but later on, you'd be like ... *oof.* More often than not, it was a very professional working environment, and I was treated like anyone else: expected to work the same hours, physically lift and move equipment, etc. I felt really lucky to have got the job.

AMBER DENKER: I had some experience with computer graphics and computer imaging, and was working with technology and art. Gretchen Bender approached me and asked if I wanted to work with her. She had some specific ideas that she wanted to do in music videos, which she was doing for Michael Shamberg and Factory Records ...

CAROLE LAMOND: [My involvement with Factory] was a combination of two things. Firstly, the technology, and secondly, because I was working in this job where they didn't really mind if I used all the facilities to make films for myself. I bought a Video8 camera, and the serial number was 002. [laughs] That was the first video camera that was handheld and very light. Up until then, most people, including myself, had been shooting on 35-millimetre and 16-millimetre, or the big-format video cameras, which were really unwieldy.

LAURA ISRAEL: There was such a divided world at that time between film editing and video editing, so if you knew video but had a film background, that was a pretty intense combination. I knew how to do both, which was really unusual, and I thought I could make some money editing.

JULIA ADAMSON: I was keen on becoming a sound technician, and I'd gone into Strawberry a couple of times, asking for a job — only to be told that women didn't do the sound engineering, that they didn't work *in the control room*. I got a couple of jobs in the meantime at recording studios, working as a receptionist, but always wanted to be in the control room working with sound. I'd met a couple of the sound engineers at the Strawberry interviews, and they said I was welcome to come and sit in on some sessions. Chris Nagle was one of the engineers and working the night sessions with Factory and Hannett was the newest and youngest engineer, so got the 'out of hours' jobs. He offered me to sit in on those sessions to see the control room and how it worked. He saw no reason why women shouldn't be working in that environment. When I first went in, it was John Cooper Clarke and the Invisible Girls recording, and Martin [Hannett] was working with them. I was just absolutely blown away — not just by the control room, but by the sound that was coming out of the speakers as well. I tried to go down to Strawberry as often as I could after that, just to witness the recording sessions in progress, from about 1980 on.

About 1984, I started working in the studio. We had these overnight sessions that were a cheaper rate. Factory just jumped on board with those straight away, and we were recording a good number of their releases. Those were memorable days, and we (the studio staff) met quite a few of the bands at that point. Tony would be at the studio quite a bit, chatting with the musicians, or with a journalist who he might have brought along, or a film crew. Factory always had that charismatic front person who was Tony Wilson. There were other record labels then, obviously, but Factory seems to be the one that's turned into the global icon . . . maybe that was the plan all along.

AMBER DENKER: I was totally self-taught. I have a BFA in painting. Carnegie Mellon now has a major in computer graphics, but at the time I was there, it was just graduate students in the computer science department writing some of the early 'paint' programs. I got exposure to that and started working with them. Art and science are always sort of unnaturally separated, but we saw them as connected. Computer graphics is the perfect example of synergy with those separated interests. Then I got a job in the NYIT Computer Graphics Lab. At the time, that was one of the only places doing that kind of work, and it wasn't particularly money-making. A lot of the people that went on to develop Pixar were all there, so it was a place of early computer graphic innovation.

The University of Utah lab had the original DARPA grants, which are Defense Department funding for research. They were basically building flight simulators out in Utah, and a lot of grad students were doing some of the first vector animations to train pilots. The brilliant people there, like Lance Williams, realised that this technology could transform film and video. Ed Catmull, Alvy Ray Smith and the who's who of the original people that developed the fundamentals of computer animation were all there. When the DARPA funding dried up, the chancellor of NYIT, Alexander Schure, decided to fund a research lab for computer animation. So ultimately, a lot of the guys, and a couple of gals, found themselves working at the lab at the NYIT campus on Long Island.

I wiggled my way into that lab and learnt how to use their equipment. They had a wing where they would develop commercials, like flying logos, to give exposure to the research work that was going on. They were also trying to sell systems and software to make movies, essentially. This is back when *Tron* was being made. I had access to that lab and image-making using that equipment. That's what I was sharing with Gretchen, my access and experience using that equipment, and that's what I used for the stuff I did on 'Bizarre Love Triangle'.

CAROLE LAMOND: I came from a technical background because I'd worked my way up through post-production. So basically, I got this Hi8 camera and shot the video on the little Hi8 cassettes, which you could then transfer up to U-matic. The whole thing was tape — nothing was digital — and obviously, as you transferred tape in those days, you got degradation. For The Durutti Column video, that actually added to the quality. By the time it got to VHS, it had been through about four passes. I shot on Hi8, transferred it to U-matic, edited it onto U-matic, and that was the master. I then copied it onto VHS and sent that up to Factory. I made two masters because I could do that through offline [part of the post-production process] as it was then, make two tapes exactly the same.

You know the pink bits in the black and white in the film? By today's standards, I found an extremely weird and archaic way to do effects. I discovered that by throwing the whole thing where you shouldn't throw it, I could pinpoint certain colours and then only show those colours. That was a long time before people could do it deliberately. It was basically jamming it with a screwdriver and winding it to places it shouldn't have gone, and it produced that effect. As long as I got Lloyd or somebody to wear a pink shirt, I could pick that out. That kind of effect now is absolutely commonplace, but then, it was only me doing it.

AMBER DENKER: At the Computer Graphics Lab, I had in-house unique graphic tools. I would have used programs that allowed me to manipulate data and create graphics. I could scan and paint before the world knew PhotoShop. That image, and the others I made for the New Order video, they're literally just data. But what you see in the video, Gretchen mangled intentionally. So the original images I made aren't *really* there because Gretchen massaged what I made until it became a new thing.

As an employee at the NYIT [Computer] Graphics Lab, I was able to learn those programs and use them to make the images that Gretchen edited into the video. Do you ever zoom in on an image on your computer? What Gretchen did with the images I made is kind of like that, where you're getting an image that's so pixelated. What she put into 'Bizarre Love Triangle' are images like that, in today's language, are so zoomed-in that the image no longer reads, so you're just seeing the data.

I would have handed Gretchen three-quarter-inch videotape with the images because she had these three-quarter-inch editing machines, these big, hulking machines. She'd use at least two, if not four, of them, and then she'd have her monitors set up and would work: cut, cut, cut, rewind, just grinding away with videotape. At the Lab, the whole point was that we were also capable of production just using bleeding-edge technology and could put this computer graphics onto three-quarter-inch videotape. We were handing these tapes over to advertising agencies, and they were running Super Bowl commercials on TV with it. We could even do 1-inch tape.

JULIA ADAMSON: Digital technology was gradually introduced while I was at the studio. We started getting more effects units that were digitised, and the advancement of them was really growing quickly. We got one of the first computers and audio software called C-Lab, an early version of Logic Audio programming. Then we ended up getting a digitised desk, one of the first Neve desks with flying faders. It was a fabulous desk, even though there were a couple of technical hitches with it. There's always new technology to learn with digital audio.

GONNIE RIETVELD: I have to painfully remember this: we were mixing one of our records, maybe the third one, and the guys were like, 'Oh Gonnie, could you make us a cup of tea?' And I say, 'But that's my music, and I want to be there . . .' and they go like, 'Oh don't give us any of that feminist stuff, don't be like that.' So, I think that sums up their attitude, really. It was Simon Topping and Mike Pickering doing a mix with the engineer, and me being in the kitchen making cups of tea . . . I think that summarises things. And I shared that experience once with my music technology students. There were twenty-two students, out of which three were female. The guys seemed angry: 'Oh well, that's nonsense . . . it's not like that!' And I go, 'But I'm telling you from my experience', and they're like, 'Ah, now that's just bollocks.' So, you know, it's something that seems endemic, not just in the Factory Records family, it's something that seemed permanently part of the music industry. I think when you hear women's stories about becoming sound engineers . . . there are more female engineers than there are female producers because, I guess, that's still a supportive role, comparatively. How many producers are there that are female, in this world? If you say that Madonna's a very good producer, the boys in my class would say something like, 'Yeah but that's just Madonna; she just dances, doesn't she? She always works with producers anyway . . .' So, I don't think it's typical for Factory Records as such, but it's something you hope is slowly changing. But then, sometimes you see things changing back as well.

CHAPTER 10
FACTORY ON FILM

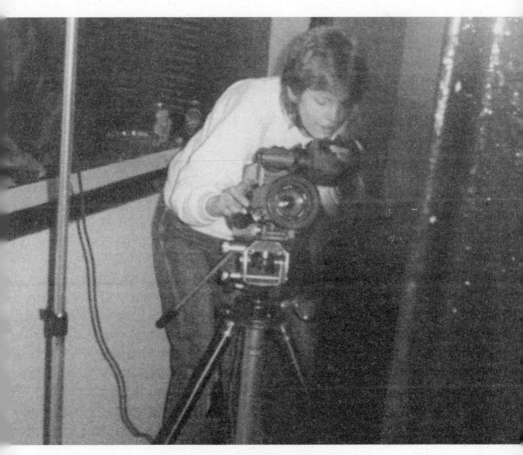

Linda Dutton behind the camera

Film and music are exquisite companions. Early on, Factory Records created IKON, a film arm that at one time was run out of a bedroom office at 86 Palatine Road. While Factory aficionados often talk of IKON, they rarely speak the name of Linda Dutton, a woman who played a key role in capturing live gigs at The Haçienda and creating Factory music videos. Speaking of music videos, Factory's frontline acts – New Order, Happy Mondays, The Durutti Column, and more – all had videos made by women: they directed, edited, produced, designed, and marketed those films that resounded both visually and aurally with viewers imbibing the Manchester scene through MTV. After Factory's bankruptcy, Carol Morley revisited the scene through experimental documentary form in *The Alcohol Years*. Collectively, these women's work reveals how the story of Factory Records is intrinsically one of sound *and* vision.

LINDA DUTTON: With IKON, it all really starts with Malcolm Whitehead, who was best friends with my husband, Harry. He was best man at the wedding, etc. Around 1977, punk started, so we started going to a club in Manchester called Rafters. I kept trying to persuade Malc to come, and eventually he did. When he comes into Rafters, we're standing across from the DJ, and Malc saw Rob Gretton, who he knew. From then, we all started going regularly to Rafters. Tony Wilson, Rob, etc. were starting Factory around that time, and included Malc, who had an interest in film. We'd helped him with things on Super 8 by that point, but everything was so expensive. We couldn't even afford a decent stills camera in those days.

When Factory started, they decided they wanted to get video equipment, and Tony asked Malc if he'd do it. I was quite in awe of Tony Wilson at the time — local TV presenter. From there, they got the equipment, and Malc was living in two rooms upstairs in my mum's attic, so all the equipment went there, and that's where he first started doing IKON. The first thing Factory wanted him to do was film Orchestral Manoeuvres in the Dark at the Hammersmith Palais. Malcolm couldn't drive — nobody could drive — so he asked me to come and drive. I guess without Malc coming into Rafters it might never have happened, so I get a brownie point for that!

BRIX SMITH: Factory had a film arm called IKON, which we were involved in. IKON did some videos for The Fall.

LINDA DUTTON: IKON was started with Claude, Malc and Tim Chambers, so I was just in the background filming the bands. I filmed Orange Juice, Simple Minds . . . all the bands that were on, really, because Rob wanted everything recorded. There were two big screens in The Haçienda, and the idea was that people who couldn't see the bands could at least watch the screens. Malc was on the main camera, and I was on the second camera. One I remember the most was Factory's 52nd Street. They were playing, and Malcolm being Malcolm decided he wasn't going to turn up. So this was the first time I had first camera. I put the camera on my shoulder. Ginger, who was manager of the club, said, 'What are we going to do? Malc's not here! What are we going to do?' This was a bit of misogyny of the day (assuming I couldn't do the job). I was stood there, and Claude said, 'She's going to do it.' So I did, and I thought I did quite a good job.

SUSAN FERGUSON: Linda (with Malcolm) videoed every live performance at The Haçienda.

SUZANNE ROBINSON: I did catering for IKON as well, which was part of early Factory and Haçienda. When they did videos on location, they would need catering, so I'd come down with a meal for the crew and obviously for whoever they were doing video shoots for. They might be in an empty warehouse, or shooting on a roof, so we'd just go to the location with trestles and take the food to them wherever they were.

ANNE LEHMAN: I started doing sales for Doublevision and IKON, which is not what I was good at, *not sales*. [laughs] Miranda was doing all of the mail order for the film arm, which was pretty much just the videos. Doublevision and IKON were both UK video. IKON was Factory's and Doublevision was Cabaret Voltaire's and Paul Smith's. It was based in the UK technically, but we were doing all of the manufacturing and distributing of those films and selling them out of New York.

LINDA DUTTON: IKON was basically to support Malcolm to make films/videos, so everybody sort of jumped in to help to do whatever needed doing. Malc would spend long nights in the bunker. Well, we call it the bunker, which was Tony's basement, where all the equipment was. We had long nights where Malc would be chain-smoking and drinking cans of beer . . . just go right through until it was done. We'd support him on that as well, which could be quite hard going.

Malcolm could also be quite secretive, so I never knew what was going on. I'm trying to turn this into a company, to do things properly, and then Malc's doing stuff completely differently. We could never pin him down to anything. That got very frustrating. In the end, that's one of the reasons I left — we had no money, and he wouldn't do things for the money. He would only do what he wanted to do. There were five of us in total, and we're all on next to nothing money-wise. But the annoying thing was that Tim, Claude and Scotty — they got some money. It was actually costing me money to go to The Haçienda, and to drive everything there, but they'd say to me, 'Oh, well, you've got a husband who can pay for you, so you don't need to get paid.' I was only given expenses. It was prevalent at the time, that sort of attitude. I got fed up with arguing. We all used to shout at each other quite a bit by that point. Even when Madonna played, they left me to do the filming. I didn't know what I was supposed to be doing, and they said, 'Who cares, she's just some dancer from New York.' It was a kind of misogyny, the idea that she was just a woman dancing and nobody knew who she was, so she wasn't important enough to be filmed. There was a lot of that sort of attitude going on at the time, the selfish attitudes. I don't want to sound bothered about it now, though; it's just how it was.

BRIX SMITH: I did the design for our IKON video with 'Eat Y'Self Fitter'. We filmed that particular video in The George, a local pub in Prestwich where Mark drank with his father and grandfather. It was literally down the hill from our flat, where our cat would follow us and wait outside the pub for us. Mark would wax lyrical about this pub before I ever got to Manchester, and I had a *really* different impression of what it was going to be like. [laughs] It was a very standard local pub, super northern, and I was a real fish out of water. I remember filming that video there and having Karl Burns in it. We made him drink this drink which looked like Guinness, but I think we might have all spat in the drink and done all kinds of awful things, like blown loogies in it and ... God only knows! He was so rock 'n' roll: he chugged it on screen, and we were just *gagging.* [laughs] I remember sitting there with, like, plastic bugs on my face for that video, too. We took a whole day to film it in that pub. It was kind of a moment.

CHRIS MATHAN: The design for the New Order video 'Pumped Full of Drugs' (FACT 177) — that's a weird story. My memory of it is this: we got the assignment, and it went on my desk. We were all a bit like, 'Pumped Full of Drugs'? ... Kind of weird, creepy even. I don't know how or why New Order came up with it. My idea, and Peter liked it, was to simulate Swiss pharmaceutical design. The Petri dish, the colours and the type made it look like a label for a pharmaceutical product. It was a tongue-in-cheek response to the title. I still have the photograph of the Petri dish.

MARGARET JAILLER: As a DOP, I was most often lighting and not camera operating, and Richard Heslop was always the camera operator on his productions. He didn't storyboard, he just created a 'happening' and then watched it down the lens — he had a very particular visual sensibility, so it would have been impossible for him to delegate camera operating to another person.

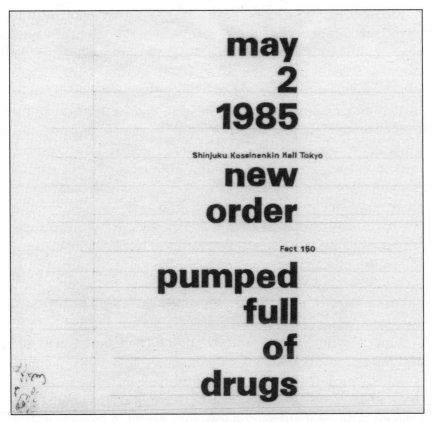

Chris Mathan's sketch for New Order's 'Pumped Full of Drugs' video

CARRIE KIRKPATRICK: I became friends with people in London that were much more involved in the art scene — Richard Heslop, especially, who was a notable artist, director and performer. I started doing some work with him, and it was through his inspiration and influence that I decided to transfer from my college to Saint Martin's. He had already left Saint Martin's, but sometimes we'd still collaborate. We knew the Grey Organisation [an artist collective] because we were on the scene, going to art openings and parties and clubs, hanging out in Soho, and various shenanigans, really. They wanted to do some filming, and a lot of that Factory IKON compilation *Fat of the Land* was clips from them, so I really had an indirect link to Factory through Richard and the Grey Organisation.

Richard Heslop included a video in that compilation we had worked on together, but I didn't really know about it at the time. My memories of it were that we did a shoot at the college, in the studio at Saint Martins, and then we did another shoot. I knew somebody that worked at a news channel and who agreed to go in after hours. We did this little shoot in that studio there in the middle of the night. She didn't really get paid enough, and it was a massive favour. I remember I was a bit frustrated that the camera work wasn't going to be more exciting, and that we weren't actually creating the art with the camera work. They wanted it very much about 'this is us just posing here like this, with cabbages on our heads'. I didn't always feel that was the most creative expression, but now looking back after all these years, it has this kind of iconic element to it, which I do really appreciate.

CAROLE LAMOND: I didn't even know my video was on a Factory IKON compilation tape!

Tony Wilson came down to London for our initial meeting, into my studio. I don't think he was expecting it would be quite a swanky outfit. I think he was expecting something a little bit more underground. We'd just had Jerry Hall in the studio, and Tony came in kind of like, 'oh my God'. I think he was expecting a bunch of students or something, and he was trying to be very 'Tony Wilson', but nobody was impressed. [laughs]

After our initial meeting, Tony left and only gave me a quick ring afterwards when it was done. That was the last time I ever heard from anybody, so I didn't even know it being shown any-where or distributed ... With The Durutti Column video ['When the World'], it was a product of just was being in the right place at the right time and having technology that nobody else had. Because with the Hi8 camera, I could do the whole thing myself. It was like having a Steadicam before the days of Steadicam. And I had the technology to edit it. I don't remember ever getting paid for it! [laughs] I got maybe 100 quid or something like that to cover basics, but I don't think Tony Wilson was known for putting his hand in his pocket if he didn't have to, so there you go. [laughs]

CARRIE KIRKPATRICK: I've got to say, we went to a big funeral a couple of years ago, of one of the guys from the Grey Organisation, Tim Burke, who unfortunately had taken his own life. It took me right back to all those years ago, and I realised how much it had always been the men who were leading in everything. It was all about the guys. Creative women were around but very much in the background. I hate to say it, but that's how it was. It was always about 'look at him' and 'look at what he's doing' and 'he's the artist'. Just to see all of those guys again at that funeral ... it really brought it home, if you know what I mean. So in terms of my involvement with it all, I feel looking back that I was very much on the peripherals. I did do a little bit of filming, but I don't know how relevant I am because I'm kind of by default in the background.

It's frustrating, actually, because when I look back, I didn't have as much confidence as I could have had. I started off with more confidence, but it just seemed like the guys got all the breaks and all the leads, and I think one begets the other. You get the opportunities, so you get more confidence. There was a general sense that everybody focused on the guys because the guys were creative and had all the talent. Nobody really paid attention to the girls.

MARGARET JAILLER: When I left film school, it wasn't possible to work in the industry unless you had union membership. It was a real struggle for me to get into the film/TV union. As a woman, I was advised by the few women I knew in the union to apply as a producer (or any of the more acceptable female roles); they advised that I would be refused membership if I applied as a DOP. So I entered as a producer/director, which would not have allowed me to work as a DOP. In the eighties and early nineties (the MTV years) I worked almost exclusively in the photography department on pop promos.

SANDY MCLEOD: I think for women, at that time when I started in the film industry in the early to mid-seventies, it was really difficult. I wanted to be a cinematographer first. I'd dropped out of college.

I THOUGHT I HEARD YOU SPEAK

I was raised in Alabama, I came to the big city and made my way. I loved photography and I knew that I had an eye, so I started learning how to load magazines. I went to the camera houses, and I started getting to know some of the cinematographers. Most of them wanted to date me, and I was like, I'm not really into that ... I really needed a job. I just really wanted to work, and I couldn't find anyone who would let me be a loader at that time. They were all like, 'You just shouldn't be schlepping magazines. It's just so wrong.' When you think about the industry in those days, it was pretty much journeyman work, passed on from father to son. It was all male. I ended up being a script supervisor because that was the only work I could get that wasn't makeup and hair as a woman at that time. It was really difficult on so many levels. Although once you got into that brotherhood, you were part of the team, and they had your back and I had their back ... it was much more complicated than just a bunch of sexist pigs working at odds with each other. And it's hard to say, being a woman from that time, whether you were complicit in ways, to where you let things slide.

CAROL MORLEY: With my film *The Alcohol Years*, the project was about feeling overlooked, but it was mostly about trying to figure out what that time had been about — for me and for others. When I was in the process of making it and getting in touch with people, the responses were generally 'that's a very narcissistic thing to do'. I never saw it as self-regarding, but as a way to unpick a musical history that was partially ignored because it was between punk and rave — at the time I made *The Alcohol Years*, that hadn't been particularly explored by many people. My initial interest was in what I didn't remember and what gets forgotten, and the people within history that get ignored, like the bartenders or the cloakroom people — people that are never asked what it was like but have a really amazing and significant point of view.

I was also fascinated by this idea of mythology, and especially the idea of mythologising young women — *The Alcohol Years* covers the time from when I was sixteen to twenty-one. I was interested in how others played into this mythology, but also in a way how I was mythologising my own life and that of others too!

A large part of what I do in my films probably has been triggered from that time in Manchester, at The Haçienda, of feeling somehow misplaced, or an outsider in that world. As a young woman, you weren't necessarily integrated into what was going on — it felt very difficult to know exactly how to be a part of it — and I so wanted to be a part of it! An insider!

LINDA DUTTON: Malc never allowed our names on any of the videos, and that was a really annoying thing. Except for The Fall — my name was on that, but I have a feeling that was probably down to Brix who would have made sure to put my name on. Otherwise, I think it was overlooked a lot, and I was very rarely mentioned anywhere.

BRIX SMITH: Working with women, in those days, women in positions of power and creativity, and in that genre, were very few and far between. I felt a camaraderie with them because it was so male-dominated and so male-heavy, these groups of stinky boys, so working with girls was like a sisterhood. Because my mother was a producer, and also in a male-dominated industry — the TV and film business — I was very aware of women that were really pushing the glass ceiling. So I would have definitely embraced Linda working for IKON, and I would have definitely made sure that she was credited as well. That would have been part of my modus operandi. So thank you, Linda, for thinking of me like that. I so appreciate it.

LINDA DUTTON: There wasn't a very typical IKON day. Usually we'd meet up in the pub around the corner first, unless it was someone special or that Factory thought was special. That would take a bit more effort than a regular band. Malc would do the main camera and I would do the second camera, and we'd try and make an edit out of it. I thought we did it really well, considering the limitations of the equipment that we had. It wasn't easy — a big camera on your shoulder and a great big battery belt slung round your waist!

CAROLE LAMOND: Because I was working for this advertising agency, I used to do quite a lot of things, and one of those was working on a film with a choreographer, Beyhan Murphy. She was married to Peter Murphy from Bauhaus. She introduced me to a chap called Lloyd Newson who ran DV8 Physical Theatre, who you see in The Durutti Column video. Because I had a Hi8 camera — they were very new to video — I made a film for them of their production entirely on Video8. I did the whole thing, shot it and edited it. Tony Wilson saw it, and he contacted Lloyd Newson of DV8 and said, 'Would you make a video for Durutti Column?' Lloyd said, 'I can't, but I know somebody.' I met Vini Reilly on the day of the shoot only. Talking today, this is only the second time I've heard the track because I made the film with DV8 as more of an artwork. The music was fitted to what we did, rather than the other way around.

It was shot in Brixton, which at the time was a run-down area of London. Lloyd and Nigel Charnock, who were co-founders of DV8, lived not very far away from where we shot. I can't remember whether I had an assistant to carry the tapes and the batteries, but it was basically just myself working with Lloyd and Nigel. There was no rehearsal. There was no script. Lloyd just said, 'Let's do this now', and I would work out how to shoot it as we were doing it, really. Vini came down and was thrust in amongst these incredibly fit and quite intimidating dance troupe. They were very, very, *very* physical. He looked absolutely terrified. [laughs] We did various things, like covering his face in plaster . . . he really just had no idea what was happening. Lloyd taught him how to move. He was shouted at quite a lot, and I think he left absolutely terrified. [laughs] Nobody paid him any attention whatsoever because Durutti Column weren't really part of the London focus musically. At least not at that point. So we shot the whole thing in a day, and then I went off and edited it to a click track, because you sort of can't do this blind. All they sent me was a drum track down from Factory.

I edited it and sent it back to Factory, and I don't think they were expecting something quite so . . . forceful, I think is the word. Tony Wilson went, 'Oh . . . we weren't quite expecting *that*.' I think they thought it was going to be a more gentle dance piece, which it really isn't. I never heard from them again!

LINDA DUTTON: We used to have to take the cameras away at the end of the night because nobody trusted leaving them at the club ... they're likely to get stolen. It was basically down to me again because nobody else could drive, so I used to transport them and the equipment back and forth from Tony's house in Didsbury, which was two or three miles away from the club. We'd just turn up there, set everything up and then probably drink too much. [laughs]

MARGARET JAILLER: The only other Factory promo that I remember working on was as DOP on Happy Mondays' 'Hallelujah' Club Mix in 1989 — it was filmed in an abandoned factory in Manchester, again, with me lighting and Richard directing and camera operating. It was co-produced by Phillip Shotton, who both Richard and I had been at film school with. I remember Tony Wilson (and his trench coat) being at the shoot for part of the day, but my overriding memory was of Shaun Ryder shamelessly belching and farting through the day.

REBECCA GOODWIN: I'm in the Happy Mondays 'Wrote for Luck' video — short dark hair, purple top, dancing with Shaun in the second half! The Bailey Brothers did that video for Factory, and they did other video work for Factory as well. They basically filmed us all having a party, and I heard that video was what got Geffen interested in the Mondays. Anyway, it was also filmed on my birthday weekend, so after we made the video, we all went to The Haçienda and had a bottle of champagne for my birthday.

LINDA DUTTON: One night Curtis Mayfield was playing at The Haçienda and I wasn't even supposed to be working that night. I said, 'Malc, I really need to do this one!' because I enjoyed it so much. I will say that Malc's hand was a bit steadier than mine for Curtis. [laughs]

NICKY CREWE: One thing I really remember about The Haçienda is the video — they had a video DJ. It was so unusual to be somewhere and to have a selection of videos, a club showing film. What I feel

I remember is a screen up above the stage with video. If you're familiar with *The Old Grey Whistle Test* and the way they used to put cartoons, animations, to a song in quite an unusual way, well, there was a bit of a sense of that at The Haçienda: juxtaposition of music with an image.

LINDA DUTTON: When John Cale was due to play at The Haçienda, they didn't want any recording to be done, but did agree to us putting a static camera on the stage just for the big screens. The DJ/VJ booth was just to the side of the stage at that time and someone decided to sit in with us to make sure that we didn't record. Claude, however, thought he would get away with connecting a hidden VHS recorder to the main U-matic recorder, but the tension in the booth soon made it obvious what he was doing and his plan was foiled. (Claude's favourite cartoon figure was Daffy Duck, and I often thought he resembled Daffy so it was quite funny for his plans to be foiled . . .)

For The Cramps, I think we'd hired a better camera, one with long distance, and the camera was up on the balcony. Malc decided he wasn't going to turn up to it, so I did it obviously and filmed the band from up on the balcony. My brother Mike was there, so I introduced him and his partner to The Cramps. They were over the moon. That was one of the best gigs I've seen and the best I've filmed. The place was absolutely packed.

There was another time when The Smiths played and they hadn't expected it to get so busy, but it was absolutely jammed. We were all actually on the stage together with the camera and with loads of people. We were having to drag people up onto the stage, throw them out the back, and then they'd let them back in at the other side.

Another good night was the gay and lesbian night on Monday night. We had the miners' strike going on in this country, and the gays and lesbians were supporting the miners, so they put the night on. Again, I think it was just me (and Tim) who were interested. We gave one of the raffle prizes — one of each of our videos. Pete Shelley played acoustic guitar, and I've got that footage on tape.

There's a story to The Pogues playing at The Haçienda. Because the crowd for The Pogues would have been quite excitable, they decided to put a fence around the stage with about three foot in front to keep the crowd back. I thought, oh, that's ideal for me with the camera. About two songs in, maybe not even that, the thing collapsed. Now I'm there with the camera, with all these people bouncing around next to me. Anyway, we didn't die. Nobody was injured. [laughs]

NICKI KEFALAS: Videos were very important in those days, so I used to go to national programmes like *The Chart Show*, or international programmes such as MTV Europe to get stuff played and on playlists. With quality shows like *120 Minutes* on MTV, it was important to get New Order and the other bands on. New Order and Factory were all over MTV, including Happy Mondays. MTV had a small office in London.

LITA HIRA: The first music video we [Stockholm Monsters] did was 'Soft Babies', and we did that in my family home where me and my brother lived. 'The Longing' we did in this pub in a place in south Manchester. I don't even like having my picture taken, so being on camera — ugh. [laughs]

The 'Soft Babies' video had all these outtakes, which was funny. We had to keep repeating everything because one of us would laugh. [laughs] I don't think we were as bad in 'The Longing'. We got through that one in about three days. But nobody knew what they were doing. We just kind of went along with it.

LINDA DUTTON: We filmed some of the ACR video 'Back to the Start', at Tony's house. The swimming pool in the video was at the YMCA building in Manchester. The pool was on the top floor and Gonnie and myself were the first women to visit, apparently. The swimmers generally swam naked, but had to wear trunks while we were there!

ANN QUIGLEY: We [Kalima] did a video for a 12-inch called 'Trickery' with Phil and Keith, who became the Bailey Brothers.

CATH CARROLL: The video for 'Moves Like You' was filmed in an old Salvation Army hostel in the East End of London. I don't know how long it had been empty but it still had a very retro institutional feel to it. The Douglas Brothers, who directed the video, brought me a straitjacket to dance in. When they first gave it to me, I thought they'd found it at the hostel.

GILLIAN GILBERT: ['The Perfect Kiss' music video] was all done in our rehearsal studio in Cheetham Hill. It was an old gas place that had no windows, so we put skylights in because otherwise it had nothing, no light. We got it because it seemed like Fort Knox. Who'd be interested? There were no windows to break, only skylights!

LINDA DUTTON: After the success of the *Video Circus* at Liverpool's Bluecoat gallery [featuring videos of Section 25, A Certain Ratio, New Order and Cabaret Voltaire] we decided to take it around the country. I can't remember how many places we showed it at, but the worst has to be in Northampton where there was only us – Malcolm, myself and my husband, Harry, a couple of people in the audience, and a security guard and his dog.

GILLIAN GILBERT: Michael Shamberg arranged for Jonathan Demme [to direct 'The Perfect Kiss'] because he'd just made the Talking Heads movie, *Stop Making Sense*. We had a Yorkshire terrier at the time called Sam, and he had one, too, so I assumed he was nice because he was also a dog lover.

SANDY MCLEOD: I got involved directing the Stanton Miranda video ['Wheels Over Indian Trails'] through Michael Shamberg. At the time, I was working a lot with Jonathan Demme, and Jonathan knew Michael. Jonathan loved music, and so did I, and we made *Stop Making Sense* together. I was looking more and more to direct. I had been producing music videos but hadn't directed any yet at that point. I remember Michael suggesting that I direct. Up to that point, I had been a script supervisor on films and had done a lot of feature films, so I had a lot of knowledge about the mechanical part of film-making. But at that time, there weren't many music videos, and I didn't really know much about the language of the music video. I met Miranda, Stanton Miranda, and she was very unusual for a performer. Jonathan and I did a music video for *Saturday Night Live* called 'Gidget Goes to Hell' with the band Suburban Lawns, and she reminded me a little bit of their lead singer, Su Tissue, who was so painfully shy that it was hard to communicate with her. Like her, Stanton Miranda was just a very shy person ... not your typical entertainer at all.

GILLIAN GILBERT: Shooting the video [for 'The Perfect Kiss'], Demme got all these old guys to do the work who'd worked on Michael Powell films, like eighty-year-olds going up the ladders and putting up lights and nets, because he wanted to use their lighting design ideas. It was quite exciting because we'd been to all the Michael Powell films and we were going to work with him − Michael Powell − at one stage. We were going to do *The Sands of Dee*. So, we met Michael, and our idea was to write some music and for him to do the video. We got as far as meeting him, but Factory said, 'We've got no money for that, I'm afraid, so you'll have to do the "World in Motion" song because that'll bring in loads of money.' Michael Powell wanted to hire helicopters and have Tilda Swinton acting in it ...

When we started recording 'World in Motion', thinking we'd do that and then get to work with Michael Powell after we'd made some money, Michael Powell died. It was really sad, but we did use his light people earlier on 'The Perfect Kiss'. Doing that video in that studio was another kind of experiment in how long we could go on with a song. I think we did it over two days, and we had to wear the exact same thing for the whole shoot. I forgot my earrings, and my dad had to come and bring them up to me because Jonathan wanted a shot of me turning up the knob on the sequencer, and my earrings would be in it because he wanted the shot from above. The idea was to make something that we could put in the cinema, to see it on a big screen, and it did go out in America like that. You can tell in the opening of the video that we're all dead embarrassed because we had a camera stuck on our face. It was very close filming, but it was fun doing it. I miss him. Shamberg was always coming up with great ideas and great artists to work with.

SANDY MCLEOD: To me, the video [for 'Wheels Over Indian Trails'] really didn't turn out that well. It was kind of a mess. It was my first endeavour, and I just kind of threw a bunch of stuff against the wall. It was kind of like that. I remember we screened it at a club, and at the time, Jonathan [Demme] and I were really good friends with Bernardo Bertolucci and his partner, Claire Peploe. They were in town and came to see it, and I remember Bernardo sort of looking at me, like 'uhhhh'. I thought, OK, he doesn't like this!

Jonathan came to the studio while I was working on it after he'd been out of town. He had no involvement in it whatsoever. It would have been useful to have had some input from him, but he wasn't there. The first words out of his mouth were, 'You really should have waited until I got back into town.' That's all he said. I thought, well, I guess I'm just a horrible fuckup and probably shouldn't be a director. Fortunately, I persevered. But it was not an auspicious start.

I had John Cale's daughter in it, a little girl then. I distorted the image, sticking those lips on her. Effects in those days were very crude. It looked ... not at all the way I envisioned it, extremely crude, which was its own look. [laughs] It was definitely an experiment, and the first music video I ever had done entirely myself, so, you know ... Sometimes you have a concept and it turns out better than you think, and sometimes you have a concept and it turns out worse than you thought. I would have to say that this was one of those examples: worse than I thought, but everyone was OK with it. It seemed like Miranda was OK with it, and Michael was OK with it, so I just went with it. It is a strange piece of work, and it looks very much of its time. It didn't transcend the moment. Let's put it that way. [laughs]

GILLIAN GILBERT: Making 'Touched by the Hand of God' was really embarrassing. [laughs] It was so embarrassing, but it was quite funny because we'd been watching MTV when we'd gone to America, and it was all White Snake, Poison, rock bands with long hair. We used to watch it continually, and we thought it'd be funny to do a send-up of it. One story goes that people actually thought we were a rock band in America. [laughs]

Michael Shamberg picked Kathryn Bigelow, and it was quite nice having a woman director. We had to wear these costumes, and we had a stylist who had to come up and do all our measurements for the costumes. She said something like, 'I've got this idea for you to have dead-woodland ethereal makeup.' So, she did this makeup and, I'm not kidding, I thought, *natural brown eyeshadow?* I'm like, I've never wanted a 'natural look' since I was fifteen! I was into punk makeup, and my dad always remembered, 'You were watching Siouxsie and the Banshees on the television, and then you and your sisters just went mad!' We'd put on loads of makeup, but just to be clear, it was just for ourselves, not for being 'pretty' or trying to be attractive to a man, but trying to be punk, wanting to be like Siouxsie Sioux. So, I said to this makeup artist, 'I've never been natural, and I've never worn brown eyeshadow, and I never will. I'm never going to be natural looking.' I told Kathryn, 'I can't look like this, I'm sorry. It's just not me.' Oh, it was *awful*, just . . . *brown*! And Kathryn said, 'Just put your own makeup on.' So, I did. I want to look punk, not horrible! [laughs] I've always done all my own makeup since 'The Perfect Kiss' video, and I did it myself in Kathryn's, too.

Anyway, we thought with this costume thing for 'Touched by the Hand of God' that we'd get somebody else to do the costumes. So, of course, the costume designer got me this corset that was too big, maybe a thirty-eight. When we had to do the choreography, I was jumping off the stage and the corset was falling down! I'm mortally embarrassed, and I thought, I'm never having anyone else do our costumes again! I saw Kathryn was wearing this jacket, a little short jacket with sleeves, and I said, 'I *have to wear your jacket* because I'm not going onstage like this.' [laughs] I got stitched back into that corset to jump off the stage. You really have to pretend to be someone else. I think we filmed it at Brixton Academy so it'd look like a concert . . . It was just a laugh, really.

GINA BIRCH: I directed music videos for New Order because I met Michael Shamberg. The Raincoats were playing at The Kitchen in New York City, and Michael was doing work for Factory in New York. I remember hanging out with him at a gig. It's funny because the first time I met him, he was wearing a white polo and black sweater, and I kept thinking he looked like a priest. [laughs] He was holy in a funny kind of way. He was very intense and very clever, but he was also very kind and gentle.

I was doing films where I'd put two cameras in the toes of my shoes. I got a really large pair of shoes from the shoemakers that hadn't been collected when they'd been repaired. I cut the toe caps off and put little cameras in there and put wires on my back that ran into cameras in my backpack. It was shot on DV cam. These were journey films, so I was making them while riding on scooters or while walking. Michael thought it'd be interesting to do something like that for a remake for a New Order video, so that's what I did for New Order's 'Crystal'.

In that video, I got a friend of mine, Simon Tyszko. Together, we were on motorbikes, whizzing through London, with just a view from the shoes. I got the idea because I heard this thing about some guy who said something about wanting to film a woman cleaning naked, and some other guy talked about putting a camera up a girl's skirt, and I thought, 'No! You're not doing that!' So in response to that, I put the cameras in the toes of the shoes, but not to look up women's skirts — in a kind of resistance to that. I took these film ideas that I felt I didn't want these men to make and applied them in slightly different ways. I was trying to take the ideas away from them.

NICKI KEFALAS: When New Order did the *Baywatch* video for 'Regret' that was Bernard's idea initially, and it started the way other ideas got started. They'd give me an idea and say, 'We want to do *this* to promote it', and I'd find a way to make it happen. I produced that *Baywatch* video, but somebody else took credit for it — probably a man! That was at the time of the London Records takeover, so it was a pretty depressing time. We went to Rome at the beginning of that campaign, and I took MTV and other TV crews out. We did lots of filming around Rome. Peter Care did the video, and I took people there to document the whole experience.

JAYNE HOUGHTON: When New Order made the video for 'Regret' in Rome, we were all on scooters, these beautiful retro Lambrettas or Vespas, charging round Rome and staying at the poshest hotel, called the Excelsior. I took David Quantick as the journalist because he's a good friend of mine, but he refused to get on the back of a scooter with me because he said it scared him. [laughs] The band was on the cover of the *NME* on those scooters, a different kind of *Roman Holiday*.

NICKI KEFALAS: Before going to Rome and the London takeover, there were many other interesting periods, but standing out in my memory right now is the 'True Faith' video with the Philippe Decouflé dancers and outfits. The band recreated it on *Top of the Pops* with the original dancers and Philippe, and then they left the costumes in our office afterwards. There are pictures somewhere of Dave and me in those outfits, being young and stupid. [laughs] We went outside to the local greasy spoon with them on and could not stop laughing!

GILLIAN GILBERT: The 'Tasty Fish' video ended up being a story about music and fashion. I think it was Rob and our financial guy who showed us a picture of a piece Issey Miyake [Japanese fashion designer and artist] had made, a corset-type piece, and asked, 'Do you want to buy it, or have a look at Issey Miyake clothes, because he could get them at cost price?' But it was like buying a piece of artwork. So, we went down to the shop and had the idea to do all of The Other Two tracks in Issey Miyake costumes since we got them at cost. We even did some interviews in Paris, and while we were there, we went to the Paris fashion show and checked out all the Issey Miyake clothes. You'd just say which of the pieces you wanted. You'd get a load of clothes like every six weeks, so it was like Christmas. It was lovely. We thought we were going to wear them for The Other Two and not for New Order, but they ended up becoming New Order clothes, too, because they were so nice.

Nicki Kefalas and Dave Harper in Philippe Decouflé designs

Anyway, I had to go on a treadmill to do the video for 'Tasty Fish' and I was being asked, 'Can you maybe do a bit of acting, maybe look a bit happier?' I said, 'No, I can't, and I don't want to do that.' A really stupid part is that they had a load of fish at the studio, and as the day went on, they were starting to disintegrate, these fish ... and *the smell*. I don't know why they had the fish there. I think they filmed the fish and used that shot on one of the backgrounds, but it was the smell of fish that I remember, so when I got asked to look happy, I just thought, 'I can't do this at all.' I think there was another shot where I had a black jacket on — not on the treadmill — and I was supposed to look 'alluring'. I don't think I pulled that off at all! [laughs]

ELIZABETH BAILEY: The 'Round & Round' video came about because of Michael Shamberg, who was basically the personal music video commissioner for New Order. He approached Paula with that 'Round & Round' video. I don't know how Michael came to know Paula, but I have a feeling he approached her because she had done that Scritti Politti video ['Perfect Way'] and those early Duran Duran videos, which used all sorts of models.

LAURA ISRAEL: Michael Shamberg met Paula Greif at the Mudd Club, and I guess Paula said, 'You should meet Laura.' The weird thing is that the first New Order video for 'Confusion' was shot by Ed Lachman — Michael got him to shoot it — and then Ed Lachman shot *Don't Blink* (the Robert Frank film) for me, so it's this great and weird connection. So many connections, and everybody was kind of learning as we went. We didn't know what we were doing, but it was really a blast. I found out recently that Lisa Rinzler, who was also cinematographer for *Don't Blink* actually shot the 'Blue Monday' footage that William Wegman directed! Also an exciting connection . . . My film *Don't Blink* is dedicated to Michael Shamberg because he actually introduced me to Robert Frank when he commissioned the video for 'Run'. He used to just pair me with directors, and I'd edit the video. That's what happened with 'Run', me and Robert Frank.

Once I moved into my studio, Paula Greif moved in across the hall, and Jane Nisselson from Virtual Beauty. All of us were there at midnight working, and Paula would be shooting things in the hallway with musicians, then Jane would do the graphics, I'd be editing, and then Michael would pop by. It was a real hotbed of creative activity.

ELIZABETH BAILEY: Paula was one of the few women directors out there at the time doing music videos. We had a very small production company, Paula Greif Inc. I met her because we both lived near Irving Place in New York near this park, and we both had dogs. We were both freelance film people — who else would be in the park in the afternoon with their dogs except artists, unemployed actors or production people waiting for their next gig? — and we became friendly. She used to do Barneys [NYC department store] commercials, and her background was as an art director. She was very much part of the whole Mudd Club scene, and eventually we formed a production company. We primarily did music videos exclusively, except we also did all the Barneys commercials.

LAURA ISRAEL: 'Blue Monday' was mainly shot on film, but it had a little bit of video in it. 'Run' had a little bit of video in it, too, and Robert said — this is one of my favourite Robert Frank quotes — and he said it during the editing of the New Order video. So there were a couple of shots on video of these guys in the audience, and I kept saying, 'These shots just don't belong with the rest of the video.' Robert said, 'You always have to leave in the shot that doesn't belong.' I was like, all right, I give up, that's obviously perfect, and I will remember that for the rest of my life. So those were the video shots in 'Run' and I wouldn't have left them in, but whatever! [laughs] 'Round & Round' was all film, and then there was '1963', which I think was on video, but you'd have to ask Gina Birch. That was right around the time where people were really switching over from film to video.

GINA BIRCH: Michael approached me about the '1963' video and said they had a budget, but New Order didn't want to appear in the video. I got this idea about baggage growing and growing and growing. We shot it in Hebden Bridge on 16-millimetre. That was a bit different for me because I don't usually shoot on 16-millimetre, it's usually Super 8 or video. I was looking for somewhere very flat, and the guy who was finding locations said, 'Let's go to Hebden Bridge!' and then of course it wasn't flat at all. [laughs] It was just around Christmas, and I remember it being all in a rush. I think that's what always happens with music videos: you don't get the go-ahead until they want it in about five days' time. It's always something like 'we're not sure if you're gonna get the job', then 'yes, you've got the job, and can you have the video done by Monday?' [laughs]

I think we had a few people in mind for the role in the video. Michael wanted to ask Tilda Swinton, but she was having some kind of operation. I found a ballet dancer who I really liked and wanted to ask, but Michael wasn't sure about her, and then we agreed on

Jane Horrocks. She plays it a little bit for laughs, which makes sense because the suitcases weren't quite what I'd hoped for, either, in terms of the baggage. That's the job of the artist — to have the dream and then be disillusioned piece by piece. [laughs] My camera man was a guy I've worked with a few times, James Welland.

ELIZABETH BAILEY: That job for 'Round & Round', honestly, it made absolutely no sense to me. Even at the time, I was kind of like, *whatever*. We were tasked with casting all these models. A very young Veronica Webb is in there, and also Elaine Irwin. This was her first hire as a model, and she was literally seventeen years old, still in high school. This was before she met John Mellencamp and wound up marrying him. I think it's interesting how culture kind of shifts and changes things. Sometimes I think about some of the videos that we did as women film-makers, and I can imagine people now watching and thinking 'they were sexist' or 'they objectified women'. The girls were young, even teenagers, and it looks like they don't have any clothes on. They all had tube tops on, of course. But we filmed it, and I think it was the first time Paula used 35-millimetre film.

PAULA GREIF: What happened is that the band wanted 'Round & Round' to look like an Andy Warhol thing. They were watching these Andy Warhol things where the camera just ran, 16-millimetre cameras. So we did that, but what we did ended up being way slicker than it should have been. We also used fancy models. I look back at it now . . . I think Veronica Webb was one of them, and Elaine Irwin. There are some really big models in there.

There was one version that was just one girl the whole time, and then another one with maybe five girls or six girls. I feel like it should have just been much more raw. If the assignment was to make it like Warhol, it should have been more raw. It was more a 'Paula and my fashion background', so it turned into a Paula thing rather than a Warhol thing. I came from Condé Nast, so that's what it turned into. Those were the girls that I knew. It wasn't, like, wacky girls off the street. Veronica was a pretty big model at that point.

ELIZABETH BAILEY: We shot it more like a photo shoot, filming these girls sitting on a stool for maybe five minutes a pop. I think we filmed about twenty girls and then picked a handful, whoever made the final edit. Then the cutaways ... you can't even tell what they are. They were colour flashes, things like a glass of milk spilling on paper, or marbles, or cutting a green apple. They were subliminal flashes. When I produced the video, part of me just thought, *I just don't know about this.*

AMBER DENKER: Gretchen was always watching TV and recording so many things, so the computer parts I did [in the 'Bizarre Love Triangle' video for New Order] are really, really small, they're these edits of literally a half a second. It was almost subliminal what she was trying to do with the imaging, and she was taking it from so many different places.

The actual computer animation I did is literally the stuff that goes by in less than one second. She's taking all these things and splicing them together to try to *ram, ram, ram* you with impulse and technology, to overwhelm your senses.

This video for 'Bizarre Love Triangle' works because of the editing. She was the first to do this kind of editing, this slicing of *boom, boom, boom.* After she did it, it gets done everywhere because you can't patent this technique. But she was the first to do this, this intense pounding through editing. That's very much what her electronic theatre was about before she edited 'Bizarre Love Triangle' and she brought that to her art. She'd run multiple television feeds at the same time, editing these images so they seemed like they were pulsating and continuously reflecting back at you what our current visual vocabulary is because of TV. That was her focus as an artist, and I think she very much brings that to the New Order video with her editing.

GRETCHEN BENDER: I think that the time limit to media-oriented artwork is an element that many media-involved artists are unwilling to confront: art as I practise it, or develop my ideas or aesthetics, has to do with a temporal limit to its meaningfulness in the culture — and that's real tough. It's hard to make art through the use of guerilla tactics, where the only constant to the style you develop is the necessity to change it. Style gets absorbed really fast by the culture, basically by absorbing the formal elements or the structure and then subverting the content. You have to make some kind of break or glitch in the media somewhere else with a different style and shove your content into it there. It's constantly having to accept the fact that your work will lose its strength. You just go on, learning to vary strategies; to recognise when to go underground and when to emerge ... Accepting the fact that your work is going to become neutralised — faster than you ever dreamt. It's a really weird feeling but it's a given, for me, at this point, so I'm just going with the given in that situation and trying to think on my feet. [Cindy Sherman interview with Gretchen Bender, *BOMB*, 1987[1]]

LAURA ISRAEL: The best editing advice — and I've read other editors saying this — is that you have to sit and watch everything. You have to have a watch party, just sit with the director. I think the first impression is going to be your impression throughout the whole editing process, so take notes! We used to use this Mitsubishi printer, a thermal printer. We used it to make boards: we'd print out all of these frames, write a little something underneath, and then put them up on the wall to become inspired by them. With all those boards up, you could see the video sort of happening by just seeing those frames. Sometimes we would go over and mess ourselves up by 'cutting' them, and then putting them back together in some way that we thought was kind of interesting — finding those abstract connections. I was really into the idea of visual humming, that you're going with certain parts of the music when you're editing. First, you'll follow the bass line, and then all of a sudden, something else will come up and you'll follow that and the rhythm.

Editing to music has always been important to me. We had this theory about turning the music off and editing just the visuals, seeing what that does, and we did that a couple of times.

So we'd talk [Alex Bingham and I] about how, sometimes, editing shouldn't go with the music so that you notice the visuals and the music becomes this other thing. Or if, by separating it, you could actually draw attention to both the music and the visuals: every once in a while, they might click and go together, and then they separate again. It can be daunting, but it's also fun to experiment, and you need to really watch everything — all the footage. I thought of the soundless editing because I did it for 'Round & Round' — the video with the girls. We purposely did that: turned the sound off, edited all the girls, and then turned the sound back up and put in the jump cuts. We actually put those jump cuts so that they didn't go with the music, to be against the grain.

GINA BIRCH: With music videos, people often want to cut to the beat and all that, but I quite like being anarchic.

•   •   •

ELIZABETH BAILEY: Soon after 'Round & Round' I started working on Elektra Records. Paula and I dissolved the production company, and I went to the music video department at Elektra.

PAULA GREIF: Looking back at it, I'd never even heard of Factory Records. My relationship was with Warner Brothers. I did all my videos for them. Was Factory Records an English label?

ELIZABETH BAILEY: My interactions with Factory itself were so limited because it was so separate — Factory in England and Elektra doing some of the US releases of Factory bands. I did go over to London to do videos with the Happy Mondays, and that was insane. But I was very independent . . . there was no one from Factory Records coming to the film shoot to tell me what to do, that sort of thing. I worked with a pair of English directors, and more often than not, I was trying to make sure that Shaun Ryder would stop disappearing to leave the set to find a dealer. That time really was at the height of their craziness, but they were fun to work with.

The terrible thing is that there just weren't a lot of women. It was really a boys' club, you know? There might have been women producers who worked on music videos for Factory Records, but you were the woman behind the man more often than not. That was what was so unusual about the production company that Paula and I had — that it was two women, and that just did not exist back then. It was a great moment in time, I have to say. Paula's music video treatments ... I'd type something up for her and she would literally give people a Polaroid. And that was it. So I'd tape it to a piece of paper and send it to the record label. Paula had a certain cachet because she really was the first person who started using Super 8 in music videos. It was very much a signature style that people copied.

LAURA ISRAEL: One thing I do want to mention, and I don't really do this that often, is that for me, back in those days, women weren't present. Now there's a lot of women editors, and it's great to see that. There were no women anywhere I went, and I have to hand it to Michael Shamberg, who didn't give a shit what other people thought and often worked with women. Otherwise that world was very male, which I never felt that uncomfortable with. If there was another woman in the room (that wasn't Paula, or another woman we'd brought), it was almost always the reception-ist. One time we had a woman video assistant at an online place, and I remember me and Paula thought, 'Cool, another woman in the room.' It was really amazing. I shouldn't have to say that, but I think you have to point that out back then. I mean, that's why it's a man's name on everything. That's why people know Peter Saville's name. Not to take any credit from him, but it's just the way the world was.

I don't think Michael worked with us *because* we were women. He just did it because he thought we had an interesting, alternate point of view. He was interested in things that were a little off the beaten path, under the radar. When I think back about it, even film school was very, very male, and I didn't feel uncomfortable in that world for some reason. But, you know, I wasn't really aware most of the time, but every once in a while, I would do a check, and there were no women except the receptionist, who quite often was very dressed up and didn't look anything like me with my T-shirt, my sneakers, my I-stayed-up-all-night attitude.

GILLIAN GILBERT: Speaking of other record companies treating women differently, it happened especially doing videos. I remember when we did 'Selfish' as The Other Two — we were on London Records then. It was an all-woman crew, the director too. The idea was a King Kong video, so they got Steve a professional gorilla suit, and I was supposed to be like Fay Wray. They had me all in pink, and it looked great. This is the thing . . . it was a big thing in those days to have an all-woman crew, and women wrote the script and everything. When we were done filming, they dressed me up in pigtails and freckles with a short dress on, and we just did it for a laugh. A guy from London Records saw the video and said, 'Why the hell do you want to look ugly in a video?' It was just a different look, I said, but he made me scrap the whole video. So we filmed a *whole video* and he was like, 'Oh no, you don't *look good* in that, so we're trashing it.' But that's never been the idea for New Order. With New Order, with Factory, it's something different. I think other record companies thought more about image than we actually did. We did arty things, and I don't think they could get their head around that at all. So that was just one of the differences — there was *never* the 'us versus them' thing at Factory. We were all treated as one big happy family.

LINDA DUTTON: In the end it was just too much . . . I'd try to do something, but I was always blocked. If I came up with an idea, it was blocked. CP Lee did a character called Lord Buckley, and that's something I would have liked to have made a film about with IKON, but my idea was blocked. So in the end, everything was kind of depressing me. The last time I was in The Haçienda, I remember seeing New Order play in the afternoon, and I walked out after that and don't think I ever went back.

I have a recent email from Tim, and he said, 'You balanced Malcolm technically with the other camera, albeit were never really allowed to do much more, despite *being* Malcolm on several occasions.'

As I say, I did try to turn IKON into more of a business, but Malc wouldn't have it. 52nd Street had moved to Philadelphia, and their record company there was pushing for a video, but Malcolm did not want to do it. They were prepared to pay good money for him to make a video promo, but he just wouldn't do it. But I will say I thoroughly enjoyed the whole thing. We all had good fun. We were all a bit anarchic, and I think some good stuff came out of it . . .

I was so lucky to have been a part of it all, and to share a stage with some amazing musicians. A lot of our (IKON) time was spent in the pub, where many meetings were conducted with various bands such as The Smiths and The Fall. Usually the Briton's Protection, which was just around the corner from the club, and became our local. Often had a drink in there before going to the club. A lot of alcohol was consumed in general. [laughs]

24 Hour Party People

A new generation of Factory Records fans came to the label through Michael Winterbottom's film *24 Hour Party People* in 2002. While the film was released after Factory had officially come to an end, Karen Jackson of Central Station Design – responsible for most of your favourite Happy Mondays sleeves – played a key design role, women like Bridget Chapman did Factory-related administrative work as the film was being made, and Lindsay Reade and other women were represented on screen. Many more women saw it as a chance to reflect on the heyday of Factory Records and, occasionally, the roles that women played at the label.

KAREN JACKSON: Michael said, 'Go on, then — do me a thirteen-second leader that will slip into the film.' So we did the leader, but in a moment of madness we decided to stick our necks out! We put together a costly four-minute main titles pitch — to the Happy Mondays track '24 Hour Party People' — knowing full well there was a big chance we were wasting our time . . . We thought it should be an art piece — hand-painted, organic, human, emotive. We just believed that when they saw it, they'd change their minds! . . . Also because we were partly responsible for creating the aesthetic and colour palette of the time — working on the film was a case of rejuvenating and recontextualizing the style we'd become recognised for. [Lola Landekic interview, *Art of the Title*, 2014[1]]

BRIDGET CHAPMAN: With regards to the filming of *24 Hour Party People*, I would say this: things were always a bit chaotic and surreal at Factory, but this took it to another level. I'd leave an office where Tony was flouncing around in sunglasses and a big black coat, and come out onto the street to find Steve Coogan, flouncing around in sunglasses and a big black coat, while being followed by a camera crew. When I saw the film after it was finished, I thought Coogan had really captured some of Tony's anarchic energy. It was an uncannily accurate portrayal.

LINDSAY READE: That film, *24 Hour Party People*, is another example of ways women are portrayed and remembered. There's the idea that women are the nurturers, they're the mothers, but then they also get inveigled into playing a sex role. When Tony came round with the film script which had me having sex with eight men in succession — and one of them was Vini Reilly, for God's sake — I said, 'Tony, look, I've never sued you before, but I'm going to sue you this time if you go ahead with this.' So he said, 'Well, we'll just have to have you having sex with someone you did have sex with, then.' I said, 'Why do I have to have sex with anybody in this film?' But I guess I had to have sex with somebody because otherwise there wouldn't have been any sex in the first half of the film. [laughs]

CAROL MORLEY: When it came out, I was asked to review Michael Winterbottom's *24 Hour Party People*, which I thought was fantastic. But I also thought the film overlooked women because there were hardly any women's stories that were known about at that time. I mean, I hardly knew many stories of women that had contributed to the times!

LINDSAY READE: For *24 Hour Party People*, I wanted to be listed as a co-founder. They wouldn't do it, and I said, 'Well, all right, you won't do it, but it was our money that started Factory.' The film-makers came back with, 'No, no, no. It was Tony's money.' Sorry, we were married — it was *our* money.

LAURA ISRAEL: When we went to the premiere for *24 Hour Party People*, Moby was DJing in New York. For some reason, nobody really got up at first to dance except Michael, Miranda, me and Alex. We just ran onto the dance floor, gone crazy. [laughs]

REBECCA GOODWIN: When *24 Hour Party People* was made, I was pregnant again. It was absolutely brilliant, and I can say that definitely because I was compos mentis since I was pregnant! We went into the film set — and keep in mind that nobody had got to say goodbye to The Haçienda — and they'd made this *fantastic* re-creation. You went in and it was truly like you were *there*: that same picture in reception of Tony Wilson, and then my friend Rachel, who used to work on the cloakroom, was *in the cloakroom*! And then I walked round and Ang was where she'd normally stand at the bar. Then I go in the lighting box, and I have a little chat with the same lighting guys who would have been there when I was working there. *Everyone's in the same place that they'd normally be*. The only thing that was a bit weird was the toilet — there was no toilet. [laughs] But other than that, everyone was there in exactly the place they were supposed to be. Jon da Silva, Mike Pickering, Graeme Park, Dave Haslam. So it was a way for all of us to say goodbye, to mark the end when we hadn't got to otherwise.

CAROL MORLEY: Around the time when I was making *The Alcohol Years*, I went to see Tony Wilson at the Factory office about setting up an interview with me and him, and I remember the receptionist was Natalie Curtis. It was when *24 Hour Party People* was in the early stages (I remember Tony going, 'It will never happen, never come about'!). Natalie was talking about how strange it was that she had met her 'dad' as in the actor (Sean Harris) that was going to play her dad. I never forgot that — going into some version of Factory, seeing Tony Wilson after what felt like a very long time, and seeing Natalie Curtis at the desk as receptionist. I was so weirded out by the whole thing, I got an eye twitch!

CHAPTER 11

MANAGEMENT AND PROMOTION

Jayne Houghton and Nicki Kefalas

Few jobs were more important to the success of Factory than the management and promotion of the artists – a role played by women from the label's earliest days until the present. Martine McDonagh did PR and managed James, Lindsay Reade managed 52nd Street, Jane Roberts was tour manager for Revenge, and Liz Naylor did promo work for New Order. Rebecca Boulton manages New Order (taking on the job following long-time manager Rob Gretton's death), and Nicki Kefalas and Jayne Houghton were Factory PR women extraordinaire. They are trailblazers and innovators in critical roles traditionally occupied by men.

REBECCA BOULTON: I graduated in summer of 1984, and then I worked with Kevin [Cummins] in 1985. At that point, I really didn't know what I wanted to do, and I was hunting around for a proper job. I spent some time at home and I learnt how to type. But just by chance, Rob and Lesley were at an opening of a restaurant where somebody I worked with behind the bar at The Haçienda worked and was a friend of theirs. We were all there, and we were chatting away, and I said that I was thinking about leaving Manchester and that I needed a job. Rob was like, 'Well, I need somebody to help me out ... do you want to do that?' And then that was it, really. After that, I just started working for him. I literally just worked in his house, giving him a bit of help answering the phone, making notes for him, telling him where he needed to be ... just general basic office admin. That was in June 1986.

I had sort of run into New Order a little bit at that point, but didn't know them at all. Obviously I knew who they were. They came to The Haçienda all the time, and I'd spoken to them or served them. But I do remember that when I started working for Rob, he took me to a rehearsal space they had in Cheetham Hill, a rough part of Manchester (or it definitely was, and I think it still is, really). They had a rehearsal space there, and I remember really vividly that he took me to meet them, and said, 'Right, this is Rebecca, and she's gonna help us out', and it was like, 'All right, OK, hello', and that was it, really.

MARTINE MCDONAGH: Brenda Kelly and I travelled up to Manchester to see James at The Haçienda on 13 February 1985. Pro-Motion was working James's second single on Factory and Brenda had arranged a meeting at Palatine Road the next day to see if we could work other Factory releases. As far as I know, they hadn't used external PR before, but I'm pretty sure they knew Liz and Pat [Naylor], who were from Manchester. I went for a walk before the meeting and bumped into Alan Erasmus, who was out jogging. A few minutes later, he came back the other way. He'd been to the baker and bought me a Valentine's biscuit! I don't remember much about the meeting — I would almost certainly have left all the talking up to Brenda, who, unlike me, was a brilliant salesperson — but we got a call soon after to say they wanted to work with us, so that was quite a coup.

JANE SAVIDGE: When James signed to Factory Records, the label had just released 'Blue Monday' (FAC 73) and *Power, Corruption & Lies* (FACT 75) so what was anyone really meant to make of their *Jimone* EP (FAC 78) in September '83? Obviously, a whole year passed until *James II* came out, and *Village Fire* was a compilation of both EPs, but the writing had been on the wall ever since Tony Wilson offered the band an album deal — when he first saw them live at The Haçienda — and they turned him down in favour of a three-track EP.

MARTINE MCDONAGH: I started managing James in '85, so I would have been in Manchester on 13 February 1985. That night at The Haçienda was the first time I'd seen James play, and was also my first time at The Haçienda. I was very obviously struck by the performance, but I was never a great clubber, so I wasn't particularly overwhelmed by that experience. I had been to Manchester before and not liked it, so there were all these complicated feelings about being in Manchester and excitement about working with the band.

I mean, I really liked James at that point — they were fantastic. With Factory, I'd never been a big fan of the label for its own sake, so I wasn't in awe. To me, it was just another meeting, but they were an interesting bunch of people.

NICKI KEFALAS: When I moved to the UK, I really wanted to work in the music industry. I was sort of thinking at the time that if it didn't work out, I'd move back to the States and get involved in film because I loved film as much as music. I guess because I love music and film so much I thought I should work in those fields, not realising how hard I'd have to work! [laughs] I moved to London in June '84, and I started working with Scott Piering who was a radio promotions person and The Smiths' manager. I did that for about six months — it was my first job in the UK. I met him through the sister of a close friend, and he just said, 'OK, start tomorrow!' My primary job was buying cigarettes for him. [laughs] He was American as well, and he was the first interesting radio promotions person. He wasn't gimmicky and old-school. Scott was very intelligent and very into the same music as I was. At some point in 1985, Scott lost The Smiths' management, and he went back to the States for a sabbatical. He did eventually come back, but I couldn't hang about and wait because I needed to earn money, so I got a job at Rough Trade.

At Rough Trade, I did the equivalent of a paid internship. I'd turn up every day, and they'd tell me what to do in the different departments — accounts, royalties, international licensing. I did about six months of work there, and I worked in every department. While I was there, I met Dave Harper, who was doing press for Factory, and he told me they were looking for a radio promotions person. Dave used to come into Rough Trade because he was doing work for another label distributed through Rough Trade. So I applied for the job at Factory.

GILLIAN GILBERT: Nicki from Out Promotion — she was in on that, you know, from the early days, and it was unusual to have a woman doing that work.

JAYNE HOUGHTON: When I was very young, I photographed Joy Division. Later on, I photographed New Order, and then I was sent to photograph Happy Mondays in 1989 at a little club in Birmingham. I was sick of being a photographer, but I was still doing live stuff for the *NME* when I got sent to photograph the Mondays. I was talking to Jeff Barrett, who'd just become press officer at Factory and Jeff was looking for an assistant. He said something like, 'God, Jayne, you know everyone . . . you know all the bands, you do all the rock parties in London, you work with all the journalists and magazine people . . . do you want a job as my assistant?' I said, 'Yeah', and within a year, he wanted to set up Heavenly Records. It was a busy office, and we were working with the likes of Andy Weatherall and The Chemical Brothers, and Jeff put out the first single by Manic Street Preachers.

MARTINE MCDONAGH: The PR came first. At that time, James were about to go on tour with The Smiths, so to get to know them a bit better, I went out to a few shows, and I got on very well with them. They called me up one day and asked if I'd be their manager. I'd always said, having worked with managers in PR, that there's no way I'd ever do that job, but I think I was just ready to do something new. I'd been working in London for quite a while. I'd been a manager and area manager for a chain of record shops called Our Price Records, which gave me some insight into how the industry worked at a marketing and retail level, which labels released what, etc. and the difference between the indie and corporate sectors. I'd done lots of business management stuff, so I thought, well, maybe it could be fun. I really liked the band, too. So, I did it! Then, after a little while, I moved up to Manchester because it felt important to be where the band were.

NICKI KEFALAS: I was interviewed for the radio and TV PR director job by all three founding members in different ways back in October 1985. Tony did a traditional interview. Alan Erasmus turned up at my flat late one night, unexpected, and asked if he could sleep on the couch of my shared flat, and he had to borrow a belt for a business meeting the next day to wear with his suit he brought down in a bag. That was all very surreal with Alan, but I never felt threatened. Then Rob 'interviewed' me on the night his son Benedict was born. It involved going out on a bender with him and various people, including Hurricane Higgins, in a pool hall in Hulme. I stayed over at Rob and Lesley's that night and had a terrible hangover the next day, of course. I think I was the favourite candidate at that stage, to have been invited on the 'wetting the baby's head' night of celebrations.

Nowadays, I think it'd be much more complicated, but back then, it was basically if you were in the right group of people, you could get somewhere. Somehow, I gravitated toward the right people who were interested in the same things as me.

MARTINE MCDONAGH: We were a very small company of four women who were put together by a woman called Brenda Kelly, and I was the last to come in. We did it because there were very few people doing PR for independent labels. Because we were based in Rough Trade's offices, our remit was to offer a PR service for independent labels who otherwise wouldn't have any promotion, particularly at radio. But we had to be selective and couldn't work for nothing and many of the small labels didn't have any budget for PR.

Liz Naylor was involved as well, and she did press. She'd worked at the magazine *City Fun* in Manchester, so Liz and Pat, her sister, did the press side of things. Brenda did national and London, which was mainly John Peel, Andy Kershaw, etc., radio, and I did regional radio. On national radio, there weren't many DJs who played that kind of music. Regional radio had a lot of indie shows because it was all non-needle time — they didn't pay to play that music, which obviously also meant no royalties for the artists or labels, but hopefully the promotion led to more sales. I remember working on ACR, but I wasn't there very long because I went off to manage James. It was mainly Brenda who dealt with Rob Gretton and Tony Wilson.

LINDSAY READE: I think it was the bass player of 52nd Street who initially asked me to manage the band, with me being based in the Factory office probably. But the very day after Tony sacked me, that same person rang me up to say, 'You're sacked as our manager.' That was pretty hurtful, except I said, 'Well, hold on a minute. There's five people in the band, you're just one. I'll hold a meeting.' In the end it was three against two to stay with me, which is why they left Factory with me and eventually went to Virgin/Ten Records. The bass player left and we replaced him. So actually, that period when I managed them while they were at Factory wasn't that long lived, compared to the five years and three albums after we left. It always struck me as ironic that the last record they made with me at Factory was called 'Can't Afford (To Let You Go)'.

MARTINE MCDONAGH: Being on tour with James was a lot of fun. We travelled in this really old ... RV, I guess you'd call it. A big kind of camper van called Katie who was very, *very* old. Katie B, actually — the car registration was KTB. Amazingly, Katie kept going but did break down sometimes, and we used to take it in turns to drive. Jimmy was the bass player, and his wife, Jenny, co-managed the band with me in the beginning. Jenny's mum used to make these amazing vegan cakes for us. It was a very big, happy family, really, in those days.

James had their first *NME* cover on that tour thanks to Liz, so it was a really exciting time for the band. They were picking up great press from The Smiths tour, so there was a lot of interest in them from major labels.

James were still on Factory at that point and the band wanted to move on. So we started to take meetings. It was all quite quick actually. We signed a deal with Sire on 11 November 1985, and we started recording in January '86 with Lenny Kaye. Factory really were not happy that the band was talking to other labels. Of course, the band had no contract with Factory because Factory didn't really do contracts. Tony Wilson really thought it was my fault they wanted to leave when, in fact, the band had made it clear to me from the start that was what they wanted. I remember one meeting in the van — in Katie the van — in Rusholme, where all the curry houses are or were. We were outside a curry house in Rusholme, in Katie with Alan Erasmus and Tony Wilson. On the one hand they were kind of saying, 'Well, you're free to do whatever you want', but on the other hand they were also saying, 'We really want you to stay with Factory.' It was kind of a funny discussion. The band were very clear that they wanted to move on from Factory, so it happened.

JANE SAVIDGE: This has always been the James way — *they always want to change us* — and that's what makes James so special. However, when James intimated publicly — at a much later date — that they'd signed with Sire (or left Factory, feel free to pick your own series of events) because they thought Factory were 'purely image-based', the move surely hid other partial truths. Back then, James was an even more loosely affiliated collection of individual spirits than they are now, and I suspect that their ever-changing line-up and sound would have sent most record companies/organisational bodies into a tail-spin/frenzy of despair. In retrospect, Factory could have been the perfect long-term fit for James — as could Rough Trade, another label they spent some time with — but the truth of the matter is that James had this *big sound* and no real image anyway — they still don't, hurrah, etc. — so something had to give.

MARTINE MCDONAGH: James were ambitious, they wanted to be huge, and they felt that Factory wouldn't get behind that particularly, or that they wouldn't be able to facilitate that. There was definitely nothing personal against anyone at Factory and they were very proud to have been on the label. James were just very, *very* ambitious and wanted to be with a more influential label. I don't think they ever regretted leaving Factory. I certainly never heard anyone say they did. They were really grateful to Factory for having picked them up and sent them on their way, but I think they thought they had reached the limit of what they could achieve with Factory.

NICKI KEFALAS: Factory was my first proper job, so I didn't realise life wasn't like that everywhere. I thought everything was always going to be that interesting, and that everyone would be that intelligent and strange. [laughs] Nothing has been like that since. I really enjoy the people I work with now, but nothing is like

Factory. They pushed the envelope in every direction, and they perhaps weren't the best business people, but I don't think they were as bad as everyone says. [laughs] They survived for quite a while and did well. It all fell apart at the end, really.

JAYNE HOUGHTON: The whole thing was like a big, dysfunctional family — Factory as a whole. Yeah. Everyone looked out for each other, and obviously it got hideously messy towards the end when it all started going wrong. Coming through it, and having been part of the New Order family for thirty years, I didn't realise until much later how special and privileged that was. I suddenly became a PR after I'd been a photographer. I always felt very heard, loved and encouraged. Whatever mad ideas and schemes, and plans for stories and articles and trips — everything was a blank canvas of opportunity. There were no constraints.

NICKI KEFALAS: It was October '85 when I started at Out. Dave was already calling himself Out Promotion, which is odd for a press officer, but I think the name was there, and he'd started maybe three months before I came on. I joined, and we got an instantly cool reputation somehow. By the time I wanted to change the name, it was too late. [laughs] Once you're established, you don't want to change the name. I talked to some colleagues about it and they said, 'You can't change the name ... you're getting "mentions" as the coolest PR company in books, you can't change it!' [laughs] So I figured I'd stick with it. Out was basically a couple of phones and some letterhead. We then splashed out on two desks, a filing cabinet and an old-style typewriter. After I got the Factory account, I started working with other labels over the next couple of years — 4AD, Creation, and Factory Benelux and Les Disques du Crépuscule ... it was very full-on, and I was doing it all myself. Dave got offered a job at BMG in 1987, so he went to do that. When Dave left, I got an assistant and that was life-changing.

CAROL MORLEY: I think we got Nicki Kefalas to manage our band, TOT! Well, we tried to! I think she did agree, along with Dave, her colleague at their Factory promotions company in London.

NICKI KEFALAS: My office was in Clerkenwell, and I had to travel everywhere in London as the radio and TV outlets were very spread out, and it was a lot of work, especially when I had vinyl or was lugging Betamax tapes. There were no fax machines so I would write and type up press releases and have to send them on motorbikes to places, so I was always running around making physical packages and sending them off on couriers. It's kind of insane to think of this now with scanning, email and digital music all being sent instantly via my laptop. [laughs] I'd take 12-inch vinyl to people, and I've got scoliosis, so I would get back pain. I was really skinny then, size 8 UK, so to carry all the stuff around was a challenge. By the time I was in my thirties, I got an assistant as I could not carry fifty 12-inch records up to the stations without my back suffering. But I used to do all that stuff on my own. I look back at pictures of myself then, and I look so tired. [laughs] Nobody really cared about 'self-care' then. [laughs]

We got the FAC 161 catalogue number because Tony really rated us and thought we did a great job. We didn't ask for it. It was *bestowed upon us* [laughs], and we were really honoured. I remember Tony came down to our office — he used to just turn up quite often. Our office was in a really cool little building at 83 Clerkenwell Road. We were the first ones in there, and then Creation moved in and a couple of other music companies followed. It was a vibey place, so Tony liked to pop over spontaneously when he was at Granada. He'd show up with ideas: 'I've decided we're going to do *this*', or 'I've decided I'm going to do *that*.' He called up one day to check we were in and if he could pop over, and when he arrived, he told us he'd decided to give us a FAC number — FAC 161. We were thrilled because it [seemed connected to] The Haçienda number, FAC 51.

JANE ROBERTS: Obviously, I went into tour managing as well because I tour-managed Revenge, which I loved. That was my sort of pressure.

JAYNE HOUGHTON: Back in the day, labels had lots of money. Factory didn't, but they thought they did. [laughs] So they'd send us on trips, and my job would be to take journalists on trips to cover the Factory bands. The first big press trip I went on was to Rio, for the Rock in Rio festival, for Happy Mondays. The journalists I took over were doing a cover feature for the *NME* written by James Brown, who was deputy editor, with photos by Kevin Cummins, our photographer friend. I also took over Dave Hogan, who was a paparazzi who worked for the *Sun*, and Piers Morgan, who was the pop column writer of the *Sun* back then. Talk about being thrown into the deep end. It was carnage, it was absolutely mad. [laughs]

The angle for Piers Morgan's piece in the *Sun*, which was tabloidy, meant we all went to Ronnie Biggs's house on the hill in Rio for a barbecue, which was crazy. It was bonkers. It was like something out of *Goodfellas* or *Scarface*, or both of those things mixed together. If we weren't all partying, I probably would have found it quite scary. Apart from Rowetta, I was the only woman.

The whole touring party and the band missed the flight home and had to stay another few days, which obviously cost Factory a fortune. At this point, I was tagging along as the only woman. We went to a club where the guests were just blokes, and the only other women there were women who would entertain Western men. Shaun Ryder credits himself with saving my life there because I didn't read the room at all. I liked to think I was a real streetwise northern lass, but in fact I was not. I'd gone to the loo and got followed by two really scary women who thought I was a Dutch prostitute encroaching on their turf, and I wasn't welcome. There were knives, and it became a crazy, scary situation where they wanted to slit my throat. Shaun and his security whisked me out and got me safely back to the hotel. With hindsight, Shaun probably did save my life that night. These war stories of life on the road ... deep learning on the job. [laughs] I think that's the best way to learn to do it.

NICKI KEFALAS: There was no typical day of work doing music PR for Factory. Sometimes Tony would be down in London as he was working as a presenter for Granada, and if Tony was down for the day, he would often take us to some posh restaurant, we'd meet people we never expected to meet, and you never knew what was going to happen. [laughs] If there was a New Order single out, I'd need to go to the radio stations — actually taking tracks in with physical vinyl records, and physical CDs. Back then, it was checking transcripts in lobbies to see what got played, hanging out with John Peel who became a friend, and lots of shows and film premieres. It was constant activity, and it's not like that any more so much. Now it's much more of a desk job. Sometimes I was in the office writing press releases and packing up records all day too. We used to write our own press releases, but press officers do that now. The whole job was much more creative in those days.

MARTINE MCDONAGH: I can't speak for all managers, but certainly in my case, I had some creative input that made a difference to the band's career. I'd occasionally come up with a line for a song, a lyric. There was one James song in particular where they were really struggling to find a chorus. I came up with something and they used it, but I never got credit for that. It was never a big hit or anything, but I did come up with the hook for the song What For'. I also designed a lot of the T-shirts and set the whole merchandising company up, which was what kept the band afloat financially for quite a while. We did merchandise for lots of other bands, too, but credit always went to the band.

NICKI KEFALAS: I worked on the *Technique* campaign relentlessly, but I didn't go to Ibiza. I was too busy doing actual work, but it was really fun to work on that record. *Technique* was such a groundbreaking record that it also promoted itself to an extent. It was always so rewarding working with Factory because I loved the music and all the visual and promotional items were beautiful and high quality. For *Technique* Tony decided to make statues — the 'Little Lewey' for 'Round & Round' — so I had like twenty of those to give to people, and they're still on a few people's desks when I go to radio station meetings.

I was very involved in Factory promotions. We would have bi-weekly meetings in Manchester at the weekends and hash out plans for campaigns with Tony, Tracey, Tina and sometimes Alan or others would be there. Vini Reilly from Durutti Column lived downstairs from the Factory office in Palatine Road and would sometimes come up to join us for a cup of tea or glass of wine afterwards. Tony was their manager, of course.

CATH CARROLL: When I went to write for *NME*, I'd been hanging around quite a bit with Vini Reilly and also Bruce Mitchell from Durutti Column. Bruce was the one who gave the *NME* editor, Neil Spencer, a copy of *City Fun*. It was the copy with the 'Normal Person's Guide to the Gay Hankie' code inside and we'd folded a coloured table napkin inside each copy so our readers could join in. Vini was a fan of *City Fun*, especially the bits that made fun of his poetic haircut. Vini is just a person who will not be replicated, not ever. He's someone who could sit there for an hour without saying anything and it wouldn't be awkward.

CAROL MORLEY: Bruce Mitchell did manage our band TOT, so he must have believed in me/us! And Vini Reilly (as you can see from *The Alcohol Years*) was a true believer in me as something! So I guess the point is, we were all of us living under a patriarchal system where women globally on the music scene/cultural scene were marginalised in some way, because that's how things were, but within that there were men who were supportive of women as artists. I was very happy when Cath Carroll was signed to Factory — a Manchester friend and someone I totally looked up to — so I guess I don't want to sound too 'them and us'! We women refused to be left to disappear! It was complicated. But histories are always skewed male because possibly men are better, and more free, to mythologise themselves and those they choose around them. But I definitely think *The Alcohol Years* was a corrective to that!

CATH CARROLL: I do remember my first front-page feature for *NME*, and oddly enough it was New Order. They sent me up there to interview them, and I was quite nervous going back to Manchester. They were in a studio. I was surprised that they actually wanted to talk to me after all the snarky stuff that we'd written with *City Fun*. I think they were always very grounded people throughout, and Manchester owes them such a lot, because they made money that definitely got invested into the community and into some other fortunate Factory artists. For me, my memory of New Order is always just a measure of grace that they let me in and were exactly who you'd think of them as. I think Rob Gretton was there as well, because it just wouldn't be the same without Rob.

JAYNE HOUGHTON: The *Big Issue* in the UK asked if they could do a cover feature on New Order. People would write about them without ever needing to interview them, but you gotta do it occasionally, and obviously this was such a good cause, so we said yes. They asked if Jeremy Vine could be the journalist to do the interview because he was a massive fan of Joy Division and New Order. At the time, Jeremy Vine wasn't quite as famous as he is now, and he was known for being a political journalist. But as a massive fan, we said yeah, that'd be brilliant. He went out partying with us and went to another after-party with Hooky, and he just got broken. [laughs] If I remember rightly, he could not do his day job the next day . . . he really immersed himself in the New Order

Jayne Houghton with New Order in Los Angeles

lifestyle for the night. [laughs] That's what happens when you pick a journalist who isn't a music journalist. They want to hang out with the band, and, well . . . He's still a fan, I believe. [laughs]

NICKI KEFALAS: Rob was really into the idea of 'mystery' with New Order, and he promoted the idea that they didn't really give interviews. Compared to bands like U2, who were *constantly* talking. [laughs] Ian McCulloch from the Bunnymen used to make fun of Bono for being like a goat running on top of the speakers, constantly available for any interview, while New Order band members were seen as very cool and detached. They didn't really do any of that on purpose . . . they just didn't like doing interviews, and it worked in their favour.

JAYNE HOUGHTON: New Order didn't need to do interviews: everyone wanted to write about them anyway. They weren't huge fans of doing interviews, so my job was to get journalists who became friends of the band; David Quantick became a good friend of the band and wrote sleeve notes. David has got a very dry, acerbic way of writing and just knew how to get brilliant copy out of the band. Of course, the more comfortable your artists are with a journalist and the more comfortable your artists are with a photographer, the better the material will be. I brought Miranda Sawyer out to Fuji Rocks festival in Japan to do a feature on New Order, and she became a close and trusted journalist who was in our camp. It was the same with photographers — we'd always choose photographers that we knew and liked: Kevin, obviously, and others. It's about trust rather than control. You want to pick a team that the band trusts where there's mutual respect. That's especially important when you have a band like New Order that doesn't like doing press. So it's not so much editorial approval from the band as much as a sort of collaboration, and that shows in the articles or photographs.

REBECCA BOULTON: I remember that New Order came into Kevin's studio because they needed some photos for something. They all came in on a Friday, late afternoon Friday or early Friday evening. There's quite a nice photo he did with everybody crouching down and Rob standing up really tall. I remember it being funny. Every-one was having a laugh ... it was really cheerful. He knew them, of course, so it was a bit like a matey thing. I can't remember what the shoot was for, but I can still visualise the photos. I don't think it lasted very long at all because they didn't really want to be there very long. They'd been rehearsing during the day, and they were just going to do some photos on the way home.

LIZ NAYLOR: I liked Rob a lot. He was perverse — and *not* in a horrible, creepy way. When I moved to London, I was doing some promotion, and Factory were looking for somebody to do promo on 'The Perfect Kiss' and *Low-Life*. It was between me and a guy called Dave Harper, who's a really great, well-known professional PR person. Dave had gone up to Manchester and done a campaign presentation to Rob. I turned up at Rob's house after smoking some dope (and I didn't really smoke dope), was sick on the carpet, and told him that I thought I didn't really like 'The Perfect Kiss' much. I passed out and he got me in a cab home, him and Lesley. Of course, I got the job. [laughs] Rob Gretton had that northern perversity, and he was always sympathetic towards *City Fun*, the plucky underdog.

GONNIE RIETVELD: I felt that Rob really supported the women of Factory. I really have to underline that: it's Rob who was always very supportive. I don't think he ever read anything to do with feminism as such. It was just because he was a genuinely nice person, and he was very much like a dad to everyone. So in his dad sort of role, however naughty and cheeky he might come over in pictures, and in anecdotes and everything, nevertheless, people say, 'Oh, he was like my dad' (which, ironically, you could say, is rather patriarchal).

ANN QUIGLEY: I loved Rob Gretton, too. I thought Rob was such a special person. His influence at the start — he was pulling a lot of the strings on all of us. If he liked you, he made sure that he got you where you were supposed to be going.

NICKI KEFALAS: Often, Rob would come up with some great idea and change our original plans.

JAYNE HOUGHTON: Working with New Order on 'World in Motion' in 1990 . . . I remember sitting in Manchester in a Chinese restaurant in Chinatown with the band, Nicki, Rob and Rebecca, planning where they could make a video for *Top of the Pops*. They were going to be on an American tour, and I can't remember, but it could even have been me who said the best place would be on the set of *Baywatch* in Los Angeles, but I don't want to take credit for that. [laughs] It came to be a thing, and that's what we did. We were in Los Angeles and got David Hasselhoff involved, so the band filmed on the sand on the *Baywatch* sets. We had a few crazy days in LA, driving around in convertibles, having this mad, crazy time. I wasn't working as a photographer then, but I still took photographs of the band, and a newspaper ran one of my photos of New Order stood with David Hasselhoff on the beach.

REBECCA BOULTON: Rob died in May 1999, but for a large part of 1998 I hadn't worked in the office because my eldest daughter was born in June of '98, so I didn't go in. I still did a few things but didn't work from there. Rob was really great. He was a bit like, 'obviously we're going to need you, so we'll just carry on paying you in full'. It was none of this maternity pay or anything, just 'we'll carry on paying you in full, we're not expecting you to do anything, unless we really need something'. So I thought, that sounds fair, great.

In early January, I went back into the office and started working, and at that stage, Rob had become busy with a few other issues to do with The Haçienda, so I was pretty busy with New Order. They had really only just started working together again (they'd had a bit of a break between '93 and '98), so I was pretty busy. By that stage, obviously, I knew them really well, and we got on great. Then Rob died in May, and it was a real shock. Really, really upsetting to everybody. He was just so young. Now that I'm fifty-eight, I think, *oh my God, he was only forty-six when he died*. That's just . . . incredible to me now.

LIZ NAYLOR: The thing I've come to appreciate about New Order is this Rob-ness, being quite sceptical. On the whole, they're quite good at taking the piss out of themselves, not taking themselves too seriously. By the time I was doing promo for 'The Perfect Kiss' and *Low-Life*, the industry around New Order took itself very seriously. I had to go to Trevor Key and Peter Saville's studio while they talked to me about the sleeve. I just thought, 'Why the hell are they telling me about the fucking sleeve?' I just didn't understand how you were supposed to take that kind of stuff seriously — because it's art? So they took me through the studio and talked me through the concept, and when I got it out to the music press, I treated it with as much respect as I'd treat a March Violets 12-inch or any old stuff that came through. I didn't really understand the reverence around it, so I can't say that I did a very good job on the promotion, but it was exactly what Rob wanted. I think, tactically, he wanted to take that music biz pomp out of it because that's what he was personally uncomfortable with. So I did a good job in terms of Rob Gretton's master plan for a low-key promo, which I'm extremely proud of. [laughs]

NICKI KEFALAS: I worked closely with Tracey. I was on the phone with her for hours every day, trying to sort everything out. [laughs] Tina was always so busy, probably doing the equivalent of three jobs, like we all were, so I got connected with Tracey. I'd also organise the acetates through Tracey, so I did more than just promo. I'd send parts to Sue at Mayking, who I still work with — she is now one of the owners of One Little Independent, Björk's label. Sue would make the acetates and test pressings, and then I would collect them and send them out for radio and TV purposes.

I also worked very closely with Rob, who was always a real team player, like a football coach. And later on I worked with Rebecca when she took over, and I still work closely with Rebecca and New Order today. All of it was *fun*, a job that consisted of a lot of relentless twenty-four-hours-a-day hard work, but not really like a normal job, because it was also fun and exciting!

REBECCA BOULTON: We were all really upset [after Rob's death], but we knew something would have to happen. Andy Robinson, who was their [New Order's] tour manager, came to me and said, 'Why don't we see if they want us to do it, manage them?' And I was like, 'Yeah, I suppose so', because even if they didn't, I knew I was going to have to do a lot of stuff to help hand everything over to somebody. So, together we decided to propose that we'd take over from Rob. We said, 'Look, we could do this, and we think we'd be pretty good at it, we know what's going on.' And they were like, 'Well, OK, we'll have a meeting.' They did, and they came back ... not unanimously, but a majority definitely wanted that. I get on really well with Gillian, obviously, and she said they didn't want somebody just waltzing in and trying to do something different. I don't think she actually said it, but I think she felt it was a bit of a family thing, really, and that it seemed obvious Andy and I would do it. So it felt natural. I didn't particularly feel that, all of a sudden, there was all this new stuff that I had to learn, or responsibilities I had to take on, because it was just a bit more of the same thing I'd always done, but I'd be ultimately responsible for all of it now. So, weirdly, it wasn't a big deal. It was quite a lot to sort out, but that was all practical stuff, and I'm quite good at that.

A lot of the way the music industry was changing at that time I had been in charge of dealing with anyway, so it was just more of an extension of my work. That's not to say Rob wouldn't have done it, but he had somebody else to do it, so he didn't do it. Please don't think that was a reflection of his abilities — it wasn't. It just happened that he had me to do that, so I was already doing it anyway. It was a period of change, and a lot of income streams were changing. Everything needed to be a little bit less ... freestyle, shall we say. We were on a major record company, we were a bit more organised, and we did start bringing in some different elements. We brought on board a live agent, and that's worked really well for us. I took over doing a lot of work making sure that income streams and international rights were being handled.

NICKI KEFALAS: Overall, promoting artists was a much more cre-ative job in those days, and Factory artists and the various teams were hyper creative, so there was always some interesting idea to work on and make happen. So every day of my job was quite different from the last.

I worked way too hard, never had holidays, and I travelled for work quite a bit to the States and Europe, and I didn't take a proper holiday until 1989. I worked flat out for about five years. I got paid quite well back then, considering. The music industry pays quite badly now unless you are at the very top, but Factory acknowledged that I was doing a great job. It was great music and interesting times culturally, so I was lucky to be part of it all.

REBECCA BOULTON: Rob was brilliant, and he had vision, but administration wasn't necessarily his forte. So a shift towards a more organised approach — especially since people were getting older and more conscious of their income streams — made sense. Don't forget that when New Order started, people were just happy to be going out playing live, making a bit of money. But they were moving into middle age and wanted to ensure that things were done properly. They've had a really rough time with The Haçienda and Factory going bankrupt. They had not been given what they should have had because of those bankruptcies, so they were very keen not to repeat those mistakes, but the music industry was also changing quite a lot at that time. Record sales were declining, and have continued to decline, but other forms of income have increased significantly.

JAYNE HOUGHTON: Proportionally, if you look at every Factory success versus every dismal, cash-haemorrhaging failure, it's a win-win every time.

NICKI KEFALAS: Dave did the original design for Out, and then it was redesigned by me when he left at some point. I think I did it for our tenth anniversary, a star in a circle. Rebecca gave me a graphic designer's contact. It might have been Central Station, but I can't remember. I've used that design ever since then, but I've changed the colour slightly for feng shui reasons. Out has now been running for [more than] thirty-eight years and is going strong!

REBECCA BOULTON: I'm really good friends with Nicki at Out — oh, she's great! I've worked with her *a lot*. God, we've been on so many promotion days together, or *Top of the Pops* ... Multiple, *multiple* meetings with her where she's taking care of her side of it. Right from the first time I met her, which must have been a long time ago, we've been really good friends ever since then, actually.

NICKI KEFALAS: I had my hair shaved with pink streaks in my hair back then, so I wasn't super feminine ... I wasn't trying to look sexy. Sometimes I'd take people out for dinner, though, and I'd have hands on knees under the table from old radio producers, and that was always quite creepy. That was unfortunately kind of normal back then, and you had to learn to fend it off without upsetting their egos. I really hope no one has to put up with that in these more aware times!

MARTINE MCDONAGH: There weren't many women managers around at the time I was managing James. There was Gail Colson, who was very successful. Other than that, I rarely came across any others. I remember once at a big arena gig we did — it might have been at Manchester G-MEX, or a venue of that size — I'd been out in the arena and needed to get backstage to sort something out, but security wouldn't let me through even though I was wearing a laminate with my name, photo and MANAGER written on it. They insisted on fetching one of the (male, obviously) road crew to vouch for me. That was not uncommon, that kind of scenario, and I'd even get it from people I spoke to on the phone. I often received letters — in those days it was mostly letters — addressed to Martin McDonagh, never Martine, even from people I'd met or spoken to on the phone. In so many ways, women were persona non grata and it didn't seem to compute that a successful band could be managed by a woman.

At one point, we employed an American manager when the band was starting to do quite well in the States. I remember being at a meeting or a gig or something with him, and an important industry person came up. He introduced me as Martine. He didn't say I was the band's manager. The implication was that I was his assistant or someone who happened to be standing next to him, nothing to do with the band.

REBECCA BOULTON: I find it really interesting that in labels most of the senior staff are men. There are always exceptions. We're with Universal Music Publishing, and obviously the worldwide head is a woman, but that's quite unusual. If you work outside the industry a little bit — management is an area that works outside it, because you're going into those places, but you're not working in them — it's much easier. Back when I started, there was a bit of a perception that being aggressive was seen as good management — shouting at people and getting your way. But that seems to have died off, and people don't really like that any more. People want to get on with the job, and they realise shouting at people doesn't get you more money because the budgets are there regardless. You're not gonna get more just because you shout. So that has gone away quite a lot, and with it some of the assumptions about males or females in management. I don't really see that sexism particularly, but have I been lucky? Possibly.

MARTINE MCDONAGH: I was always very mindful of the fact that — and this is very cynical — maybe the reason Tim was in a relationship with me was to try to have greater influence over management decisions. So, I was very careful to be democratic, to make sure that everyone had a say and that I wasn't just there as Tim's mouthpiece. I made great steps to avoid that, but I can't really claim to know how the others perceived it.

NICKI KEFALAS: I remember there was a guy who was doing the same job as me, and he said to me once, 'You're only succeeding at this job because you're an attractive woman.' I was quite shocked at the jealousy, and I don't even know how I responded to him, but it was shocking that he just assumed I wasn't good at my job. I don't think I was conventionally attractive, very Greek-looking with a big nose and skinny. [laughs] I think Factory, to their credit, hired me because I didn't have self-limiting beliefs, and many people did. There were people who thought indie music was a fringe thing and that it should only show up on indie charts. Most independent things didn't get airplay or much press coverage. I think Dave and I were the ones who turned that around. Scott Piering did 'Blue Monday', and obviously he did quite well with that! But then he stopped working with New Order to become The Smiths manager. Factory decided to finally get their own promotions director, which was when I got hired.

MARTINE MCDONAGH: I think the music industry is really misogynistic, and I don't know how it's got this far without its own 'Me Too' scenario blowing up. Maybe it's on the cusp. Every now and again something comes up and I think, here we go, here we go, and then nothing comes of it. Certainly, at the time when I was working with James, record companies were mostly run by white men with very few women around. Women would be in the sales department basically — so PR and international licensing. But in any kind of so-called glamorous role, like the A&R department, there were never women. Actually, there *was* a woman in A&R at Phonogram, but she never got any credit for anything. She was the person who arranged all the studio time and negotiated the deals with studios and producers. Men would get executive producer credits and financial bonuses for doing nothing.

NICKI KEFALAS: Factory were . . . sexist in their own way, by which I mean there was a lot of masculine energy. They did not hire me because I was a woman, or make decisions not to hire someone because they were a woman, not like that. But as I'm sure others can say, too, women didn't get credit in the same way. I'm talking about Tracey and Tina, who really did all the work while Tony swanned around the world. There's a thought of 'oh, that's the way it was back then', but that's not good, so let's correct that.

MARTINE MCDONAGH: Someone — a journalist I think — contacted me after Tony Wilson died to ask if I knew Wilson had said some quite nasty things about me in print and if I wanted to respond. I hadn't been aware of it and didn't see the point in getting into a spat with someone who was no longer around. But it was upsetting because I always thought we got on OK . . . I knew he wasn't happy that James left Factory, and I knew he kind of blamed that on me a bit, but I didn't realise he held on to that.

LIZ NAYLOR: I kind of feel a bit like you shouldn't speak ill of the dead, but my basic take on Tony is that he was a bully, and that's a bit uncomfortable. He was very much a big fish, a big man in Manchester, and I think responded really badly to our little fanzine occasionally saying Factory are a bit shit, or 'Who do they think they are?' The relationship with Rob Gretton was very different, so it wasn't Factory per se for *City Fun*. It was Tony who we just thought was an insufferable, pompous bore. I can remember late '79, Tony drove me around Manchester, in his ridiculous car, monologuing at me about Le Corbusier. I had no fucking idea who this guy was, so I'm just like, whatever. But it was a monologue, right? You could either go 'wow, that's really amazing' or not. It was always a bit of a testy relationship with Tony. When Joy Division played the Osborne Club and Tony announced it as a benefit for *City Fun*, that was a sarcastic thing. I can't even remember if we ever got any money for it, but it felt like a slap.

CAROL MORLEY: Liz would always say that Tony Wilson, the Factory owner, was like the mill owner and we were all just workers. [laughs] It was extraordinary to have someone like Tony Wilson in your midst because he was so fiercely intelligent. He believed in scenes and thought about how scenes are created always through a place, which is why he created The Haçienda. But as a woman, I don't think you were taken seriously — it felt as if your artistic aspirations weren't as important as, say, the way you looked.

BRIDGET CHAPMAN: Tony liked chaos. He never ever liked it when things were running smoothly. He liked a bit of conflict, and if things were running smoothly, he would always drop sort of mental bombs into the situation to disrupt things. I'm not sure that I could live like that permanently, but he made things happen. He really did make things happen.

MARTINE MCDONAGH: With Wilson, it was all about him. He took credit for everything, but Alan and Rob Gretton weren't like that. And Wilson didn't just take credit for the women's hard work. I heard him tell people he was the Happy Mondays' manager, but he never was — Nathan McGough was. I don't think he was a bad person. I think he just had a very strong sense of his own superiority, especially with that whole Mister Manchester thing. There's a lot of mythology, a lot of mythmaking in Manchester about Factory and Tony Wilson and all of that — a lot of it created by him. But it's great that Manchester has so much pride in its culture, and Factory did release some really amazing bands: Happy Mondays were fantastic, A Certain Ratio I loved, New Order, obviously Joy Division. What a roster! So of course there was going to be some mythology around the Factory bands, and I think Tony Wilson really encouraged that kind of thinking. It might sound like I didn't like him — I did.

JAYNE HOUGHTON: Tony was such a massive, larger-than-life character who obviously adopted legendary status. So in a way, nearly everybody, men and women, were supporting cast to the star of the show. And that's mostly how it was, really. But with Factory Records, the perception was that it was a very male-dominated company. You've got Rob Gretton managing New Order, Nathan McGough managing the Mondays, and most of the bands were male. That's how everyone sees it, but that's not the whole story, right? There are women in bands that might just look like male bands. Obviously Gillian's done it with New Order, and after New Order, the Mondays were the next biggest Factory band, where Rowetta was the only female in a male band.

REBECCA BOULTON: There was one instance where we [New Order] were in Paris, and we happened to be there at the same time Warner's had all the heads of A&R from the different departments worldwide there having a meeting. Quite a scene of people, obviously, and they were having this social dinner. They booked out this restaurant and invited us as sort of 'special guests' at the time. It's like, 'Oh wow, you're in town' and all of the 'everybody loves

New Order' sort of thing. They asked us to be guests at the dinner. We were like yeah, yeah, great we'll come, no problem. We went, and we all sat down, and it was actually a very nice evening. But I remember for about half an hour at the start, in this enormous room full of people, I thought, I'm actually the only woman in this room, *the only woman in this room*. Gillian wasn't there because she had taken a bit of a break. I sat next to Bernard and said, 'You know what, look around, I'm the only woman here.' And he was like, 'Oh my God, that's ridiculous.' That wasn't sexism directed at me, but I still thought, is this really right?

MARTINE MCDONAGH: In Mark Kurlansky's book *1968*, there's a fantastic first-hand account of a woman, Suzanne Goldberg, a leader in the Free Speech Movement, who was deeply involved in the protests in Chicago that year. She talked about how she'd suggest something and everybody would just ignore it. Then, ten minutes later, a guy would suggest the same thing and everyone would say, 'Oh, that's the best idea I ever heard.' I couldn't begin to count the number of times that happened to me as a manager, and I remember reading her quote and thinking, 'Oh my God, it's not just me that had this experience.' I used to think maybe it was my voice, or it was something about me. I'd think, is it the pitch of my voice and they can't hear it? Then I read that and I realised that's the female experience.

So while there was a lot to enjoy about music, that world and that period of my life, it was also extremely frustrating. And it could be miserable at times, absolutely miserable. While the guys in James all would claim to be feminist and 'right on' and all of that, I don't think their perception was quite in line with mine, really. [laughs] That's often the case — to not actually have any sense of how their own behaviour fits into those theories, those ideas, that they'd like to have about themselves.

NICKI KEFALAS: Maybe as an American, I never felt limited by being a woman. I didn't have a sense of the class system in England, or the sexism there. I really felt at the time like I could do anything, and maybe I should have been aware that others thought I'd be limited because I was a woman. As an American woman coming from a working-class family, I never felt less than, and if I wanted to do something I was allowed to do it. If I wanted to go to England, I knew I could do it, as long as I was able to save the money, which I did with several jobs I worked at through high school and university. When I came to London in '84, it was only supposed to be a vacation, but I stayed. [laughs] I was never afraid of taking risks and was very ambitious back then ...

REBECCA BOULTON: Constantly, until fairly recently, there's a sense of women working on the margins. All the time. For example, I've never dealt with a female head of department. They exist, don't get me wrong. They do, but it's rare. It's generally men. I still find that promoters are much more interested in talking to Andy than me. There's always a general sense that he's the one making the decisions, and that he's more important than me. A lot of the time it doesn't bother me particularly because when we're on tour, I'm really busy. So I really don't want to sit and talk to promoters anyway, or hear all their stories about this band or that band — I don't have time for it. But I suppose I could be bothered, but now I'm in a position where I don't have to prove myself or justify anything, so I *really don't care*. If that's what they want to think, fine. The people that I work with directly are all very supportive and very respectful, and that's always been true.

NICKI KEFALAS: I also arrived at the right time, and got swept up in the upward trajectory of Factory. It was all very electric. Everyone involved really felt like anything could happen. If anyone had a good idea, it could become reality. When Factory fell apart and I was working with London-based labels and other European labels, it was more business as usual. None of those labels focused purely on creativity as Factory had. With Factory, we all worked our asses off, but it was pure synergy. I have to say that now the labels I work with are very creative again, but much more based on reality and budgets than Factory ever was. But I suppose that's why they are all healthy and viable businesses!

REBECCA BOULTON: I don't think there's many of us that would suggest that we are the visionary ones, but what we would say is that we absolutely made sure, or tried to make sure, that the best was done with those visions that could be done. And I think for me, that's how I see my role now: to direct the visions of the past and current and future in their best and most commercial way possible, without detracting from the vision.

MARTINE MCDONAGH: Maybe there are more women around now in the music industry . . . I don't know. I stayed in the music industry until quite recently, just doing bits and pieces. I managed another band after James, Fujiya & Miyagi, who were absolutely lovely. They were the antithesis of James, so that was a good, positive, corrective, shall we say, experience. But I wouldn't recommend it to another woman, really, not until men's attitudes change. I do think things are changing, but slowly.

Wrangling
the Mondays

The Happy Mondays photographed by Jayne Houghton

The task of managing the Happy Mondays more often resembled wrangling (in the American Old West, outlaw sense). For those women charged with overseeing Shaun and Bez, the job often required patience, planning, and sheer grit. But for the most part, their stories are hilarious. With these recollections, the women who wrangled the Mondays cement the Factory mythology – all the stories are true! – as they reflect on their experiences with humour and levity.

JAYNE HOUGHTON: Working with the Mondays was a different thing entirely. That was literally shambles. Absolute shambles, completely bonkers. How it all came together *ever*, I have no idea . . .

God, doing press for the Mondays was very, very different from doing press for New Order. It was like herding sheep, doing the Mondays. Miranda Sawyer was writing for *Select* magazine, and we flew out to New York and got put in the Paramount Hotel because the Mondays were going to be doing some press there. We were there three days before we'd even seen them. It's one thing going up to Manchester and having to wait a few hours for them, but it's another thing entirely being flown across to New York and waiting days. In theory, it sounds great, right? It's like you're on holiday. But of course, on the other hand . . . While we're waiting for them to do photos, somebody said to me, 'Shaun shaved all his hair off. He just shaved all his hair off.' Right, absolutely great, of course he did. We didn't know where they were, we're all waiting for hours, and then a really big flash car pulled up outside the hotel we were staying in. It had blacked-out windows and I thought, *finally they're here.* One of the windows in this car was half down, and I remember running out and seeing this stubbly shaved head, just the top of it. I thought, 'Right! Shaun!' So I went up to the car and shouted in it, 'Where the fuck have you been!' The rest of the window wound down and it was Sinéad O'Connor. God, and then what do you say? It's not gonna sound OK to say, 'I'm terribly sorry. I thought you were Shaun Ryder!' [laughs]

ANGIE CASSIDY: The Happy Mondays actually came to America to do a tour when I was living in New York, and I was tasked to sort of look after them while they were there. It was absolutely insane. It would have been set up through Anne [Lehman]. The Mondays were ... dangerous. Not to others, but to themselves. They thought they didn't need anybody looking after them, but *they did*.

TRACEY DONNELLY: Joy Division and New Order were my favourite Factory bands, but Happy Mondays came to the label right around the time I did, so I got to work with them from the start. When I left in 1990, they had their first *Top of the Pops*, so I felt like I saw something through from start to finish. I was probably more involved with the Mondays than anyone else. I got sent to Ibiza with them, London ... Ibiza was crazy, but London was crazier! [laughs]

JAYNE HOUGHTON: [Factory thought] *Yes Please!* would be an album that was best recorded in the crack capital on the other side of the world? Really? You're going to send Shaun to Barbados? We still had to do press around the album's release because, obviously, it did come out, but the stories of Shaun and nothing coming together as Chris Frantz and Tina Weymouth were hoping ... They must have thought, *What's happening?* The expenses for Factory were extraordinary, especially when you've had two Talking Heads for production.

I didn't go over there, but everything seemed to be falling apart, and everyone came back with all these horror stories. Shaun was struggling to write any lyrics, so I hear they deposited him in some shack with literally no money and no phone or anything somewhere on the island. I don't know that they literally locked him up, but they put him with his notepad in this shack to go write lyrics. The next morning, they're all taking breakfast on the veranda of the main house and see some Rasta kid wandering on the beach, wearing all of Shaun's clothes and his jewellery. Shaun had managed to score by selling his clothes. Nathan and the band went to get him and he's sitting in this little shack, bollock-naked because he'd sold everything. I can just picture it, but it all might be just another Mondays myth. [laughs]

CHRIS MATHAN: When Happy Mondays came to New York, they landed at Newark Airport, New Jersey. Ruth Polsky picked them up and the first thing the band wanted was to get high. They weren't even permitted to bring their instruments to the US to play the gig at the Limelight Club on 6th Avenue. How she managed them is beyond me.

JAYNE HOUGHTON: Nobody had the ability to control the Mondays and it was bonkers, it was chaos. But behind all of that, morally, they were gentlemen, they were chivalrous, and they were trustworthy. They were decent, solid people. They obviously weren't trustworthy when you say, 'I'm going to be meeting you at two o'clock in the Paramount Hotel', and they said, 'Yes, we'll meet you then.' But that's not what a moral compass is, and the moral compass is ultimately what's important. They always, always had your back. Whatever insane situations we would find ourselves in, they were very protective, very decent, and there was a really tight bond. No matter what state they were in, as a woman, you always felt safe. Yes, it's bonkers and chaos, but not in a way that you didn't trust them morally. Aside from Ro, there were only a handful of women around them for all those years, and I knew I could trust them where it counted.

TINA SIMMONS: There's a video clip with Granada TV, and I was interviewed for it. I had very short, spiky hair then, so you can recognise me in the video. Those were the days! [laughs] I said we didn't need to advertise or promote Happy Mondays because they promoted themselves, so over the top. You almost didn't even have to employ promoters to promote Happy Mondays because everybody wanted to know what crazy thing they were doing next.

ELIZABETH BAILEY: The Happy Mondays video [I produced] was for 'Step On'. For me, oftentimes, working with bands and being a woman video commissioner was where it felt like people were dismissive or sexist. But with the Happy Mondays, they weren't really engaged in terms of picking the music or the video treatment. Shaun was Shaun, and Bez was ... whatever it is that he was, a dancer? They were funny, but drugs were really an issue.

With Shaun, we were literally filming at a soundstage in London. Monty Whitebloom and Andy Delaney of Big TV! were directing, and Big TV! always had kind of very elaborate sets. They'd previously done a New Order music video for 'State of the Nation'. Invariably, we were always running into overtime and shooting until four o'clock in the morning. It was always that kind of a scene with them, although they were super talented. But Shaun Ryder would literally disappear. It's like, *he's the lead singer.* [laughs] So we'd have to stop filming, and I'd have to say, 'All right, where did he go? What happened?' I was literally out walking through London trying to find him. It was impossible to corral them, Shaun and Bez, and they certainly weren't going to listen to me in terms of someone telling them what to do. There was very little I could do to control them. But the video was great, and it was a big success on MTV.

Even back then, considering what people spend now on videos, the budgets were huge. I think the Happy Mondays video was maybe $200,000, and that was 1990. So it was a big deal when Shaun disappeared on this $200,000 music video set. Everyone was sitting around at two in the morning wondering, you know, where the lead singer was. [laughs]

JAYNE HOUGHTON: The thing about the Mondays is that they were honest. They never had PR training — with them, there's no such thing. They had me — their PR — but you couldn't ever coach or guide on what is OK to come out of their mouths and what definitely *is not.* With the Mondays, what you see is what you get, and it was really refreshing. Certain publications were not right for covering the Mondays. [laughs] I remember *Jackie* magazine, which was a real squeaky clean, younger-girls' magazine, sent a journalist to Factory to do an interview with Shaun, and he just didn't turn up, and didn't turn up, and didn't turn up. He was staying at a mate's flat nearby and eventually shows up, and this young girl from *Jackie* is really starry-eyed and obviously new to the job. We'd been there a minute and he said, 'I'm starving, I want to get some food. Let's go back to the flat.' This girl's clearly thinking, 'Wow, it'll be a bit of a glimpse into a rock star's life.' We come back to this flat and he disappears. I started to feel a bit anxious. So he disappears, then comes back out, and I say to the *Jackie* girl that he won't be long. He's got some tinfoil in his hand and the girl asks me, 'What's he doing?' I remember I said, 'Oh, well, he's really hungry. He's just going to make himself a jacket potato.' [laughs] How gullible! [laughs] Seriously, though, it wouldn't have been appropriate to discuss what he was actually doing.

MELANIE WILKINSON: The event for G-MEX stands out in my memory, which was when Tony Wilson had an issue with the person who was running the event for the Happy Mondays and New Order. It was a big, massive weekender kind of thing. Me and Pauline got approached: 'Do you think you can do it?' We looked at each other and went, 'Yeah, c'mon, let's do it!' We managed to get an event together, get all the food, get it staffed, and go around and get all the supplies we needed. We'd never had that much money in our bond bags. I remember being solidly awake for something like seventy-two hours. I was just running on adrenaline. We got free champagne on the last night, backstage listening to the next Happy Mondays song that nobody had heard yet. The Happy Mondays were very simple eaters: steak and chips, and steak and chips, and steak and chips. [laughs]

NICKI KEFALAS: When New Order were recording *Brotherhood* in London, Dave and I would go nightclubbing with them. We often went to Taboo, which was Leigh Bowery's legendary club, and Café de Paris and others. And I went to the infamous wrap party at Peter Gabriel's studio. Happy Mondays had just been signed and were there giving everyone pills. Ecstasy had just arrived in the UK at this time, I think. As everyone knows, it became a massive club drug a few years later. I'm always the first one to go off to bed, so I left around two or so and slept in one of the studio bedrooms. The party went on until 7 a.m. and the next morning, I found out they blamed Dave Harper for axing a urinal off the wall in the men's toilets, but I'm sure he didn't do it.

JAYNE HOUGHTON: I've got some bonkers photos of Shaun Ryder in the shower [laughs] . . . dripping wet, wearing an *NME* T-shirt. The *NME* produced this logo T-shirt and asked if I'd get Shaun to model it — they'd occasionally get some big names to model the shirts because it would help them shift a bit of merch. So after a very big night out, Shaun decided it was a good idea to jump in the bath and stand in the shower, pretending to adopt some pinup-boy poses, which obviously was not a good look for him. [laughs]

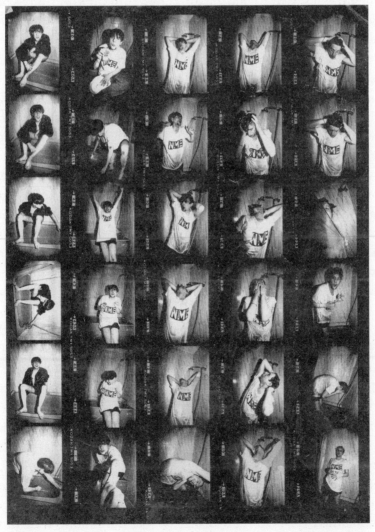

Shaun Ryder in the shower, photographed by Jayne Houghton for *NME*

CORINNE DREWERY: ACR let us [Swing Out Sister] share their rehearsal room in Manchester at The Boardwalk. There was the venue upstairs and then the rehearsal room downstairs, and there was also a pool table. I can't play pool really, but while I was just waiting for Andy to finish rehearsing with ACR, I used to go swimming at the YMCA or play pool with anyone who came in. I bumped into Shaun Ryder at Tony Wilson's funeral and said, 'Good to finally meet you.' He looked at me and said, 'You fucking know me! You used to play fucking pool with me every day at The Boardwalk!' [laughs] I didn't know that the boys I was playing pool with were to become the Happy Mondays. He said to Andy, 'And it's me who's supposed to be the fucking drug-addled lunatic — she can't even remember me!'

JAYNE HOUGHTON: In the early days of the Mondays I was having to think on my feet a lot. It became a well-documented thing, the Mondays' lifestyle. Of course, all the journalists loved it because they could live their lives vicariously through this mad bunch of working-class, rough-and-ready northerners. So all the music journalists — the more middle class and pompous and pretentious the better — adored them and wanted to be in their slipstream, even for a short time. They thought this is what rock 'n' roll was meant to be like . . .

The Mondays were constantly welcoming journalists in, and there weren't inner sanctums or anything like that. It was like some sort of touring Victorian circus freak show, going on the road with them and the sort of people who'd surround the band and would be always hanging around. Everyone was welcome, and it was absolute chaos, you know? It was like herding sheep — but feral sheep.

CHAPTER 12

ART AND DESIGN

Factory/IKON poster designed by Chris Mathan

Masterful design is, quite rightly, at the heart of any Factory Records story. Art made the label. Yet so few existing narratives emphasise the creative vision and artistic works of women. Women are rarely recognised or spoken of among Factory collectors and aficionados, yet they were partners and innovators at design firms. Chris Mathan was a partner at Peter Saville Associates (PSA), the design firm that became synonymous with Factory, and Karen Jackson co-founded Central Station Design. Ann Quigley's paintings appeared on ACR sleeves, while she did additional design work for her own records. Jackie Williams, an animator by day and spouse of Bruce Mitchell of The Durutti Column, painted rhythmic watercolours for some of the band's best-loved albums. Meanwhile, in architectural design, Sandra Douglas co-designed The Haçienda with Ben Kelly. At Ben Kelly Design, she went on to contribute to plans for Dry 201 and Factory's Charles Street office along with Elena Massucco. Kelly originally met Douglas and Massucco as design students at Kingston Polytechnic (now Kingston University), where Kelly is now a professor in interior design. Sandra Douglas died in 2010, but her design work still speaks powerfully.

ANN QUIGLEY: The Factory at the Russell Club opened in, maybe, June 1978. Around that time, I was going to what could be called a discotheque (called Devilles), and me and my friend got to know two boys there. One was Peter Saville and the other was Barry Adamson (who would later be in Magazine and the Bad Seeds). One drunken night, Peter Saville came back to my house so he could look at my portfolio — I was applying to art school, and I wanted to know what people thought of my work. So, all I knew was that he went to Manchester art school. I knew nothing else about him. He came back and it's something like three in the morning, and we sat on my mum's horrible, swirly, patchy carpet.

We've got my portfolio out and Peter's got all my pictures, and he seemed to like my work. The following night, I went round to his flat and, lo and behold, that yellow poster was on the desk, piled high — a lot of copies of the yellow poster for FAC 1. And I suddenly realised that he was the artist that had done that poster! I'd seen that poster from when I was on the bus going into town, and because the writing was so fine and delicate on it, all you saw was the flash of yellow, and you didn't know what it was for. In a way, that was the sort of Situationist thing: that you could see the poster but couldn't see the writing, so you couldn't know what the poster was for. That was my first introduction to Factory in any shape or form.

LINDER STERLING: I made the photomontage for 'Orgasm Addict' late in 1976, but it was one of a series. Buzzcocks had asked me to be their designer, but typography never came easily to me at that time. The typography lessons were always on Thursday mornings, and on Wednesday evenings I used to go to the poly disco, which was one of the few places in Manchester at that time that played interesting combinations of music. Therefore, Thursday I was always a little frayed around the edges, and found it difficult to concentrate on point sizes and typesetting. I asked Malcolm Garrett to help me with the Buzzcocks design. I vaguely remember some democratic process of selection and my photomontage was the favourite of all. UA paid me £75 with which I bought some bondage trousers. A little known fact is that Anthony Wilson subsequently asked me to design for Factory, but I was moving on by then and passed the job on to the young Peter Saville, who was in the year below me. [John Robb, personal interview with Linder Sterling, 2006[1]]

CHRIS MATHAN: During the 1980s, I was very lucky to be working as a designer first at the prestigious Chermayeff & Geismar Associates, then in the graphic design department at Knoll Furniture — pretty much dream jobs for any young designer. By then, of course, I was totally familiar with Peter's work. I travelled to London in 1985 to visit some friends. Having contacted Peter beforehand, I met him

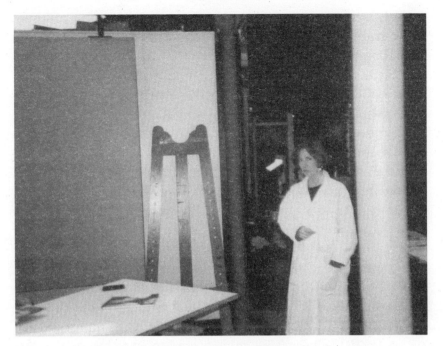

Chris Mathan in the Peter Saville Associates studio

at his studio on Kensal Road (shared by Peter Saville Associates and Trevor Key). We talked for a good while and I told him, 'I'd love to come work with you.' I returned to New York, sent Peter a set of my portfolio slides but never heard back from him. Later, working with him, that seemed completely normal. [laughs] I decided to move to London anyway, with plans of working as a designer in the independent music business.

I moved to London in 1985 and called Peter to arrange to pick up my slides. He and Canadian designer Brett Wickens, who was already working with Peter, were going to an art opening at the Royal Academy and we arranged to meet there. By the time we parted that evening, I was in a partnership with them.

NICKI KEFALAS: Factory excelled at creating beautiful artwork and interesting promotional items, using great designers such as Peter Saville and Central Station and others, and I used to think of things and ask them to make them, too. Tony came up with most of the ideas I think, but since he was always down in London, we'd have those lunches and collaborate on ideas. I think he felt as stimulated by us as we did by him at the time.

JAYNE HOUGHTON: When I was promoting New Order's releases, Peter Saville had a very relaxed approach to deadlines, but the brilliant work his studio did ... When the band's catalogue went to London, one thing that I always used to stamp my foot about was that the albums were special and the fans loved them. One thing journalists especially loved was the artwork. Everything looked brilliant, with untouchable sleeves and designs, but they'd barely make it on time if they did at all. When the albums were ready to be pressed to go on the shelves in record shops, I could never really work with them because I'd only have the white label and generic white packaging – the actual artwork was never ready in time to be able to use it as part of the promotions.

CHRIS MATHAN: I don't remember who ordered the metal sheets for the New Order *Brotherhood* album and its singles]. They were samples from wholesalers. Sheets of various metals were delivered to the studio during the course of a week or so. I remember the delivery of a thin sheet of silver-grey textured zinc that was stamped 'BILLITON TITAANZINK'. That became the *Brotherhood* album jacket. The other metals were for the singles ... I don't remember exactly what they looked like, but not that interesting or unique from one another. One evening, Peter and I were in Trevor's adjoining studio. I don't know who thought about getting a blowtorch – I'm guessing Trevor came up with that idea – but we were literally holding up sheets of metal and blowtorching them. The heat distorted the surface and made the marks and colours that you see on 'Bizarre Love Triangle' and 'State of the Nation'.

Originally the entire front and back *Brotherhood* jacket was foil stamped but it broke the foil-stamp machine at the printers. They were not very happy and refused to do any more. The process of foil stamping isn't intended for an area anywhere near that big; usually it's just a bit of type or a logo mark. So those first album jackets actually had the texture of the zinc, but in the end that didn't even work out because the metallic foil ink rubbed off. On top of that, it cost a fortune, so we had to go back to printing it offset, which wasn't very successful. It had a bluish-purplish tinge which didn't resemble zinc. Anyway, I don't think it was anyone's favourite New Order album or jacket, though the singles were quite good . . . I designed the typography for *Brotherhood* and the singles 'Bizarre Love Triangle' and 'State of the Nation'. The bold sans serif is Franklin Gothic and the text is Bodoni. They are proportioned similarly and complement each other well . . . something you just feel.

GILLIAN GILBERT: I remember being at an airport with everybody to go on tour, and Peter Saville brought the sleeve around when we were in the airport lounge to ask if we liked it, but by that time it was too late since the record was coming out soon.

CHRIS MATHAN: If there was a single phrase that defined working with Peter, it was 'see you in a bit'. If I had to call Pete about something during the day when he was still at home he almost always ended the conversation with, 'see you in a bit'. It was never just 'a bit' [laughs] . . . it was an ongoing jest. Trevor Key, who knew him much longer than anyone, told some hilarious anecdotes of working with Peter and his seeming obliviousness to time. They were close collaborators and friends . . . but like Mutt and Jeff as personalities. Anyway, Peter showed up in the studio often as late as 5 p.m. or even later, having spent the day conceptualising about some project we were about to take on. By the time he came to the office, there were ideas he'd thought about all day and we had to explore, so we'd inevitably start working again at 5 p.m.

Of course, it'd get to be well past 10 p.m., and everything in London was closed or closing by then. Peter and Brett were members of the Groucho Club in Soho, so Peter, Trevor, Brett and I would call in our dinner order before leaving the studio or we'd get there too late to order food. We sometimes did this three or four times a week so my work day often ended at two in the morning. I'd get a few hours of sleep and be in the office by 9 a.m. the next morning.

But I will always look back on that period as exceptionally creative. It was all business, [but] we had a lot of fun too. It may not have always seemed that way then ... the long days, late nights, not enough sleep, etc., but looking at the design profession today, I'm immensely grateful to have had that experience.

BRIDGET CHAPMAN: I remember being in London with Tony on a business trip, and he said, 'We're going to go and meet Peter Saville.' Peter Saville was this name you knew but you weren't sure he was a real person. It was like hearing about a unicorn. [laughs] He was living in Mayfair in this incredible apartment. I think somebody said it had belonged to a member of the Saudi royal family. Some of the walls were covered in dark blue velvet ... it was really like something out of the movie *Blue Velvet*. By the time we went in it was maybe four o'clock in the afternoon and his assistant said, 'Peter will be with you in a moment', and sat us on this high-end-design sofa. Then he brewed a cup of espresso and got some very expensive-looking cigarettes out and laid them down next to a silver lighter. Only then did he go wake Peter Saville, who was still in bed. Peter finally came out in a smoking jacket. To Tony, this was all perfectly normal. I thought, oh my God, this is another world.

CHRIS MATHAN: I don't think there could have been a Factory the way we know it without Peter. There were several other designers who worked for Factory bands, but they didn't have the impact that Peter had, or his visionary connection to the culture. Excellent designers — certainly Brett Wickens went on to become a hugely successful and innovative designer in San Francisco. But Peter is unique, he's very perceptive and had his finger on the pulse of what was going on in culture, art, fashion and music. I studied cultural anthropology in college, so the merger of art and culture really fascinated me. After I left, I believe Peter made some forays into the corporate design world but I'm not sure it ever worked out. He certainly required a certain lifestyle and surrounded himself with beautifully designed objects, so he was by no means opposed to making the money his talent deserved, but 'to design' with the primary objective being profit, he could never fit into that paradigm. Neither did I.

GILLIAN GILBERT: *Low-Life* had a great sleeve. When I went to Japan, people thought Stephen was the singer because he was on the cover. We each had to pick our style of photography — Peter Saville had the idea that each of us should be photographed the way we wanted in the style we picked. So, Stephen picked his style, Barney and Hooky picked theirs, of course. I went to Stephen's photo shoot where I was a bit annoyed or even jealous, perhaps, because Peter Saville had brought his model girlfriend, and she was talking to Stephen. It's stupid now, but at the time I was a bit annoyed. I never saw Barney and Hooky's shoots, and they never saw ours. Peter Saville wanted to do a 'messed-up Polaroid' with me, so we did some in a studio on a chaise longue, all smoky, black and white. It wasn't really working, so we went to the warehouse where it was very dark. I put a big coat on and he took some of these weird Polaroids. I think it was slightly warped in a way, so of course he said the warped one was one of the best photographs, so Stephen's went on the front and mine was on the back. Barney and Hooky were in the middle. I don't think they were very pleased, but especially not with Stephen on the cover. It was ultimately a very New Order thing to do — not to have the singer on the cover — and I thought that was a great concept. That's what he's great at doing, Peter Saville — something brilliant but always last minute.

CHRIS MATHAN: Factory, by that time, was releasing albums on CD, but the older albums had not been released in that format or on cassette. They decided to release the entire back catalogue on both. I worked on reinterpreting Peter's original artwork. Because a CD and an album are both essentially square, the CDs were mostly just a 'translation' of the album artwork. But in some cases — for example, with New Order's *Low-Life*, which is actually one of my favourites, because the front and back of the album jacket, and the inner sleeve are sort of interchangeable — we made photo cards and slipped them in a transparent folder.

Factory Records cassette boxes

The linen-textured cassette boxes for Joy Division (FACT 10c, FACT 25c), A Certain Ratio (FACT 16c), Section 25 (FACT 45c, FACT 90c), New Order (FACT 100c) . . . that was a way to release the cassettes as a 'family' of Factory music. The linen-textured paper that wrapped around the cardboard boxes came in a variety of colours that were used to identify each band. So, for example, purple was Joy Division, New Order was white, and so on. Conventional cassette packaging couldn't accommodate the character of the album artwork, so we did something unique. The box encased both the cassettes and some printed piece — some semblance of the album jacket and inner sleeve. For example, with *Unknown Pleasures*, the CD is pretty much the album cover, but the cassette insert 'translation' of the album was printing metallic silver ink on white linen paper.

REBECCA BOULTON: Putting together those [New Order] box sets and reissues [from 2019 onward] is quite complex. It all started a very long time ago with this idea that everything would be contained in a box. The idea kicked around, and it developed into what you've seen with *Movement* and *Power, Corruption & Lies*. So we started off with *Movement*, and we brought in a consultant, James Zeiter. He knows more about Factory's history, and New Order and Joy Division's history, than New Order and Joy Division do themselves, that's for sure. He's been brilliant at compiling spreadsheets of what would be available. So that's the starting place, and then the band members that are interested in being involved take a look. Steve's absolutely brilliant. He's really helpful and really keen on making sure things are good and right, but also has a sort of fan sensibility because he personally enjoys box sets and the way they are approached. He knows what he likes and what he doesn't like. Hooky's pretty good, he's got quite a lot of opinions about how things should be presented. Bernard's not really very interested. He's always been incredibly forward-thinking, so for him, his attitude is, 'I'm really proud of what I've done, and I always want it presented in the best light, but I don't really want to spend my time looking backwards.' He's always the one who wants to instigate new music, new ways of doing songs. It's just a different approach, and I don't think one's right or wrong. In a band like New Order, it's quite useful to have both.

TRACEY DONNELLY: I don't think Tony or anyone else ever made anything with the idea that they'd be collectable, but they realised later on that people were actually collecting the stuff . . . If I'd known then what I know now, I would have taken one of everything! [laughs] I'd never have guessed how Factory would become what it is today, but there were little things that made me know it was something special, even early on.

CHRIS MATHAN: As far as archiving Factory artefacts, they were commercial products, and except for the art world — where archival papers have always been used — commercial printing papers were/are not acid-free. No one thought, 'Well, these things are going to be worth something', or 'People will want to collect them as art objects in a half-century, so we should produce them in a way they won't deteriorate.' Peter was definitely pushing the envelope anyway at Factory but that kind of guaranteed permanency could not have been accomplished without causing them to be insanely expensive to produce. For example, the card stock record jackets were offset-printed on were manufactured for specific printing presses, scoring and folding processes and, of course, to be inexpensive. Having said that, to preserve artefacts in reasonable condition now, sensible precautions like using archival mattes and glass would certainly help. There are commercially printed objects that are considerably older that have been preserved simply by keeping them dry, clean and out of direct light.

MICHELLE MANGAN: Factory was one of those labels that was making collectible records, so you wanted to buy the vinyl. I've lost so many records over the years that are probably worth a fortune from early Factory releases. The sleeves are always so magnificent, so I never bought tapes or CDs — always vinyl. There's the original 12-inch 'Blue Monday', and The Durutti Column albums were always so carefully and artistically presented. So buying the records was a big thing for me . . . Factory Records were one of the labels that really took the time on the sleeves. It was art. So for me, it was a religious experience opening a new album — absorbing the music, but also going into a new world when you looked at those covers.

ANN QUIGLEY: Obviously, when ACR came around to the flat after the shows, they'd see my artwork because it was stuff I was working on. Simon asked me to do the cover for 'Flight', A Certain Ratio 12-inch, and he described what he wanted me to do, like a sort of a strange, eerie angel, in some sort of setting. I did what I thought was the best, which was an eerie angel that was laid on her head with her wings in the air, and you couldn't tell whether she could fly or not. I tried to take the mood of what 'Flight' was, and that was obviously my first ever commission. I remember I had done the painting, but my style was still quite naive since I was still an art student. I wasn't an accomplished artist, and my final idea had to get taken to this club Rafters in central Manchester, where I had to show it to Tony Wilson, who was ACR's manager at the time. So I turn up at Rafters with this cover artwork and I'm really nervous because I've never met Tony Wilson before. He was a local celebrity, and I'd shown the picture and he didn't seem to respond, so I thought, *oh, he doesn't like it*. It's in the dark in this nightclub, so you couldn't see anyway. But ACR took it and it was put on the 12-inch sleeve, but the funny thing was that Pete Saville was obviously the designer of the album, and he put my picture on the front but did it in a really tiny little corner. It's a full-sized picture, and the thought did go through my mind: did Pete Saville know I'd done that painting and that was why it was small — because he didn't like it — or because he thought it looked good? I didn't know but I thought it was quite funny, and then the Italian 12-inch had the full-sized painting of the angel.

CHRIS MATHAN: People are intrigued by things that deviate from the norm ... certainly in the spheres of culture and music.

I don't know the simple way to talk about it, but juxtaposing elements from one world that don't appear to belong in another world is powerful. Like when you look at Joy Division's *Closer*, when you bring that kind of funerary imagery into the world of rock 'n' roll music, it takes on a different meaning. I think Peter liked the idea of bringing my corporate design background into the mix.

BRIDGET CHAPMAN: I think the last time I saw people was probably at Tony's funeral. You know, I really didn't expect him to die. I think everybody was in a state of shock at the funeral. I have the invitation made to the funeral by Peter Saville, and I often think, 'I wish he'd been there because he really would have appreciated that as a bit of design.'

•   •   •

ANN QUIGLEY: I did the album sleeve for *So Hot*, and this is how primitive we were at the time. That sleeve was done by me going to WHSmith stationery and buying this Letraset, and the lettering was done by me by hand on the back, and it's really badly done! The picture was just a picture I found in a library book that was literally *so hot*: it was a desert that said 'so hot'. I wasn't saying we were so hot, which was what people seemed to interpret it as. It was that the desert was so hot, or the jungle was so hot.

Then I did the sleeve for *To Each* ... for A Certain Ratio, which was really complicated because Simon had come round and said, 'I've got an idea! We want to have a trumpet and we want to have these boys in it.' I did my best to fulfil the request, but it was basically going to be the first idea I came up with because of the short time frame I had to work in. So the hand that's blowing the trumpet is based on Miles Davis's fingers I painted from my perspective. It's not ACR's fingers, it's Miles Davis's fingers. That painting, there are things I'm happy about with it and things I'm not happy about ... It was really hard to do because I didn't have enough time. I gave Simon what I had and hoped for the best, really. I don't know what Tony Wilson thought because he had two other artists doing things as well for ACR. I'm not sure how I feel about the whole of the sleeve, but if I see it in a shop, it's really recognisable as an ACR sleeve.

JACKIE WILLIAMS: The Durutti Column album artwork came about because I got to know Vini through Bruce. He brought him home one day, we got on well and he was interested in my paintings. Next time they were recording, he just said, 'I'd like to use your paintings.' I think he went to Tony Wilson and said, 'I'd like to use Jack's paintings', so Tony came around and looked and said, 'Sure.'

I was really taken with Vini's music when I first heard it. I didn't know it beforehand, and the moment I heard it, I just loved it. It was so atmospheric. When he asked me to do something to go on the albums, I thought, where do you start? My work in the past was very different from what I painted for The Durutti Column albums, but I wanted it to reflect how I felt about the music. I played the music over and over again and tried to work automatically, to have the images come to me from the music. The images that went through my mind mainly had to do with space and colour, and the way those things play with all the vibrations of the music. That is how the splashes of colour came about. Some of the parts that have walls and columns ... it's all the way I felt listening to the music. I saw the colours moving and bouncing off in space because there's a lot of spacious feeling in Vini's music. That's how it was, almost doodling and using my imagination.

I started painting and drawing in the 1960s when I went to art college, and that work was quite minimalistic. I think that was the thing in the sixties and especially at Manchester art college. Very minimal, and my pieces were quite large things. They were often done by me not with canvas as such, but done with materials like Perspex, aluminium and glass. I did a big glass piece in the sixties that was exhibited in a gallery here in Manchester. By the eighties I got work at a place called Cosgrove Hall, an animation studio, where I worked for twenty years. I did *Danger Mouse*. I didn't actually do the figure drawings because that's not my thing, but I did special effects. If there was a building blown up, or things like fire or rain storms ... that sort of abstract thing is what I worked on.

I did very hard shapes and colours, and it was only Vini's music that made me softer and interested in organic shapes. *LC* was just doodling with watercolour with my imagination running, just playing the music over and over.

MARTINE MCDONAGH: You know the little flower design [for James]? I drew that, and I added it to a poster because it was a really boring poster otherwise. I put it on the poster and the band hated it, but the fans loved it. So, we put it on a T-shirt, and we sold thousands of T-shirts with that design on it. When I wanted to leave the band, I asked if they were going to continue using the flower and if they wanted to buy the rights for the design off me. They said they weren't ever going to use it, and then about two years later, a 'Best Of' album comes out, and it's just the flower design. It's everywhere. They completely used it. I ended up having to sue them, which took years to resolve.

JACKIE WILLIAMS: I did an album cover [for Life, *Tell Me*, FAC 106] that had a sort of double helix on it. It was just a piece Tony saw and said, 'Can I use this?' and took it away with him. It was just a piece of paper designed as a cover with somebody else working on it. But that's all I ever did, and I didn't plan on making any other album covers . . . because The Durutti Column's covers aren't like normal album covers anyway. What Factory found interesting about them was that they were pieces of artwork really.

ANNA DOMINO: Benoît Hennebert did the sleeve art for both 'Summer' and for the *Anna Domino* LP. One day, Benoît and I were wandering around Brussels and I invited him to come over and see my new apartment. The place had been in awful shape when I rented it but had been fixed up some by then, and I was pretty proud of the results. One of us suggested watching a movie and at the video rental store Benoît picked out *Faster Pussycat! Kill! Kill!* I didn't know anything about Russ Meyer or Tura Satana till then. We watched it with Benoît commenting on the cinematography and the bizarre plot — he had seen it before, more than once. For me it was a bit disturbing, I had to wonder why he'd picked out such a thing to watch on a quiet afternoon. He, himself, was a very quiet, introverted guy. Then later on he did this absolutely beautiful painting of that apartment! He made it even better by including an imaginary grand piano. He got the light of an overcast afternoon sky and the feeling of the place at that moment perfectly [and that painting became the album cover for the self-titled *Anna Domino* LP]. By the time I got up the nerve to tell him I needed that painting, he'd already given it to another friend. I was so sorry not to have asked sooner.

JACKIE WILLIAMS: I actually wasn't too happy that the album covers were going out as my work . . . it wasn't necessarily the stuff I'd be proud of. My typical work is quite hard and cold, much the opposite of the paintings I did for The Durutti Column covers. I used to use things like big American trucks for inspiration, so you couldn't get more opposite, really. The art I did — and do — for me is much stronger.

I do like the paintings now for The Durutti Column albums, but they weren't on a big scale, and I like to work on a big scale. They were mostly done on paper. It wasn't a wild enough style for me. I am much more hard edged. It was just the soft side of me that came out during that time, making those covers to Vini's music.

Meeting Vini and listening to music I'd never heard before, it just struck a chord. It had an atmosphere and I was trying to make the feel of the atmosphere and the sound of the notes come out through colour and shape. After those albums, I didn't do any more work like that, really. I went back to my own work and style. The music must have just had some sort of effect on me. That softness, the way the music made me feel, just isn't typical of me.

ANN QUIGLEY: I stopped doing sleeves and just let Trevor [Johnson] do them, and I think we'd gotten a photographer to do the *Kalima!* exclamation mark album where there's a picture of me on the sleeve. It was a tongue-in-cheek thing that we didn't know at the time because he was a *Vogue* photographer, James Martin. He charged a fortune, but we were oblivious to anything about business. Luckily, the Japanese sales of our records paid for the session, which was great because I don't think Tony Wilson was happy with how much was being spent on photographs, sleeve or not.

KAREN JACKSON: At some point you need an incubator and a home for all this energy, which for us became Factory Records, Dry Bar and The Haçienda. Tony Wilson articulated the value of this energy, people like Kevin Cummins photographed and documented it, the bands soundtracked it, and we tried to paint it. The city has contributed a lot to our work and we hope we have contributed to the city. [Lola Landekic interview, *Art of the Title*, 2014[2]]

ALISON KNIGHT: We [Baylis & Knight fashion designers] used to work out of 42 to 44 Sackville Street, which was a building where Trevor Johnson had his studio, and he used to do graphics for Factory. He was on the top floor, we were on the second, and Central Station Design was also in there. The Bailey Brothers who were quite involved with Factory and did videos for Happy Mondays, like the one on the roof in Ibiza, they were in there as well. It was a very exciting and creative building to be working from, and I had a New York-style loft apartment in there, where we sewed from. I have absolutely zero photographs of that loft, which is so frustrating. I used to have all The Haçienda posters on the wall of my flat, gig posters. We used to have to hide when the firemen came because I was living there illegally and ad hoc, but other people were as well. We had a bathroom, so it was all quite good.

KAREN JACKSON: We loved Tony. He always fought in our corner and if anyone questioned the value and importance of the cover art, he used to say, 'Does the Catholic Church pour its wine into mouldy earthenware pots? I think not.' [Lola Landekic interview, *Art of the Title*, 2014[3]]

CHRIS MATHAN: When I left Peter Saville Associates a couple of years later, I knew I would likely never have the opportunity to work with such an inspiring group of creatives again. It was an exciting time in my life as a designer, having worked almost exclusively for corporate clients prior to that. I collaborated with amazingly talented people on fabulous music, art, and fashion-related projects. And much of the music was what I was passionate about. It was pretty crazy, too. I never went to sleep before one o'clock in the morning. To me, London was a hotbed of creativity . . . and Peter, despite his eccentricities, had his finger on the culture and was a force of innovation.

TINA SIMMONS: Cath Carroll was out in the States, and when she did her first album with Factory, she wanted to use Chris Mathan to do the photography and design [for *England Made Me*]. She wanted to use Robert Mapplethorpe to take photographs later on.

CATH CARROLL: I was very familiar with Robert Mapplethorpe and his work, and I understood that this was an incredible opportunity, but it was quite daunting. Paul worked very hard to get Robert

Mapplethorpe to do those photos, and it was quite difficult because he wasn't well, but there was also very little wiggle room with his copyright and usage.

I think working with Robert was above my level of comfort. I wasn't someone who loved the camera, so my memories are small. Robert Mapplethorpe had this coffee with cinnamon, and I'd never had coffee with cinnamon before. I went to their apartment and his partner Jack was there, too, and he was the one who helped me to understand what to expect, because Robert Mapplethorpe's energy levels were not great at the time. In between shots I was just staring at Robert Mapplethorpe's shoes — they were these very elegant monogrammed slippers, very costumey. Jack was just so welcoming and kind, and then we did the shoot super quick. Robert just did his thing. I was like a deer in the headlights with my sailor hat, and then it was over quite quickly. Jack told me then that they were going to go on to a club, and I wish I'd gone, but I was absolutely terrified of socialising with people.

But what a great gift, to be photographed by Robert. Thank you, Tony Wilson, and thank you, Paul Smith. I actually had a copy of the prints for quite a while, but then I sent them back to Factory for the box set, and unfortunately they never made it back. I think that's sort of quite poetic because I don't think the prints were ever really mine to keep.

TINA SIMMONS: Chris was back in New York at that point, and I got in a lot of trouble with Tony about her doing the design for Cath's album. Even though the contract with Cath existed — and Factory didn't really have contracts before that, as I'm sure you know, which was one of the bizarre things about them, including no contracts with Joy Division and New Order — the contract had all kinds of bizarre and quirky things. By the time of Happy Mondays, Cath Carroll, Northside . . . they all had contracts. One of the quirky things about those contracts was that the bands should have the right to choose themselves whoever they wanted to do their artwork.

CATH CARROLL: My manager, Paul Smith, set it up initially. Just after I moved to the US, we had a photo shoot in New Orleans and around there. So Chris and the photographer, Julian, met me down there, and we spent a few days going around.

TINA SIMMONS: This was where I got in trouble because Cath and her two managers wanted to use Chris Mathan and photographs that had been done, and I said, 'Sure, that's fine.' What I didn't know was that Tony Wilson had already been talking to Peter Saville about doing Cath's album cover, to which Peter turned around and said, 'Chris Mathan's already doing it', and Tony blew up at me: 'You've got no right passing this stuff onto your mates!' I said, 'Tony, she might be a mate, and she might be in America rather than here, but it was *Cath's choice*, and it says she can choose that in her contract!' So we did have our ups and downs, quite a few of them. [laughs]

CHRIS MATHAN: Cath Carroll's *England Made Me* cover was shot on the porch of historic Homeplace Plantation House, built in the late 1700s, located in Hahnville, Saint Charles Parish, Louisiana — about an hour up the Mississippi River from New Orleans. It's listed in the (US) National Register of Historic Places. London photographer Julian Broad did the photo shoot. The album was recorded in São Paulo, Brazil. We did a previous shoot in Julian's London studio before any of us heard the music. When I finally had the opportunity to listen to the music, I knew the studio shots just didn't work and we needed to do another shoot . . . outdoors and somewhere warm. I had a friend from New Orleans, so I thought, let's do the shoot in south Louisiana since my friend could help direct us to possible locations. (She was a chef, so she would tell us the best places to eat!)

CATH CARROLL: My memories of Chris are that she was very sensitive and very kind. I didn't feel as vulnerable as I might have in that situation. She had a vision for the album, and I remember doing a photo shoot at an old house. The manager of the house was this guy called 'Cowboy'. That was my first exposure to certain kinds of southern white people. To say he was massively racist is putting it lightly. He seemed like he was trying to bait everyone and seemed really pleased with himself. I don't know how Chris managed to get through it — and we didn't need to deal with him too much — but she did. She really took care of me in a way that I never really had any moments where I felt vulnerable.

CHRIS MATHAN: Julian and I met a day before Cath flew in and drove up the Mississippi from New Orleans to scout out places. I had an idea I wanted to explore of a close-up of Cath leaning on a white column, with columns fading away behind her. We came upon an old plantation house with a porch all the way around that looked like it would be perfect. The building was in some disrepair and there didn't seem to be anyone there so we stopped to take a closer look. While on the back porch, a fellow who turned out to be the caretaker rode up on his paint horse [an American horse breed]. He introduced himself as 'Cowboy' and later invited us to the local fair to watch him show his prize hogs. [laughs] We were tempted! He told us the place was owned by a gentleman called 'the Colonel' and we'd have to come back to get his permission to take the photographs. He also told us that a Hollywood film crew had been there a month or so ago filming a movie starring Robert Duvall. Very cool but we figured he was going to charge us a fee to take the photo on his porch.

We returned the next day with Cath, met the Colonel — who was a well-educated man who'd studied agriculture in my then home state of Maine. He gave us a tour of the interior of the house — it had been a sugar plantation — and told us of its history and how it fared through the Civil War and he graciously allowed us to do our photo shoot for no charge.

Julian sent me the prints I had requested from looking at the contact sheet. They were gorgeous. I lovingly designed the sleeve, sent the artwork to England and, well, I was horrified with the result. It was designed to have a Japanese-style transparent paper belly-band. The text 'England Made Me / Cath Carroll' ran vertically up the belly-band, printed in metallic blue ink. It was very subtle. I don't know who made the changes but there was no attempt to get input from me. It was a huge disappointment. It did make me admire Peter all the more for his never-compromising attitude about his design with Factory.

CATH CARROLL: We had a budget, so Chris and Paul thought we could do something interesting by sending me to New Orleans, but then it ended up just looking like I'm next to a pole that could have been anywhere. [laughs] The same thing happened with the Robert Mapplethorpe photo shoot, where you're in an interesting situation but it doesn't necessarily make for an interesting photograph. I still think Julian and Chris did a gorgeous job with that sleeve and I was grateful to have that artwork for the album. There was a little school-monitor-style badge that came with that album that said, 'England Made Me'. I haven't kept much from that time, but that's one of the things I have kept.

• • •

TERESA ALLEN: I loved it when Ben and Sandra [of Ben Kelly Design] used to come up to Manchester to visit. She and Elena made a big impression on me.

CLAIRE DE VERTEUIL: I got to be friends with Elena Massucco, one of the designers [of Dry]. We used to spend loads of time together hatching plans, so I felt very involved and invested in the project. That's probably why I ended up working 110 hours a week for the first six months! It was *all* I did. I was sleeping or I was at Dry. It was great to see something go from an idea to what it became, and for the two years I was there, it just got bigger and better.

ELIZABETH BAILEY: When I was at Elektra, I worked with Factory, with Tony Wilson on the Happy Mondays, because they were signed to Elektra in the US. Very coincidentally, a very close friend of mine at that time, Elena Massucco, was working for the architecture firm that did The Haçienda and Dry, Ben Kelly's firm. She was always going to Manchester to work on that stuff.

TERESA ALLEN: The Ben Kelly Design (BKD) team didn't come to the club very many times, obviously being London-based, but they certainly did when there was a project on the go. I think I probably saw them more when Dry 201 was being designed and built, and then again with the Factory headquarters. However, I wasn't involved directly in the work they were doing apart from paying their bills! It was always a pleasure to see them — they were so lovely — really friendly.

I can still picture them, Sandra always smiling, all of them in black! I was a little bit in awe.

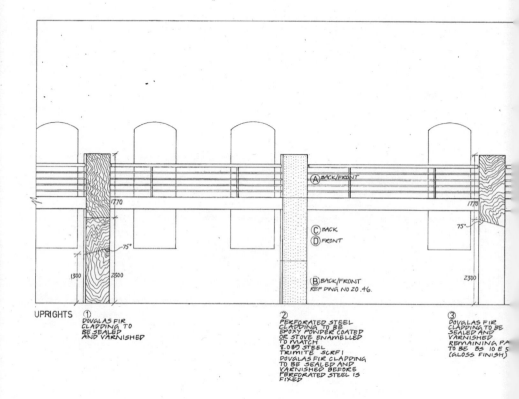

UPRIGHTS

① DOUGLAS FIR CLADDING TO BE SEALED AND VARNISHED

② PERFORATED STEEL CLADDING TO BE EPOXY POWDER COATED OR STOVE ENAMELLED TO MATCH T.089 STEEL TRIMITE SCRF1 DOUGLAS FIR CLADDING TO BE SEALED AND VARNISHED BEFORE PERFORATED STEEL IS FIXED

③ DOUGLAS FIR CLADDING TO BE SEALED AND VARNISHED REMAINING PA TO BE BS 10 E 5 (GLOSS FINISH)

Sandra Douglas at BKD (Ben Kelly Design): front elevation drawing
of The Haçienda balcony, drawn by hand by Sandra

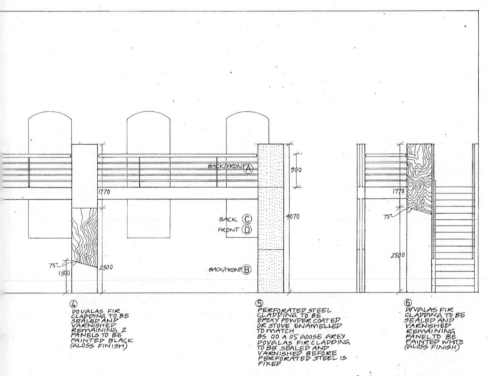

BACK/FRONT Ⓐ

1770

900

BACK Ⓒ

FRONT Ⓓ

4070

75° 2300

1300

BACK/FRONT Ⓑ

1770

75°

2300

④ DOVALAS FIR
CLADDING TO BE
SEALED AND
VARNISHED
REMAINING 2
PANELS TO BE
PAINTED BLACK
(GLOSS FINISH)

⑤ PERFORATED STEEL
CLADDING TO BE
EPOXY POWDER COATED
OR STOVE ENAMELLED
TO MATCH
BS 00 A 05 GOOSE GREY
DOVALAS FIR CLADDING
TO BE SEALED AND
VARNISHED BEFORE
PERFORATED STEEL IS
FIXED

⑥ DOVALAS FIR
CLADDING TO BE
SEALED AND
VARNISHED
REMAINING
PANEL TO BE
PAINTED WHITE
(GLOSS FINISH)

Ben Kelly Design

FACT 51
11-13 WHITWORTH STREET
MANCHESTER

DWG NO. 20 53
SCALE 1:50
MARCH 1982

BEN KELLY DESIGN
47 49 CHARLOTTE RD
LONDON EC2
01 729 5168

CHAPTER 13

THE HAÇIENDA
MUST SURVIVE

Ang Matthews with staff at The Haçienda

The Haçienda existed in physical form from 1982 to 1997. During those years, the club went from being a cold and often empty music venue, to a space that thrived with cultural production, to an ecstasy-fuelled party, and then to something else altogether. As a new generation of fans gravitated to the sounds of Factory in the Madchester years, a new generation of women came to work for the club, while others took on more complex roles. Ang Matthews became assistant manager and later went on to fill the crucial role of manager and licensee. Marcia Pantry continued running Hicks after bringing her sister Sidnie and her cousin Anne-Marie Copeland into the mix. Teresa Allen's role shifted over the decade-long work she did at the club. Alison Agboola, Judith Foster, Rebecca Goodwin, and Ruth Taylor also became Haçienda employees. Many worked at the club during the years of historical hyperbole involving the police, gangs, and violence. Yet as the women's voices reveal, some of it happened and some of it didn't. The club is ultimately the stuff of both truth and legend. And the memory of The Haçienda persists into the present, in the minds of the women who worked there and in events like Haçienda Classical that have arisen to celebrate the club's legacy today.

DJ PAULETTE: Women actually ran Factory, and they ran The Haçienda. Women *ran it*. From the cloakroom to the kitchen to the bars, to managing it. Absolutely not enough is made of Ang Matthews's role in running The Haçienda, and she *ran it* ... She was the one who was taking the money in big black bin bags at the end of the night. She was the one that was handling the distributors and the licences because the boys were just spending the money. It was the women that were running it. It was the women that were making sure that the relations with the police were such that it stayed open. And the women that ran the kitchen, and the women that were in the cloakroom, and the women that cleaned the toilets — all those key major jobs — they kept it running. Ordering in the beers, wines and the spirits, and making the deals with the distributors. That was Ang. It wasn't Peter Hook, and it wasn't Tony. The person that was signing the cheques and making the deals was Ang Matthews.

KATH MCDERMOTT: Nobody fucked around with Ang Matthews, and she'd always have an eye out for the girls.

ANG MATTHEWS: When I asked why they wanted me for the job, Tony said, 'We heard that you were an anarchist like us, darling.' And that's how I got the job. But I've since found out, I didn't *actually* get the job initially. They had offered it to someone else first, and he had refused. They always said years later how glad they were that he didn't do it because I brought a whole different vibe.

YVONNE SHELTON: A lot of women were involved in the keeping together of The Haçienda — the networking, bobbing and weaving between the egos, keeping it running. The women were really holding it together.

ALISON AGBOOLA: It's not something I've thought about consciously, but women are usually the mainstay of these types of things, and that's true of The Haçienda. I think Manchester has bred strong women, and women who want to be involved at the heart of things, and The Haçienda was the beating heart. So of course women were at the centre.

DJ PAULETTE: You always have to scratch under the surface of what's going on because even if you only went to The Haçienda two or three times in its entire existence, you will have seen Ang at the corner of the main bar! It was impossible to miss her. She was there handling everything from the door, to the bar, to the money. She was involved in absolutely *every* step of the organisation, so there's no way you can tell The Haçienda story without giving her that credit. I'm not saying she made the club — she didn't make the club. Tony Wilson, Peter Hook and the rest of New Order and

Factory, they made the club. And Ang didn't design it, but when it comes down to running it — that was *all Ang.*

ANG MATTHEWS: After I'd finished my degree, I started working at Manchester Metropolitan University as a student union representative, as the social secretary putting on gigs and events. I stood out because I think I was only the second woman in the UK to do that job, so that was quite unusual. I was there for a year going to two or three gigs every night, so I became known to Tony Wilson and Alan Erasmus, Rob Gretton. I'd done a very mini tour with New Order with the band I managed at the time, so I was getting to know them and they were getting to know me. I stood out because I was a woman. When I finished my degree, I was totally out of Manchester, but I came back and started running The Boardwalk club a couple of times a week to give their manager nights off.

It was during this time that I started getting noticed. The Boardwalk was like a 300-capacity venue. Various people stood at the bar, such as Tony Wilson and Paul Mason, who was the operations manager at The Haçienda and Dry Bar. I was starting to feel self-conscious of them staring at me, thinking, 'Why are they here?' I thought, 'Why would they be at The Boardwalk when The Haçienda was open?'

Then I just got a call out of the blue and someone said, 'Would you be interested in being interviewed for the position of assistant manager at The Haçienda?' I said yes, of course. I mean, I hadn't worked at what I'd call a proper job. I went for an interview with Paul Mason. He talked about bars and selling beer because there were actually three bars in The Haçienda. I just thought, well, I don't want a job selling beer, *I'm into music. That's what I like.* A couple months passed, and I'd heard nothing. There was a Happy Mondays gig, and I was sat in the dressing room. I saw this man again, Paul Mason. I said, 'Oh, hi Paul', and he said, 'Oh, hi. You need to ring in on Monday and speak to me about the job.' I said, 'Well, I don't know anything about bars' and he replied, 'It doesn't matter.' So, I rang in on Monday and he wasn't in. He never called back, so I forgot all about it. I bumped into one of the receptionists later who said, 'Why haven't you started? You didn't show up for work.' So, I actually got the job, but that sort of gives you the impression of how life would be working for them: I got the job and nobody told me.

TERESA ALLEN: Ang ran the bar after Leroy moved to Dry. I remember when we moved the office upstairs to the top floor of the building, it had windows. It was a revelation because we'd spent years below ground. Ang used to have power naps in the room at the end ... she used to nap and that would keep her going.

MARCIA PANTRY: I was running Hicks at one point.

SIDNIE PANTRY: My sister Marcia was working at The Haçienda when an opening came up at the hatcheck, and she asked if I wanted to do some work there. She'd been working there for a long time. It must have been 1985 when I started.

ANNE-MARIE COPELAND: My cousins at the time — two sisters, Sidnie and Marcia — one worked in the cloakroom and one worked at Hicks. Sidnie was a fashion designer, so I was like, 'Why are you working here when you have your own store?' She was like, 'It's just to get the vibes.' I didn't get it — just to get the vibes? Then around that time, I got really into indie music. I was seventeen at the time, and when I went to my first Haçienda student night, the Temperance Club, I was *hooked*. When I heard The Haçienda were looking for help with the cloakroom, I was like, 'Yeah, *of course, I'll do it!*' I'd just turned eighteen and thought, well, that's the perfect job for me because it means I get to go out. My parents were really strict, so I wasn't really allowed to go out, but if I had a job that meant I *had* to go out, they wouldn't say anything about it.

RUTH TAYLOR: Then there was the cloakroom staff, and Anne-Marie Copeland on the cloakroom. So she actually set me up on my first date with my husband! He used to play the saxophone, and he used to do a little gig in The Cornerhouse on a Wednesday night and then bring the saxophone down to The Haçienda. Anne-Marie was like, 'Just ask him out!' [laughs] I wanted to but I couldn't, so she did it. In the end, Anne-Marie asked him out for me, and there you go. Thirty-four years and four kids later, we're still here. So I have The Haçienda to thank for my husband as well.

MARCIA PANTRY: I got Anne-Marie and Sidnie their jobs at The Haçienda, and even my brother was working there at a point. But I don't think people knew we were family. For instance, Sidnie and I don't look alike. Sidnie's very, very slim, about a size 8. I was always bordering on a size 14 when I was young, so I'm on that spectrum. I always say I don't let the size of me dictate my fashion, my dress sense.

SIDNIE PANTRY: Working on the hatcheck, I'd have to deal with people who would try to come behind the counter and I'd have to stop them. I remember one night, the guy from Simply Red tried to come behind, and I had to get quite militant with him! 'No, *no*, you can't come behind here!'

You'd take a few tickets at a time and get a few coats at once. When you brought people their coats after they gave you their tickets, it was like people refused to recognise their own coats! [laughs] *Bring your brain with you when you come at the end of the night!* I remember running after a guy because he's taken his coat and somebody else's coat just because I brought it out! *Keep your brain in check!* [laughs]

RUTH TAYLOR: I started going to The Haçienda when I was about sixteen, and as soon as I turned eighteen, I applied for that job on the cloakroom. The doormen were like, 'How old are you? You've been coming here for years!' [laughs] They actually used to call me 'Swing Out' because they thought I looked like [Corinne Drewery of] Swing Out Sister. I had very black hair and red lips.

CORINNE DREWERY: The Haçienda definitely influenced me and that's where my relationship with Manchester began, as I met Andy [Connell] there. I suppose The Haçienda was responsible for Swing Out Sister, as it kicked off our career.

RUTH TAYLOR: I worked with so many women at The Haçienda: Rebecca Goodwin, Judith Foster, Fiona Allen, Ang, of course ...

ANG MATTHEWS: You know, it's quite a big job to have, and it was only like five bullet points — I've got them somewhere actually: 'turn up for work on time' was the first one. So that was how it all started. I started there in June 1989, and I actually remember the day because it was my birthday, June 19.

REBECCA GOODWIN: I was an indie kid, so I went to The Haçienda a couple times before I went to university — I left Manchester to go to university in Leeds — but I'd come back for Haçienda trips and bring my new university friends to the Thursday night, which was student night. In the summers, I'd come back to Manchester and get a bar job in town somewhere, and I'd go to The Haçienda all the time. I was there as much as I could be. I ultimately left university in Leeds and came back and did a degree in Manchester. In the summer before that started, I was working at a bar in town. I used to go into The Haçienda loads, and I'd chat to Dave Haslam. He recommended me for a leafleting job in publicity: to flyer the queue and all the bars and cool shops in town. I thought yeah, I'll do that, it's a bit of money. I started doing that and going around town, doing the leafleting — pre-internet PR. The woman who worked on the door, taking the money at night, then suggested I come and help her because she needed somebody, so I started doing the door as well. I used to do three nights a week, sometimes four nights a week.

The reason I got employed for promotion in the first instance was because — I was annoying Dave [laughs] — there was a new night going on called Zumbar, which was quirky, a little bit camp, and had cabaret. It needed a lot of promoting for who was on cabaret. That was the beginning of the Balearic sound, music that had been played in Ibiza ... it was unusual and new in a club environment.

ANG MATTHEWS: Another person I worked with on a daily and nightly basis was Rebecca Goodwin. She was very involved. Like a lot of people who worked at The Haçienda, she had many jobs.

She worked on a fanzine called *Beautiful2000*, which was linked to Dave Haslam's Thursday student night, playing indie music. During the early days she was on the door, taking money, and she was a receptionist for a few years.

REBECCA GOODWIN: When The Haçienda reopened [after the first closure due to police pressure], the nights booked were supposed to deter the parties and the drugs, so there was a lot of student focus. We did a new night called Beautiful2000 with Dave DJing and a guy called David Knopov did the artwork. I did a fanzine for that night every week and interviewed people like Johnny Marr just after he'd left The Smiths, etc., and it was a free handout on the way in. I've definitely got a few of those still knocking around my house.

JUDITH FOSTER: I moved to Manchester from Yorkshire for university when I was seventeen. I met a friend, Rebecca, in my first year who was already working at The Haçienda. She used to leaflet the queue and she asked, would I be interested in doing that? I said I would, so she went to reception, taking money, and I started leafleting. Alongside that, every Saturday I would have to carry a massive box of leaflets around town, dropping a pile of leaflets off at the trendy shops where young people used to go. That was my task at the time.

RUTH TAYLOR: I started on the cloakroom and did about a year there, and then I started doing the door, selling the tickets. I started in 1988 and finished in 1996. Just before we shut down, the last job I was doing was on the security cameras, which was a bit grim. To be fair, it was just staring at screens for hours on end, but it's a reminder of how it all just changed massively over those years. When I look back — and because I've got kids older than that — I just think, oh my God, being at the front of it on the door with all the gangster stuff that was going on in the background . . . just mental. But it was also great fun.

I can't remember what the capacity was — 1,200, I think — and we'd get 1,200 people through that door in an hour. *Bang, bang, bang*. One of my friends used to laugh at the speed I could get people in because the queue was massive, and all people wanted to do was get in to dance. We'd print off all tickets beforehand and give them the ticket, get the money, get them through. It was so much easier when they had a tenner because that was perfect — no change, no messing around with change, which would massively affect your throughput.

Working on the door was a dream because you got everything done. When you cashed up, it was like ten o'clock, and then you went out into the club and danced and partied. The faster you got them all in and the faster you got the money counted, the faster you could get out there and dance. I was at university the whole time as well, and I continued working there after I graduated.

MARCIA PANTRY: Hicks was upstairs, and we called it the can bar because that was the only bar that sold cans at the time, and it sold cans from all over the world. There was Chinese beer, Chilean beer, beers from all over the globe. There were also a couple of pinball machines that the guys used to play on.

We were part of the scene as well because we're working, but we're vibing at the same time, so it wasn't work. Working at The Haçienda was not work. At any time we could leave the bar, go downstairs or go upstairs. There was a walkway from one part of the building to the next, and the DJ booth was upstairs as well. So we could go and chat to any of the DJs. My favourite DJ was Hewan Clarke. And then the guy from Quando Quango, Mike Pickering, I used to go ask him all the time to play a record by The Whispers. We'd use that as a sign-off at the end of the night.

ANNE-MARIE COPELAND: The first time I met Tony Wilson was at my cousin Marcia's house, and she was having a party. I was thinking, 'Wow, what's Tony Wilson doing here? This is the guy from television.'

MARCIA PANTRY: Tony Wilson used to take me home from time to time. At the time, I was living at my mother's house. When he'd come to my house to drop me off, we'd sit there with a cup of tea and have a quite adult chat. I used to call him TW. I thought I was just a girl, a nobody person, but he wanted to talk to me and didn't mind taking me around in his Mercedes. I remember the first time I saw a mirror in the sun visor of a car and a light on the mirror, it was in his car and he had to show me how to use it. [laughs]

I used to take Tony to parties as well. I'd tell him, 'I'm going to this party', and he'd want to go, so I'd take him. I took him to lots of Black people's parties as well. He was quite cool that way. I remember I took him to a party at my sister-in-law's, but I was breaking up with my husband, and my husband just happened to be there. He thought Tony was my boyfriend. [laughs] Tony also used to come to my parties in Hulme.

ANNE-MARIE COPELAND: I'll never forget the first night I started working at The Haçienda because that was with Alison [Agboola], and she was showing me the ropes: this and that, tearing the tickets, and waiting for the customers to come. I was always into visuals, I was always into fashion and I was always into music. I was overwhelmed by the whole situation because that was the first time that I was out ... and I was earning money! After that, it just did not feel like work anymore. It was like I was paid to enjoy myself.

ALISON AGBOOLA: Marc Almond was playing at The Haçienda on a Thursday night, and bear in mind that I was only a seventeen-year-old then. I remember going into this place, which was nothing like the nightclubs I'd ever been to before. The club blew me away and I thought, 'The next time I come in here, I want to be working here.' So not long after, I got in touch with Paul Mason, who was the general manager at the time, and it was just a normal enquiry — like you do. I wanted to know if they'd got any part-time work and was quite willing to do anything. I had to fabricate my age, and I said I was a year older. [laughs] So obviously I put my date of birth back a year, like you do when you're that age, and I got a Saturday-night job in the cloakroom. I worked there for five years, and it was one of the best jobs in the club because after you get the initial rush of people coming in, you don't have to do anything until everybody's going out. You got a few hours in between where you could socialise and dance.

I first started working with Sidnie — Sid, she was called — which I thought was a really cool name for a girl back in the eighties. Sid had an older sister working there too, Marcia. Sid was really cool, and we had our own type of system for the coats. It was basic, but we had little books of like lottery tickets we'd rip out and give, and put the other half on the hanger with the coat. At the end of the night, people were coming in dripping in sweat, having lost these tickets or, if you did get them back, they would be extremely wet. [laughs]

The next person who came to work with me was Anne-Marie Copeland. She was in the band Kiss AMC, and she had these bright-green contact lenses and this amazing big hair, because obviously she was in the music business and wanted to make a statement.

ANNE-MARIE COPELAND: I was in a band, Kiss AMC, and we had a recording contract and promotional obligations. I always tried to keep my day job at The Haçienda — don't lose your day job! — but because I turned up late once or twice, Paul Mason, the manager at The Haçienda, said I'd have to decide what I wanted to do — whether I wanted to work in the club or be a popstar. That was so sad, that night. I'll never forget on the train journey back from London, I was like, 'I can't be late for work. I just can't be late for work!' Nobody understood why I wanted to get back to the club, but it was because I enjoyed it. I had made friends, and there was always something going on.

MARCIA PANTRY: They brought a new manager in — Leroy [had been] the manager, but they brought another manager in from some other town. Two weeks before they introduced him to the place, I remember this guy came up to me at the Hicks bar and ordered a can. I'd never seen him before. I think he was sussing out what was going on with the club, so he came in anonymously. Two weeks go by and then they have a meeting to introduce him: Paul Mason. He was serious about turning The Haçienda around. This was late '87. I said to him, 'You came to my bar and ordered a can of Red Stripe.' Hicks was *always* busy, so he was bowled over that I remembered him. But he came in and immediately started making changes, putting structures in. But Paul Mason is also the one who increased my wages.

The first thing Paul Mason did was sack a guy called Terry from downstairs who was working at the Gay Traitor. He had to go. Glenn was working with him, so Glenn said he's walking out. So Glenn walked out. Then Brendan, my friend who was Glenn's partner, he's walking out as well.

Before Paul Mason, it was anything goes at The Haçienda. They'd give you a float, some money in the till. At the end of the night, you'd put some money in the till. That was how we did it. Then Paul Mason came and started putting structures in. He'd give you a £50 float, and you had to count the float. End of the night, you'd count back and take the £50 out of what was made. Then you'd count the money, which we didn't have to do before, and Paul would notate the receipts at the till. This was a proper running of the club now.

SUSAN FERGUSON: Angela Matthews came in when Paul Mason was brought in from Rock City, Nottingham, to turn the fortunes of the club around. I think she probably did more than him. I think he just got into all the bad ways of the original management.

ANG MATTHEWS: There was no typical day, really, and it would depend what event was on that night. I was very career orientated, and I was quite hard in how I worked, and perhaps how I was with people. 'That bitch at The Haçienda' is a phrase I think that comes up quite often.

My average day was split in two. I went in at about half past ten in the morning and would come back home at about three o'clock or four o'clock, and then I would sleep again for a couple of hours. I'd go back about half seven, eight o'clock so I could reopen. In the daytime, I'd be doing things like rosters because there were thirty-two staff I had to sort out. There would be money to sort out. Thursdays were directors' meetings. I had all the beer to order. It was that kind of thing — me sorting out maintenance. It was quite full-on, really. At night time, I literally stood in one spot from when the club opened to when the club closed, and I just dealt with things that cropped up. I would have checked that there was enough to drink, and everything was in place, and enough staff to run it all, and everybody knew where to find me. It was instances that could not be planned for that I dealt with in the night time.

I would stand at the main bar — in front of the door that led to the main bar, that led to the lift to go down to the cellar and also could go up the stairs. It was at the bottom of the stairs, leading to the DJ boxes and across to the next bar. And there was another thing: Paul Cons was the person who was the promoter and was responsible for the look of the club and different things like banners up until '92 when he left. From then on, that was also part of my job, and I became responsible for booking all the DJs as well.

REBECCA GOODWIN: When I was finishing my English degree, they very kindly gave me five weeks off work full-pay to do my finals, and then I started full-time at The Haçienda the day after my last final as Paul Cons's assistant. I was press and PR, but I was still doing the door at nights as well.

ALISON AGBOOLA: I worked in the cloakroom until 1991, and then I went to the States, nannying, on the East Coast. When I came back in 1993, I'd spoken to Paul Mason to ask if there was any job I could do. He got me a job on the door, just checking passes — I wasn't a doorwoman or door person as such. If anybody wanted to have a fight with me, I'd be running the other way. [laughs]

Working there in the eighties, we had the legacy of door people still wearing bow ties — the epitome of the doorman image. When I came back, things had changed. It was a lot tenser, more money-orientated, more political in terms of local politics and the gangs. I didn't particularly want to be on the door, but I was there about twelve months. It started to become uncomfortably tense, and my life was moving on because I was trying to get into nursing. I'm glad I moved away from it before it all went significantly downhill.

RUTH TAYLOR: The door was held up at gunpoint one day when I was working there. There was a front door into the club, and then there was a door at the back that basically took you down to the basement, which is how you got up to the office. We ran to the back, and the girl I was with was like, 'What about the money?' *The money!* We had to run back in, get the money, and run back out again. When it was all over, everything carried on as you were, so it seemed normal. Looking back, it was quite bonkers.

TERESA ALLEN: In the later days, working on the door was hard work. We had to run tickets off and clear the till because we had to pay protection money to all the bad guys ... doing things that didn't sit well with me on the legal front.

JUDITH FOSTER: Working reception was quite a bit more intense because we were handling a lot of money. At the end of the night, we couldn't be up on money and we couldn't be down, obviously — you're in trouble either way because you'd obviously done something wrong. Maybe I'd have sold too many tickets, or a ticket had been dropped and you sold it again. Halfway through the night, one of us had to go upstairs to the safe and take some of the money out, because you had to be careful, you could have been in the firing line. No one ever actually tried, which amazes me, but I was very aware that we could be robbed.

ANG MATTHEWS: When they had closed down before — because the police wanted us shut — I was assistant manager and I'd been in the club every night. The police kept going on and on about various things — that if I had walked past somebody smoking a spliff and not said anything to them, or asked for them to be thrown out ... They were always picking up on things, and they were constantly watching me. I was aware of that. So the police said, 'We're going to shut you down unless you get stricter.' Everybody was in a complete panic, and it was decided that on Friday and Saturday night, we were going to search all our customers for drugs, and we were going to get really strict on the door.

SUZANNE ROBINSON: When the club closed down, I had two young boys. I was still on the catering staff, but we didn't have any income, so I set up this New York deli-style takeaway. I had a friend in New York faxing me menus over. The kitchen was quite a good size, so we all went from there. We did that from The Haçienda during the day, and that went on for quite a few years. We didn't plagiarise one of those New York menus ... Obviously there's some ingredients you couldn't get here at the time. We did a Reuben, a triple decker ... American sandwiches. We also did some British deli-style sandwiches. Soup was very popular, and we'd do a fresh homemade soup every day and send that out in flasks. Because we knew the people we were catering for, more often than not, they came back the following day.

REBECCA GOODWIN: FAC 51 Productions happened later, when the club got shut down due to the criminal activity and the council wanting to build flats. It became a branch of Factory that developed in that kind of gap. So Ang was kept on during that shutdown and was moved to Dry with Leroy, and I got kept on at The Haçienda. Everybody else was made redundant, basically. I was there because I was part of this FAC 51 Productions thing, which wasn't necessarily my skill set: it was an events business that involved staging, barriers and crew.

One particular event, Carl [Ryder, who established FAC 51 Productions] couldn't do for personal reasons. So we had the first big event to do and it was a nightmare. [laughs] The first big, live music, three-day festival in Manchester's Heaton Park − the biggest civic park in Europe − that would be the first of its kind. We had to design and build a whole new bit of fencing for the park ... so we made a huge fence! It was produced in conjunction with a company called Star Hire. I went up to oversee where the fence was being constructed in the north of Manchester − the riveting, steel work and panels. They're all to be erected around this huge arena, with about seven gates for punters. At this point, Jake was crew boss and stage manager, and he couldn't be there either because his girlfriend went into labour! So I got called up to run it. [laughs] I was in charge of all the crew and various crowds of people trying to crush through the gate. People kept radioing me with 'Rebecca, GATE FOUR!' or, 'Rebecca, you've got to get to Gate Six!' It was an exciting thirty-six to forty-eight hours where I was suddenly doing all the stuff I didn't normally do — all the practical stuff. That fence we built is still being used at various festivals.

For FAC 51 Productions, I went with Carl down to a company in London called Steel Deck that made staging units for scaffolds where you could adjust the heights and build up modular stages. They did a lot of theatre work at that point, and they were looking to expand into rock 'n' roll. We were their conduit into that, so we marketed it to arenas and venues as staging first, and then we added areas — because there'd been a horrible barrier incident where people had been killed — so they started doing this thing called a Pop Code [Code of Practice on Environmental Noise at Concerts]. It was all run by cowboys, the whole industry, but they started this thing called a Pop Code to encourage the professionalisation of events, and especially safety for production and equipment. So we did the staging and went into the industry of rock 'n' roll and barriers. You don't hear much about it, but in a way, Factory helped get that started with FAC 51 Productions, and Star Hire were involved, too.

TERESA ALLEN: I left in early '91, but I didn't really leave — quite a few of us were made redundant. I kind of lost my way a bit after that because it had been such a massive part of my life, and it took a long time for me to actually find myself, you know, find *me* at all again. But by that point, working at The Haçienda was not fun any more. That was when the knives started appearing, the ecstasy, and a girl died. Then there were guns turning up. It wasn't a nice place to work any more, and I wouldn't have lasted much longer because of that. Factory also had brought in some new business people around that time, and they wanted to change things, and quite a few of us realised it wasn't the same.

ANG MATTHEWS: Because Paul Mason believed it was house music that was causing this problem, he changed the policy and we got another DJ in on Friday nights instead of Mike Pickering. Unfortunately that DJ has since died, Dave Booth. Now, it's no reflection of Dave Booth — he played indie music — but in changing the music, in searching all our customers, we disrupted their lives and it just killed the trade. So Tony Wilson decided we were going to go on strike. It was a strike against the police, and I think he thought it would gain a lot of publicity. He went on the radio — and I have the recording somewhere — stating that we were going on strike, so we were closing down. Of course, ultimately, that decision in the end killed The Haçienda. They'd bought the building at a period when mortgages were sky-high in the UK, so it really killed them in the end, trying to get that paid when there was absolutely no income. I had to make forty-two staff redundant that weekend.

REBECCA GOODWIN: In the early nineties, there was an attempt to make it all new again — part of an attempt to stay open. Squeaky clean. People were coming in wearing dresses and high heels again like the early days, whereas before they'd just been dressed to sweat. We had a big metal detector on the door by that point, and the reception area was smaller. We also had more doormen. It wasn't as good as in the really good days in '88, '89, '90 when it was all going off, but it was still a startlingly exciting place to go. Anytime you'd walk in, the whole place was moving.

LIEVE MONNENS: I think the girls working there might have been a bit less bothered with all the male attitudes because they came across a lot of other stuff that was much less pleasant. I wouldn't have wanted to work at The Haçienda at all because of all the violence. It was OK in the beginning when I started to go there, with alternative music, but if you have to go through a metal detector to get into a club, deal with bouncers who are armed . . . no. That came with the territory of Manchester at the time.

ANG MATTHEWS: In the early days, The Haçienda was like an indie club. It wasn't making any income, surviving on New Order's money. House music happened in '88, '89, first imported to Manchester and brought to The Haçienda by Mike Pickering. He was already DJing there, and then the Mondays started. When ecstasy arrived in Manchester — and I don't know how true it is, but they say the Happy Mondays brought it back from Ibiza, while London Records say it was them that brought it over, so who knows — that changed everything. People started dancing. There was nobody sat in the alcoves. It was more like *dealing* in the alcoves in The Haçienda. I was selling alcohol, but with that cultural shift, I became the biggest seller of bottles of water in the UK for about a four-year period when house music hit. I used to have a lorry arrive separately from the beer and the soft drinks just filled with bottles of water.

MARCIA PANTRY: Hicks was always busy. It was always, *always* busy in the can bar. I remember when Red Stripe came in for the first time. Oh my God. People climbing over each other for Red Stripe. [laughs]

There was a little table and couple of chairs under the stairs to the Gay Traitor, and that's where people used to 'partake of party'. I say to people that I never saw any drugs in The Haçienda and they don't believe me, but it's true because my drug was vodka. I never saw people taking drugs because I was never a drug taker myself. But I know they used to do it just under the stairs. I used to love dancing at The Haçienda. People always asked me what I was on, and I used to say, 'Vodka and lemonade!' [laughs]

ANG MATTHEWS: But then there was another change when we started selling things like brandy. Brandy and coke became the drink in Manchester anywhere you went, and that seems to be linked in with the later stage of The Haçienda, or what I saw myself socially. Cocaine seemed to become the drug of choice, and from my perspective, that started creating violence. Of course, The Haçienda was going through its own problems with the gang stuff in Manchester. For the last six months, I just didn't want to work there any more. I did hand my notice in, but Peter Hook and Rob Gretton refused to accept my notice and asked me if there was a role I could create within the company so I wouldn't leave. Rob was adamant I didn't leave because he said I was the only person left who had a connection with the past and to the history, and he wanted me there because I'd been there so long.

ANGIE CASSIDY: Up to that point, Factory had not been heavily associated with drugs ... it was associated with excellent music and really beautiful artwork. A different doorway was opened up into The Haçienda because that drug crowd came in.

ANN QUIGLEY: It wasn't until the mid- to late eighties, when the Madchester scene arrived and a different kind of music, that The Haçienda changed.

ANG MATTHEWS: Things changed in mid-1989 when coaches used to arrive, and the peak years were probably '89 to '94. People came from all over, and because we were a small club, by law I was only allowed to let 1,200 people in. So, that's not many when you think now they have 10,000 to 15,000 in the Warehouse Project legally. I used to break the law and let in up to 1,800 people. You can print that because I'm not going to be licensing anywhere else. And 1,800 is not a lot of people! That's why there were so many queues outside, and that's why people used to start queuing from about six on a Friday to try to get in.

ANN QUIGLEY: When the Madchester scene arrived, Kalima had moved in a completely different direction ... We were still making music and getting great responses round the country, and it was weird to see the difference between the dance scene we were part of and the scene in Manchester, which came out of The Haçienda.

REBECCA BOULTON: Obviously, there was a change in atmosphere during the whole Madchester thing because it was always crowded and the music changed. But initially, it was great and everyone was really happy, whether they were on drugs or not. Much is made of that, but it didn't really matter. But then there was a change, because inevitably that is one of the issues with drugs, isn't it? That with drugs come those who are prepared to be involved with illegal activities. So there was a change in atmosphere, and that was quite hard to see because it was sometimes quite frightening. There were times when it wasn't nice.

ANG MATTHEWS: Obviously, music changed through the whole period, and because it was open so long, it eventually had a different generation of punters. I can remember from '94 to '95, from the New Year's Eve to the next New Year's Eve, I didn't actually know the customers like I had previously because that first generation of house music was now ten years old. That brought those customers almost to thirty [years old], and they were changing their lives. So, the customers actually changed.

MARCIA PANTRY: And the queue at The Haçienda! It was *the place* to be. Everybody wanted to be on the guest list.

ANGIE CASSIDY: Then The Haçienda closed, New Order split . . . it was such a sad way for something so majestic to finish. It should have been better because it was worth more and it was better than that. But people's egos get in the way, don't they?

LINDSAY ANDERSON: You always think someone or something's going to be there forever, so when The Haç got changed into flats, it was kind of shocking.

ANNE-MARIE COPELAND: I came to Germany in 1994, to study at an art school in Frankfurt (Städelschule). I made a very good friend from Madrid, and I used to talk about The Haçienda because I just complained about the nightlife in Frankfurt where people stood in corners just staring at each other. I was like, where I come from, you talk to people, you interact. Nobody cared what you looked like, nobody cared what you wore. Nobody cared what skin colour you had, nobody cared what religion. I even had a friend who was like, 'After Shabbat, I'm coming to The Haçienda.' My friend said, 'If that's true, then I'll come with you to Manchester.' We got on the plane to Manchester, but because it was 1996, 1997, The Haçienda vibe had died down by then. She turned around to me and said, 'Everything that you were telling me was just fantasy.' It seemed too unreal to be true.

• • •

ANG MATTHEWS: I've spent more time in The Haçienda than any other living person. That's my claim to fame! [laughs] I used to count, but when it got to over a thousand nights, I just gave up. I've been there more than anybody else.

SUZANNE ROBINSON: I think I've spent more hours in that club than anyone else because I would be the first in and I would be the last out. I had one New Year's off in all that time, in fifteen years of working there. I worked and worked and worked. Even when the kids' grandma was dying, I used to drive to Devon where she lived on Sunday morning and come back on a Wednesday morning ready for the club, so it was a massive part of my life. For years I was known as Suzanne from The Haçienda.

ANNE-MARIE COPELAND: The Haçienda was the place where gay people, Black people could go without discrimination, and there was no misogyny. It was just a completely different space.

CORINNE DREWERY: What I noticed when I came to The Haçienda was how no one made a big deal about anyone being Black, white, gay, straight, male, female — it was a collective of people. It was so diverse, and everybody was well represented.

ANNE-MARIE COPELAND: I have to add here that I spent most of my summers in New York with my grandparents and one summer at Hofstra University, and Manchester felt more homey and completely different. When you live in Britain and watch all these American films, and then you see all these college campuses and how the American youths live, it was just a completely different experience from what I knew in Manchester and in The Haçienda. It was so weird, so different and so segregated as well. I have to add that one. That was quite new to me. It just wasn't like that in Manchester at all.

BEV BYTHEWAY: It's also interesting to think about the relationship of The Haçienda to the city. I'm thinking about SuAndi, a Black poet that lives in Manchester and used to run a Black arts organisation — still does probably. She's said it took years for the Black community in south Manchester to feel that they could come into the city, and I would think — would hope — The Haçienda was one of the spaces that pulled Black youth into the city centre or gave them a space to come into.

STELLA HALL: In the eighties, The Haçienda felt like a very open space. As the Green Room, we were absolute pioneers in ensuring that queer, disabled, Black artists and audiences were encouraged into the space, and that was the same at The Haçienda then. It was a 'come all ye'. Obviously people would choose their particular nights, but it was really an eclectic mix. It's certainly the last club that I ever felt really comfortable in, wandering about. I usually went with girlfriends, but probably I would have been happy to go in on my own.

JUDITH FOSTER: Ruth and Rebecca and I are still really good friends, and I think The Haçienda forged quite strong relationships among a lot of women.

RUTH TAYLOR: So many of the friends I made working at The Haçienda, they're still my friends today. It gave you a place to belong. Everyone used to laugh about the sound because the acoustics weren't great, but it didn't matter. We didn't care. It was this big, huge, open space — and *it was ours*.

ANNE-MARIE COPELAND: The Haçienda was a different environment. There wasn't anything macho about it. I really felt safe. There was always respect coming from everybody who worked there. It was like family . . . everybody looked out for each other.

JUDITH FOSTER: One night, I got off the bus and was walking down for work at The Haçienda. A car drove past me and I was gonna say it was partly my fault, but it bloody wasn't. He drove past, honking and grimacing at me. I shouldn't have but I did just give him the finger. He stopped his car and ran across the road after me. Luckily, The Ritz nightclub was halfway between Oxford Road and

The Haçienda, so I ran into The Ritz and said to the doorman, 'That bloke's chasing me', and he said, 'Well, you must know him, then.' I said, 'I don't', but he kept saying, 'Oh, I think you must.' He didn't believe me. He did let me into The Ritz to ring The Haçienda, and Fiona was working. I told her what happened, and she said she'd come get me in her car and bring me back safe. There were dodgy people everywhere, and people who didn't believe you when you said you weren't safe. I was probably more cavalier than I should have been about it all.

CLARE CUMBERLIDGE: The background is that Manchester was a very violent place. My flat was broken into three times, and a number of my friends were raped. There was an undercurrent of violence. But then there was this space of creative play that happened in The Haçienda, The Cornerhouse and the Green Room from probably '86 to '88.

MARTINE MCDONAGH: I never felt safe there [in Manchester]. I always felt like there was this aggressive undercurrent, particularly in the city centre. I travel a lot and I go to lots of different places, but Manchester has always felt a bit . . . not my place. This got worse as the band [James] became more successful. I didn't live anywhere flash, but my house was broken into several times – a couple of times when I was home alone with my infant son, which was scary – and my car was stolen a few times, so we had to move.

ANG MATTHEWS: Tony was aware of how unusual it was, being a female manager of The Haçienda. Well, not 'a female' but *the* manager of The Haçienda who was female. He was worried about any risk of repercussion that could come on me because he was aware of . . . well, the obvious thing – he was aware that rape could happen at the end of the night if we were broken into or they tried to get money. There was an added element of my security, and he felt somewhat responsible for that.

REBECCA GOODWIN: I should say that at the time, as a female, the 'dress code' at The Haçienda was about comfortable clothes or quirky clothes. I wore a lot of charity shop or second-hand clothes, and I didn't feel sexualised at all. *At all*. It felt like everybody was equal and you didn't get groped, you didn't get propositioned, you didn't get sexually threatened, you didn't feel remotely vulnerable in The Haçienda. That might have been happening outside The Haçienda, but inside, it felt like equal politics to me.

CLARE CUMBERLIDGE: Factory Records always had a laddie element to it. Not necessarily macho, but laddie in a kind of northern white boys' culture, and everybody who wasn't a white boy knew that. Yet The Haçienda didn't actually *feel* like a Factory space for that reason — because it felt like it was shaped by the communities in it rather than by Factory.

• • •

YVONNE SHELTON: When I talk to people who I know were involved in Factory, in bands and as producers — even looking at Hooky during The Haçienda Classical [events] — it is about building on the legacy of Factory in the present. You're thinking about The Haçienda, and then it is about putting that in the present by doing Haçienda Classical shows. The first official Haçienda Classical was the second one done after Ibiza. People were asking them to do The Haçienda for ages before the Ibiza Classical happened, and they kept saying how wonderful that the Ibiza one worked. Then they took on it, making Haçienda Classical. So when you talk about it building on the legacy of Factory Records, it really is.

REBECCA GOODWIN: There's a lot of Haçienda-related stuff going on now, still going on, and I'm honestly not that interested. I understand why people do Haçienda Classical, revisit those memories in a new way, because it was the most exciting part of their life — and it was extremely exciting. We did feel like we were at the centre of the world culturally, and there was nowhere else we'd rather be. But the new stuff, at least to me, feels like squishing it all a bit, turning it into something it was never supposed to be. Maybe I'm too old for it. [laughs]

YVONNE SHELTON: A lot of auditions were going for Haçienda Classical, and I thought, well, I don't really want to audition, so I don't mind passing the audition onto other people. Finally, the manager of Haçienda Classical says, 'Do you want to do it, do you want to sing in this?' I said, 'Yeah, I don't mind singing it. I'm not interested in doing the audition and trying to see if I can get it, to be quite honest. But if you just want me to do it, then let me do it.' It wasn't that I wasn't interested in the songs — I was. And my voice goes right down that road. But I just wasn't going to audition at this point.

Graeme Park likes the songs to be sung as close to the original as possible. The conductor, too. Then I think Hooky likes to experiment if you want to, and so does the manager. So as a singer, you're cutting and splicing between the two rules, those two schools of thought. I deliver what I know they'll want, and then depending on if it's outside, or if you've got a morning slot or evening, or if you've got back-to-back gigs, well . . . then it depends on my voice and the conditioning of my voice.

ANNE-MARIE COPELAND: When you think about it, something like The Haçienda can't really happen, but The Haçienda has been built and it's there. It's still present in everything that I do.

Big Sister Is Watching

As criminal activity surrounding the club during the Madchester years (late 1980s through to the early 1990s) brought intense police and city surveillance, you might say Big Brother was watching. But in fact it was a resistant, benevolent Big Sister. After a brief closure brought on by high-handed policing, the women of The Haçienda set up their own surveillance system upon reopening, took control of the cameras, and contended with the law.

ANG MATTHEWS: We closed for six months because of all the trouble with the police. I was one of the few people they kept on, and Hooky's argument was that I could go to the newspaper and sell my story, so they may as well pay me the amount I would get if I sold the stories about what had gone on. So, I just helped out during that six-month period, doing whatever needed doing.

REBECCA GOODWIN: I had to go into Bootle Street police station, which was the central police station in Manchester at the time, because something had happened. It was all videoed, so I had to go in and talk about that. But I didn't see the police as being on our side. We'd asked the police for help, but they wouldn't. They wouldn't put police on the door like they would for football matches, nothing like that.

ANG MATTHEWS: During the closure, as I say, I was kept on, and I helped out at Dry because that was kept open. But the bar didn't take enough money to keep a building the size of The Haçienda and pay the mortgage on it. I don't think that they realised how much money there was available to New Order and Factory Records at that given time — because big money was coming in. We had the best top lawyer in the UK who fought the case against the police and won. It was during this period that the police said if the place was to reopen, I was to be the manager and the licensee. It was a form of promotion, but they were not going to be open if I didn't do it. The police didn't exactly make my life comfortable after that. They were always on our case, waiting for anything, because we'd made them look fools, I suppose.

REBECCA GOODWIN: The police were building a challenge against us because they wanted to get The Haçienda shut down. I think the council were complicit because they wanted the real estate for flats, which is what it is now. So the police would sit in the pub opposite in an upstairs window, record the doors and take notes. That wasn't great.

JUDITH FOSTER: We had the police in the pub opposite The Haçienda, and they had a camera set up from the windows, trained on the doorway of the club all the time. I don't know what the police's responsibilities were, but I can imagine they were probably quite frightening. I think they knew that they had a job to do, and they knew that we did, too, so there was an uncomfortable understanding there.

REBECCA GOODWIN: At that time, I was doing the door less because I'd go upstairs and do the cameras. I was manning (or, womanning!) the CCTV cameras in the club and had a radio to say, 'OK, guy in whatever hoodie just sold this', and they'd go and grab them to take them out of the club. But I was also watching the police watching us — on instruction. I was noting down, for example, how you could see them in the window of the pub with a telephoto lens. They were just looking to record wrongdoing rather than coming in to help us with wrongdoing. It all culminated when everything shut down, and the court case followed. I was one of the only people still working there, so I was asked to compile all the evidence we had of the police not being helpful and observing. It was a foregone conclusion because the powers that be in Manchester — coming out of the early eighties, post-industrial decline, when property was at a premium — wanted us shut because they wanted it residential, and they didn't want the trouble of the club. What was good about us being the trouble was everyone was contained and the police knew everybody were there. The police did say afterwards that once we shut, the trouble dispersed around the city and it was harder to contain.

RUTH TAYLOR: There was a little room in the cellar and for probably the last two or three years, they converted the basement into a gig area. So they always had the downstairs bar, and then there was a room on the other side of it (where they had the gigs). The camera room was tiny, in the corner of what was the dressing room. There were four screens and four cameras. There was one on the front door, one on the stairs, one over the bar, and then I think there was another one downstairs. So there's four of them, round about, and they were put in place because of the drugs. It was pitch black, so there was very little you could see. [laughs] The idea was that it had to be done, and I ended up working those cameras three or four nights a week. By the end, I was literally going cross-eyed because it was like four o'clock in the morning and still staring at the same screen. But it was funny because I also got to see all of the drama happening. [laughs]

ANG MATTHEWS: I also then had legal duties to fulfil, being a licensee. The police actually told me I was the first woman in the UK to hold a licence for a venue that size. I'd been dying to go public with it, and I don't know if they wanted me to or didn't want me to. But I said, 'Well, we're not bothering, we're not even putting my name on the outside.' We felt at that time we couldn't because of threats going on from gang people and that it would be best if my name wasn't on anything.

Anyhow, my relationship with the police was that they wanted all the drugs confiscated, but then they were complaining that I was giving them too many drugs and that it must be a really bad place, 'all these drugs'. So then we had the ridiculous situation where I was flushing drugs down the toilet. You know, I'd monitor how much drugs came in, split it, put half down the toilet. Hooky said to me then, 'I can't believe you're flushing drugs down the toilet.' Well, what else was I going to do? At any given moment, I knew the police could be waiting for me outside and search me to make sure I hadn't taken them home. The Haçienda lawyer also pointed out that on the walk from The Haçienda to the police station, at any given time, I might be arrested because I was actually carrying drugs on me, so I refused to do it. The police had to come to The Haçienda.

JUDITH FOSTER: Sometimes the doormen would confiscate drugs from young people coming in. They were passed to us to keep in reception, and we were tasked to find the police in Manchester to collect them from us — that was an agreement from our management.

ANG MATTHEWS: There was one night they decided I was going to get arrested in the club, and this idea, 'Ang at the bar is going to be arrested by the police.' Customers just jumped over the bar so they couldn't arrest me. Tony once phoned me and said, 'Are you aware that someone was shot at The Haçienda last night?' I said, 'No', and he said, 'Don't come into work, the police are looking for you.' There'd be all that sort of thing. I couldn't be just an ordinary girl doing her job, playing records at a club, because there was all this nonsense going on behind the scenes.

RUTH TAYLOR: I don't know how effective the security cameras could have been, and putting me on them . . . I was hardly security trained! The training was literally, 'OK, right, so this is how you make the cameras move around, this is the remote, press this button on the walkie-talkie to speak to one of the guys and tell them to go look at something you see on the camera.' And at the beginning of the night, I'd put the videotapes in to record. Every now and again, the police would come back for the videos, and I don't know how long we kept them, but we'd have however many videos for each night, with a day of the week written on. So you'd have the Wednesday ones, and then the following Wednesday you'd just have a 'Wednesday' video, so the tapes would only be kept until the following Wednesday. Crappy old VHS tapes. I can't imagine the quality was that great.

Security inside – apart from the door – was me just scanning the cameras around, looking out for trouble. Flesh night was probably the night where you would have the least drama because the gangs would stay away. They'd stick out like a sore thumb at Flesh.

There was a very, very, very small minority of the bad stuff at The Haçienda, and it didn't impact most people. You hear the stories now and there were a few awful nights, like the horrific day where one of the doormen got stabbed, but that wasn't the norm.

ANG MATTHEWS: But I do think that sometimes people focus on that too much – the drugs and the violence – and it was a very small part. I think it's a masculine focus. There was an article in *Vice* about The Haçienda, and you'll see that a lot of the guys they interviewed went absolutely crazy on the violence – talking about sliding in blood on the dance floor. I don't even know what they're referring to, you know. That's just changing history.

CHAPTER 14
DRY 201

Dry 201 coaster (beer mat) and flyer

Dry 201, or Dry Bar, or FAC 201 – the bar and restaurant that sprung out of the Factory universe. A BKD design, Dry 201 was imagined as a place to go before heading to The Haçienda, and it made bar culture aesthetically sublime while also serving as another gathering spot for Factory scene-makers. When Dry 201 was in its formative stages, Sandra Douglas suggested that BKD bring on Elena Massucco for the massive project, and the two women played a major role in the bar's creation. Meanwhile, women took on essential roles in management, promotion, and culinary arts. Claire de Verteuil had the multifaceted position of assistant general manager. Melanie Wilkinson was Dry 201's first chef, and she worked closely with Pauline Harrison on all things food.

TINA SIMMONS: Don't forget about Dry Bar! Factory had The Haçienda, so what else could they want? A bar, of course, that sells food, so you have somewhere to go before The Haçienda. [laughs] It was designed by Ben Kelly and had the weirdest bar that was like an aeroplane wing shooting out the front and out into the sky. How we got it past the building regs I don't know, but we did somehow. It was a nice place but totally bizarre. It was really before its time.

CLAIRE DE VERTEUIL: I went to Manchester Poly in 1984 and I graduated in 1987. Like many students, I was equipped with a piece of paper, no real plan and an overdraft. A lot of my friends at the time decided to go to London, but me and my boyfriend at the time liked Manchester too much to leave. Manchester was run-down — those were the Thatcher years — but it was full of great spirit. My boyfriend at the time got a job behind the bar at The Haçienda, so I joined him and ended up working four nights a week behind the main bar for what turned into two years. Leroy promoted me to bar supervisor, so I worked there every night it was open. The fun kicked off during summer of '87 when everything changed, work was busy, hot and sweaty, but the atmosphere was amazing.

It was soon decided that Factory were going to open a bar called Dry 201. Probably about a year before it opened, they asked if I would like to be assistant general manager, and Leroy and I were going to move over there and start that up. At the time, there was nothing happening in the Northern Quarter at all. Socially, it was pretty much a dead space, apart from the fact that we used to sometimes have a drink up behind the *Daily Express* building on [Great] Ancoats Street. There were lots of little pubs that used to stay open all night to serve the newspaper workers and you could always get a drink and spy a character or two.

Factory decided they wanted to explore Ancoats, but at that time they couldn't get a licence because there were so many little hole-in-the-wall pubs there. The licensing authority said, basically, 'there's enough, and we don't need any more'. Factory had to go to court and get that reversed. They found this fabulous old furniture warehouse, so they asked me to put together a campaign for that. It involved lots of market research and doing a full plan of the whole area and visiting all these hole-in-the-wall pubs to break down what they were offering and what sort of crowd it appealed to. We took this big campaign to court and we won! So that was it — all systems go from about a year before Dry opened.

PAULINE HARRISON: It was a very trendy place to be. The reason they took that site in the first place was that they were told the area around it was going to get a grant and be up-and-coming. That never happened — they never got the grant — but Dry was already there, so they couldn't move. They just missed their time.

REBECCA GOODWIN: Factory opened Dry, and Dry became the pre-Haçienda place to go. I came up with their happy-hour slogan, and I was quite pleased with it: Drink Dry.

MELANIE WILKINSON: I was working at a bar in town called Corbières, and I was getting a bit fed up there. My friend Maria, who I was working with there, came in one day and said, 'There's a new bar opening. It's called Dry Bar, and my boyfriend's doing the graphics. Do you want to try and get it?' I said yeah, and so the Factory people opening Dry planned to come into the bar where I was working because I did all the food. Maria said, 'I know who they are, so I'll tell you when they come and you can make sure the food is really good.' She did, and that's how I got the job. After they had the food I made, they said, 'Yeah, she can come and work at Dry.' I went to work at Dry Bar as the chef, and that's where I met my friend Pauline. On the day of the opening of Dry Bar, I met everyone at Factory, and that's how it all started.

PAULINE HARRISON: When I was with Vini, I was catering, and they said they wanted somebody for the new café, Dry. Vini suggested I put myself forward for it, so I did. I was working with Laurent Garnier, the DJ, and he set the café up. We used to drive around and try people's baguettes and stuff like that. We ended up headhunting Melanie Wilkinson, who was the chef at Dry. Then, of course, the way things were, nobody wanted to eat because it wasn't that type of place. [laughs] Everybody was off their face, it seemed, on one substance or another, so food was the last of their desires as it were.

CLAIRE DE VERTEUIL: With Leroy and the Factory guys, I put together the general way that things were going to run on a practical level at Dry. They were very keen to make it a more stylish place and to brand it in their way. So that planning was everything from producing beautiful glasses that had the acid-etched Dry logo on it, to little chocolates in paper envelopes to serve with the coffees on the all-new Italian coffee machine ... We all had to take lessons in how it worked, it was so new. We gave out little black boxes of matches with the logo on and the orange and purple beer mats, it was all beautifully designed and considered, but all the kinds of stuff that everyone wanted to take home and we were always running out of glasses. The uniform was a logo T-shirt for the staff with a long, black, French-style waiter's apron, which was so completely new at the time. We researched every possible drink that you could find, and behind the bar we ended up with seventy-five different whiskies, endless Polish and Russian vodkas that weren't seen anywhere else. We really put together a package of something that was totally different and very, very stylish to match the beautiful space that Ben Kelly's firm designed.

PAULINE HARRISON: There were women working all over the place for Factory in all sorts of different areas, absolutely. Most of our staff at Dry were women, managers were women.

REBECCA GOODWIN: Me and Paul Cons did the promo for Dry. And when he was in the States for six weeks, I did his job.

MELANIE WILKINSON: I'd always been interested in cooking. It's just one of those things that I'd always loved doing — dinner parties for friends and cooking generally. I had a passion for it. I got cooking in The Corbières wine bar where I worked because the chef walked out one day. I said, 'I can do that', and afterward the owner said to me, 'Do you mind just staying in there and cooking? You did a good job.' 'Yeah, that's fine,' I said, and that was how I started cooking before going to Dry.

We had a lot of freedom with the menu. We were allowed to do what we wanted mostly, and there didn't appear to be any kind of budget. It was a nice time for me to experiment with different things. We did a lot of 'home cooking'. I used to do quite nice dishes for lunchtime, chicken with brandy and cream, and sautéed potatoes, that kind of pub lunch but a bit more upbeat. We used to have a cheese selection, we used to cook a lot of vegetarian food, and there were French bakers that we used to buy from. We could source our food from good places as well, which was nice.

I had a friend who was a butcher who we'd source from. I like to give business to local and organic places, which were mostly Cheshire produce, local farms, other local shops. I mean, they were more expensive, but it was nice to be able to buy quality things. But I'm also quite a resourceful person. I can turn a whole meal into another meal the next day. So we were just careful about what we did, but it was a bit free-for-all, I must admit. I remember once having to have a go at members of the staff because there was cheese missing out of the fridge, so we had to start locking the door.

Leroy Richardson was usually who I'd ask about trying something for the menu. He was the guy who was running Dry Bar at the time, and he was very flexible. He was a meat guy, so he'd say, 'As long as you do that roast beef every day . . .' [laughs] I think it went a bit too far, trying things on the menu, because we weren't making a lot of money. We were buying all kinds of things without even thinking about a budget. At one point I thought, 'We need to slow it down a bit and think about the costs.'

PAULINE HARRISON: There used to be pastries. There was a French guy that me and Laurent sourced who had a French bakery in Chilton. We used to get croque-monsieur and pastries from him. That was the morning. Then Mel would sort out a menu for the afternoon. Dry was never open in the evening for food as a late-night place. It was more of a daytime thing.

MELANIE WILKINSON: Everybody said that my chilli was great, so I got a reputation for the best chilli. I was really proud one day when I heard somebody say about my chilli, 'That's the best chilli I think I've ever had.' I was like, *yes*!

Some of the menu was already planned out because Factory had seen some things in other places that they wanted, so we followed those guidelines. But they were also very good at giving me freedom to create. There was a brunch that they were quite happy for me to create the menu for, and I'm convinced I invented the Stilton and cranberry croissant. It was delicacies like that which I was allowed to try out, and that worked well. People liked them. Sunday brunch was usually very healthy. It was all fruit and eggs, but having to make scrambled eggs for one hundred people could be quite tiresome. It was backwards and forwards at Dry Bar with the menu: we were asked to do things, or we would say, 'Can I try this thing?' and they would almost always say yes.

PAULINE HARRISON: We had a lot of Factory people come in, like the Mondays and New Order. It became their watering hole, which was great in itself because they're all good people. Factory was run by good people, and it surrounded itself with good people. So it was a lot of fun. Too much fun. [laughs]

CLAIRE DE VERTEUIL: Day to day, you never knew who was going to pop up at the bar. Andy Connell from Swing Out Sister, Steve Diggle, Central Station, DJs, bands and artists were all regulars ... Manchester was full of wonderful crazy, talented people and real characters and they all treated Dry as their second home. In the days before mobile phones, the landline behind the bar was constantly ringing, with messages for Sasha or a call for Sean or Bez. Tony would turn up at the bar after he'd been in New York, talking about seeing this band or that. Tony turned up one day with a handful of CDs of all the Factory Classical stuff, Durutti Column, Brian Eno, and at first that became the soundtrack for the Sunday breakfast.

BRIDGET CHAPMAN: Tony loved going to Dry Bar. At any time, there would be somebody terribly famous having a drink in there, and somebody who obviously didn't know that these people were terribly famous, but nobody bothered anybody. It was really a place where everybody could be anonymous.

ANG MATTHEWS: Tony used to walk through The Haçienda, but he didn't dance and didn't party or anything. He'd come in at night to say hello. Peter Hook and some of them used to party there, so I have a closer relationship with them than anybody else, particularly with Peter Hook. We used to meet in Dry Bar and then go out. So my closest relationship still to this day is with Peter Hook. I was friends with the others but especially with Peter. So it was one of equality, really; there was no hierarchy.

TINA SIMMONS: Dry was about attracting bands but also people on the street. For people on the street coming in, they might be rubbing shoulders with Bernard, Hooky, Shaun, Vini Reilly ... It was always a feeling that you were part of something, and that the Factory bands didn't think themselves too important to talk to their fans or people off the street, and Dry Bar was a place for that.

ANG MATTHEWS: I used to be sat in Dry Bar, because I'd go there socially when The Haçienda wasn't open, and a message would come from the door staff: 'Alan Erasmus is outside and he'd like to speak to you.' I'd go outside, and he was actually in his car, not parked — he'd stopped all the traffic with the door open and said, 'Get in.' He'd ask me some questions about business, I'd answer him, he'd say, 'Get out', and then off he'd drive. [laughs] Yeah, it was quite strange. He used to say to me, 'You're the only person in that building who knows what's going on.'

CLAIRE DE VERTEUIL: It was all quite sophisticated, with Sunday newspapers, good food and great coffee, but it didn't really appeal to the crowds that stumbled in, wrecked after a night of partying! But Factory were always about doing things with style and though never the most popular time to work as a staff member, it was different. At that time, when we first opened, Laurent Garnier was our kitchen chef, and then Pauline and Melanie took over the kitchen just a bit later when he had to go back to France to do his national service.

MELANIE WILKINSON: Laurent Garnier was big then, and he has done really well for himself. It was very male-dominated. I remember one day he changed the name of my chilli. Instead of 'Mel's Chilli', he put 'Laurent's Chilli' and thought it was funny. I got really annoyed and he was like, 'C'mon I'm joking', and I said, 'No. There's enough men doing stuff around here and taking credit. Get your name off there.' There I am, agitated, and he thought it was really funny. I said, 'I'm not angry that you're stealing my chilli. I'm angry that you think because you're a guy, you can just put your name up there and everyone will buy it.' That's really annoying to me, and that's just one example of how it was very male-dominated.

I wasn't particularly ambitious at the time, so I wasn't necessarily trying to climb any ladders. As a result, I was never put in a position where I would think 'oh, they're not letting me do that because I'm a woman'. I never felt that way then. But thinking back now, women who were there were working really hard, and I can't say that they got the recognition.

We were in a place where we were very experimental, so there were situations where people turned around to say 'they don't know what they're doing', but at least we were trying something new. And if it had been a male chef, would it have been different? I don't know, maybe . . . it's interesting to think.

CLAIRE DE VERTEUIL: At the end of the night at Dry, no one wanted to go home; it was impossible to make people leave. We had this fabulous sound system, which was state of the art. In the cavernous space that was Dry, the sound was huge. Anyway, one of the CDs that Tony brought over was the soundtrack to the film *Diva*. One night, to get rid of people at the end of the night, I decided to put on 'La Wally' from *Diva* really loud and fade the lights up. Everyone knew it was time to go home because they didn't want to listen to it! So that became something we did and it became the soundtrack to the end of the night. I used to love it when everyone left because I'd turn the lights off, turn the sound system up really loud and dance in that huge empty space.

PAULINE HARRISON: We'd have some events at Dry. We had an auction of memorabilia for a charity, and we did Martin Hannett's wake, the catering for that.

MELANIE WILKINSON: We did a couple of Dry Bar functions. We did a funeral, and it was a last-minute thing . . . 'Mel, Pol, can you do this?' Yeah, we could do it. We were very . . . *instant*, I have to say. [laughs]

The auction is a strong memory. Factory did a charity event at Dry Bar where everybody auctioned some of their things — like a guitar would come in, or a T-shirt, or a poster.

We did an event for Dizzy Gillespie, and we did his rider — all he wanted was fried chicken! He was a really nice guy. He was really getting on and was very appreciative of what we did.

• • •

CLAIRE DE VERTEUIL: Because there was so much going on in Manchester and Dry was such a fabulous venue and popular space, I started doing little exhibitions there. One of the customers approached Leroy with an idea for some Christmas decorations and it was a bit potty. The next thing we knew, a truckload of car tyres and half of Halfords arrived and Leroy and Mike O'Leary the cellar man had to put it all together and built a Christmas tree made of gold-painted tyres and 'festive' decorated tyres to hang behind the bar . . . all a bit unusual, but it worked. We had a few photographic exhibitions, big-sized blow-ups of things that people had done, behind the bar. We did a fashion show for Red or Dead when they launched their 'Space Baby' collection. Third Estate (the contemporary dance group) put on a performance there, and the bar hosted TV shows and events.

TERESA ALLEN: For Dry, Rebecca and I commissioned roses on big spikes, made of metal or porcelain. We went on a road trip to go and pick them up. We would just get money from petty cash, go and buy a load of stuff, and then we'd go back to the club and decorate it.

CLAIRE DE VERTEUIL: For Dry's first birthday my friend the artist Wayne Simmons put together a video of all the events that we'd had in Dry and set it to Durutti Column and other Factory band soundtrack, and we built this enormous tower of TVs to show it on.

MELANIE WILKINSON: The most social time at Dry Bar would have been around the World Cup in 1990. I'm not a football person, but I remember my partner said to Leroy, 'You're not putting the screen up for the World Cup event?' The next day, there were screens *everywhere*. That actually created a really nice vibe, and everybody was really enjoying it because, of course, New Order was doing the theme tune 'World in Motion' for it!

CLAIRE DE VERTEUIL: There were three or four floors to the space above the bar, and I think Factory always planned to develop them, but at the time they were kind of like empty warehouse spaces and the Happy Mondays and Northside made music videos up there.

MELANIE WILKINSON: On an average day, we used to open about 10 a.m. Myself and Pol opened most mornings because we used to get there quite early to start prepping. That was always my favourite time of the day because it was quiet — no customers and music blasting. We'd all decide what we were going to listen to while we were prepping. We'd all make tapes. I remember making tapes, taking some songs in and sharing music. The guys would be doing the bottle bins out the back. Then all the customers would come in and it got busy with orders. We joined a health club, myself and Pol, so we'd go for a swim after the lunch orders, and then go back to the bar and get drunk. [laughs] Sometimes we'd get roped into doing a few things because we were there. Those swims — that was one of the memorable weekly things that we did.

PAULINE HARRISON: Oh, God, I was at Dry all the time. We used to finish at about five, maybe half five, six o'clock. Then we'd go over to the Piccadilly Hotel because they had a gym in the basement. Me and Mel joined the gym, so we used to work, go for a swim and then go back to Dry for happy hour. That tended to last for a couple of hours, and sometimes I'd be in there all night because I knew a lot of the bands. I could sit and I didn't ever have to worry about being on my own for very long. It did a pretty fair trade at night.

MELANIE WILKINSON: I left Dry because I got pregnant, basically. I had to think about taking some time off. But me and Pol were both kind of made redundant at the same time, in a sense. I just don't think they knew what they wanted to do at Dry. We got a bit of a golden handshake and were given some redundancy money. Since I was pregnant at the time, I was happy to take it. I don't know what happened at Dry after that, to be honest. I didn't go back in for some time.

PAULINE HARRISON: I worked at Dry for two or three years. Me and Melanie got called to Tony's office and we were made redundant in the nicest possible way. He gave us a cheque and explained that it really wasn't working. And it wasn't, so we couldn't argue with that. It wasn't working because people just weren't eating. Factory were paying people to cook food that was going in the bin.

CLAIRE DE VERTEUIL: I'd actually gone out and secured funding from [the restaurateur] Oliver Peyton, since that was at the time when Absolut Vodka was really starting to do well. He was doing promotions all around the country, one-off events, and I think he did something at The Haçienda. I approached him about sponsoring events at Dry, but Paul Mason, who worked at The Haçienda, was not at all encouraging. We didn't see eye to eye on a lot of things and at that 'Think About the Future' meeting in 1990, where everyone from Factory came together, I put forward this idea of doing more events at Dry with sponsorship. It wasn't really discussed at the meeting, and after that, I started getting a lot of negativity from Paul Mason, who was basically just slapping me down, saying, 'Why are you getting big ideas? You just need to do the job and run the bar.' So that meeting in 1990 wasn't great for me. The next thing I know, Tony turns up and says, 'Come and have lunch with me.' We go up to The Cornerhouse, which was on Oxford Road, and Tony says, 'Listen, I don't necessarily think that what you want to do is a bad idea, but Paul does, so I'm afraid we're gonna have to knock it on the head for now.' It was really a bit crushing. In '91 the whole of Factory was having money problems, and they brought in this money guy, a guy with a big red pen. He came in and started putting his big red pen through lots of things, and they made me redundant.

MELANIE WILKINSON: I remember feeling like I was in a very misogynistic environment quite a lot of the time at Dry. A lot of women were pandering around to the men, and I wasn't going to do that.

PAULINE HARRISON: They did serve food again after we were made redundant, but they went in a completely different direction. Initially, what Factory wanted was restaurant-type foods in a café setting, but they completely changed tack after that, and I think they did tapas.

CLAIRE DE VERTEUIL: I did handmade Christmas decorations for Dry one year and it was great to work there again [after the redundancy].

My times at The Haçienda and Dry are incredibly cherished, and I always think now, it would have been so nice to have a video camera on your shoulder to document everything. It's a shame we can't scan the inside of our heads for those images, isn't it?

Mothers of Invention

The word 'mother' is often loaded, reflecting cultural assumptions about women's roles and bodies in patriarchal societies, but it's also multifaceted. A quick delve into the denotation says it's a noun to describe a 'female parent'. Yet it's also a term for 'the title of a woman who is in charge or who has a high rank' and 'the largest or most extreme example of something'. Further still, it's a verb: 'to treat someone with kindness and affection and try to protect that person from danger or difficulty'. The women at Factory Records defied the norms and did the work (and often had children while doing it). They persevered as versatile, pragmatic, and polymathic people.

JANE ROBERTS: Tina was in charge of the office. I think she was Tony's right- and left-hand woman. She might have seemed like a scary mum, but she was actually wilder than any of us. [laughs]

TRACEY DONNELLY: I remember being absolutely blown away when Tony listed 'Tracey's Baby' on the 'Think About the Future' meeting advertisement. He didn't tell me he was doing it, and I was blown away when I saw it . . . I got pregnant in 1990. They'd just bought the new building on Charles Street, and Tony'd be taking me round there in a hard hat, showing me my office, but I always knew I wouldn't go. When I was there initially, I ended up with the best job in the country, as I saw it. On my last day, they all took me to the pub (I couldn't drink, of course — I was pregnant!), but they were just the best bosses ever. To work for Tony, Rob and Alan — they were amazing. They changed a lot of things for a lot of people, almost like father figures.

GILLIAN GILBERT: It was only after Factory that I realised how special it was to be an equal, treated the same as everybody else ... When I was pregnant with [my daughter] Grace, a London Records company guy said, 'That's a bit inconvenient of you.' For me to have a baby? I thought, *no*. That never would have happened at Factory.

ANN QUIGLEY: As early as art school, I got the gist of what girls could and couldn't do, or more like the idea circulating of what they'd been allowed or not allowed to do. I also found out that it's really hard to be a mum and to be a singer in the band. The way we used to rehearse for these gigs that we did, it was like athletes with music. It was quite intense and complicated, and I realised after I had my daughter that I couldn't maintain that lifestyle.

GILLIAN GILBERT: At Factory, Lesley left to have a baby, and she didn't go back to work, and it was *her choice* — that's the difference. But in some ways, you sort of drop off the radar even if it is your choice.

SUZANNE ROBINSON: Over the years I had quite a few staff. At one point, I think I had fifty. A lot of them were students and some were artists. My first team were friends, and then I had four gay men working for me who were just the best. When I did get pregnant with the twins, Chris, one of these guys, he managed it for me because I had high blood pressure. He told me that I shouldn't be working because I'd had two miscarriages previous to this, so I had to stay at home, which killed me. When I did go back to work, because I breastfed the twins, I'd first breastfeed the twins, then I'd go to work, come back, breastfeed them again, and then go back to work. The boys were born in February 1990, so this was just after that ... I don't think they knew how hard it was to go to work, go home to breastfeed, come back to work. I think I was one of the first in our gang to have kids. Tony Wilson had got children, and so had Rob Gretton, that were a little bit older than my boys.

CLAIRE DE VERTEUIL: I actually gave birth to my daughter wearing my Hot night T-shirt from The Haçienda. There's a photograph of me wearing this T-shirt, in labour, sucking on gas and air. [laughs]

MARCIA PANTRY: I took on a young man called Roger, a student, because he used to come to Haçienda a lot anyway. But by the time that happened, I was now pregnant. So the last time I worked at Hicks was the New Year's of 1988. I had my baby that March. Working at The Haçienda while I was pregnant? [laughs] I was *partying* in The Haçienda, I would say. Those Friday and Saturday nights weren't really work. [laughs]

NICKY CREWE: Later on, when I was married and had little ones, I lived next door to Bruce Mitchell, who joined Vini Reilly in The Durutti Column. My daughter, my first baby, was born at home in the room that adjoined Vini Reilly's bedroom, so he was playing guitar through the time I was giving birth, completely oblivious to the fact that somebody was giving birth next door. We've always had this great story. We didn't tell my daughter for years, but yes, she was born to the sounds of Vini Reilly playing guitar ... When my children, who were born in '85 and '87, became teenagers, they got an interest in The Haçienda and Factory. They discovered Durutti Column, and of course then the story came out about my daughter's birth and Vini's guitar. [laughs]

MARTINE MCDONAGH: That was a big part of my decision to leave James. The band was on the road a lot, particularly in America. I used to take my son with me when I travelled. He would come everywhere with me, but we weren't allowed to travel with the band, so I would drive us all over the US and sometimes my assistant would come with me. Because his dad was in the band, I was a single parent in some ways. His dad was around but not *around*. When my son was approaching school age, I thought, If I'm going to leave, this is the best time to do it because, once he starts school, he needs stability. He needs somebody to be around all the time, a parent to take him to school, pick him up, give him his lunch, all that day-to-day stuff that a kid needs.

LINDSAY READE: At the beginning, Factory Records was like our baby, mine and Tony's baby. We didn't have a physical baby, but we did give birth to Factory Records. There was a lot happening in Manchester in '76 to '78, musically speaking. Tony and I didn't entirely agree on musical taste and Factory initially started with Tony and Alan Erasmus managing a band that Tony named The Durutti Column. That led to the Factory gig nights at the Russell Club. We'd already seen Joy Division at Rafters and they played at the Russell too. Tony also put them on his Granada TV show.

The gig nights went really well and then Tony and I had a discussion about making a record — featuring four acts who'd appeared at the club, including Durutti Column and Joy Division. This was the Factory Sample. It involved spending all our savings. While it's true that it was from money that his mother had left him, we were married and I was working. I was a school teacher, and it was all the savings we had, and we decided to do it together. Hence, I call myself a co-founder of Factory. I hadn't found my voice then, but I have now. I took on more of a mothering role then, providing support and nourishment. I was involved with all manner of other things: feeding musicians, driving them about — such as to the Factory Club, going to the studio, packing up the records. Me and Tony spent hours and *hours* just wrapping these records up, and I haven't even got one 'cause I smashed mine up in anger. [laughs]

CHAPTER 15

FACTORY HQ: THE CHARLES STREET YEARS

Lieve Monnens at Factory HQ

Factory Records eventually outgrew the Palatine Road offices and worked with Ben Kelly Design on the new headquarters, Factory HQ (FAC 251), located at the corner of Charles Street and Princess Street in Manchester. As building plans became a reality, the label invited all of its employees to a 'Think About the Future' conference in July 1990. Shortly thereafter, in September 1990, most of the office employees moved to the new headquarters, joined by new hires such as Georgina Trulio. Expectations were high, and the women – as they had done at Palatine Road – performed critical work that kept the label running. Despite their sweat, agony, and perseverance behind the scenes, the financial insolvency of the label became a reality. By November 1992, Factory Records was bankrupt and the women whose work had helped define Factory were forced to redefine themselves and their relationship to the music industry.

TRACEY DONNELLY: They were always about the future and not the past. *It's all about the future.*

LIEVE MONNENS: That 'Think About the Future' conference was me just starting at Factory and feeling wowed. We were going to move from the apartment office on Palatine Road into a big building, and there was a feeling that it was going to be a new phase and a new future. I thought it was going to become a bigger and more professional company.

ANG MATTHEWS: There were twenty-six of us at that 'Think About the Future' meeting and three unfortunately have since died. It was at Mottram Hall in Cheshire, so it was all posh, and it was very serious. Well, that's what we expected, anyway: that it was a really posh place we were going to. We walked in and there was a big white paper board, the kind business conferences have, and

F A C 3 0 1

THINK ABOUT
THE FUTURE
JULY 5TH 1990
Mottram Hall, Cheshire.

F A C 3 0 1

Factory

Stationery from Factory's
'Think About the Future' conference

I thought, 'Oh, we're going to be organised here.' And then Tony had written, 'How do we kill Peter Saville?' So that was the first thing on the agenda, and it was something to do with a design he'd done or was trying to get too much money for. [laughs] There were other things on the agenda, too, of course.

TERESA ALLEN: The agenda said everyone should expect to contribute 'except Teresa'. I know why this would have been, but I'm so angry with my then-self now because now I'm a much more confident person. I'm not afraid of speaking my mind in a workplace situation, but I wasn't that person then.

LIEVE MONNENS: At the gathering, there were people from the record company, from Dry, from The Haçienda. I was still very hopeful then, looking ahead to the future. We had the New Music Seminar lined up, and we went to Glastonbury, so it was nonstop interesting things happening for the first months I was working there. I had a good feeling, especially since everybody was together from all the parts of Factory and a New Order album was supposed to be coming out . . . We were all looking to the future. That feeling should have continued, but it didn't — and three years later, that New Order album still hadn't come out.

ANG MATTHEWS: Alan Erasmus decided, 'I've noticed nobody's actually been trained or even interviewed properly for the jobs they've got.' So it was then decided I would take some sort of training for another job I wasn't qualified for. It was decided that, perhaps because I was in charge of forty-two staff, I should do a post-baccalaureate degree in management and business, which was very kind of them. They then paid for me to do my post-grad. Of course, compared to everyone else who was on the course, it was just madness — my job compared to theirs. They were working for things like the British Electricity Board and things like that. So, ultimately, the 'Think About the Future' meeting was a really good meeting, and I suppose it brought us all together.

• • •

Factory HQ (FAC 251) compliments slip

LIEVE MONNENS: Going from Brussels to the Factory office in Manchester was like arriving on a new planet. But those last two and a half years put me in a position where I was observing the label going down the drain. The sad thing was that they'd moved to a really expensive building at the height of the property market — just before a big recession — which meant that the mortgage was actually costing them a lot more than the building was worth. I wish they'd kept it small because the overheads would have been smaller. They didn't seem to recognise that some records sell, some don't, and that bands will be bands and mess things up, and if you have big overheads, you can't collect. There were four accountants. I don't even know what difference they made. All I know is that they had to deal with the messy set-up that was The Haçienda, Dry Bar and Factory Records, all dipping into each other's funds.

At some point, Factory thought moving would make it more professional, but in my mind, the majority of them didn't really *feel* music as I felt it. They just couldn't keep it small because there were so many more people working for the record company. It was very ambitious. You can be ambitious if you don't put all your eggs in one basket, which in their case, at that time, was the

Happy Mondays' new album. Considering the band's history, you *can't* put all your eggs in *that* basket.

GEORGINA TRULIO: I was there towards the end of Factory, at Charles Street. I came in later than everybody else and never actually worked at Palatine Road, although I visited the office when I was working for Tony Michaelides and working for Hooky and Revenge.

When I started working for Tony Michaelides Promotions (TMP, one of the biggest independent radio and TV promotions companies in the UK, back in the day), Tony was plugging New Order and the Happy Mondays. Hooky wanted us to manage Revenge for him. I ran the Revenge office next door to the TMP office and assisted Tony with combined TMP business.

From there, a job opened up at Factory on Charles Street. We all knew each other because we worked in the same industry, and many of us were good friends. Manchester was more like a village: everyone knew everyone in the music scene and if you were known and trusted, you got the job. Alan Erasmus told me I was liked and trusted, I didn't have a groupie or star-struck mentality and still don't to this day, so I was hired. I've always been a good communicator and professional; people can trust me.

Georgina Trulio at Factory HQ

ALYSON PATCHETT: When Tracey left, most people thought she'd come back since she'd been there so long. But I stayed in the role of PR co-ordination. I'm not sure if Tony thought I was always good enough. I always got the impression that because I wasn't particularly an outgoing-type person − not an 'over-enthusiast' he'd say − he didn't think I was good enough for it. But I heard he thought I was doing a good job, so I stayed after we moved to the new building.

GEORGINA TRULIO: Back at TMP, Tina Simmons was across from me, and this was after she'd left Factory. Tina is a really strong, amazing woman, a friend and inspiration. She taught me to have confidence in myself, and I am forever grateful to her. The Happy Mondays and Simply Red were downstairs . . . It was a *hub* of music people. I eventually took over management of the Revenge office with Tony. I ran the whole office independently on my own: liaising with the band, record label, promoters, getting all the specs for everything, the equipment for Revenge tours, and of course dealing with the money and refusing a certain member of the band (not Hooky) a pair of leather trousers on expenses. He never forgave me! [laughs] I learnt how to do all of that and brought that over with me to Factory.

SEEMA SAINI: The way I got the official job at Factory on Charles Street is a sad story. The girl who was going to be the receptionist and clerical person was Tracy Farmer. I met Tracy when I was there for my dissertation, and she was so sweet to me. I think people didn't realise that the people working for Factory were just regular, down-to-earth people. But Tracy Farmer passed away from an aneurysm after she'd had her baby, and I met the baby one time when she came into the offices. After she passed, I was sitting in Dry Bar − I went there after one of my temping jobs − and I saw Chris Smith, the Factory accountant. He asked what I was doing, and I told him I had finished my Higher National Diploma and was now looking for a job. He said, 'We have an opening at Factory for a receptionist, do you want it?' 'Heck, yeah!' I said. That was at Charles Street, so they were in transition at that point. I was at Palatine for a bit and then moved over to Charles Street.

LIEVE MONNENS: There was no room for me at Palatine Road, really. I think I sat on the other side of Tony, sharing his desk. But when he was there, he was talking so loud on the telephone all the time that I had to take my chair and go somewhere else. They *had* to move. There was no room, no space. The meeting room upstairs was an old bedroom. It was . . . cosy. [laughs]

The funny thing about the move was that everything was going to be so organised there, or that was the idea. We had this metal box at the new office on Charles Street, and at the end of the day all our desks had to be empty — everything had to fit in that metal box. Anything that didn't fit had to be thrown out because it must not have been worth keeping. I had so much stuff and I needed it to do my job. That idea was supposed to keep the space looking beautiful, but it was not practical. I think they had a lot of good concepts, ideas, but getting them to work is another story.

SEEMA SAINI: I think Palatine was very down to earth. You'd never know you'd walked into a record company, this incredible music hub. With Charles Street, there was much more of an appearance, and there'd be people there coming in from Elektra, from London Records, that kind of thing.

ALYSON PATCHETT: I was based downstairs in the basement, where the records were now in a cage. I don't know if it's because loads had been taken and they realised that they were losing stock, but you needed a key to get into this cage.

LIEVE MONNENS: There were several women working at Factory, and I felt we had to prove ourselves a little bit more. That surprised me, that attitude coming from Factory, because you'd think they'd be more progressive, more open-minded. This was 1990. I didn't have that feeling in the record companies in Europe before Factory. To make it worse, they hired an executive director who was especially chauvinist. I was supposed to be head of international, and we were supposed to go on a trip to all the licensees in Europe. Just before that happened, a lot of responsibilities were taken away from me, and I was left just sending the tapes out, and one of the other guys went on the international licensee trip with the new executive director. That had been *my* job. When they came back from that trip, I got my old responsibilities back. It was like, OK, I wasn't fit to do these responsibilities before and to take the trip, but now that you're back, you want me to do them again? That executive director was only there for maybe a year, and at that point financial issues were already bubbling up. Maybe he was supposed to fix things, but I think he was way too late to fix anything, if that's what he was there to do.

GEORGINA TRULIO: I worked with Chris Smith as his PA — he was Factory's accountant — and also with the new managing director. We were in this beautiful building designed by Ben Kelly. Tony sat in the middle of the room. His desk was always adorned with beautiful fresh flowers, bought and arranged weekly; the rest of our desks surrounded him. There was a nice camaraderie between everyone, although definitely a man-woman divide. I don't think this was on purpose, but it was a sign of the times.

LIEVE MONNENS: Before things really turned bad, I went to France with The Adventure Babies. (They only had one album, but they had no chance in the end because the company went bankrupt.) In France, they needed someone who could speak the language, and I also went with Northside to Midem in France. They wanted to eat steak tartare because they thought it was steak, but it's raw meat of course, so they wanted to send it back because it wasn't cooked. I was like, 'No, this is steak tartare, guys.' [laughs]

The local licensees and press officers all spoke English, but it's more when you're in a cab or a situation like that, when it's good to have someone who speaks the language. I wouldn't say I was babysitting the bands — they had their manager — but sometimes I did have to pay for things for them. [laughs] I was also representing the record company in that capacity.

GEORGINA TRULIO: For me, it was quite a tricky position, because I'd get people ringing and saying, 'Georgina, this money is owed', or, 'Georgina, is Chris there?' and, 'Please do make sure I get this money.' They would ring and ring and ring and ring *and ring*. Then I'd have to issue a rubber cheque . . . a tricky situation.

SEEMA SAINI: I was supposed to help with merchandise with Fiona Allen, but that never took off with me. I mean, she did a great job, don't get me wrong, but it was hard to do that when I'm answering the phones all the time.

LIEVE MONNENS: My role in the last two and a half years was as head of international. Just me. I was the head of my own department, which basically involved talking with the minor licensees. Not America — that was too big/important a territory, and Tony Wilson liked to handle that himself — so I dealt mostly with smaller licensees like the Rough Trades of Europe and Australia and Japan, as well. I liked working with those licensees because I had a respect for what they were doing, and they didn't get that much support. I sent them all the production materials so they could produce the records themselves, and all the marketing materials so they could promote the bands.

I was supposed to be a kind of replacement for Tina, but I think they only gave me some of the things Tina was responsible for. Anything that was more business-like, finances, or anything to do with America, they kept that work for themselves.

SEEMA SAINI: Every morning we'd have a meeting in the conference room, and Tony would want the phone shut off. But, otherwise, my job was basically to answer the phones, send out smaller shipments going to promotional agencies, like down to Nicki Kefalas, greeting business acquaintances, and other clerical duties like photocopying.

ALYSON PATCHETT: On the top floor, where they had meetings, I remember how impractical the table was. I'm sure you've heard about that table. It moved. So if you would try to write on it, it'd sort of swing one way and then swing back. I can't remember any specific metres [table length], but it was suspended by little wires. There was a lot of storming out in those days. I can't remember all the times, but I remember The Adventure Babies, maybe the last band to sign to Factory, storming out of one of the meetings on the top floor. The police were also coming in all the time.

ANG MATTHEWS: The Factory directors' meetings . . . oh, dear. [laughs] I've never been involved in other directors' meetings, but I'm sure they were nothing like that! [laughs] There were always silly little things that would go on. The first thing would be that two crates had to be brought up from the cellar, and this was only one or two o'clock in the afternoon, and there'd be cigarette smoke, alcohol . . . I was the only woman at the directors' meetings because Gillian from New Order stopped going years ago — she'd probably had enough! [laughs] But I obviously had to because I was relaying all the information about The Haçienda. So it would be me, Tony Wilson, Rob Gretton, Peter Hook, Leroy Richardson (who was then manager of Dry Bar) and Paul Mason (who was sort of between me, Leroy and the directors if you were looking at it from a formal business view). I'm just thinking somebody must have taken the minutes. The accountants were also there, and I don't know what these stray accountants used to think of us. [laughs] To give you an example of the kinds of ridiculous things that we'd be discussing: how we were going to buy drugs to give to the DJs, and should we account for that in the budget? And then we'd discuss the drug box, which I used to lock in the safe, that we had to hand over to the police, full of drugs that were confiscated on the door. Hooky used to be arguing because he wanted the drugs for himself, but I'd already registered them. We did discuss serious things as well, but that gives you an example. There were minutes taken at each meeting, which would have been taken by Andy Jackson. Hooky's got the biggest collection of the minutes — he's actually got the hard copies of the minutes.

In my early days, more people would be at those meetings. You'd have Gillian and all of New Order would be there. Bigger business people would be there, but then as problems started up, people couldn't be bothered with the whole thing. I think Gillian gave up her shares in The Haçienda and so did Bernard and Stephen. They'd bet on how many people would be coming into The Haçienda on Saturday nights, and they'd bet their shares, so then they were no longer involved if they lost. [laughs]

TINA SIMMONS: Directors' meetings could be bizarre [laughs], but nine times out of ten, there was actually business that needed to be discussed.

LIEVE MONNENS: My day would usually start by communicating with the licensees (faxes or letters — remember, no email yet!). Say we had a new release coming out of a more minor artist — so, not Happy Mondays or New Order, but Revenge, Kalima, Northside, etc. (New Order didn't release an album while I was there, by the way. I think they were waiting on the New Order album that would save them, but it arrived too late.) Anyway, say a new record was coming out. I'd ask the licensees if they wanted to manufacture it locally or import copies from us. I'd mail promotional materials and photographs, which they'd usually reproduce locally. If it was an especially small release, they'd just want to import the English product, so I'd arrange for their order to be sent.

There was always an issue to get the materials to them so they could reproduce locally before imports came. It used to take a long time for me to get to films or duplicate tapes, by which point there were already imports from the UK in the international markets. For a big release like 'Step On' for Happy Mondays, imports flooded the international markets before they even had a chance to produce the single. There was always that friction. Through all this, I'd be in touch with the licensees, ask how the release was doing in their market, whether they wanted any interviews with the band, etc. Well . . . [laughs], an interview with the Happy Mondays only if you could pin them down. They'd do interviews, but they'd maybe just send their bass player . . .

I'd also report back to management. We'd have a roundtable maybe every two weeks, where we'd report back, like: 'Japan sold ten copies of Kalima.' They'd push back, 'Can't you get them to sell

more?' and I'd have to say, 'It's not even selling in this country.'
Everybody on staff would be at the roundtable, so salespersons,
accountants, and we'd be up in the attic around the famous suspended table that cost £30,000. Is that a myth, the cost of that
table? I've never seen the receipt for that. I hated getting put on
the spot at those meetings, which happened constantly, because
I'm an introvert. But the people working on UK sales usually had
the most interesting things to say, and then there was me with my
sad export sales ... We were all trying to contribute as much as
we could. We got questions like: 'Who would be a good producer
for the new Happy Mondays album?' For me, it was hard to speak.
It was a table full of music fans and bad accountants. Most of us
were there because we loved the music, not to talk about bands
in terms of money.

REBECCA GOODWIN: You know, Factory was not great with money.
[laughs]

GEORGINA TRULIO: One day I remember vividly: 'Is Martin Hannett
coming in?' The accounts team shot out of the back door. Martin
asked where Chris was. I knew where they were — the Lass O'Gowrie! Martin sat down and told me he wouldn't be moving from that
seat until he got paid the money he was owed. He sat for over two
hours right in front of me. I made polite conversation and got him
drinks. He was a really lovely guy; I felt awful. There was no way
he was going anywhere. The accounts team kept ringing to see if
he had left. In the end, they told me to bring the chequebook over
to the pub and they would sign it. I snuck out the back door, ran
over to the pub, got it signed and handed it back to Martin (praying
it wasn't another rubber one!). I believe he would have sat there
all day if they hadn't obliged.

LIEVE MONNENS: The music used to be on all the time at the office,
on MTV. There were always people coming in and out, and in the
end when money was really tight, we used to have two doors: a
back exit and one at the front. If a band was coming in or someone
who wanted money, one of the accountants or the head accountant

would leave through the back door. Anyone who had authority to sign cheques would exit through the back. 'No, no, I've not seen them!' we'd have to say. [laughs, sighs]

GEORGINA TRULIO: Another time Shaun Ryder rang asking for Tony (about money again). I forgot to switch the phone to silent, and I shouted across to Tony, telling him Shaun was on the phone. He said, 'Tell him I'm out and will call him later.' Shaun at the top of his voice shouted, 'I can fucking hear him, tell him I'm on my fucking way!' [laughs]

LIEVE MONNENS: The big realisation — when Factory realised they were actually in really, really deep — was when they sent me to their London attorney's office, where they kept all the contracts with all the bands. They wanted to see what assets they had, which record deals they still had with bands, and what they could use to show the profitability of the company. Most of the contracts had expired, it turned out, or they didn't have them at all, even with New Order. A lot of the contracts were record by record, and even those had expired. They had nothing, no record deals at all. Originally, the idea of not doing a five-record deal with a band where they're stuck with you (like with a major label), but instead an album-by-album agreement, that's a great deal for the band and that's a great idea. But that idea meant Factory basically had nothing, just a record contract with Adventure Babies. When I went down to London, I made a list and they asked me three times, 'Is that really all there is?' and I said, 'Yes, that's really it. Unless you have a hidden archive somewhere with record deals . . .' It was a shock. I spent two days going through everything, and it was one contract after the other that was expired. It was an eye-opener for me, and I think it was even a bigger eye-opener for them because there were no spreadsheets, no master records. And nothing to sell to London Records — so they signed with New Order directly and Factory went bust.

ALYSON PATCHETT: I ended up staying with the job until the redundancies started in September '91. That started maybe a year before Factory went under completely, when they made quite a few people redundant. I think it was me, Lieve, Seema and Georgina. I remember I was on holiday when I heard.

GEORGINA TRULIO: The finances kept getting worse and worse. So I was made redundant in summer of '92 before Factory folded.

LIEVE MONNENS: This is my anecdote that sums up that time: we hadn't even been paid but we still had fresh flowers in the office up until the last week. A florist who'd never get paid for it had made a nice bouquet. The image, the concept, over the practical.

GEORGINA TRULIO: Seema and I were the first people to go. It was really awful. We were actually quite lucky when we left, though — everybody was very kind to us and I know that in the end when everybody else left, when Factory went bankrupt, people hadn't been paid wages, so it was a really terrible and depressing period for everybody.

SEEMA SAINI: When Factory was going out of business, they wanted to cut positions. Rebecca [Boulton] told me years later that Rob was really angry. 'Get rid of the flowers, not Seema's receptionist position!'

GEORGINA TRULIO: When I was made redundant, I kind of had an inkling because I was last in, so first out, and there's a pecking order in any job environment. So one day, we just got in and Tony, Rob Gretton, Alan Erasmus and Chris Smith said, 'Can we have a chat with you?' I thought, this isn't good. They sat me down, very serious and just said, 'We're really, really sorry. Things are not good at the moment. We don't want to do this, but we have to let some people go, and you were last in.' I burst into tears! It was terrible, I sobbed my heart out and set Tony off crying! I knew they didn't want to do it, and by November, it was all over.

LIEVE MONNENS: When Factory were trying to cut costs at the end, some people were made redundant. Georgina was made redundant and Seema, as well. It was clear it was not going to end well, but I was there until the end. We actually discovered, arriving at the front door, they'd changed the locks and they hadn't told us. We were standing there at the door, and there were cameras from a TV station trying to interview us. Great, right? I didn't even know. For me, that was really bad. Like, this is how you treat staff? I think by then it was completely out of their hands. The receivers might have told them they had to change the locks. We were told that everything would be arranged by the receivers, and that they'd be in touch.

When we finally got inside the building, we were told the stockroom was open and people could take what they wanted. People were grabbing all the records. I think I took a bag of Factory badges. Some people took framed gold records. Those are all probably sold on eBay now. We didn't know if we were going to get paid, so we were told to take any of that – all of it – because it hadn't been counted by the receivers. They weren't going to pay anyone with money, and they owed money to so many people. I think that's what happens when you know you're going to go bust – you keep ordering things from people, trying to keep up appearances. Fortunately, I did get some of the money I was owed through some government fund, so I was compensated . . . enough. It was the fact that they didn't tell us. I'm sure that might have been legal advice, but they could have done something to let us know, a little meeting, or even telling us the morning of . . . but changing the locks? For me, that was the end of the music business. I never wanted to work in the music business again, and I didn't. This was an alternative industry that should be treating people differently. But when you try to play the big game, having all these accountants, an executive director . . . that's what you get. They'd had a good thing going and I felt they could have kept it smaller. It's good to be ambitious, but you have to have the skills to run a company. You can't *just* be a music fan. It becomes a balancing act of doing well with your artists while making sure you pay all of your overheads.

ALYSON PATCHETT: A friend from Halifax was living in LA, and I'd never been to America, so I was out there staying with my friend and we travelled up to San Francisco. I'd phoned Jane [Lemon] to find out about getting some tickets for a gig in San Francisco, and she said, 'There's been some redundancies.' I was like, 'Oh my God. What and who?' She reeled off names like Seema, Georgina, Simon . . . I kept asking, 'Who else?' I sort of felt that she wasn't telling me everything. Eventually she said, 'You've been made redundant as well.' So that's how I found out, and I was absolutely broken. I was away, I didn't have a job to come back to, and I'd lost the job that had become part of who I was. I sobbed in a hotel in San Francisco for about a day. I was just devastated. They gave me some redundancy money, which was about one and a half grand, which I suppose at the time was pretty generous. But I do remember coming back to Manchester, and some of the people around Factory, like a member of Central Station Design and Northside's manager, had apparently heard I'd been made redundant and they came into the office saying, 'You shouldn't have made Alyson redundant. She's part of the team.' They knew everyone else that was made redundant had been taken on later than me. So, that really touched me, this part of my little Factory gang stood up for me. That's what I try to remember the most.

LIEVE MONNENS: In 1992, when all of this had happened with Factory, I was unemployed for nine months. There was a recession, and you can imagine that someone who'd only been employed in the music industry up to that point, well . . . I learnt to type in one of those 'job-ready' courses, and that was a good skill to get. I still go to shows, I still go dancing, I'm still in touch with a number of artists — they're the reason that I got involved in the music industry. But when the attorneys and the accountants start taking over, for me, that's just . . . no.

KAREN BOARDMAN: I was already working at London Records when Factory went bankrupt and London Records came in. That was indicative of how different the ethos was — of Factory's DIY, do it ourselves, we'll keep it in Manchester. Then, as soon as things go bad, the traditional record company comes in and behaves how you would expect them to behave. Not in a very nice way. Thank God

I'd already left London Records by the time they acquired Factory. I missed that by about three months.

GEORGINA TRULIO: It wasn't all doom and gloom! None of us wanted it to end — we loved the music.

LIEVE MONNENS: I do still have friends from Factory, and I became close with women there, like Jane Lemon and Georgina Trulio and Seema Saini.

GEORGINA TRULIO: I think we, the women at Factory and The Haçienda, really held it together. It was the women who made sure everything ran smoothly and got problems solved. A lot of it might have been behind the scenes, but we were there doing it. At the end of the Factory road, we had to fend everybody off while the men were just having a drink and hiding in the Lass O'Gowrie. So the women were very strong. We worked really, really hard to keep things going, and at the end, the women took the brunt of what was going on. We were the infantry, holding the fort for everybody, so we had a huge role there and were never properly acknowledged.

TINA SIMMONS: I'm sad Factory ended the way it did. Alan did try to get Tony to make up with everybody because, by the end, he'd fallen out with a lot of people. His heart was always in the right place, but his brain wasn't sometimes. [laughs] We were at Midem [an annual music conference] in Cannes, probably two years after I'd left Factory. I'd set up my own consultancy business and was working for independent bands on management contracts and record labels. Anyway, I saw Tony there, and he snubbed me! [laughs] I was there with one of the guys who I was working for as a consultant, and he said, 'Tony Wilson's acting like a woman scorned!' [laughs] I knew there was no good reason, but I think it was because I'd told the truth about the finances — he'd realised by then I wasn't rocking the boat as he'd said, and that I knew what I was talking about — and he'd have hated to admit that I was right, to say that to me ... That would have been too much of a climb-down for Tony. At that point Factory must have been just a few months from going down.

I wish Tony had listened to me, I wish Chris had understood finances better, and I wish very much that Rob hadn't been so poorly because he was actually in hospital when I handed in my resignation. Alan was trying to get Rob to persuade me to stay. He was in his hospital bed and Rob turned and said, 'I don't want Tina to be as ill as I am.' When you're part of something that has been growing and blossoming ... we could have done so much more! It's like having the carpet pulled out from underneath your feet. I really wish Tony had listened to me because Factory could have continued well beyond 1992. Factory might still be here. But you can wish a lot of things, can't you?

REBECCA BOULTON: I think it was just assumed that they [New Order] couldn't repeat the financial mistakes of The Haçienda, of Factory, even though they didn't necessarily speak of it directly. They did talk about their unhappiness at the way things had gone, but no one ever said 'we must not repeat this'. It was just assumed that there would be no repeat of that.

CHAPTER 16

FACTORY TOO?

Bridget Chapman and Tony Wilson signing
the Space Monkeys to Factory Too

Factory Communications Limited – Factory Records – collapsed in November 1992. In the years that followed, Tony Wilson imagined various new incarnations of the label. Factory Too was the first of those, technically under London Records (which had become the label of Joy Division and New Order) but based in Manchester. Women again took frontline roles in operating the new venture, with Bridget Chapman running the office and Bindi Binning serving as Factory Too's A&R 'man'. Factory Too released records by The Durutti Column, Hopper, the Space Monkeys, and The 6ths between 1994 and 1998. An offshoot of Factory Too, Factory Once released archival material from the original Factory Records days via London Records. The fourth and final Factory incarnation, F4, ran briefly from 2004 to 2005.

BINDI BINNING: Factory Too never reached the dizzying heights of Factory (one). That was always going to be a tall order.

BRIDGET CHAPMAN: It never ever occurred to me for a minute that I would end up working with Tony Wilson. When I was at university, in 1992 or 1993, I was already a fan of the music, and I was also a really, really bad student. I kind of thought that if you really wanted me to attend a nine o'clock lecture, you wouldn't have put it on at nine o'clock in the morning. I could spend my entire time going to see bands instead. I remember Wednesday was a big day because *NME* and *Melody Maker* came out. So, I would get up, put my coat on over my pyjamas, go to the shop and then come back and read [them] cover to cover — when I'm supposed to be doing an English degree. In those days when I was a fan, to me Factory was like some kind of magical creation — this amazing, crazy record label where the more popular the record was and the more it sold, the more money it cost them. It was just a bonkers thing. For me, it was really about Joy

Division and New Order — they were the bands that I loved then and still do.

Getting to how I ended up at Factory Too ... My dad was a senior civil servant working in the northwest of England, and he was working for the Department of Trade and Industry. When I was coming up to graduate with my English degree, he started wheeling me around cocktail parties, introducing me very point-edly to his friends and saying, 'This is my daughter, and she's just about to graduate.' I really wasn't interested in any of the jobs that might have come my way. I didn't really know what I wanted to do. If you'd asked me, I would have said, 'Yeah, I'd love to work in the music industry.' But I didn't think it was possible. Then I met this guy called Dr James Grigor, who was a professor of biochemistry, but he also was part of something called the Central Manchester Development Corporation, and Tony Wilson was on the same board. He was the only interesting person at this particularly boring party. He knew all about the Reading Festival, and he said he'd been to The Haçienda. He asked if I'd be interested in some unpaid work experience, and the next thing I knew I was in Atlas Bar on Deansgate in Manchester and Tony Wilson swept in. He was exactly like you'd imagine him, in a sort of black cape with sunglasses. We had a bit of a chat and he said, 'Come and have some work experience, darling.' It was for Factory Too.

BINDI BINNING: I was a fan of the music, and I loved New Order. They were probably my first taste of proper music. I grew up in the south of the UK near London, and I went to Manchester to go to university. A lot of my friends were in bands, so when I finished my courses, somebody asked me if I wanted to manage their band. I thought, wow, that could be fun. Rather than getting a proper job, I could do that for a while and see where it goes. So I did manage this band, and they signed to London Records. When I first came across Tony, I was working on a big event called Cities in the Park, which was run by Alan Wise and Matthew Cummings, who was one of the Stone Roses' managers. I came across Tony and we hit it off, and I think he realised that I knew music. A few months later, he was setting up In the City and was looking for somebody to run the gigs and find new talent. He gave me a call and I started working on In the City. So I wasn't part of Factory (the first one), but after the original Factory went by the wayside and Tony was focusing on In the City and his TV career, he was really using In the City as a tool to put on the new talent as a tool. So many bands got signed off the back of it, and it gave him the urge to start Factory Too.

ALYSON PATCHETT: After being made redundant at Factory, I think Jane told Tony I was still looking for a job. I'd obviously kept in touch with Jane. The only good thing about In the City, really, was that I made a friend, Bindi, who did A&R for In the City [and Factory Too].

BINDI BINNING: I was doing Factory Too at the same time I was doing In the City. We had the In the City office, and that's where I was based, and in the next room were Tony and Bridget. That was essentially Factory Too. My job was really doing two jobs in one. Because I'd been doing In the City, people were sending me demos. I became absolutely *deluged* with demo tapes − and they were cassettes at the time, piled high on my desk. Tony used to have a real thing about people's desks being tidy, so he'd look at mine and go, 'Darling, you're OK but your desk is atrocious, but it's fine − you're a creative!' [laughs] What could I do with these mountains of tapes? I'd have a series of scouts around the country. For Factory Too, I had somebody in Liverpool and somebody in Leeds, and a lot more for In the City, and many were London-based.

I'd travel to see bands everywhere, and I'd travel whenever there was anything happening like a music convention. There used to be this annual thing called Sound City, and Radio 1 put it on in a different city every year. I'd go on my own every year as a woman to these events, which was quite unusual back in the day, but because you knew everybody in the industry, it didn't feel so daunting. I was literally on my own going out each night to see bands, not knowing anybody. It's quite a lonely job, A&R. Even though I always felt like I could take anybody on if anybody were to try to mess with me, I probably couldn't have. Going out on my own at night, looking back now, was quite a brave thing to do. That was part of the job, and I guess that's also a reason why more men do it, A&R.

RUTH TAYLOR: For In the City, I worked in the office in an admin role. There was so much going on back then, and Manchester was a really fun place to be. I didn't get a proper job till I was in my thirties. It was me and Bindi, and then Tony and Yvette. Alyson Patchett had gone when I started, and I think I probably replaced her, to be honest . . . I think she'd started work for the BBC already at that point. It was in this tiny little office right at the top of Manchester Town Hall, and then they got this funky new office, just down from The Boardwalk on Little Peter Street. First, I was scheduling the catering, sorting the riders out for the bands. I think that was '93. By '94, I was working in the office and handling more behind the scenes.

BRIDGET CHAPMAN: It was me and Tony in a little office on Little Peter Street, where a guy called Chris owned the building and had his recording studio downstairs. We were upstairs. It was just really exciting and you never knew quite what was going to happen next. After two weeks, I was thinking this was all going to end, and Tony said to me, 'Are you enjoying it, darling? I really need to make this permanent, darling.' I never thought for one minute I'd end up working there, and it still feels a bit like it was a very weird but wonderful dream. I was there from 1994 to 1996.

The Factory Too office had a huge sofa from a trendy shop in London called Aram. It was a ridiculously big sofa and Vini Reilly was tiny. I remember him in there on this sofa, like a little doll.

BINDI BINNING: So on an average day, I would listen to demo tapes, and I'd be on the phone all the time to the scouts, on the phone to the bands, on the phone to the studio doing the production, recording studios for production companies, designers, etc., etc. I used to rock in — now when I look back at this, it was so cushy [laughs] — about eleven o'clock every morning. Everyone else had been down for a couple hours by that point. In the evening,

I'd go out to watch bands, whether they were in Manchester or in London. There was no typical day at all, looking back. I think, wow, what a job I had. It was just amazing. I was answerable really to nobody because I was fully trusted by Tony.

BRIDGET CHAPMAN: There was really no such thing as a regular day and that was the most amazing thing about it. I did everything — from emptying the bins and changing the loo roll in the toilets, to booking recording sessions, to digging out tapes from the Factory archive (by this stage London Records had put the money behind Factory Too, so they owned the Factory archives). There was a lot of babysitting of bands, both bands that had been around for a while and new bands, booking studios, liaising with the radio pluggers (who were in the office downstairs, called Red Alert), and there was a lot of cross-pollination between Factory Too and In the City. Sometimes it was just making the tea. Vini from The Durutti Column — who is a very talented man but not great at the day-to-day business of living, like paying bills — would turn up with gas bills and electricity bills that were overdue, so we'd sit down and we'd go through them. I had to deal with members of New Order, Happy Mondays, that turned up to argue with Tony. Tony drove me absolutely mad, but he was also a tremendous character who was fun and made things happen, and I miss him terribly.

BINDI BINNING: I got a very, very early demo tape from Oasis and it was utterly shocking, so bad. That first demo didn't get any traction from anyone. I eventually recorded over it, which now in hindsight was a terrible, *terrible* faux pas. By the time their second demo came out, Oasis had asked me to manage them. I was really excited because I'd heard this demo and it completely knocked my socks off. I was talking to Noel and Liam, saying, 'Yeah, I'm really interested in managing', but it wasn't to be. That same week Noel met Johnny Marr, his hero, and he said, 'Why didn't you go with my manager, Marcus Russell?' — and the rest is history.

To be honest, most of the time when I listened to demos, they were so raw that you couldn't really tell if you liked some songs. If you went to see the band play live, they might be atrocious, or you'd see a band that were amazing despite a terrible demo. It's really about seeing them live.

I remember a particular band Pullover I really loved. They were amazing, sort of in a storytelling mode. I took Tony to see them one night and he absolutely loved them, but he said to me, 'Darling, you know I can't sign them. Nobody's having a nervous breakdown. I need a band where someone's having a nervous breakdown!' [laughs]

BRIDGET CHAPMAN: It did get more and more hectic as time went on, and it was always busy. I don't want to make it sound more than it was. We started off with a small roster, and it was hard work but it was doable.

BINDI BINNING: We did sign a band called Hopper, and they had a female frontwoman, Rachel. She was the quintessential popstar in the making. I was looking through some notes yesterday and I couldn't believe, firstly, that we used to have weekly minutes — because this was Factory! [laughs] It was actually Tony writing the minutes by hand, and then he'd type them up to send to London Records. But I bring this up because somebody wanted to interview Rachel, and the way they framed it seemed quite derogatory to me, so I kyboshed that. If they wanted to interview her, they'd have to take a different tack where she was seen differently than a play thing. Of course, it was somebody at a record label who'd suggested this as a way of marketing Hopper, which to me felt lazy.

RACHEL MORRIS: My memories of Tony are fond ones. He was a generous man and he believed in us, sometimes more than we did ourselves. It was a bit of a strange situation to be in [signed to Factory Too] as I guess typically the Manchester music scene was more male dominated and he picked this southern, bespectacled and geeky-looking girl to sign. I remember one time he marched us into The Haçienda, smiled to the security guards and said, 'Step aside — these people are going to be huge.' I said, 'Which people Tony?' quite bemused. [James McMahon interview, jamesjammcmahon.com, 2020[1]]

REBECCA GOODWIN: With Factory Too, Tony Wilson had this band Hopper with a female lead singer, and he asked me what I thought of them. He was thinking of signing them and he knew I'd been around the band scene. It was always about the bands for me — about the music — and I went to The Haçienda when it was half-empty and freezing for the music, when people were wearing long coats just to be around the music. So he knew I knew music. That would have been in '95, or '96, absolutely in The Haçienda when he asked me for my opinion on Hopper. I think I was pregnant at the time. (I was pregnant and working part-time at The Haçienda in the final days.)

BRIDGET CHAPMAN: I'd have a list of necessary equipment that the bands had to have, and then it would be a question of matching that up with studios that were in the right budget. I didn't know what I was doing to start off with, and in the beginning a lot of the time it was nice people in the studios talking me through it. Then it was just a question of negotiating rates to make sure that we could get it for the right price. The Factory name opened a lot of doors, I'm not gonna lie. People were keen to work with bands that Tony had his eye on.

BINDI BINNING: I was trying to sign this band called Northern Uproar. They were all underage, sixteen and seventeen, but they were fantastic and I loved them with a passion. Tony loved them with a passion. We went all out to try and get them. In the minutes we used to send to London Records, there'll be references to things like taking Chris, their manager, out, or doing loads of substance abuse with the band to try to sign them. We tried everything. Then London said to Tony, 'OK, so here's your budget for the next year. How do you want to split it up?' Tony had my line and various other lines: a car for Tony, overseas travel for Tony [laughs], but he asked, 'Can I get a general overhead lump sum that I can use for bands or managers to ply them with drink and drugs?' Worth a try! Anyway, eventually we were very much the first option for Northern Uproar because they loved us, and they loved everything Tony and Factory stood for. They wanted a bit more money, and I said, you know, we're an indie, you're not signing to Sony. But I left, and the deal ended up going to Heavenly Records.

RACHEL MORRIS: Tony made sweeping gestures of kindness which I sometimes was a little bit shy to fully accept. I do remember that one time we played a gig and he sent me a bouquet of ten red roses. The band Northern Uproar were onlookers and couldn't fathom it. 'She looks like a teacher,' one of them said. [James McMahon interview, jamesjammcmahon.com, 2020[2]]

BRIDGET CHAPMAN: The day that Factory Too signed the Space Monkeys to the label, they did it in the archive. I think I have a photo of me, Tony and the Space Monkeys on the day they signed in the upstairs part of the bank.

The archive was in the Midland Bank in Manchester, which is a Lutyens building. It was a bank vault exactly like you'd see in a heist movie. One of these big doors was opened, and there were these great tapes of pretty much everything that Factory had ever done, in no particular order. It was a dusty job, finding things . . . it was all just sitting in this incredible bank vault in the middle of Manchester. Bit by bit they were transferred to London and, I'm guessing, digitised. So yeah, I was literally going down into a bank vault and I'd never been in a bank vault before. I'm not the kind of person that has a lot of diamonds or gold bullion. [laughs] It was like being in an Agatha Christie novel.

BINDI BINNING: I think it was difficult because there was so much to live up to. When people thought of Factory Records, aside from the bands, they thought about Tony Wilson. So when Tony has another record label, also called Factory, everyone immediately assumes it needs to be the same. But, unlike at Factory, with Factory Too he didn't have complete control because he was under London Records. But without London, it would have been even more difficult and maybe impossible to do — because Tony would have had to get a distribution deal, which would all be fine, but there was no money to actually run the day-to-day. So to be able to make it happen, we needed London, but they were and are a very commercial organisation. Tony was not very commercial at all. That's not what he was led to. He was led by talent, passion, the music and the characters. If the character was there, the music wasn't that important. If the music was there but the characters weren't, then it wasn't a Factory act. [laughs] So there was this disconnect from what he wanted, from what he wanted Factory Too to be, to what they wanted Factory Too to be. They wanted all the New Orders and the Happy Mondays — the finished product of the New Orders and the Happy Mondays — when they're already selling records as opposed to the years and years of being nurtured. So I think the fans wanted it to be Factory, London wanted it to be Factory already having succeeded, and Tony wanted to start from scratch.

BRIDGET CHAPMAN: It was a very male environment. I think the women that were around were quite strong characters. Bindi, for example, is a strong character. I think you have to be to work in that kind of environment. I'm sure I did experience sexism, but I don't know if I would have recognised it at the time. I was straight out of university and I was just so grateful to be there.

BINDI BINNING: I can't say that I felt discriminated against for being a woman at all, but what was lucky for me was I had somebody who was enormously supportive — Tony — who really pushed me to the forefront. Secondly, what helped me was that I wasn't in London. There was a time when I was thinking about moving to London and Tony didn't want me to go. Tom Zutaut from Geffen Records had asked Tony if he would let me go and work for him, but Tony said he didn't want to let me go. He wanted me to stay and do Factory Too, so he negotiated for London Records to pay me. This was in the minutes Tony wrote, so I'll read it: 'London happy to help with keeping Bindi in Manchester.' He knew there were so many A&R people in London, and what a lot of people used to say to me was, 'You're a big fish in a small pond here. Don't go there because you'll be swallowed up.' When I eventually did go to London, it was really difficult. I couldn't get a job, even though at the time — when I was doing In the City and Factory Too — I used to have people coming to me, wanting to know my thoughts on bands, always being very complimentary. But when I went down to London to try to do the same job that I was doing in Manchester, I wasn't supported like I was by Tony.

BRIDGET CHAPMAN: I went off to work in the marketing department at Polydor in London, where I was from. I'm a London girl. Working with Tony at Factory Too was great fun, but I was missing friends and family, and was kind of ready to come back. But, you know, it was a wrench to leave after three years.

BINDI BINNING: How did I leave Factory Too? This is where it all goes horribly wrong, and it's actually a very long story. Tony and Yvette were together, and Tony brought on Yvette to run In the City without any music experience. It was quite difficult to be working with somebody with no music experience, and they used to bring some of their relationship into the office. There were a lot of tears and tensions in that office. After that first In the City, Alyson and I basically said, 'We can't work like this, we're done.' Tony came around to my house with all sorts of promises. He said Yvette wasn't going to be coming to the office any more, and he, Andy Dodd and Elliot Rashman (Simply Red managers as well as In the City directors) decided they wanted me to stay in my role and that they would move Yvette into a nonexecutive board role instead, so she wasn't in the office or working with the team. They had decided this as not only had they lost the team, but Tony was finding it difficult to work with her, too. Of course, how that translated was his taking my side over hers, so there was a lot of friction between myself and Yvette ... I was supported in my career, but Tony didn't know what to do about this dynamic. He had somebody he wanted working for him desperately, and he had somebody he loved. Now this is where it all goes horribly wrong. Looking back now, Yvette and I were set up badly. The guys had decided how they wanted the set-up of the business, but between us, we were paying the price in our own ways ...

I was totally ignorant ... It was somebody who I used to work with closely who really hated Yvette, and said to me, laughing, 'You know, once I chucked paint on Yvette's car and I did this and

I did that, and you took the blame.' It was unbelievable. All these things that I was accused of doing, which was somebody else's doing, who had me take the fall . . . It's terrible. I was absolutely gutted because Tony — who was my supporter and my mentor for several years — suddenly cut me off. I couldn't get my head around it for years and we didn't speak for a fairly long time. I was out at a festival and saw him; he smiled a genuine smile and looked really pleased to see me and said, 'How are you, darling?' But Yvette was also there and suddenly he stopped talking and we never spoke again.

I lost my confidence after that happened. I moved to London and it took me a long time, years, to get out — because I genuinely didn't know what I'd done and why he hated me so much. It was baffling to me. So I lost a lot of confidence and I really fell out of love with the music industry.

I never got the chance to say, 'Tony, I now understand what happened — and all those things you thought I did, I didn't do, and I now know who did.' I did actually go and visit his grave the last time I was in Manchester . . . I felt a bit stupid, but I thought, this person was a huge part of my life, and I need to do it, so I did manage to tell him then.

RACHEL MORRIS: It ended too soon and I feel we could've stuck together more. It was disappointing. London Records pulled funding from Factory Too. Tony hawked our demos around, but no one took him up on it. [James McMahon interview, jamesjammcmahon. com, 2020[3]]

BINDI BINNING: With the original Factory, it makes my skin tingle when I think about the amount of great music and great characters it produced. If I didn't work at Factory Too, I don't know that I'd have known it existed! I don't think London Records believed in it enough to renew their deal.

Factory Fuckups

We thought that we could tell you about 'New Order – Substance', the double LP twelve inch singles compilation for world release in August. We could tell you about the Hacienda's fifth birthday party. We could tell you about the property plans of Factory Australasia, Vini Reilly's new project, Happy Mondays' gigs, 'Young Popular and Sexy', Diggle's latest painting, The Railway Children deal, the TV show of the Tenth Summer concert, or the beautiful Cath Carroll.

But we decided we'd tell you about

the mad fuckers

...the new film by the Bailey Brothers for Factory Communications Limited, Manchester, England for release in Spring 1988.

Ad for *The Mad Fuckers*

If you've heard anything about Factory Records, you probably know some of the more infamous myths and legends: the 'Blue Monday' 12-inch cost more to make than its price tag, Tony Wilson wrote Joy Division's contract in his own blood, Linder designed a 'Menstrual Egg-Timer' (FAC 8) that never materialised, the label spent £30,000 on the suspended 'Temporary Contemporary' table (FAC 331) at Factory HQ . . . But wait, there's more! Women at Factory remember more FAC numbers that never came to be – some good ideas, some not – and sunk costs. Factory fuckups or Factory fables? You decide.

ANGIE CASSIDY: Factory was very organic, and style and music as an art form was more important than running it like a business . . . it really lost money. The poster for one of our gigs in New York cost more than we got paid for doing the gig. It's like, what the hell? . . . You'd hear people say 'Factory fuckup' like, 'Oh, it's another Factory fuckup.' That was like a regular saying for gigs or when albums were coming out. And it wasn't just us, Section 25. There were other bands that had difficulties and probably lost money because of the way it was run.

FIONA ALLEN: Business-wise, it couldn't have gone further unless we had done the Factory clothing. In fact, at that stage Factory was in trouble with money so there was no way that that was gonna be possible, although in an ideal world it was brilliant. It was just one of those things — the money wasn't there and there was nothing we could do about it. [John Cooper, *Scream City*, 2010[1]]

LIZ NAYLOR: Tony must have asked me to write the script for FAC 20 ['Too Young to Know, Too Wild to Care'], and at the time I was living with Cath in a flat in north Manchester on a really rough estate. I can't tell you how poor we were . . . we were just insanely poor. I didn't have a typewriter, I didn't have a stereo, I didn't own anything. So Tony says to me, 'You can write a script for this film.' I was like, 'Sure', though I didn't know what a script was, in terms of how to construct one.

ANN QUIGLEY: Tony Wilson wanted this film made, 'Too Young to Know, Too Wild to Care'.

LIZ NAYLOR: For some reason, Jon Savage was involved and brokered the payment, because I think Tony thought, 'Oh, she can do it for the glory', and Jon must have said, 'No, you have to pay her.' To this day, I can't remember how much it was. It might have been 150 quid, it might have been 100 quid. It wasn't a massive amount of money, but for somebody who had nothing it *was*, so I thought, brilliant, give me the money. I remember Tony gave me a cheque for Coutts Bank, which is the Queen's bank in England. I'd never heard of this bank, and I'm not too sure I even had a bank account, but I got given this stupid fucking cheque, this pretentious cheque from Tony, which is very much what the relationship was like. Then I thought, Oh fuck, I've got to write this film script. I hand wrote about two pages of gibberish. I have no idea what I wrote, but it was complete fucking nonsense, and I gave Tony these two pages of handwritten garbage.

I don't even have a copy of it — in a way, it might as well not exist, which is probably the most perfect Factory story. Jez Kerr [of ACR] asked me about it because he wanted to buy it, and I'm like, honestly, it doesn't really exist. I have no idea what I wrote. I was probably on drugs at the time. Tony was really aggrieved that he had paid me this money and was still going on about it for the last years of his life. He was still banging on about the 100 quid or whatever he paid me, like the Happy Mondays hadn't cost him a *little bit* more. People are asking like it's under my bed or something, this film script. But it doesn't exist, right. It happened because I was an idiot and Tony was an idiot. So there you go, that's the word on it. It was just an idea that didn't happen.

ANN QUIGLEY: The Bailey Brothers — Phil Shotton, Keith Jobling — and a film they were working on with Tony Wilson at some point had the title *The Mad Fuckers*, I think?

TINA SIMMONS: We also got involved in trying to get a Bailey Brothers script published. They came up with a script for *The Mad Fuckers*, which had to be changed because the censors didn't like the name of it. It was actually quite a good script, and Tony did try to get it made, but it never materialised. That was Tony's world, really, since he was on television. A lot of work was done around that, especially in the office. I've still got my copy of that script!

CHRIS MATHAN: The design for *The Mad Fuckers* (FACT 181) print ad, the Bailey Brothers' screenplay, that's something Tony asked me to do. It was already called *The Mad Fuckers* and I thought, well, then let's just make 'Fuckers' really big. That's all, and Tony loved it. The word really has no shock value any more, but in print — in a sophisticated-type treatment — the context changed entirely.

ANN QUIGLEY: The Bailey Brothers were going to be Factory's film producers. Tony could never get the funding, but Phil and Keith were then on board the Factory family, and that's how it tended to work. It was friends of friends of friends. If you were talented, if you showed interest and talent, people like Tony and Rob would encourage you and give you a big chance to get things going.

ANGIE CASSIDY: It's laughable, but mistakes got made that, in hindsight, they didn't have to make. Perhaps things might still be going now, but it would be a different beast now, wouldn't it?

CODA

WOMEN AT
FACTORY RECORDS

Tina Simmons's Happy Mondays pass

From the beginning of Factory through to its legacy in the present, women have been central to the work. Yet the story of women at Factory Records has long been a history on the margins. Intentionally or not, women haven't been captured fully in the existing narratives of the label and, by default, they've been written out of its legacy. The women's voices included in *I Thought I Heard You Speak* reflect on the vestiges of misogyny, and they stand collectively in resistance to preceding chronicles of the label. At the same time, these voices shine a light on stories of indomitable work ethics, massive creativity, laughter, friendship, and the long-lasting inheritance of Factory Records. This is indeed a story of a happening that became a label that became an (inclusive) cultural phenomenon, in spite of itself.

NICKI KEFALAS: I don't think anyone who was actually involved in Factory could say that the story of Factory *isn't* a story of women. The women who were in the office might not have been doing the 'front-line' stuff of going on tour or being the figureheads for the label, but they were really doing the critical work.

SANDY MCLEOD: If we don't tell our stories, we lose our voices. We don't want to happen — not for ourselves and not for the next generations. Why not empower those girls of the next generation to have their voices?

MARGARET JAILLER: It's terrible the way older people become invisible — older women especially — and I do think that the struggles of women who challenged gender stereotyping by entering professions which they were not largely welcomed into by their male counterparts *are* worth telling.

ALISON SURTEES: It has always been a challenge for women to have a voice in any industry that is outside of the home, and sometimes not even there. As a result, women are often overlooked, underrepresented and not acknowledged for the part they play in many industries, certainly in music. One of the founding principles of Manchester Digital Music Archive was to provide a platform that would allow anyone to share their perspective of history and tell their own stories, not mediated by archivists and gatekeepers, not amended and extracted, but raw and real. History is all about perspective, but if we leave out a majority of voices and only share certain views, we skew the reality of what happens ... [W]e as women should also take up the act of recording our own stories. That in itself is an act of change, being prepared to put ourselves out there and acknowledge the work we do and why. It is vital that women are seen and heard; this is a way of encouraging future generations to be present and counted.

MICHELLE MANGAN: I think women get written out of Factory Records quite a lot. Yes, yes, there's Tony Wilson, but, for me, when I think of Factory Records I think of Gillian from New Order.

DJ PAULETTE: It's like that question about female DJs. As much as I would like to think that question would be less important or would disappear, the longer I do this job, it's still here. And the reason it's still here is because the things that we're trying to undo are so deeply ingrained – the processes and the ties and the restrictions are so deeply ensconced in society that it's almost impossible. I've been DJing nearly thirty years, and it is still actually a thing that there aren't any women on the line-ups, there aren't any women in the boardroom. There aren't enough female radio presenters, there aren't enough Black female radio presenters, and there definitely aren't enough Black female and LGBTQ presenters. You can go all the way with that, but in the thirty years that I've been DJing, as much as things have changed a tiny little bit, we've got so far to go. We've got many, many miles to go before even the changes that we're making now will make any difference. But this is why we have to make as many changes as we can. This is why we have to tell as many stories as we can − if we don't tell the stories, whenever and wherever we can, those stories stay closed and 'other'. We have to bring those stories into the canon, bring them into the discussion.

ANG MATTHEWS: My thoughts are even if my gender has no relevance to the story, it still sort of has relevance because it's my story and it's a female story and it's bound to be slightly different. And, if nothing else, in the telling of my story, if you're a young woman, even to this day you are going to clubs and everything, there are still more men there than there are women, and this is important for women my age to talk about − what we did in our past − to let people know that it can be done and it's normal. And in that short time to be the first woman who was licensee at The Haçienda, to be the second woman in a student union to do that job . . . I think it is important that we say that. It's important to tell your story.

GONNIE RIETVELD: Secrecy has always been the hallmark of Factory, which is why it's so hard to make a sensible book about it, as well. To some extent, it sort of reminds me of a Mafia movie: you keep things in the family but don't involve the women. In that sense, there was an informal gender politics that put me in a precarious position. I was active as a creator and I was married to Mike Pickering, and then I ended up working there, as well. But there were things that were said 'only amongst management', which is fair enough, but also certain things that seemed to be just amongst the blokes. I think Rob Gretton to some extent had quite a good idea about posterity . . . well, now we are talking here! I think he had quite a good idea that eventually something might leak out in a way that he had no control over. There's something also with Factory about being self-mythologising . . .

LIEVE MONNENS: I felt the guys at Factory used to hold the cards very close to their chests. If there was anything important to discuss, they didn't want us to know. I'm actually not talking about

Tony Wilson, because he was quite free with sharing information, or at least it wasn't obvious and in your face when he *wasn't* sharing information. But there were guys who'd go across the street to the pub, like the accountants, and leave us to 'man' the fort. I decided to go over there one day. They saw me coming in and were talking about something related to the business. All of a sudden, they switched to talking about cricket. You bastards! There was an underlying feeling that was weird.

GONNIE RIETVELD: The men would talk with each other, it seemed, but there were a lot of supporting women there — Tracey Donnelly being one of them, Rebecca Boulton, a very strong woman, and the perennial, caring Penny Henry. So it was all about the 'strong woman' who supports the guys. I was actually told, when I was complaining about the way I was positioned, 'Yeah, Gonnie, but you need to be a strong woman — I expect you to support me, you should be proud of me', as Mike may have put it. I thought, I don't want to be strong, I just want to be part of the process — I don't want to be excluded.

LINDA DUTTON: Women film-makers are constantly overlooked, and us women at Factory have been overlooked. There was recently an exhibit on Factory Records, so I went to have a look. They had the films that we'd done playing, and yet the only mention of IKON was Malcolm Whitehead and Brian Nicholson. I wasn't mentioned at all, which I found a bit annoying, really, because I was there from the very first day of The Haçienda. The very first day it opened, Malc said to me, 'Do the second camera.'

LINDSAY READE: I think that if I had been born much later it would have been very different. For one thing, I would have been a named director of Factory, no question. Tony and I fell out in much the same way that bands fall out if they don't share ideas and royalties with one another . . . It didn't even occur to me, at the outset, to say I wanted to be named as a director! I didn't have that voice in my own head that I should have had.

MELANIE WILKINSON: One of the things I do remember quite vividly is that it was a very male-dominated environment.

LIZ NAYLOR: My bottom line is, I think Factory was a very male environment ... the built environment, the gig environment, the labour. It didn't feel like there were women around Factory at all ... it didn't feel like a very welcoming space.

JULIA ADAMSON: I got the impression it was a boys' club with Factory, even from the studio side of things. The very first time I went to see John Cooper Clarke and the Invisible Girls, women weren't allowed to work in the studios as sound engineers. The female representation tended to be backing vocalists, or an occasional singer-musician, but rarely a singer-songwriter. It's possible girls shied away, perhaps, as I did, when Tony Wilson said, 'Oh, no way, I'm not doing that kind of thing.' I just didn't pursue it.

ALYSON PATCHETT: From the outside, Factory looked very male, I think, especially in the time I was there, because it was the Happy Monday laddishness of it that created an image of a very blokey sort of scene. But there were a lot of women ... So it always felt like a level playing field.

CATH CARROLL: I never, ever personally got any kind of sexist vibes at Factory or the *NME*, but I think it's the culture of the time that surrounds Factory and the way that some journalists were. And the fact that the successful bands were mostly just men. I'm hesitant to say, well, it's just a boys' club, because that was what people said about everything then. In most cases it was true, but with Factory I just don't think that was the case. That was just my experience because, most of the time that I was associated with them, certainly in the early days before Miaow, I didn't necessarily see myself as a woman. So, I wasn't really that tuned into that. Perhaps that afforded me something else, allowed the sexism to pass me by. If something didn't work out, I'd assume it was because I was a weirdo.

TINA SIMMONS: There were always women on the periphery of the music scene, of Factory and elsewhere. At the time, there seemed to be more women emerging as managers of bands and as owners of PR companies, and that's a good start, but as record company executives, they were fewer and farther between. A few may have crept into A&R, but you did find a lot more women becoming involved in publishing, but then you've also got women as artists, on that side. That's where we were then, and that's quite a glass ceiling, isn't it?

BRIX SMITH: Being a female was my superpower. I mean, yes, I have scars all over my hands from punching the glass ceiling the whole time.

GILLIAN GILBERT: There were a lot of women there, and I think they were all pretty clever and did loads of great things. Like Lesley ... I don't know how to describe how important she was, really, and of course Tina. Tina was one of the true professionals. She'd already worked in the industry when she came to Factory. We used to have a lot of meetings with her where she'd say things like, 'I don't know why that's happening', or 'Why is that *not* happening?' It was a bit disorganised, and I think it was only the women that came and sorted it all out. Tony was basically writing stuff on the back of his hand and not being 100 per cent. Factory needed someone dependable, and I think the women did fill that role of sorting it all out ... So, behind it all, there was a hub of women sorting out all the practical everyday stuff that needed to be done, like ordering all the records and all the finance stuff. That's what I know!

SEEMA SAINI: There were a lot of women there! I mean, the whole thing about Factory Records was that the women were very supportive of one another. I was the youngest, and all the women looked out for me.

GILLIAN GILBERT: Factory actually picked women ... I think they embraced women. So even though things were different at Factory,

I still think there was a sense that you don't blow your own trumpet for the women. But to say it again, the day-to-day running of Factory, it was the women who sorted it all out, as usual!

TINA SIMMONS: I was competent at my job and I was very good at it. I'm blowing my own trumpet here [laughs], but I had a good business head on me, and that's the difference. Factory needed someone with a business head, and as we grew, we needed a financing person with a business head, too. Chris wasn't the right person for that job. He was a good bookkeeper, but he'd have needed to understand the royalty model and that may have been asking a bit too much. I think, though, if you're in the music industry, you need to have a knowledge of what's required of the accounts, the royalties, and the financial and payment models. If you can't grasp the technicalities of what royalties meant and how much you have to pay out, then you need to get someone else who can do that. I think it's also fair to say that a lot of the women at Factory were good multitaskers, and I'd been able to multitask. In terms of the day-to-day routine, there were certain things that had to be done, but other important matters would come up and those would have to be handled as well. It's about prioritising, understanding where you're coming from, and knowing what you didn't know as well.

CATH CARROLL: Going back to the eighties, I think it was still a time when women would be in extremely necessary positions — not just logistically, but socially, keeping things together and working with personalities that may not always get along — but weren't always visible. The women at Factory especially might not have been visible to, say, readers of the *NME*, but as far as I can tell, towards the end when all of the money was going out and maybe coming in, it was the women on the staff who were keeping Factory alive.

JULIA ADAMSON: The women are always there, aren't they, just invisible in history much of the time.

GEORGINA TRULIO: I'm really thrilled to think that the women, for once, will get the limelight because all of us were often like shadows. The men had the limelight most of the time, and even in the bands the men would get the most attention. It's nice to think that the women who were huge behind the scenes, that somebody wants to highlight that — us — girl power! Yeah, that's good, long overdue and about time.

• • •

BRIDGET CHAPMAN: Factory was such a key part of Manchester, but it was much more than that. A large part of the Western music world was influenced by the sound that came out of Manchester, and a lot of that can be traced back to Factory Records, for better or worse.

CLAIRE DE VERTEUIL: I think I was an eyewitness to an awful lot of things that went on with Factory that became so important — not just for Manchester, but for popular culture. Factory affected my musical tastes and catapulted me into working for another seven years in nightclubs and being creative. It was a bubble of creativity that was going off every single minute. Every day, somebody was doing something remarkable and I got to be a part of it. I'm grateful for each day of it, and even the negativity because, in the end, there really wasn't so much of that.

KAREN BOARDMAN: When I think about it, we're all constrained as women because if we have kids, we have to take a break from the work . . . I took a break to have my two children. But in Manchester, the women support each other. We've got a network for women in the music industry, SheSaidSo. I want us all to strengthen the music infrastructure here, to get it back to what it was with Factory — the idea of 'stay here, be successful here and invest here'. It's like Tony Wilson's ethos . . . you don't have to go to London to make it in the music industry.

STELLA HALL: I met Tony Wilson because I was invited to sit around a table with the great and the good to talk about the future of the city and what we, as the cultural sector, could contribute to it. I was twenty-five, twenty-six years old, about to open up a little art centre, and there I was sitting with these other major players — and my voice was heard. They had this vision for where Manchester was going and they wanted to hear a real range of voices. I think to this day, that inclusivity is a real hallmark of Manchester.

GEORGINA TRULIO: I have used my experience at Factory and in the music industry — and still use it to this day — to help promote our vibrant music scene here in Manchester on our own indie TV show *MancuniaTV*, where I give bands, artists and visual art a place to play.

TERESA ALLEN: There was nothing else like Factory, there's never been anything like it since, and I don't think there ever will be, to be perfectly honest. But at the time, it was just our day-to-day life. We weren't thinking 'we've got to remember this for posterity' because years down the line your kids will be bragging to their friends, 'My mum used to work at The Haçienda!' My eldest son is a videographer, and he works with big-name DJs. He was telling them about me and they Googled me, and they said, 'Why can't we find your mum anywhere if she worked at The Haçienda?' That's one of the reasons I agreed to speak for this book — because there is no historical record. Peter Hook mentioned me briefly in one of his books, but he spelt my name wrong and got my job wrong. He didn't even know what I did, and I worked there for ten years, nearly. I find that quite insulting, to be perfectly honest. We all worked incredibly hard and got very little thanks for it, but we did it because *god damn it was fun.*

Notes

Foreword

1 Breanna Williams, 'Women are constantly being overlooked in history classes and it's an issue', 12 April 2021. *The Lane Tech Champion* <https:// lanetechchampion.org/10990/opinion/women-are-constantly-being-over- looked-in-history-classes-and-its-an-issue/>, last accessed 2 February 2023.

2 Bernice Reagon, reported by Audre Lorde, 'Learning from the 60s': Harvard University, 1982. Published in Audre Lorde, 'Learning from the 1960s', *The Master's Tools Will Never Dismantle the Master's House*: Penguin Random House, 2018, 42.

Introduction

1 Alessandro Portelli, *The Death of Luigi Trastulli and Other Stories: Form and Meaning in Oral History* (SUNY Press, 1991), 53

2 Reinhart Koselleck, 'On the Meaning and Absurdity of History', in *Sediments of Time: On Possible Histories*, eds Sean Franzel and Stefan-Ludwig Hoffmann (Stanford UP, 2018), 185.

Chapter 3: The Musicians

1 Directed and shot by Alison Surtees for Manchester Digital Music Archive, part of Rebel Music: The Sound of Politics and Protest in Manchester, 'Woman: Breaking the Rules: Part 5: Denise Johnson', 15 May 2018, <https:// www.youtube.com/watch?v=ewPiGJPkh0A>, last accessed 11 December 2022.

Chapter 5: Live Gigs

1 Directed and shot by Alison Surtees for Manchester Digital Music Archive, part of Rebel Music: The Sound of Politics and Protest in Manchester, 'Woman: Breaking the Rules: Part 5: Denise Johnson', 15 May 2018, <https:// www.youtube.com/watch?v=ewPiGJPkh0A>, last accessed 11 December 2022.

Linder's Meat Dress

1 Linder Sterling, 'Northern Soul', in *Linder: Works 1976–2006*, ed. Lionel Bovier JRP Ringier, 2006), 40.

2 John Robb, personal interview with Linder Sterling, 2006. Printed in part on 14 March 2011, on Louder Than War, as 'Linder: Interview with the Greatest Artist from the Punk Generation', <https://louderthanwar.com/ linder-interview-with-the-greatest-artist-from-the-punk-generation/>, last accessed 11 December 2022.

3 Ibid.

Notes

Chapter 6: The Haçienda: More than Music

1   Iain Key, 'Factory United — A Chat with Fiona Allen', 14 May 2020, <https://
    inkey69s.blogspot.com/2020/05/factory-united-chat-with-fiona-allen.html>,
    last accessed 11 December 2022.
2   John Cooper, 'The Absence of the Object Becomes a Presence You Can Feel:
    An Interview with Fiona Allen by John Cooper', *Scream City* Issue 5, n.d.,
    2010, <https://factoryrecords.org/cerysmatic/sc5-absence-of-the-object-be-
    comes-presence-you-can-feel.php>, last accessed 11 December 2022.

Chapter 7: Hey, DJ!

1   Kamila Rymaldo, 'The Women Who've Been Written Out of Manchester
    Clubbing History', *Dazed Digital*, 25 September 2018, <https://www.
    dazeddigital.com/music/article/41536/1/women-hacienda-manchester-
    clubbing-lgbt-history>, last accessed 11 December 2022.

Chapter 8: Factory Goes Global: New York and Benelux

1   Ruth Polsky, *The Aquarian*, 22 – 29 August 1979, 40(20-B)/Guggenheim
    Memorial Library, Monmouth University Special Collections.
2   Ruth Polsky, *The Tube*, Channel 4, 1983, NYC clubbing special/interview with
    Jules Holland and Leslie Ash.
3   Akiko Hada, 'Annik Honoré/Les Disques du Crépuscule: An Article by Akiko
    Hada', *Rock Magazine* (Japan), September 1981, translated by Akiko Hada
    2019, <http://www.bunnies.de/akiko/Music/interviews/annik.html>, last
    accessed 11 December 2022.

Chapter 9: Technology

1   Stacy L. Smith et al., 'Inclusion in the Recording Studio? Gender and Race/
    Ethnicity of Artists, Songwriters & Producers Across 900 Popular Songs from
    2012 – 2020', March 2021, USC Annenberg Inclusion Initiative, <https://
    assets.uscannenberg.org/docs/aii-inclusion-recording-studio2021.pdf>, last
    accessed 11 December 2022.

Chapter 10: Factory on Film

1   Cindy Sherman, 'Gretchen Bender by Cindy Sherman', *BOMB* Issue 18, 1
    January 1987, <https://bombmagazine.org/articles/gretchen-bender/>, last
    accessed 11 December 2022.

24 Hour Party People

1   Lola Landekic, '24 Hour Party People', *Art of the Title*, 21 October 2014,
    <https://www.artofthetitle.com/title/24-hour-party-people/>, last accessed
    11 December 2022.

Notes

Chapter 12: Art and Design

1 John Robb, personal interview with Linder Sterling, 2006. Printed in part on 14 March 2011, on Louder Than War as 'Linder: Interview with the Greatest Artist from the Punk Generation', <https://louderthanwar.com/linder-interview-with-the-greatest-artist-from-the-punk-generation/>, last accessed 11 December 2022.

2 Lola Landekic, '24 Hour Party People', *Art of the Title*, 21 October 2014, <https://www.artofthetitle.com/title/24-hour-party-people/>, last accessed 11 December 2022.

3 Ibid.

Chapter 16: Factory Too?

1 James McMahon, 'I Wish People I Like Would Stop Dying', on Spoook — The Substack of James McMahon, 28 February 2022, <https://spoook.substack.com/p/i-wish-people-i-like-would-stop-dying>, originally published online as 'An Interview with Rachel Ratajski of Hopper', 29 September 2020, on James McMahon's personal website, <https://www.jamesjammcmahon.com/-indie-heaven-1/hopper>; most sites last accessed 11 December 2022.

2 Ibid.

3 Ibid.

Factory Fuckups

1 John Cooper, 'The Absence of the Object Becomes a Presence You Can Feel: An Interview with Fiona Allen by John Cooper', *Scream City* Issue 5, n.d., 2010, <https://factoryrecords.org/cerysmatic/sc5-absence-of-the-object-be-comes-presence-you-can-feel.php>, last accessed 11 December 2022.

Acknowledgements

An enormous and unending thanks to everyone who agreed to speak with me for this book and to have their memories included here, creating a new historical record. Your voices matter in so many ways, and they've always mattered to the story of Factory Records.

When I first mentioned the idea of writing this book to Tracey Donnelly, she not only encouraged me to do it, but she connected me with dozens of women who worked for and around Factory (and, I suspect, convinced many of them to speak with me for the project). Throughout the interviewing and writing process, she fielded what must have been thousands of questions, always warmly and thoughtfully. Without Tracey, this book truly would not have been possible. Not only am I beyond grateful for everything she did to make this book happen, but I'm also incredibly grateful for her friendship.

A million thanks to Martine McDonagh who connected me with Lee Brackstone at White Rabbit. This book, quite literally, might not have found its home at White Rabbit without Martine. Knowing that Martine believed in this project has meant more to me than she may know. I'm forever grateful to her.

Chris Mathan's work at Peter Saville Associates (PSA) has always been an inspiration to me, and I'm grateful for her incredible design work, her voice, and her friendship.

I'm so grateful to DJ Paulette for recognising the value of this project and writing a truly incredible foreword.

An eternal thank you to Lee Brackstone for believing in this project and for deftly editing the manuscript. I'm also grateful to everyone at White Rabbit who worked on this project, including Susie Bertinshaw, Alice Graham, Ellen Turner, and Nat Dawkins.

The fierce and amazing Jen Otter Bickerdike gave me the most incredible pep talk when I really needed it, and she helped

Acknowledgements

enormously with the process of writing the proposal for this book. A million and one thanks to Jen.

I had some fabulous research assistants who helped with some early transcription work and who delved into library archives for me: Hannah Chestnut, Lori Kholomyanskaya, and Lily Incantalupo.

I am incredibly grateful for the assistance that so many people provided — fielding questions about Factory, connecting me (or trying to connect me, even if it didn't work out) with women interviewed for this book, and more: Julia Adamson, Alison Agboola, Teresa Allen, Elizabeth Bailey, Ursula Baylis, Michael Butterworth, Beth Cassidy, Bridget Chapman, Phil Cleaver, John Cooper, Anne-Marie Copeland, Clare Cumberlidge, Kevin Cummins, Claire de Verteuil, Tracey Donnelly, Brian Gempp, Paula Greif, Stella Hall, Pauline Harrison-Duggan, Dave Haslam, Jan Hicks, Lita Hira, Chris Hughes, Ben Kelly, Jez Kerr, Iain Key, Anne Lehman, Chris Mathan, Ang Matthews, Kath McDermott, Gerard 'Caesar' McInulty, Liz Naylor, Sidnie Pantry, Spike Priggen, Gonnie Rietveld, John Robb, Melanie Smith, Alison Surtees, and Anthony Zannino.

Thank you so much to everyone who supplied photographs and images (including some that didn't make it into the book): Julia Adamson, Carolyn Allen, Karen Boardman, Michael Butterworth, Angie Carpenter (née Cassidy), Beth Cassidy, Bridget Chapman, Kevin Cummins, Tracey Donnelly, Parker Dulany, Linda Dutton, Mark Eastwood, Jan Hicks, Bindi Houghton (née Binning), Jayne Houghton, Angel Johnson, Nicki Kefalas, Ben Kelly, Alison Knight, Chris Mathan, Kath McDermott, Lieve Monnens, Marcia Pantry, Sidnie Pantry, Vini Reilly, Gonnie Rietveld, Suzanne Robinson, Tina Sproson (née Simmons), Lindsay Thomas (née Anderson), and Peter Walsh.

Many thanks to Bruce Holsinger and Niki Hemmer, who helped me to think through various issues concerning non-fiction writing and publishing.

I'll be forever grateful to John Robb for giving me a venue — *Louder Than War* — in which to share interviews with musicians and artists I've long admired, and for all of the editors there who have encouraged and published my writing. I can't imagine I would have had the confidence to begin working on this book if,

- 488 -

years ago, Nigel Carr hadn't accepted my first pitch, and if Melanie Smith hadn't been interested in my book reviews (thank you both so much). The world of academia, where I spent a number of years, tends to discourage writing about things you love so that a wider public might find joy in them, too. Becoming a writer at *Louder Than War* showed me that a more fulfilling and meaningful life in music writing was possible.

Thank you to my family, who have always encouraged me to write, especially my mom, and both my dad and Aunt Sue who have left this world for another one. I'm also grateful for my cousin, Brian Jones, for all the music conversations we've shared. He gave me a mixtape in the early '90s that introduced me to the Sex Pistols, and I don't know if there's anything much better than that.

Several people read early drafts of the introduction and other parts of this book, and I'm grateful for their feedback and their friendship: Lauren Turek, Sarah Joslyn Wahl, Lydia Fash, and Iain Key.

For their friendship and support throughout the process of writing this book, including reading portions of my writing and being willing to field a variety of neurotic questions, a million thanks to Sarah Witt and Siobhán Chambers – maybe someday we'll become the 'disco' versions of ourselves we can only imagine.

And thank you forever to my husband Evan McCormick, who must be the most supportive partner on this earth. He has believed in this book, and in my ability to write it, more than anyone. He talked through various oral history questions and complications with me, and he read multiple versions of every single piece of this manuscript while providing a thoughtful and expert editorial eye. He has also championed every Factory Records purchase I've made over the years and has supported my insatiable record-collecting habit. He didn't bat an eye when I mentioned I was thinking of spending way too much money on a 1982 membership book from The Haçienda, which someone had fished out of a skip more than two decades ago. 'Get it!' he said. And I did.

Credits

White Rabbit would like to thank everyone at Orion who worked on the publication of *I Thought I Heard You Speak*.

Editor
Lee Brackstone

Ellie Bowker
Alyx Hurst

Copy-editor
Sue Lascelles

Design
Nick Shah
Liam Relph

Proofreader
Victoria Hunt

Helen Ewing
Joanna Ridley

Indexer
Nic Nicholas

Picture Research
Nat Dawkins

Editorial Management
Susie Bertinshaw
Alice Graham
Jane Hughes
Charlie Panayiotou
Tamara Morriss
Claire Boyle

Finance
Nick Gibson
Jasdip Nandra
Sue Baker
Tom Costello

Inventory
Jo Jacobs
Dan Stevens

Audio
Paul Stark
Jake Alderson
Georgina Cutler

Production
Katie Horrocks

Contracts
Dan Herron

Marketing
Lindsay Terrell

Credits

Publicity
Ellen Turner

Operations
Group Sales Operations team

Sales
Jen Wilson
Victoria Laws
Esther Waters
Group Sales teams across
Digital, Field, International
and Non-Trade

Rights
Rebecca Folland
Alice Cottrell
Ruth Blakemore
Ayesha Kinley
Marie Henckel

Index

Illustrations are denoted by the use of *italics*.

Index

Index

Index

Index

Montgomery, Steve 244
Morgan, Piers 330
Morley, Carol
  on *24 Hour Party People* 316, 317
  on Factory women 63, 117,
    188–189
  on The Haçienda 129, 164
  on Joy Division 20
  TOT 199–200, 328, 332
  on Wilson 93–4, 343
  The Alcohol Years 187, 194, 292–3,
    332
Morris, Rachel 460, 462, 465
Morris, Stephen 55, 275, 367
  Gillian and 10, 12–13, 63, 365
  The Other Two 81, 91–2, 312
Morrissey 39, 127
Moscrop, Martin 62, 105
Murphy, Beyhan 294
Murphy, Paul 86

Nagle, Chris 279
Naylor, Liz 137–9, 156–9, 468–9
  Cath and 18, 72–3, 88–9, 198
  on Gretton 335, 343
  on The Haçienda 1, 112, 477
  on New Order 337
  press and 325
  Unknown Pleasures and 20–1
  Wilson and 10, 19, 343
Naylor, Pat 327
Neville (friend of Wilson) 189
New Hormones 64, 198
New Music Seminar, NY 40, 254–6
New Order 70–1, 332–4
  American tour programme 178–9
  Apple Mac 45
  'Blue Monday' video 56–7, 305,
    306
  contractless 47
  'Disorder' party (FAC 208) 4
  and Dry Bar 421–2
  Festival of the Tenth Summer 196
  gigs 150
  Haçienda shares 445
  Happy Mondays and 200

in Paris 344–5
PR and 333–4, *333*
press and 334
solo projects 91–2
support acts 64, 142–3
tax issues 254
tours 242–3, 244, 268–70
US recording 244
'Age of Consent' 82
'Bizarre Love Triangle' 280–1, 308,
  362–3
'Blue Monday' 3, *53*, 54–7, 218,
  342, 368
'Confusion' 305
'Crystal' 302
'Fine Time' 78, 242
'Leave Me Alone' 82
'Love Vigilantes' 78
'Love Will Tear Us Apart' 149
'1963' 306
'Pumped Full of Drugs' 288, *289*
'Regret' (*Baywatch* version) 302–3,
  336
'Round & Round' video 305, 307–8
'Run' 306
'State of the Nation' 353, 362–3
'Subculture' 79
'Sunrise' 143
'The Perfect Kiss' 78, 298, 299,
  335, 337
'Touched By the Hand of God'
  300–1
'True Faith' 303
'World in Motion' 174, 299–300,
  336, 425
Brotherhood 362–3
Low-Life 335, 365
Movement 74, 77, 367
Power, Corruption & Lies 55, 367
Republic 70
Substance 40, 48
Technique 47, 78, 79, 331
New Osborne Club, Manchester 9
Newson, Lloyd 294
Nicholls, Pip 19
Nico 152

Index

Index

Index

8 C#. 4b. 8 C#. 8b. 2 C#.

4 C#. 2b. 6 C. 2b. 4 C#

4 C#. 2b. 6 C#. 2b. 4 C#.

4 C#. 2b. ~~##~~. 6 C#. 2b.
co:4C.

8 C#. 2b. C#. . . . till end

Atomrock
Revolution